A READER
FOR
DEVELOPING WRITERS

SECOND EDITION

A READER FOR DEVELOPING WRITERS

SANTI V. BUSCEMI

MIDDLESEX COUNTY COLLEGE

McGRAW-HILL, INC.

New York   St. Louis   San Francisco   Auckland   Bogotá   Caracas
Lisbon   London   Madrid   Mexico   Milan   Montreal   New Delhi
Paris   San Juan   Singapore   Sydney   Tokyo   Toronto

A Reader for Developing Writers

Acknowledgments appear on pages 405–409, and on this page by reference.

1 2 3 4 5 6 7 8 9 0 HAN HAN 9 0 9 8 7 6 5 4 3 2

ISBN 0-07-009343-1

This book was set in Times Roman by ComCom, Inc.
The editors were Lesley Denton and David A. Damstra;
the designer was Rafael Hernandez;
the production supervisor was Annette Mayeski.
R. R. Donnelley & Sons Company was printer and binder.

Library of Congress Cataloging-in-Publication Data

Buscemi, Santi V.
    A reader for developing writers / Santi V. Buscemi.—2nd ed.
        p.   cm.
    Includes index.
    ISBN 0-07-009343-1
    1. College readers.   2. English language—Rhetoric.   I. Title.
PE1417.B855   1993
808'.0427—dc20   92-26976

*For Joseph and Theresa Buscemi
and for all the other Sicilian heroes
who came to this country to make a better
life for their children*

ABOUT THE AUTHOR

Santi V. Buscemi chairs the English Department
and teaches reading and writing at
Middlesex County College in Edison, NJ.

CONTENTS

Chapter 3
DEVELOPMENT

SECTION TWO

WORD CHOICE AND SENTENCE PATTERNS   **109**

Chapter 5
WORD CHOICE: USING CONCRETE, SPECIFIC, AND VIVID LANGUAGE   **111**

Chapter 9
DESCRIBING PEOPLE **210**

SECTION FIVE

Chapter 13

TO THE INSTRUCTOR

The first edition of *A Reader for Developing Writers* was received with kindness, encouragement, and enthusiasm, for which I will always be grateful. In its second edition, the text retains its primary purpose: to help students read carefully, react thoughtfully, and use these reactions as creative springboards for writing. Research in the theory of composition continues to confirm the need to provide beginning writers with a program of critical and committed reading that increases their appreciation of language, that provides inspiration for their own creative efforts, and that reinforces the teaching of basic rhetorical strategies. In short, no basic-skills program in English makes sense without the integration of reading and writing.

As in the past, the reading selections have been chosen with an eye toward helping students use their own experiences and perceptions as sources of information and insight in writing that explores questions suggested by if not drawn directly from the reading. However, this edition is an even stronger and more versatile teaching tool than the first, for it provides an expanded and more diverse table of contents. Additional selections by and of interest to African-, Arab-, Asian-, Caribbean-, Latino-, and Native-Americans have widened the text's appeal and enriched its texture, as have pieces depicting cultures and lifestyles that will be unfamiliar to some student readers. Introductory materials in Chapters 3, 4, and 7 have been expanded and now better illustrate important principles and techniques. In addition, the reading selections are now more varied in length. Included in all but the last chapter is at least one short, readily accessible piece designed to promote confidence in beginning writers/readers and to prepare them for longer, more challenging selections.

Another major change in the second edition is the addition of a chapter on persuasion, which comprises four essays on diverse topics. Carefully considered, the inclusion of this material comes in response to a demand by some faculty that developing writers practice the full range of academic discourse. Indeed, this concept helped determine revisions to other parts of the text as well, especially Sections One and Two, which now offer additional reading selections and prompts for writing to help students learn more about exposition and persuasion.

In addition, the second edition places greater emphasis on the notion that writing is a process of discovery to be approached with care, commitment, and energy. In this connection, the revised Getting Started section, which opens the text, traces the evolution of an essay from prewriting through the editing of a final draft, with each stage fully explained and illustrated via samples from the work of a first-year college student. The notion that writing is a process is reinforced in the Suggestions for Writing, which appear at the end of each chapter. With only a few exceptions, the suggestions refer to journal entries students make after reading the selections, and they encourage the use of this information to begin and develop sustained projects. As revised, however, they also remind students that composing is more than simply gathering information and arranging it on a page. Indeed, woven into the fabric of each Suggestion for Writing is a persistent reminder that successful writing demands a commitment to careful planning, to the creation of multiple drafts, to frequent reorganization and revision, and to painstaking editing.

The table of contents continues to address a variety of academic disciplines and a wide range of social, political, economic, and scientific concerns. While I have chosen selections appropriate to the reading abilities of developmental students, I have included several that promote healthy intellectual stretching and help students prepare for more advanced work. (Of course, the text continues to offer easy-to-follow aids designed to foster comprehension.) While most selections are non-fiction prose, fiction and poetry continue to play a prominent role. The second edition also contains several inspiring pieces of student writing. Some are new to the text; others have been revised and expanded from earlier versions. All are the products of careful, sustained effort through which the writers' forceful and distinctive voices address engaging topics through various modes of discourse.

Behind the design of *A Reader for Developing Writers* remains a belief that there should be a natural and clear connection between what students are asked to read and what they are asked to write. This is not to say that reading selections must serve as blueprints for student writing. They should certainly illustrate important principles and techniques clearly, but they should also inspire students to use writing as a way to explore ideas, emotions, and issues they find meaningful. This essential connection is fostered by the text's instructional apparatus. Section and chapter introductions discuss fundamental principles and strategies of composition seen in the reading selections that follow. In addition, each selection is accompanied by materials that help students learn and practice those strategies. Apparatus for each selection includes Looking Ahead (comments to help students preview reading selections); Vocabulary; Questions for Discussion; and Suggestions for Journal Entries. As mentioned earlier, Suggestions for Writing (prompts for sustained projects) appear at the end of each chapter.

Since developmental students often find collecting detail difficult, special attention is paid to the early stages of the writing process. In this regard, perhaps the most useful piece of apparatus is Getting Started. As revised, this brief introduction to the text traces the evolution of a student essay from beginning to end. It also explains prewriting strategies that are recommended in Suggestions for Journal Entries and that help students gather details for longer projects described in Suggestions for Writing.

As in the first edition, the instructional apparatus is fully integrated. Items under Looking Ahead and Vocabulary help students preview the contents and structure of the paragraph, essay, poem, or short story they are about to read. At the same time, they prepare them for the Questions for Discussion, which follow. Finally, as mentioned earlier, there is a clear connection between the Suggestions for Journal Entries and the Suggestions for Writing. The latter make direct reference to details, insights, and ideas students have recorded in their journals, and they encourage the use of such materials as springboards for sustained writing.

No textbook, even one that carries a single byline, is the product of one person alone. I am indebted to several good friends and fellow teachers whose counsel, direction, and encouragement helped make this book what it is. For their careful reviews and helpful suggestions, I would like to thank several colleagues from across the country: Camille Bundrick, University of Illinois; Lawrence A. Carlson, Orange Coast College; Barbara Chandler, St. Charles County Community College; Linda J. Daigle, Houston Community College; Peggy Karston-Borden, Willmar Community College; Marjorie Keil, Cleveland State University; Eric R. Pedersen, Butler County Community College; Christie F. Rubio, American River College; Ann M. Salak, Cleveland State University; Lawrence C. Sather, St. Louis Community College at Florissant Valley; Bernadette Wilkowski, Seton Hall University; and R. J. Willey, Oakland Community College.

Among my friends and colleagues at Middlesex County College, I want to extend my deepest gratitude to Jacky Abromitis, Connie Alongi, Betty Altruda, Jim Bernarducci, Loretta Burd, Joe Cardone, Gert Coleman, Laura di Pasquale, Sallie Del Vecchio, Virve Ettinger, Barry Glazer, Jim Keller, Jane Lasky-MacPherson, Jack Moskowitz, Bernice Osborne, Georgianna Planko, Renee Price, Ken Rader, Joseph Sikoryak, Yvonne Sisko, Sonia Slobodian, and Richard Strugala for their support and counsel. Special thanks must go to Emanuel di Pasquale and Albert Nicolai, splendid colleagues and even better friends, who brought me advice, comfort, and light. I also want to express my gratitude to members of my McGraw-Hill family, especially Emily Barrosse and Bob Redling, who believed in this book from the very start, as well as Lesley Denton, David Damstra, and Laurie PiSierra, who guided me through the second edition. Finally, I thank my wife, Elaine, for her patience and support during the many times she had to vie with this and with other projects for my time and affection.

Santi V. Buscemi

A READER
FOR
DEVELOPING WRITERS

GETTING STARTED

The reading selections in this book illustrate principles and strategies that you will want to learn as you develop your skills as a writer. Some of them will even serve as models for the kinds of writing you will complete in other college courses. More important, because of the interesting topics they discuss, these essays, poems, and short stories might very well inspire you to use writing as a way to explore, understand, and communicate your ideas on a variety of subjects important to you.

Ideally, then, everything you read in this book should serve as a springboard to help you get started on your own writing projects. Some selections will supply you with useful facts and ideas that you may want to include and make reference to in your own work. Others will motivate you to write paragraphs and essays about similar themes, questions, and concerns by drawing details from what you know best—your own experiences, your own observations, and your prior reading. In short, *A Reader for Developing Writers* has been designed to help you recognize and use the important connection between reading and writing, and it will help you strengthen your skills in both areas.

HOW TO USE THIS BOOK

At the heart of this book are the reading selections—82 paragraphs, essays, poems, and short stories by students and professional writers. In addition, *A Reader for Developing Writers* contains a complete set of instructional materials to assist you in making the most of what you read and in beginning your own writing projects. The book is organized as follows:

1. Each of its five sections and sixteen chapters is introduced by an explanation of the principles and techniques illustrated by the reading selections and important to your development as a writer.
2. Every chapter contains several reading selections. Each of these is prefaced by a short biography of the author and by a list of vocabulary words designed to help you increase your understanding of the selection and to strengthen your command of language.
3. Following each selection are questions for discussion, and following these are suggestions for writing notes in your journal (a record of your personal responses to the readings).

4. At the end of each chapter are suggestions for writing paragraphs and full-length essays.
5. Important terms used throughout the chapters are gathered in a glossary at the end of the book.

SUGGESTIONS FOR JOURNAL ENTRIES

Keeping a journal of your responses to this book's essays, poems, and short stories is one of the most important things you can do to improve your reading and writing skills. Making regular journal entries will help you increase your understanding and appreciation of what you have read. Even more important, it is an easy way to gather details and ideas for the paragraphs and essays that you will be developing as you respond to the Suggestions for Writing at the end of each chapter. In fact, most of the Suggestions for Writing refer to the Suggestions for Journal Entries earlier in the chapter, and they discuss ways to use journal material as the starting point for longer projects.

Keeping a journal is not difficult. First, buy a notebook in which to record your journal entries; ask your instructor about the type that is best for your class. Next, carefully read the essay, poem, or short story that your instructor has assigned, and answer all the Questions for Discussion (you might even want to write your answers in your journal). Finally, write in your journal responses to one or more of the Suggestions for Journal Entries that follow the assigned reading selection.

PREWRITING TECHNIQUES

Prewriting, also called "invention," is an important part of the writing process. For professional and student writers alike, prewriting techniques are especially useful during the early stages of developing a long project's ideas and details, and many writers rely on them for short projects as well. Five of these techniques are described below, and in many cases the Suggestions for Journal Entries will direct you to use one or more of them. Because these techniques are so useful, you will want to master them; the best way to do so is to use as many as you can in your journal.

Listing

You can use your journal to make a list of details by recording what you think is most important, most startling, or most obvious about your topic. Sometimes, in fact, you can compile a useful list of details simply by putting down whatever comes to mind about your topic. Here's a list that student writer Aggie Canino made when she was asked to describe a recent storm and its effects on her community:

Cloged rain sewers overflowing
Giant tree limbs across the road
Flooding
Strong winds
Birch trees bent duble in the wind
Cracked utility poles
Downed power lines
Loss of electric
Lasted only one hour
Dog hidding under bed
Flooded basements
Thunder/lightening
Loss of power
Frightning sounds—howling of the wind, crash of thunder
Complete darkness in the middle of the day
Old oak on corner struck by lightening—bark ripped off

This list is repetitious and has spelling errors, but don't worry about such problems at first; you can correct them later. Just concentrate on your topic and record the details as fast as they pop into your head.

Make sure to read your list after—but only *after*—you run out of things to say. Doing so will allow you to eliminate repetition and correct obvious errors. More important, it will help you make various items more specific and even come up with a few new details. For instance, Aggie expanded her mention of ''cracked utility poles'' by describing the ''white sparks that flew from downed power lines'' and by detailing the terror she felt as she heard the ''splintering of a utility pole struck by lightning.''

Brainstorming

This method of gathering details is like making a list. Usually, however, brainstorming results in a collection of words and phrases scribbled across the page just as they come to mind. Another difference is that brainstorming is usually done with friends or classmates. As the saying goes, ''two (or more) heads are better than one.'' Brainstorming will help the group come up with the number and kinds of questions and answers about a topic that would have been impossible had each of you worked alone.

You can begin brainstorming by asking questions to help you understand why your topic is important to you and what you want to say about it. Various questions can be used to generate details. Among the most common are those journalists use to decide what to put into a news story: ''What happened?'' ''When did it happen?'' ''Where did it happen?'' ''How and why did it happen?'' ''Who was involved?''

Questions like these work best if you want to tell a story or explain how or why something happens or should happen. However, you will probably have to think of different kinds of questions if you have other purposes in mind. Say you want to describe Uncle Charlie. You might ask: ''What does he look like?''

"How old is he?" "What details best describe his personality?" "What are his friends like?" "What kinds of clothes does he wear?" "What does his car look like?" "What kind of work does he do?" In any case, remember that prewriting is also called "invention," so invent as many kinds of questions as you like.

Not all the questions you ask will yield useful details—the kind that best describe Uncle Charlie, for example. However, the answers to only one or two might suggest other thoughts and opinions among the people in your brainstorming group. In a little while, a kind of mental chain reaction will occur, and you will find yourself discussing facts and ideas that seem to pop up naturally. Working together, then, you can inspire each other to come up with information for a fine journal entry and even for a more formal assignment based on that entry.

Focused Freewriting

Freewriting is a very common technique to help overcome *writer's block,* a problem that results in staring at a blank piece of paper while trying unsuccessfully to come up with something to say. Freewriting involves writing nonstop for five or ten minutes, simply recording ideas that come into your mind at random. Focused freewriting is similar, but it involves concentrating on a predetermined topic.

Let's say that you want to do some focused freewriting on a storm. The results might look like this:

> The clogged rain sewers were overflowing, and there was a lot of flooding with strong winds knocking down power lines. Thunder crashed, and lightning flashed. Giant tree limbs fell across the road and a birch was bent double, and there were lots of flooded basements. Even though the storm lasted only one hour. Several downed power lines threw threatening sparks and flashes across the road. My street was blocked; a large oak had fallen across it. We lost our electricity. The crash of thunder shook me to my bones. My dog hid under the bed. We were terrified.

Again, don't worry about grammar and other such errors at this point in the process. Simply try to focus on your topic and record your ideas quickly and completely.

As always, read your journal entry as soon as possible after you've recorded your ideas. Doing so will help you cut out repetition, rework parts that require clarification, and add more details that come to mind in the process.

Interviewing

Asking appropriate questions of people who know about your topic is an excellent way to gather detail. Like brainstorming, interviewing gives you other perspectives from which to view your topic, and it often yields information that otherwise you might never have learned.

The kinds of questions you ask should be determined by your purpose. If you are trying to learn why something happened, what someone did, or how something works, for example, you might begin your interview with a group of questions like those journalists rely on and that you read about under Brainstorming. As you just learned, they have to do with the *who, what, when, where, why,* and *how* of a topic. Again, however, you might have to decide on your own set of questions.

Just make sure that the person you interview is knowledgeable about your subject and willing to spend enough time with you to make your interview worthwhile. People who can give you only a few minutes might not be good sources of information. When you make the appointment to meet with the person you want to interview, tell him or her a little about your topic, your purpose, and the kinds of questions you will ask. This will give your subject a chance to think about the interview in advance and prepare thoughtful responses to your questions.

Finally, come to the interview prepared. Think carefully about the questions you need answered ahead of time. Write them down—at least those you feel are most important—in your journal or on a piece of notebook paper. Bring them to the interview, and use them to get your subject talking. If your questions are clear and interesting, you should gather more information than you bargained for. On the other hand, don't get upset if the interview doesn't go exactly as you planned. Your subject might not answer any of your questions but simply discuss ideas as they come to mind. Such interviews sometimes provide a lot of useful information. Just take good notes!

Summarizing

This prewriting method involves condensing another writer's ideas and putting them into your own words. It is especially effective if you want to combine information found in your reading with details you have gathered from your own experiences or from other sources. Just be sure to use your own language *throughout* the summary. In addition, if you plan to use any of this information in an essay, make certain to tell your readers that it comes from the work of another writer by mentioning the writer's name. For instance, if you decide to summarize the paragraph from Rachel Carson's *The Sea Around Us* (a selection in Chapter 1), you might begin: "As Carson explains in her study of the ocean's origins . . ."

THE MAKING OF A STUDENT ESSAY: FROM JOURNAL ENTRY TO FINAL COPY

The next few pages trace the writing of a full-length essay by Deborah Diglio, a first-year nursing student. They show that Diglio sees writing as a process of several important steps. These steps include:

- Gathering information.
- Writing a working draft.
- Revising the working draft several times.
- Editing the final draft for presentation.

Gathering Information in the Journal

Diglio was inspired by Carl Sandburg's "Child of the Romans," a poem in Chapter 11 that describes the difficult life of a laborer. Responding to one of the Suggestions for Journal Entries after the poem, she completed ten minutes of focused freewriting on an experience she had had while working as a waitress. Here's what Diglio wrote in her journal:

> People ordering food. The night was going by fast. Nervous. First nights can be scarry. Keep a pleasant attitude. I could do the job easily. Training period over, I was on my own. I needed this job. We needed the money. I felt confident, too confident. I can now laugh at it. Not then. Society may not place waitressing high on the social ladder, but you have got to be sure-footed, organized, you have to have a sense of humor, and a pleasant personality. You have to be able to learn from your mistakes. Eventually, I did learn but then I thought I would die. This old woman left her walker in the corner. How did I know it wasn't a tray stand? Still I should have! Why didn't I just look more closly. Why did'nt my brain take over. And the old folks didn't mind. We should look back at ourselves and laugh sometimes.

As you can see, there is no particular order to Diglio's notes and, like most freewriting, it contains errors in spelling, sentence structure, and the like. Nonetheless, an event that might make interesting reading is coming through. So is the idea that Diglio learned something from the experience and can now look back at it with a smile.

Writing a Working Draft

After discussing her journal entry with her teacher, Diglio decided to tell her story in a full-length essay. She reviewed her notes and thought more about her central idea, the point she wanted her essay to make. After taking more notes, she made a plan, or outline, to organize and write the working draft of her essay.

As she began writing this first draft, more and more ideas and details came to mind; she put them into the draft wherever she could. After she stopped writing, she read her work and began squeezing even more information between paragraphs and sentences and in the margins of her paper.

The result was messy. So she made a clean copy of her first draft. This is the version you are about to read. It contains more detail than her journal entry and is better organized. Still, it is only a first, or working, draft.

Waitressing

It was a typical Saturday night. I was standing there, paying no attention to the usual racket of the dinner crowd. The restaurant was crowded. I was waiting for my next table. I try to listen to the sounds around me. I hear the stereo.   1

In come my eight oclock reservation, fifteen minutes late. There is an elderly woman with them. She reminded me of something that happened when I started working there many years before. Recalling that story taught me to look back and laugh at myself.   2

When my second child was born, it became clear that I needed to find a part-time job to help make ends meet. A friend said I should waitress at the restaurant where she worked. I thought about it for a few days. I decided to give it a try. I bluffed my way thru the interview. A new chapter in my life began. Since then, I have learned from many mistakes like the one I am going to describe. My friends told me that, someday, I would look back and laugh at that night. I guess after fifteen years that day has come!   3

I followed another waitress for a few days and then I was released on my own. All went well that first week. When Saturday night came, I had butterflies in my stomache. I was given four tables not far from the kitchen. It was an easy station. Oh, God, was I happy, however I still felt awkward carrying those heavy trays. Before I new it, the restaurant was packed resembling mid-day on wall street. I moved slowly organising every move. I remember the tray stand in my station. It looked a little different then the one I was trained on. It had nice grips for handles of which made it easier to move around. I was amazed at how well things were going. I was too confident. I remember thinking that I was a born natural. Than, this jovial looking old man came over, and taped me on the shoulder, and said ''Excuse me, dear, my wife and I loved watching you work. It seems your tray stand has been very handy for you, but we are getting ready to leave now, and my wife needs her walker back.'' I wanted to crawl into a hole and hide. What a fool I made of myself. I was so glad when that night ended.   4

Since then, I have learned from many mistakes such as the one I just described.   5

Revising the Working Draft

The essay above makes for entertaining reading. But Diglio knew it could be improved, so she revised it *several times* to get to the last draft of her paper, which appears below. Although this draft is not perfect, it is more complete, effective, and polished than the one you just read.

Lessons Learned

It was a typical Saturday night at Carpaccio's Restaurant. I was standing there, paying no attention to the usual merrymaking of the dinner crowd. Just two of the restaurant's twenty-five tables were vacant. As I waited for my next table, I absorbed a few of the sounds around me: clanging trays, the ringing of the cash   1 register. I could even hear Dean Martin belting out a familiar Italian song in the background.

Finally, in come my eight o'clock party. As they were seated, my attention was drawn to an elderly woman with a walker slowly shuffling behind the others. She brought back a memory I had locked away for fifteen years. 2

After the birth of my second child, I needed a part-time job to help make ends meet. A friend suggested I apply for a waitressing job at a new restaurant where she worked. After considering it for a I a few days, I decided to give it a shot. I bluffed my way through the interview and was hired. A new chapter in my life began the next evening. 3

After trailing an experience waitress for a few days, I was allowed to wait tables on my own. All went well that first week. When Saturday night came, the butterflies in my stomach were set free. I was given the apprentice station that night, four tables not far from the kitchen. Oh, God, was I relieved, however I still felt awkward carrying the heavy trays. 4

Before I new it, the restarant was packed; it resembled mid-day on wall street. I moved slowly, organising every step. I remember how impressed I was with the tray stand in my station, it looked different than the one I was trained on. It had nice grip-like handles on it, of which made it easier to manuver. I was amazed at how well things were going, I began to believe I was a natural at this job. 5

Then, a jovial, old man approached, tapped me on the shoulder, and said, ''Excuse me, dear, my wife and I loved watching you work. It seems your tray stand has been very handy for you, but we are getting ready to leave now, and my wife needs her walker back.'' 6

At first his message did not register. ''What was he talking about!'' Then, it sank in. I had set my trays on his wife's orthopedic walker. I stood there frozen as ice, but my face was on fire. I wanted to crawl into a hole; I wanted to hibernate. 7

Since then, I have learned from many mistakes such as the one I just described. I have learned to be more observant and more careful. I have learned to guard against overconfidence, for no matter how well things are going, something will come along eventually to gum up the works. Most of all, I have learned that the best way to get over honest embarrassment is to look back and laugh at yourself. 8

As this last draft shows, Diglio made several important changes to improve her essay:

1. She changed the title to make her purpose clearer; ''Waitressing'' didn't say much about the point of her story.

2. She moved the central idea—the point she wants it to make—to the end. This allows her to tell her story first and then to explain its importance in a way that is both clear and interesting. It also makes her conclusion more effective and memorable.

3. She added details to make her writing exact and vivid. Just compare the beginnings of each draft. In the later version, Diglio names the restaurant, and

she explains that just two of its "twenty-five tables were vacant," not simply that it was "crowded." She even mentions that "Dean Martin [was] belting out a familiar Italian song."

4. She reorganized paragraph 4 into several new paragraphs. Each of these focuses on a different idea, makes a new point, or tells us another part of the story. Thus, the essay becomes easier to read.

5. She removed unnecessary words to eliminate repetition and make her writing more direct.

6. She replaced some words with more exact and interesting substitutes. In paragraph 1, the dinner crowd's "racket" is changed to "merrymaking"; in paragraph 4, "I was happy" becomes "I was relieved."

7. She combined short choppy sentences into longer, smoother ones to add variety and interest.

8. She corrected some—but not all—problems with spelling, verb tenses, punctuation, sentence structure, and mechanics.

Editing the Final Draft

Although Diglio's last version is much better than the draft with which she began, she owed it to her readers to review her paper once more. She wanted to remove annoying errors that could interfere with their appreciation of her work. Using a pencil, a dictionary, and a handbook of college writing skills recommended by her instructor, she corrected problems in grammar, spelling, punctuation, capitalization, and style in her final draft. Here's what just two paragraphs from that draft looked like after she edited them. (If you want to practice your own editing skills, you can go back and correct the rest of Diglio's paper after you review her changes in what follows.)

After trailing an experienced waitress for a few days, I was allowed to wait tables on my own. All went well that first week. When Saturday night came, the butterflies in my stomach were set free. I was given the apprentice station that night, four tables not far from the kitchen. Oh, God, was I relieved; however, I still felt awkward carrying the heavy trays.

Before I knew it, the restaurant was packed; it resembled mid-day on Wall Street. I moved slowly, organizing every step. I remember how impressed I was with the tray stand in my station; it looked different from the one I was trained on. It had nice grip-like handles on it, which made it easier to maneuver. I was amazed at how well things were going, *and* I began to believe I was a natural at

this job.

Of course, an entire paper full of such corrections is too sloppy to submit in a college composition class. Therefore, after correcting her final draft in pencil, Diglio prepared one last, clean copy of her paper. It was this copy that she gave her instructor.

Each of us is unique in the way he or she writes. The methods you use to put together a paper may be different from those Deborah Diglio used. They also may be different from the ways your friends or classmates choose to write. And no one says any of the steps outlined above has to be done separately from the others. In fact, some folks revise while they edit. Some continue to gather information as they write their second, third, and even fourth drafts. Nevertheless, writing is serious business. Completing just one or two drafts of an essay will never allow you to produce the quality of work you are capable of! You owe it to your readers and to yourself to respect the process of writing and to work hard at every step in that process, regardless of the way or the order in which you choose to do so. (If you want to learn more about the process of writing, read Richard Marius's ''Writing and Its Rewards'' in Chapter 1.)

SECTION ONE

ORGANIZATION AND DEVELOPMENT

In "Getting Started" you learned several ways to gather facts, ideas, and opinions about the subjects you choose to write about. Collecting sufficient information about your subject—making sure that you know as much about it as you need to—is an important first step in the writing process.

Next, you will need to determine what it is about your subject that you wish to communicate and how to use your information to get your point across clearly and effectively. Learning how to make such decisions is what the four chapters of Section One are all about.

In Chapter 1 you will learn that two of the most crucial steps early in the writing process are *focusing* and *limiting* the information you've collected so that you can begin to decide upon a *central idea.* Sometimes referred to as the "main" or "controlling" idea, the central idea of a paragraph or essay expresses the main point its writer wishes to develop.

The process of determining your central idea begins with carefully reviewing the information recorded in your journal (information collected through brainstorming, freewriting, or the other prewriting activities explained in "Getting Started"). You must then evaluate these details in order to determine not only what they say about your subject but also exactly what you want to tell your reader about it. Therefore, always keep your journal handy; the more information you collect about a subject, the easier it will be to find an interesting central idea to write about. And once you have found it, this central idea will help you choose the kinds and amounts of detail needed to develop your main point most effectively.

Chapter 2 introduces you to *unity* and *coherence,* two key principles to observe in organizing your information. The section on unity explains how to choose details which best accomplish your purpose and which relate most directly to your central idea. The section on coherence shows you how to create connections in and between paragraphs in order to maintain your reader's interest and to make your writing easy to follow.

Chapter 3, "Development," explains how to determine the amount of detail

11

a paragraph or essay should contain. It also describes several ways to arrange these details and to develop the ideas you wish to communicate.

Finally, the last chapter in this section, ''Introductions and Conclusions,'' explains the importance of introductory and concluding paragraphs, and it will offer suggestions to help you write these units of composition more effectively. In short, Chapter 4 will explain a number of ways to start and to end an essay.

The reading selections in Section One contain examples of the important principles of organization and development explained in the chapter introductions. They are also a rich source of interesting topics you might want to develop in your own writing. However, like the other selections in *A Reader for Developing Writers,* each has an intrinsic value—a value all its own—which goes far beyond its usefulness to any textbook. Whether written by professionals or by college students like you, these paragraphs and essays discuss people, places, or ideas that you are sure to find interesting, informative, humorous, and even touching. Here's hoping they will inspire you to continue reading and writing about a variety of subjects, especially about those you care about most!

CHAPTER 1

THE CENTRAL IDEA

An important concern for any writer is the ability to organize information in a form that is easy to follow. The best way to do this is to arrange, or focus, the details you've collected around a central idea.

IDENTIFYING THE CENTRAL IDEA

The central idea is often called the "main idea" because it conveys the writer's main point. It is also called the "controlling idea," for it controls (or determines) the kinds and amounts of detail that a paragraph or essay contains.

You might think of the central idea of a paragraph or essay in the same way that you think of the foundation of a building. It is the major idea upon which all other ideas and details are based; it holds the entire piece of writing together, just as a foundation keeps the rest of the building standing. To be more accurate, the central idea of an essay or paragraph is the focal point to which every detail must relate and which every bit of information must develop.

Notice how the central ideas (shown in italics) let us know from the very start exactly what the student authors of the following paragraphs have in mind:

Talk about bad days: today is a classic. First, I woke up to hear my parents screaming in my ear about a bill I have to pay. Then I went to school to find out I had failed my art project. After that, I called home to learn that I might have my license revoked, and the accident wasn't even my fault. Finally, while walking out of the cafeteria, I tripped over somebody's book bag and made myself look like an ass. And it's only two in the afternoon! (Donna Amiano, "Bad Days")

Upon reaching mid-life, many people feel a sense of panic, but I am only getting my second wind. I often feel like Janus, the two-faced Roman god who greeted each new year by looking both forward and behind at the same time. Although it is a time for reflection, it is not a time for idle moments because the future is now just as long as the past. A person without a future is not someone of advanced age, but someone who has no vision. Each day brings a future, every yesterday a tomorrow, and each step brings a new view of the horizon. (Donna Becker, "Second Wind")

In most cases the central idea of a paragraph is expressed in a *topic sentence,* and the central idea of an essay is expressed in a *thesis statement.* In some pieces of writing, however, the central idea is so obvious that the author does not need to state it in a formal topic sentence or thesis statement. In such cases, the central idea is said to be implied. This is often true of narration and description, the kinds of writing you will read in Sections Three and Four. However, it can apply to all types of writing. In this chapter, for example, a paragraph in which the central idea is only implied appears on page 21; it is entitled ''Women in Early Islam.''

Nonetheless, as a developing writer, you should always try to express the central idea outright—as a topic sentence when you write a paragraph or as a thesis statement when you tie several paragraphs together in an essay. Doing so will help you focus on specific ideas and organize information.

Very often, authors state the central idea early, placing the topic sentence or thesis statement at the very beginning of a paragraph or essay. However, this is not always appropriate. Sometimes it is necessary to provide the reader with explanatory details or background material before revealing the central idea; in such cases you will want to place your topic sentence or thesis somewhere in the middle or even at the end of a paragraph or essay. Another good reason for not revealing the central idea right away is to fill your writing with a sense of expectation or suspense. Finally, waiting until the end of a paragraph or essay to reveal your central idea is a good way to avoid offending or antagonizing a reader who may not at first be in favor of the idea or opinion you are presenting.

WRITING A PRELIMINARY TOPIC SENTENCE OR THESIS STATEMENT

As a developing writer, make sure that you have a good grasp of the central ideas that will control the paragraphs and essays you write. You can do this early in the writing process by jotting down a working version of your central idea on a piece of scratch paper or in your journal. This will be your *preliminary* topic sentence or thesis statement. It is called ''preliminary'' because you can and often should make significant changes in this version of your topic sentence or thesis statement after you've begun to write your paragraph or essay.

Of course, before you draft a preliminary topic sentence or thesis, you must choose a subject to write about. Keep in mind that by its very nature a subject represents a kind of thinking that is abstract, general, and incomplete. A central idea, on the other hand, is a concrete, specific, and complete expression of thought. For example, notice how much more meaningful the subject waterskiing becomes when you turn it into a central idea: ''Waterskiing can be *dangerous.*''

In order to turn any subject into a central idea, whether it winds up as the topic sentence of a paragraph or the thesis of an essay, you will have to *focus* and *limit* your discussion of a subject by saying something concrete and specific about it. Focusing and limiting are important thinking processes that will help you begin to organize the information you've collected about your subject. Here's how they work.

Focusing Your Discussion

A good time to think about focusing on a central idea and drafting a working thesis or topic sentence is immediately after you have reviewed your journal for facts, ideas, and opinions that you gathered through one or more of the various prewriting activities discussed in ''Getting Started.'' While these important details are still fresh in your mind, ask yourself three questions:

1. *Purpose:* What do I want this piece of writing to accomplish?
2. *Main Point:* What is the main point I wish to communicate about my subject?
3. *Details:* What details can I use to develop this main point?

Purpose   As well as you can at this stage in the writing process, determine your purpose—what you want your essay or paragraph to do. For instance, it may be to entertain the reader with a humorous event from your childhood, to describe a beautiful forest, to explain an interesting idea, or to compare two automobiles.

Once you've determined this purpose, it will become easy to decide what the main point of your writing should be, for you will already have begun determining which of the details you've gathered will be useful to you and which will not.

Let's say that your purpose is to describe the forest you hiked through last autumn. You begin by reviewing your notes, and you decide that it makes sense to include details about the symphony of colors—the brilliant reds, the burnt oranges, the subtle yellows—against which you saw a family of deer prance through the wilderness. It might also be appropriate to describe the old truck tire someone had dumped by the side of the path or the party of hunters you saw as you entered the woods. On the other hand, it might not be appropriate to explain that you traveled three hours in an old pickup to get there, that you bumped into a high school friend in a clearing, or that one of the forest rangers you met once dated your great-aunt Matilda. These last three details would not likely help you describe the forest.

Main Point   The next step is to determine exactly what you want to say about your walk through the woods. Ask yourself what for *you* is the most interesting or important aspect of the subject. This will be your *main point,* the point that will help you tie all the details together logically.

In short, you can turn a subject into a central idea by making a main point about the subject. If you decide that the most interesting or important aspect of your walk in the forest is that it was *inspiring,* your central idea might read: ''The forest I hiked through this autumn was inspiring.''

As you learned earlier, focusing lets the writer turn an abstract, general, incomplete subject into the central idea for a paragraph or essay. Notice how much clearer, more specific, and more complete the central ideas on the right are than the abstract subjects on the left:

Subject	Central Idea
The forest I hiked through this autumn	The forest I hiked through this autumn was inspiring.

Cross-country skiing	Cross-country skiing is good exercise.
The Battle of Gettysburg	The Battle of Gettysburg was the turning point in the Civil War.
My great-grandmother	My great-grandmother was very resourceful.

As you can see, focusing on a main point helps change an abstract idea into something specific and concrete—into a central idea.

Details   Finally, focusing also provides a starting point for a first draft of an essay because it guides you in selecting the kinds of details that you should and should not include. If you decide to focus on the inspirational aspects of the forest, for example, you certainly ought to include a lengthy description of the changing leaves and of the family of deer that crossed your path. But should you also mention the old tire and the party of hunters? These details are certainly a part of the experience, but do they relate to the idea that your hike through the forest was inspirational? Probably not.

Limiting Your Discussion to a Manageable Length

Typically, students are asked to write short essays, usually ranging between 250 and 750 words, with paragraphs seldom longer than 75 words. That's why one of the most important things to remember when writing a thesis statement or topic sentence is to limit your central idea as much as you can. Otherwise, you won't be able to develop it in as much detail as will be necessary to make your point clearly, effectively, and completely.

Let's say that you are about to buy a new car and want to compare two popular makes that you know a great deal about. In a short essay it would be foolish to try to compare these automobiles in more than two or three different ways. Therefore, you might limit yourself to cost, appearance, and comfort, rather than discuss their performance, handling, and sound systems as well. You might even want to limit your central idea to only one of these aspects—cost, for instance. You can then divide cost into more specific subsections, which will be easier to organize when it comes time to write your first draft. The thesis for such an essay might read:

I chose the 1992 Whizbang over the 1992 Dream Machine because it costs less to buy, to operate, and to repair.

CONTROLLING UNITY AND DEVELOPMENT

At the beginning of this chapter, you read that the central idea can be called the "controlling idea" because it helps the writer determine the kinds and amounts of detail that a paragraph or essay should contain. This is explained further in Chapters 2 and 3.

For now, you should know that the kinds of details that a piece of writing contains determine whether it is unified. A paragraph is unified if each of its ideas relates directly and ummistakably to its central idea, whether or not this central idea is expressed in a formal topic sentence. Similarly, an essay is unified if each of its paragraphs relates directly and unmistakably to its central idea, whether or not this central idea is expressed in a formal thesis statement.

The amount of detail that a piece of writing contains determines whether it is well developed. A paragraph or essay is well developed if it contains all the detail it needs to prove, illustrate, or otherwise support its central idea.

REVISING THE CENTRAL IDEA

One last and very important bit of advice. As mentioned earlier, always remember that you can and often should revise the working, or preliminary, versions of your thesis statements and topic sentences during the writing process. Like taking notes or writing a first draft of a paper, writing a preliminary version of a thesis statement or topic sentence is intended only to give you a starting point and to provide you with a sense of direction. Don't be afraid to reword, edit, or completely rewrite your central idea at any point. Like all processes, writing involves a series of steps or tasks to be completed. However, there is no rule that prevents you from stopping at any point along the way, looking back upon what you've already accomplished, and changing it as thoroughly and as often as you like. What's more, the process of writing always includes discovery. And the more you discover about your subject, the more likely you are to understand it better and to revise what you *thought* you had wanted to say about it.

The reading selections that follow illustrate the important organizational principles discussed in this chapter. Read them carefully, and take some time to respond to the Questions for Discussion and the Suggestions for Journal Entries that accompany them. Doing so will help you develop a more complete understanding of the central idea and its importance to organization.

From *The Sea Around Us*

RACHEL CARSON

Rachel Carson (1907–1964) was one of the founders of the American environmental movement and one of its most eloquent spokespersons. It was she, more than anyone else, who helped convince people of the terrible effects of chemical pollution. In 1951 she won the National Book Award for The Sea Around Us, *from which this paragraph is taken.*

Looking Ahead

1. Carson begins with a statement of her central idea. As you read this paragraph, ask yourself what main point she is making about the sea in her topic sentence.
2. You've learned that before deciding on a central idea you must ask yourself what you want to accomplish. Try to determine Carson's purpose when she wrote this paragraph from *The Sea Around Us.*

Vocabulary

accounts   Reports, stories.
cosmic   Of the world, of the universe.
testimony   Written or spoken evidence.

Beginnings are apt to be shadowy, and so it is with the beginnings of that great mother of life, the sea. Many people have debated how and when the earth got its ocean, and it is not surprising that their explanations do not always agree. For the plain and inescapable truth is that no one was there to see, and in the absence of eyewitness accounts there is bound to be a certain amount of disagreement. So if I tell here the story of how the young planet Earth acquired an ocean, it must be a story pieced together from many sources and containing whole chapters the details of which we can only imagine. The story is founded on the testimony of the earth's most ancient rocks, which were young when the earth was young; on other evidence written on the face of the earth's satellite, the moon; and on hints contained in the history of the sun and the whole universe of star-filled space. For although no man was there to witness this cosmic birth, the stars and the moon and the rocks were there, and, indeed, had much to do with the fact that there is an ocean.

Questions for Discussion

1. What is the paragraph's subject? What is the author's purpose?
2. Reread Carson's topic sentence. What one word in that sentence establishes her focus and reveals her main point about ''Beginnings''?
3. What details does she use to develop or explain her main point later in the paragraph?

Suggestions for Journal Entries

1. Review your answers to the Questions for Discussion above. In your own words, explain Carson's purpose and central idea. Then list the details and ideas that she uses to develop this central idea.

2. Think about a familiar subject. Then list some of the reasons why this subject is interesting or important to you. Use each of the items in your list as the main point of a topic sentence in what could later become a complete paragraph. Write as many topic sentences as you have items in your list; for instance, if Thanksgiving were your subject, you might end up with the following topic sentences:

Thanksgiving is a time for overeating.
Thanksgiving at my grandmother's house was a day filled with love and laughter.
Watching football on TV is a Thanksgiving ritual at my house.
Preparing a Thanksgiving dinner takes a lot of work.

Four Paragraphs for Analysis

The selection by Rachel Carson you just read shows the importance of focusing on a central idea. The same is true of the four paragraphs that follow. Written by various authors, they discuss four different ideas, but each focuses clearly on a main point developed through detail.

Gilbert Muller and Harvey Wiener are English professors and scholars. "On Writing" first appeared in a textbook they wrote for college students.

Richard Marius, the author of "Writing Things Down," is the director of Harvard University's expository writing program. Another selection by Marius appears at the end of this chapter.

John Naisbitt and Patricia Auburdene predict social, technological, and cultural changes. They wrote Megatrends 2000, *from which "Jobs in the 1990's" is taken.*

Naila Minai is the author of Women in Islam, *a full-length history in which the last of these four paragraphs appears.*

Looking Ahead

As the paragraphs that follow show, a writer who wants to express a central idea in a topic sentence need not put that sentence first. Depending upon the paragraph's purpose, the author might provide a few sentences of background or explanation first. He or she might even wait until the end of the paragraph to reveal the central idea and, in this way, create suspense or emphasis. In fact, as you will see when you read "Women in Early Islam," the last of the four paragraphs, writers sometimes choose not to express central ideas in topic sentences at all. Instead, they allow readers to draw their own conclusions about the facts and ideas they present. In such cases, as you know, the central idea is said to be implied.

Vocabulary

anticipated   Expected, predicted.

caravan   Line of pack animals used to transport goods across the desert.

colleagues   People engaged in the same profession.

discipline   Academic subject, area of study.

flourishing   Prospering, growing, successful.

liberal arts   Branch of academic study including subjects such as language, literature, philosophy, and history.

Mecca   Place of Mohammed's birth and Islam's holiest city.

random   By chance.

rifle through   Search through vigorously.

scandalized   Shocked, offended.

zeal   Excitement, eagerness.

ON WRITING by Gilbert Muller and Harvey Wiener

Few writers begin without some warmup activity. Generally called prewriting, the steps they take before producing a draft almost always start with thinking about their topic. They talk to friends and colleagues; they browse in libraries and rifle through reference books; they read newspaper and magazine articles. Sometimes they jot down notes and lists in order to put on paper some of their thoughts in very rough form. Some writers use free-association: they record as thoroughly as possible their random, unedited ideas about the topic. Using the raw, often disorganized materials produced in this preliminary stage, many writers try to group related thoughts with a scratch outline or some other effort to bring order to their written notes.

WRITING THINGS DOWN* by Richard Marius

In our zeal to think of writing as communication, we may forget how much writing helps us know things—to arrange facts, to see how they are related to one another, and to decide what they mean. Nothing helps the mind and memory more than writing things down. Everyone who has taught a discipline such as history, literature, economics, or philosophy has had at least one student who protests, "I *know* it; I just can't *write* it." In fact, a person who cannot write about a discipline in the liberal arts rarely knows anything about it except a disconnected jumble of useless facts.

JOBS IN THE 1990'S* by John Naisbitt and Patricia Aburdene

In the next decade, 14 or 15 million new jobs will be created, not as many as the 20 million created in the 1980's. It's a good thing, because there are not

* Editor's title

enough people to fill the anticipated new jobs. The labor supply will increase less than 1 percent a year, the slowest growth since the 1930's. The 1990's will be the tightest labor market in decades.

WOMEN IN EARLY ISLAM by Naila Minai

Khadija, an attractive forty-year-old Arabian widow, ran a flourishing caravan business in Mecca in the seventh century A.D., and was courted by the most eligible men of her society. But she had eyes only for an intelligent and hard-working twenty-five-year-old in her employ named Muhammad. "What does she see in a penniless ex-shepherd?" her scandalized aristocratic family whispered among themselves. Accustomed to having her way, however, Khadija proposed to Muhammad and married him. Until her death some twenty-five years later, her marriage was much more than the conventional Cinderella story in reverse, for Khadija not only bore six children while co-managing her business with her husband, but also advised and financed him in his struggle to found Islam, which grew to be one of the major religions of the world.

Questions for Discussion

1. What are the topic sentences in the first three paragraphs?
2. What, in your own words, is the central idea in the fourth paragraph, "Women in Early Islam"?
3. Would "On Writing" have been as effective and easy to read if the topic sentence appeared in the middle or at the end of the paragraph?
4. What important information does Marius provide before the topic sentence in "Writing Things Down"?
5. What is the main point in "Jobs in the 1990's"? Why do the authors wait until the last line to make it?

Suggestion for a Journal Entry

This journal entry is in three parts:

First, pick a limited subject you know a lot about. Here are some examples: waiting on tables, last year's Fourth of July picnic, your bedroom at home, feeding a baby, your car, studying math, your Uncle Mort, going to a concert, watching baseball on television.

Second, decide what are the most interesting or important points you can make about that subject. Choose *one* of these as the main point of a central idea. Write that central idea down in the form of a topic sentence for a paragraph you might want to write later.

Third, do the same with three or four other limited subjects you know about. Here's what your journal entry might look like when you're done:

1. Limited Subject: Feeding a baby
   Main Points: Sometimes messy, always fun
   Topic Sentence: Feeding a baby can be messy.
2. Limited Subject: Uncle Mort
   Main Points: Old, handsome, outgoing, considerate
   Topic Sentence: My Uncle Mort was one of the most considerate people in my family.
3. Limited Subject: Last year's Fourth of July picnic
   Main Points: Much food, many people, lots of rain
   Topic Sentence: Last year's Fourth of July picnic was a washout.
4. Limited Subject: Working at Bernie's Auto Service
   Main Points: Hard work, long hours, a lot of dirt and grease
   Topic Sentence: Working at Bernie's Auto Service is a dirty job.

Three Passions I Have Lived For

BERTRAND RUSSELL

One of the most widely read philosophers and mathematicians of the twentieth century, Bertrand Russell (1872–1970) is even better remembered as a social and political activist. For many years, he was considered an extremely unortho-dox thinker because of his liberal opinions on sex, marriage, and homosexuality. Politically, Russell was a socialist and pacifist. In the 1950s and 1960s he became one of the leaders of the ban-the-bomb movement in Europe, and later he helped organize opposition to U.S. involvement in Vietnam.

Among his most famous works are Principles of Mathematics, A History of Western Philosophy, *and a three-volume autobiography in which the selection that follows first appeared. Russell won the Nobel Prize in literature in 1950.*

Looking Ahead

1. The first paragraph contains Russell's thesis. Read it carefully; it will give you clues about the topic sentences on which he develops three of the paragraphs that follow.
2. The word "passions" should be understood as deep, personal concerns which Russell developed over the course of his life and which had a significant influence on the way he lived.

Vocabulary

abyss   Deep hole.
alleviate   Lessen, soften, make less harsh or painful.

anguish   Grief, sorrow, pain.

consciousness   Mind, intelligence.

mockery   Ridicule, scorn.

prefiguring   Predicting, forecasting.

reverberate   Resound, repeatedly echo.

unfathomable   Unmeasurable.

verge   Edge.

Three passions, simple but overwhelmingly strong, have governed my life: the   1
longing for love, the search for knowledge, and unbearable pity for the suffering
of mankind. These passions, like great winds, have blown me hither and thither,
in a wayward course over a deep ocean of anguish, reaching to the very verge
of despair.

I have sought love, first, because it brings ecstasy—ecstasy so great that I   2
would often have sacrificed all the rest of my life for a few hours of this joy. I
have sought it, next, because it relieves loneliness—that terrible loneliness in
which one shivering consciousness looks over the rim of the world into the cold
unfathomable lifeless abyss. I have sought it, finally, because in the union of love
I have seen, in a mystic miniature, the prefiguring vision of the heaven that saints
and poets have imagined. This is what I sought, and though it might seem too
good for human life, this is what—at last—I have found.

With equal passion I have sought knowledge. I have wished to understand   3
the hearts of men. I have wished to know why the stars shine. . . . A little of this,
but not much, I have achieved.

Love and knowledge, so far as they were possible, led upward toward the   4
heavens. But always pity brought me back to earth. Echoes of cries of pain
reverberate in my heart. Children in famine, victims tortured by oppressors,
helpless old people a hated burden to their sons, and the whole world of loneliness, poverty, and pain make a mockery of what human life should be. I long
to alleviate the evil, but I cannot, and I too suffer.

This has been my life. I have found it worth living, and would gladly live   5
it again if the chance were offered me.

Questions for Discussion

1. The title gives us a clue about why Russell wrote this selection. What was his
purpose?

2. Russell expresses the central idea—the thesis—in paragraph 1. What is his
thesis?

3. In your own words, explain each of the central ideas—topic sentences—in
paragraphs 2, 3, and 4. In other words, what three passions did Russell live
for?

4. How do these three passions relate to the thesis?

5. What details does Russell use to develop the topic sentence in paragraph 2? In paragraph 3? In paragraph 4? Explain how these details relate to their topic sentences in each case.

6. You've learned in this chapter how to limit your discussion to a manageable length. In what ways did Russell make sure to limit his essay's length?

Suggestions for Journal Entries

1. In your own words, summarize the three reasons why Russell has "sought love."

2. In Looking Ahead you read that Russell used the word "passions" to describe the deep, personal concerns that determined the way he lived. Using Russell's essay as a model, write a series of topic sentences for paragraphs that describe the passions—at least three of them—that *you* live for. The kinds of passions you mention should be personal and real. Remember to limit each topic sentence to one and only one passion. If you're embarrassed to write about yourself, write about someone else's passions. Here are some examples:

One of the most important concerns in my life is getting a good education.
My religion is the cornerstone of my existence.
My brother lives to eat.
My grandmother's most important concern was her children.
Mother Theresa's sole purpose in life is to serve the poor.

Echoes

MARIA CIRILLI

Born in a small town in southern Italy, Maria Cirilli immigrated to the United States in 1971. She earned her associate's degree in nursing from a community college and is now an assistant head nurse at the Robert Wood Johnson University Hospital in New Brunswick, New Jersey. Cirilli is also completing her bachelor's in nursing from the University of Medicine and Dentistry of New Jersey. Since writing "Echoes" for a college composition class, she has revised it several times to add detail and make it more powerful.

Looking Ahead

1. Cirilli chose not to reveal the central idea of this essay—her thesis statement—in paragraph 1. However, the first paragraph is important because it contains information that we can contrast with what we read in paragraph 2.

2. Paragraph 2 mentions the ''graciously sculptured seventeenth-century church'' in Cirilli's home town. The reference to the seventeenth century means that the church was built about 300 years ago, between 1600 and 1699.

Vocabulary

distinguished   Made different from.
exuberance   Joy, enthusiasm.
manicured   Neat, well cared for.
mediator   Referee, someone who helps settle disputes.
negotiating   Bargaining, dealing.
placate   Pacify, make calm.
siblings   Sisters and brothers.
solemnly   Seriously.
tribulation   Trouble, distress.
vulnerable   Open, without defenses.
with a vengeance   Skillfully, earnestly.

I hardly remember my grandmother except for the fact that she used to bounce   1
me on her knees by the old-fashioned brick fireplace and sing old songs. I was
only four years old when she died. Her face is a faded image in the back of my
mind.

In contrast, I remember my grandfather very well. He was 6' 4" tall, a   2
towering man with broad shoulders and a pair of mustaches that I watched turn
from black to gray over the years. He also possessed a deep voice, which
distinguished him from others whether he was in the streets of our small picture-
perfect town in southern Italy or in our graciously sculptured seventeenth-
century church. He appeared to be strong and powerful. In fact, he used to scare
all my girlfriends away when they came over to play or do homework, yet he
was the most gentle and understanding man I have ever known.

I still see him weeping softly as he read a romantic novel in which his   3
favorite character died after many trials and much tribulation. And I will never
forget how carefully he set the tiny leg of our pet bird, Iario, who had become
entangled in a fight with frisky Maurizio, our cat. Once, my brother and I
accompanied him to our grandmother's grave at a nearby cemetery that was
small but manicured. As we approached the cemetery, my tall grandfather bent
down from time to time to pick wild flowers along the road. By the end of the
journey, he had a dandy little bouquet, which he placed solemnly at my grandmother's grave while bountiful tears streamed down his husky, vulnerable
face.

My grandfather was always available to people. Mostly, he helped senior   4
citizens apply for disability or pension benefits or file medical-insurance claims.

Several times, however, he was asked to placate siblings who had quarreled over a family inheritance. Many angry faces stormed into our home dissatisfied with what they had received, but they usually left smiling, convinced by my grandfather that their parents had, after all, distributed their possessions fairly.

At times, he could even play Cupid by resolving disputes between couples   5 engaged to be married. Whether the problem concerned which family would pay for the wedding or who would buy the furniture, he would find a solution. As a result, our family attended many weddings in which my proud grandfather sat at the table of honor.

On Sundays, there was always a tray of fresh, homemade cookies and a pot   6 of coffee on our oversized kitchen table for visitors who stopped by after Mass. Seeking advice about purchasing land or a house, they asked my grandfather if he thought the price was fair, the property valuable, the land productive. After a time, he took on the role of mediator, negotiating with a vengeance to obtain the fairest deal for both buyer and seller.

I remember most vividly the hours we children spent listening to our grand-   7 father's stories. He sat by the fireplace in his wooden rocking chair and told us about the time he had spent in America. Each one of us kids would aim for the chair closest to him. We didn't want to miss anything he said. He told us about a huge tunnel, the Lincoln Tunnel, that was built under water. He also described the legendary Statue of Liberty. We were fascinated by his stories of that big, industrialized land called America.

As I grew up and became a teenager, I dreamt of immigrating to America   8 and seeing all the places that my grandfather had talked about. His exuberance about this land had a strong influence on my decision to come here.

A few months before I arrived in America my grandfather died. I still miss   9 him very much, but each time I visit a place that he knew I feel his presence close to me. The sound of his voice echoes in my mind.

Questions for Discussion

1. What important information does Cirilli give us in paragraph 1?
2. What is her thesis? Why does she wait until paragraph 2 to reveal it?
3. Pick out the topic sentences in paragraphs 4 through 7, and explain what each tells us about Cirilli's grandfather.
4. What evidence does the author give to show that her grandfather was ''gentle''? How does she prove he was ''understanding''?
5. What about Cirilli's grandfather scared her girlfriends? Why does the author give us this information?
6. Why is ''Echoes'' a good title for this essay?

Suggestions for Journal Entries

1. Use focused freewriting to gather information that shows that someone you know practices a particular virtue. Like Cirilli's grandfather, your subject

might be gentle or understanding. Then again, he or she might be charitable, hardworking, generous, or considerate of others. Reread paragraph 3 or 4 in "Echoes" to get an idea of the kind of details you might put in your journal.

After completing your entry, read it carefully and add details if you can. Finally, write a sentence that expresses the main point you have made and that might serve as a topic sentence to a paragraph using this information.

2. Think of someone special in your life, and write down a wealth of details about this person. Use brainstorming, interviewing, or any other information-gathering techniques discussed in "Getting Started." Then, discuss this special person in three or four well-written sentences. Like the topic sentences in "Echoes," each of yours should focus on only one main point you want to make about your subject or about your relationship with this person.

Writing and Its Rewards

RICHARD MARIUS

Richard Marius directs the expository writing program at Harvard University. He began his career as a historian and has authored biographies of Thomas More and Martin Luther. He also has written four novels and several books on writing, including The McGraw-Hill College Handbook, *which he co-authored with Harvey Wiener. "Writing and Its Rewards" is from* A Writer's Companion, *Marius's splendid guide for both experienced and developing writers.*

Looking Ahead

1. Writing is a process of drafting and revising, Marius tells us. As you probably learned in "Getting Started," *drafting* means putting down facts and ideas in rough form, no matter how disorganized your paragraph or essay might seem at first. *Revising* involves rewriting, reorganizing, adding to, deleting from, and correcting earlier drafts to make them more effective and easier to read.

2. In paragraph 5, Marius mentions three writers whose work you may want to read: Geoffrey Chaucer, Leo Tolstoy, and W. H. Auden. To learn more about them, look up their names in an encyclopedia or reference book recommended by your college librarian.

Vocabulary

eighteenth century   The 1700s.
embodied   Contained.
enduring   Lasting.
lexicographer   Writer of a dictionary.
parable   Story with a lesson or moral.

profound   Deep, extreme.

weighing   Carefully considering.

Writing is hard work, and although it may become easier with practice it is   1
seldom easy. Most of us have to write and rewrite to write anything well. We
try to write well so people will read our work. Readers nowadays will seldom
struggle to understand difficult writing unless someone—a teacher perhaps—
forces them to do so. Samuel Johnson, the great eighteenth-century English
writer, conversationalist, and lexicographer, said, ''What is written without
effort is in general read without pleasure.'' Today what is written without effort
is seldom read at all.

Writing takes time—lots of time. Good writers do not dash off a piece in an   2
hour and get on to other things. They do not wait until the night before a deadline
to begin to write. Instead they plan. They write a first draft. They revise it. They
may then think through that second draft and write it once again. Even small
writing tasks may require enormous investments of time. If you want to become
a writer, you must be serious about the job, willing to spend hours dedicated to
your work.

Most writers require some kind of solitude. That does not mean the extreme   3
of the cork-lined room where the great French writer Marcel Proust composed
his huge works in profound silence. It does mean mental isolation—shutting
yourself off from the distractions around you even if you happen to be pounding
a computer keyboard in a noisy newspaper office. You choose to write rather
than do other things, and you must concentrate on what you are doing.

In a busy world like ours, we take a risk when we isolate ourselves and give   4
up other pursuits to write. We don't know how our writing will come out. All
writers fail sometimes. Successful writers pick themselves up after failure and
try again. As you write, you must read your work again and again, thinking of
your purpose, weighing your words, testing your organization, examining your
evidence, checking for clarity. You must pay attention to the thousands and
thousands of details embodied in words and experience. You must trust your
intuitions; if something does not sound right, do it again. And again. And again.

Finally you present your work to readers as the best you can do. After you   5
submit a final draft, it is too late to make excuses, and you should not do so. Not
everybody will like your final version. You may feel insecure about it even when
you have done your best. You may like your work at first and hate it later.
Writers wobble back and forth in their judgments. Chaucer, Tolstoy and Auden
are all on record for rejecting some of their works others have found enduring
and grand. Writing is a parable of life itself.

Questions for Discussion

1. Reread Marius's introduction. What is his thesis?
2. In which of the paragraphs that follow is the topic sentence *not* the first
   sentence?

3. In paragraph 4, Marius says "we take a risk when we isolate ourselves and give up other pursuits to write." What does he mean?

4. In what way is writing "a parable of life itself" (paragraph 5)? Does this statement make a good conclusion?

Suggestions for Journal Entries

1. Marius says "Most writers require some kind of solitude." Do you? Use your journal to describe the place in which you write or study most often. Is it comfortable? Can you concentrate there? Should you find another place to work?

2. Summarize (put into your own words) the central idea of each paragraph in this essay. Make each statement a complete sentence. When you are through, you should have five different sentences.

3. "Writing and Its Rewards" contains advice to make us better writers. Use your journal to list three or more specific pieces of advice to help you or a classmate become better at an important activity you know a lot about. Here are examples of such an activity: studying or doing homework; dressing for school or work; driving in heavy traffic or bad weather; communicating with parents, children, teachers, or classmates; maintaining a car; losing weight; sticking to a nutritious diet; or treating members of a different race, age, group, religion, or sex with respect.

Express each piece of advice in a complete sentence, the kind that can serve as the topic sentence to a paragraph you might write later on to explain that piece of advice more fully.

SUGGESTIONS FOR WRITING

1. You may have responded to item 2 of the Suggestions for Journal Entries after the paragraph from Carson's *The Sea Around Us.* If so, you wrote several topic sentences on a particular subject, each of which was to explain a reason you found that subject interesting or important.

    Write one paragraph each for at least three of these topic sentences. Make sure that the details you include support or explain the central idea expressed in the paragraph's topic sentence. Here's what a paragraph like the ones you are being asked to write might look like (the topic sentence is in italics):

    > *Preparing a Thanksgiving dinner takes a lot of work.* First you'll have to prepare the stuffing. This means peeling and cutting up the apples, chopping up and soaking the bread, mixing in the raisins and the spices. After you're done, you'll have to stuff the turkey with this gooey mixture. While you're waiting for the bird to roast, you should peel, boil, and mash the potatoes, and cook any other vegetables you will serve. You'll also have to bake the biscuits, set the table, pour the cider, and put the finishing touches on the pumpkin and apple pies you spent three hours preparing the night before.

    As you learned in "Getting Started," don't be satisfied with the first draft of your work; rewrite it several times. Then, correct spelling, grammar, punctuation, and other distracting problems.

2. If you haven't done so already, complete the Suggestion for a Journal Entry after "Four Paragraphs for Analysis." Use *each* of the topic sentences you were asked to write as the beginning of a paragraph in which you explain the main point you are making in that topic sentence. You should wind up with the rough drafts of four or five paragraphs, each of which is several sentences long.

    Rewrite these rough drafts until you are satisfied that your topic sentences are clear and that you have included enough information to help your readers understand the main point in each paragraph easily. Complete the writing process by editing your work just as student writer Deborah Diglio did with her paper in "Getting Started."

3. In "Three Passions I Have Lived For," Bertrand Russell explains three deep, personal concerns that have "governed" his life. If you responded to item 2 in the Suggestions for Journal Entries following this essay, you have probably written a few topic sentences about the passions you or someone you know well lives for.

    Use each of your topic sentences as the basis or beginning of a fully developed paragraph about each of these passions. Next, take the main points expressed in your topic sentences and combine them into a sentence that might serve as the thesis statement to an essay made up of the paragraphs you have just written.

    Refer to Russell's essay as a model. Remember that his thesis statement mentions three passions: "the longing for love, the search for knowledge, and unbearable pity for the suffering of mankind.'' These three passions are used individually as the main points in each of the topic sentences of the paragraphs that follow and develop his thesis.

You should end up with the draft of an essay that contains a thesis statement followed by a few paragraphs, each of which develops one of the points mentioned in that thesis. Don't forget to revise and edit this draft.

4. Write a short essay in which you explain three reasons that you are doing something important in your life. Include these three reasons in a central idea that you will use as your thesis statement. Let's say that you decide to explain three of your reasons for going to college. You might write: "I decided to attend Metropolitan College to prepare for a rewarding career, to meet interesting people, and to a learn more about music and literature." Put this thesis somewhere in your introductory paragraph.

Next, use *each* of the reasons in your thesis as the main point in the topic sentences of the three paragraphs that follow. In keeping with the example above, you might use the following as topic sentences for paragraphs 2, 3, and 4. The main point in each topic sentence is shown here in italics:

Paragraph 2: The most important reason I decided to attend Metropolitan College was *to prepare myself for a rewarding career.*

Paragraph 3: *The opportunity to meet interesting people* was another reason I thought that going to college would be a good idea.

Paragraph 4: My decision to continue my schooling also had a lot to do with my desire *to learn more about literature and music.*

Try to develop each of these in a paragraph of three or four sentences that will help you explain the main point of your topic sentence completely and effectively. Finally, as with other assignments in this chapter, revise and edit your work thoroughly.

5. In item 2 of the Suggestions for Journal Entries that appeared after Maria Cirilli's "Echoes," you were asked to write three or four sentences, each of which was to focus on a single aspect or characteristic of someone special in your life. Make each of these the topic sentence of a paragraph that describes or explains that aspect or characteristic. If necessary, reread "Echoes." Many of the paragraphs in the body of this essay will serve as excellent models for your writing.

Next, write an appropriate thesis statement for an essay containing the three or four paragraphs you've just written. Make sure that your thesis statement somehow reflects the main points found in the topic sentences of the three or four paragraphs in your essay. Make this thesis part of your essay's first or introductory paragraph.

Again, approach this writing assignment as a process. Complete several drafts of your paper, and don't submit your final product until you are satisfied that you have dealt with problems in grammar, spelling, punctuation, and the like.

6. If you responded to item 3 in the Suggestions for Journal Entries after Marius's "Writing and Its Rewards," you have probably listed three or four sentences that give advice on a particular activity you know a lot about. Use *each* of these sentences as the topic sentence of a paragraph that explains the advice you are giving in detail. For example, if you are trying to help a friend lose weight, one thing you might suggest is that he or she "get a lot of exercise." That would make a good topic sentence of a paragraph that goes like this:

> *Get a lot of exercise.* Wake up early and jog two or three miles. Use the weight room in the college gymnasium several times a week or ride one of the stationary bicycles you will find there. If all else fails, walk the three miles to school every day, do sit-ups in your room, or jump rope in your backyard.

After you have written three or four such paragraphs, decide on a thesis statement that might express the central idea of the essay in which these paragraphs will appear. Make your thesis broad enough to include the main points you made in all three or four of your topic sentences. Use the thesis statement as the basis of a paragraph that comes before and introduces the three or four body paragraphs you have just completed.

Now, rewrite your paper several times. Make it as clear, well organized, and free of distracting errors as you can.

CHAPTER 2

UNITY AND COHERENCE

Chapter 1 explained the importance of focusing on a central idea. As you learned, the central idea is also referred to as the controlling idea because it controls, or determines, which information a writer uses to develop a paragraph or essay.

Deciding how much information to include in a piece of writing has to do with development, a principle discussed in the next chapter. Deciding what kinds of information to include and making sure that such information fits together logically have to do with the two important principles of organization discussed in this chapter: unity and coherence.

CREATING UNITY

A piece of writing is unified if it contains only those details that help develop—explain or support—the central idea. You probably remember from Chapter 1 that a central idea contains both a subject and a main point the writer wishes to make about that subject. In the following paragraph, student Craig Pennypacker uses every detail to explain that ''love and infatuation'' (his *subject*) are ''quite different'' (his *main point*):

> *Many people feel that they are in love when they are really only infatuated, but love and infatuation are quite different.* First, infatuation leaps into being, while love takes root and grows one day at a time. Second, infatuation is accompanied by a sense of uncertainty; one is stimulated and thrilled but not really happy. Love, on the other hand, begins with a feeling of security; the lover is warmed by a sense of nearness even when the beloved is away. Third, infatuation tells us to ''get married right away.'' Meanwhile, love advises: ''Don't rush into anything; learn to trust each other.'' These are important differences. Unfortunately, too many people overlook them and wind up getting hurt in the end.

In contrast to what you read in Craig's paragraph, beginning writers sometimes mistakenly include information that is irrelevant—information that does not help explain or support the central idea. Guard against this problem. Including irrelevant material only sidetracks the reader, drawing attention away from your main point and toward details unimportant to your central idea. With such unrelated material, your writing will lack unity, and your reader will thus have difficulty determining exactly what it is you want to say.

The following paragraph about seventeenth-century Moscow is taken from Robert K. Massie's biography of Peter the Great, the famous Russian czar. However, it has been modified, so you will notice that it contains many details unrelated to its central idea. This material was added to the paragraph (as were the bracketed sentence numbers) just to prove the point that irrelevant details and ideas can destroy the focus of a piece of writing and make it difficult to follow.

> [1]Not unnaturally in a city built of wood, fire was the scourge [devastation] of Moscow. [2]In winter, when primitive stoves were blazing in every house, and in summer when the heat made wood tinder-dry, a spark could create a holocaust. [3]Some of the homes had beautiful carved porches, windows, and gables, which were unknown in other parts of Europe, where buildings were made of stone. [4]Caught by the wind, flames leaped from one roof to the next, reducing entire streets to ashes. [5]Moscow was also subject to terrible Russian winters, which often caused severe damage to the city's wooden structures. [6]In 1571, 1611, 1626, and 1671, great fires destroyed whole quarters of Moscow, leaving vast empty spaces in the middle of the city. [7]These disasters were exceptional, but to Muscovites the sight of a burning house . . . was a part of daily life. [8]So were the heavy wooden planks that covered the streets, which had become filled with mud after the heavy autumn rains.

Massie establishes his focus—states his central idea—in a topic sentence at the very beginning of the paragraph. His subject is "fire"; his main point about that subject is that it was "the scourge of Moscow." This is what he sets out to develop in the paragraph. Therefore, each detail *should* relate directly to that point. With the added material, however, this is *not* the case.

Let's analyze the paragraph to determine which details belong and which do not:

- Sentence 1, the topic sentence, expresses the central idea.
- Sentence 2 details the causes of fire in winter and summer, so it relates directly to the topic sentence.
- Sentence 3 explains that some wooden homes in Moscow displayed beautiful carvings seen nowhere else in Europe. This sentence tells us something about Moscow, but it doesn't help explain the topic sentence's main point that "fire was the scourge of Moscow." Therefore, sentence 3 should be removed.
- Sentence 4 shows how fire spread in the city. Like sentence 2, it relates directly to the topic sentence.
- Sentence 5 explains how severe the Russian winters were, but it doesn't relate to the point that "fire was the scourge of Moscow." Sentence 5 is thus extraneous and should be removed.
- Sentences 6 and 7 show how often and to what extent fire endangered the city. Therefore, like sentences 2 and 4, they contribute relevant information and thus help develop the topic sentence.
- Sentence 8 discusses another aspect of daily life in Moscow, but it makes no mention of the threat of fire. Since it is unrelated to the central idea, sentence 8 should be removed in order to keep the paragraph unified.

This analysis demonstrates that the details added to Massie's original paragraph are irrelevant. Compare the disunified version above with his original version below. Notice how much more focused and easy to read the paragraph becomes with the extraneous material removed:

Not unnaturally in a city built of wood, fire was the scourge of Moscow. In winter, when primitive stoves were blazing in every house, and in summer when the heat made wood tinder-dry, a spark could create a holocaust. Caught by the wind, flames leaped from one roof to the next, reducing entire streets to ashes. In 1571, 1611, 1626, and 1671, great fires destroyed whole quarters of Moscow, leaving vast empty spaces in the middle of the city. These disasters were exceptional, but to Muscovites the sight of a burning house . . . was a part of daily life.

MAINTAINING COHERENCE

The second principle important to organization is coherence. A paragraph is coherent if the sentences it contains are connected clearly and logically in a sequence (or order) that is easy to follow. An essay is coherent if the writer has made sure to create logical connections between paragraphs. The thought expressed in one sentence or paragraph should lead directly—without a break—to the thought in the following sentence or paragraph.

Logical connections between sentences and between paragraphs can be created in two ways: (1) by using transitional devices and (2) by making reference to words, ideas, and other details that the writer has mentioned earlier.

Maintaining Coherence by Using Transitional Devices

Transitional devices, also called "transitions" or "connectives," are words, phrases, and even whole sentences that establish or show definite relationships in and between sentences and paragraphs. As seen in the following, transitional devices can be used for many different purposes.

To Indicate Time   You would be describing the passage of time if you wrote: "Henry left home just before dawn. *After a short while,* sunlight burst over the green hills." Other connectives that relate to time include:

After a few minutes	During
Afterward	Immediately
All the while	In a few minutes (hours, days, etc.)
Already	In a while
As soon as	In the meantime
At that time	Meanwhile
Back then	Now
Before	Prior to
Before long	Right away
Before that time	Soon

Still	Thereafter
Subsequently	Until
Suddenly	When
Then	While

To Indicate Similarities or Differences   You can also use transitions to show that things are similar or different: "Philip seems to be following in his sister's footsteps. *Like* her, he has decided to major in engineering. *Unlike* her, he doesn't do very well in math." Other transitions that indicate similarities and differences include:

Similarities	Differences
And	Although
As	But
As if	Even though
As though	However
In addition	In contrast
In the same way	Nevertheless
Like	Nonetheless
Likewise	On the other hand
Similarly	Still
	Though
	Unless
	Yet

To Introduce Examples, Repeat Information, or Emphasize a Point   You would be using a transition to introduce an example if you wrote: "Mozart displayed his genius early. *For example,* he composed his first symphony when he was only a boy."

You would be using a transition to repeat information if you wrote: "At the age of 21, Mozart was appointed court composer for the emperor of Austria. This event was *another* indication of how quickly the young man rose to fame."

You would be using a transition to emphasize a point if you wrote: "The end of Mozart's career was hardly as spectacular as its beginnings. *In fact,* he died in poverty at age 35."

Other transitional devices useful for these purposes include:

Introducing Examples	Repeating Information	Emphasizing a Point
As an example	Again	As a matter of fact
For instance	Once again	Indeed
Specifically	Once more	More important
Such as		To be sure

To Add Information   If you wanted to add information by using a transition, you might write: "When Ulysses S. Grant and Robert E. Lee met at Appomattox Courthouse in 1865, they brought the Civil War to an end. *What's more,* they opened a whole new chapter in U.S. political history.'' Here are some other connectives you will find useful when adding information:

Also	Furthermore
And	In addition
As well	Likewise
Besides	Moreover
Further	Too

To Show Cause and Effect If you wanted to explain that an action or idea led to or was the cause of another, you could indicate this relationship by using a transitional device like ''consequently,'' the word that draws a connection between the two thoughts in the sentences that follow: ''During the early days of the Revolution, General George Washington was unable to defend New York City. *Consequently,* he was forced to retreat to Pennsylvania.'' Other transitional devices that show cause-effect relationships are:

As a result	So that
Because	Then
Hence	Therefore
Since	Thus

To Show Condition If you need to explain that one action, idea, or fact depends on another, you might create a relationship based on condition by using words like ''if,'' as in the sentences that follow: ''Professor Jones should arrive in a few minutes. *If* she doesn't, we will have to go on without her.'' Some other transitions that show condition include:

As long as	In order to
As soon as	Provided that
Even if	Unless
In case	When

Maintaining Coherence by Making Reference to Material That Has Come Before

Two common and very effective ways to connect details and ideas in one sentence or paragraph with what you have discussed in earlier sentences or paragraphs are (1) to use pronouns to link details and ideas and (2) to restate important details and ideas.

Using Pronouns to Link Details and Ideas One of the best ways to make reference to material that has come before is to use *linking pronouns,* pronouns that point clearly and directly to specific names, ideas, or details you've mentioned earlier. Such pronouns direct the reader's attention to nouns in earlier sentences or even in earlier paragraphs; these nouns are called ''antecedents.'' Relying on pronouns to maintain coherence also helps you avoid mentioning the same noun over and over, a habit that might make your writing repetitious and boring.

The most important thing to remember about using linking pronouns is to make sure that they refer directly and unmistakably to the nouns you want them to. In other words, all pronouns of reference should have antecedents that the reader will be able to identify easily and without question.

Notice how well freshman Helen Giannos uses pronouns (shown in italics) to establish coherence in the opening paragraph of "AIDS: An Epidemic?":

> In the winter of 1981, Dr. Michael Gottlieb, an immunologist at the Harbor-UCLA Medical Center near Los Angeles, was among the first physicians . . . to notice that something strange was going on. In just three months, *he* treated four patients with an unusual lung infection. Each of *these* men was approximately 30 years old, and *they* were avowed [declared] homosexuals. *Their* immune systems were extremely depressed, although *they* had previously enjoyed excellent health. "I knew that I was witnessing medical history, but I had no comprehension of what this illness would become," commented Dr. Gottlieb. *He* was talking about a new virus, *which* was later named AIDS (Acquired Immune Deficiency Syndrome).

Helen's paragraph includes only a few of the pronouns you might want to use to make your writing more coherent. Here are some others:

Personal pronouns   These are pronouns that refer to people and things:

I (me, my, mine)   We (us, our, ours)
He, she, it (him, his; her, hers; its)   You (your, yours)
                                         They (them, their, theirs)

Relative pronouns   These are pronouns that help describe nouns by connecting them with clauses (groups of words that contain nouns and verbs):

Who (whose, whom)   Whatever
That   Which
What   Whichever

Demonstrative pronouns   These are pronouns that precede and stand for the nouns they refer to. Sentences like *"Those* are the best seats in the house" or *"That* is my worst subject" make use of demonstrative pronouns. The most common demonstrative pronouns are:

This   These
That   Those

Indefinite pronouns   These are pronouns used for general rather than specific reference. You can make good use of these pronouns as long as you are sure that the reader can identify their antecedents easily. For instance: "Both Sylvia and Andrew were released from the hospital. *Neither* was seriously injured." In this case, the antecedents of "neither" are Sylvia and Andrew. Here are other indefinite pronouns:

All	Neither
Another	Nobody
Both	No one
Each	None
Either	Several
Everybody	Some
Everyone	Someone

Restating Important Details and Ideas   The second way to make reference to material that has come before is to restate important details and ideas by repeating words and phrases or by using easily recognizable *synonyms,* terms that have the same (or nearly the same) meaning as those words or phases.

In the following paragraph from "How the Superwoman Myth Puts Women Down," Sylvia Rabiner repeats the word "women" three times but for the sake of variety also uses easily recognizable synonyms:

> *Women* are self-critical creatures. We can always find reasons to hate ourselves. Single *women* believe they are failing if they don't have a loving, permanent relationship; *working mothers* are conflicted about leaving their children; divorced *women* experience guilt over the break-up of their marriages; *housewives* feel inadequate because they don't have careers; *career women* are wretched if they aren't advancing; and *everyone* is convinced she is too fat!

The paragraph holds together well because Rabiner was conscious of the need to maintain coherence through the careful repetition of words and ideas.

This chapter has introduced you to two very important principles of organization: unity and coherence. A paragraph or essay is *unified* if all its ideas and details relate to and contribute to the central idea. A paragraph or essay is *coherent* if the reader can move from sentence to sentence and paragraph to paragraph easily because the writer has connected the ideas clearly and logically.

Look for signs of unity and coherence as you read the following selections. More important, apply these principles in your own writing as you respond to the Suggestions for Journal Entries and the Suggestions for Writing.

From *The Anatomy of an Illness*

NORMAN COUSINS

Norman Cousins (1915–1990) was the editor of Saturday Review, *an important literary magazine, for four decades. In the early 1960s he became stricken with an illness that left him almost totally paralyzed. His doctors told him he would never recover, but Cousins refused to believe them and prescribed his own cure. Above all, he remained steadfastly optimistic, believing that a strong will was the surest way to recovery.* The Anatomy of an Illness *is a book about his successful struggle to regain his health.*

Looking Ahead

1. Using what you learned in Chapter 1 about the central idea, identify Cousins' topic sentence, which contains the central idea of this paragraph.
2. After reviewing the transitional devices and other ways to maintain coherence discussed in this chapter, identify the methods that Cousins uses to maintain coherence throughout his paragraph.

Vocabulary

overzealous   Too eager, too enthusiastic.
pain suppressants   Painkillers, drugs used to relieve or diminish pain.
sustained   Over a long period.

Professional athletes are sometimes severely disadvantaged by trainers whose job it is to keep them in action. The more famous the athlete, the greater the risk that he or she may be subjected to extreme medical measures when injury strikes. The star baseball pitcher whose arm is sore because of a torn muscle or tissue damage may need sustained rest more than anything else. But his team is battling for a place in the World Series; so the trainer or team doctor, called upon to work his magic, reaches for a strong dose of butazolidine or other powerful pain suppressants. Presto, the pain disappears! The pitcher takes his place on the mound and does superbly. That could be the last game, however, in which he is able to throw a ball with full strength. The drugs didn't repair the torn muscle or cause the damaged tissue to heal. What they did was to mask the pain, enabling the pitcher to throw hard, further damaging the torn muscle. Little wonder that so many star athletes are cut down in their prime, more the victims of overzealous treatment of their injuries than of the injuries themselves.

Questions for Discussion

1. What is Cousins' topic sentence? What subject does that topic sentence discuss? What main point is Cousins making about that subject?
2. You've learned that a paragraph is unified if all its details relate to and contribute to the central idea. For instance, when Cousins talks in the third sentence about ''The star baseball pitcher whose arm is sore,'' he is making a direct reference to the term ''professional athletes'' in the topic sentence. Examine each of his other sentences, and make sure you understand how it relates to or supports the central idea.

3. As you know, a good way to maintain coherence is to use transitional devices or "connectives." Reread pages in this chapter that explain how to use such words and phrases. Then, identify a few of them in Cousins' paragraph.

4. Another good way to keep your writing coherent is to use linking pronouns. Reread the pages in this chapter that discuss such pronouns. Then, identify a few of these pronouns in Cousins' paragraph.

5. Still another way to maintain coherence is to restate important details and ideas. Which ones does Cousins repeat in order to make his writing coherent?

Suggestions for Journal Entries

1. Look for a paragraph of about 75 to 100 words in any of your other textbooks or in a popular magazine. Write its topic sentence in your journal. If the paragraph's central idea is not expressed in a topic sentence but is only implied, put the central idea into your own words. Then, explain how each of the other sentences in the paragraph relates to the central idea. You can do this sentence by sentence in a manner similar to the way the paragraph by Robert K. Massey was analyzed on pages 34–35.

2. Find another paragraph like the one mentioned in item 1. What has the author done to maintain coherence within this paragraph? What linking pronouns has he or she used? What transitional devices do you find? What words or ideas are repeated?

From *People of the Deer*

FARLEY MOWAT

Farley Mowat was born in Ontario, Canada, lived two years in the Arctic, and writes about the people and creatures of the northern Canadian wilderness. His most famous work is Never Cry Wolf, *a study of Arctic wolves upon which a popular film was based.* People of the Deer, *from which this paragraph is taken, describes the Ihalmiut people and tells of Mowat's travels.*

Looking Ahead

1. Mowat states his central idea clearly. As you read the paragraph, ask yourself what general impression or main point he communicates about his subject. Then, pick out the sentence that best expresses that main point.

2. The writer maintains coherence in this paragraph well. Look for linking pronouns and connective words and expressions.

3. About the middle of the paragraph, Mowat mentions the "Barrens," a subarctic area of Canada.

Vocabulary

bleak   Harsh, gloomy, empty.

caribou   Large deer of the North American Arctic.

evading   Escaping, getting away from.

frantic   Desperate.

hordes   Swarms, masses.

malevolent   Evil, harmful.

surcease   End.

Equipped with pack dogs, it took us better than a week to cover the same sixty miles that the Ihalmiut cross in two days and a night. I shall not soon forget the tortures of that march. While the sun shone, the heat was as intense as it is in the tropics, for the clarity of the Arctic air does nothing to soften the sun's rays. Yet we were forced to wear sweaters and even caribou skin jackets. The flies did that to us. They rose from the lichens at our feet until they hung like a malevolent mist about us and took on the appearance of a low-lying cloud. *Milugia* (black flies) and *kiktoriak* (mosquitoes) came in such numbers that their presence actually gave me a feeling of physical terror. There was simply no evading them. The bleak Barrens stretched into emptiness on every side, and offered no escape and no surcease. To stop for food was torture and to continue the march in the overwhelming summer heat was worse. At times a kind of insanity would seize us and we would drop everything and run wildly in any direction until we were exhausted. But the pursuing hordes stayed with us and we got nothing from our frantic efforts except a wave of sweat that seemed to attract even more mosquitoes.

Questions for Discussion

1. What is Mowat's topic sentence? What word in that sentence expresses his main point?
2. Where in the paragraph does the author echo his main point by repeating that word or by using other words that relate to it?
3. Why does Mowat say that he and his companion had to wear sweaters and jackets? Does this fact make the paragraph less unified, or does it help explain his main point?
4. What linking pronouns do you find?
5. What connective words and phrases does Mowat use?

Suggestion for a Journal Entry

Think of a time when you felt physical discomfort or even pain. Using the journalists' questions you learned about in ''Getting Started'' (page 3), gather details that describe that experience. For example, you might ask yourself:

1. When did this happen?
2. What or who caused the discomfort or pain?
3. What kind of discomfort or pain did I feel?
4. How did I react?

Say you had a difficult time getting to sleep last night because of all the noise in your house. Here's how you might answer those questions:

1. When did this happen?
   Between midnight and 3:00 A.M. last night
2. What or who caused the discomfort or pain?
   Sister's stereo blasting
   Dad slams front door at midnight
   Neighbor's dog attacks my cat—barks/squeals
3. What kind of discomfort or pain did I feel?
   Loud pounding rhythm in my ear
   Walls throbbing
4. How did I react?
   Covered my head with pillows, blankets
   Started to doze off; got knocked out of bed when I heard and felt door slam
   Wide awake, I heard animals fighting, rushed outside to save cat, got scratched, bitten, fell in the bushes

   Your answers will contain words, phrases, and even sentences that might be the makings of a good paragraph because they relate to the same main point. Read the details you have recorded carefully. Then, ask yourself what the main point is. Put that main point into what could be the preliminary topic sentence of a paragraph you might write later. For example, the details above might lead to a topic sentence like one of these (the main point is in italics):

   Getting to sleep last night was *impossible.*
   Trying to fall sleep in my house last night was *like being tortured.*
   Loud music, doors slamming, and animals fighting made trying to get to sleep last night a *nightmare.*

Waste

WENDELL BERRY

Writer, teacher, and Kentucky farmer, Wendell Berry is concerned about our effect on the natural environment. He is also a champion of simplicity, arguing that relying on ''labor-saving'' gadgets like personal computers and power tools can make life less fulfilling than using simpler devices. Berry's works include a book of poems, The Wheel; *a book of short stories,* The Wild Birds;

and a collection of essays, Home Economics. *"Waste" is from another book of essays,* What Are People For?

Looking Ahead

1. The author expresses his feelings about the way we manage our waste in a strong topic sentence. Look for this topic sentence and identify its main point.
2. Berry uses transitional devices and repeats words and ideas to make connections between sentences. Underline or write down words and phrases you think help maintain coherence.

Vocabulary

abundance   Great amount of.

imperishable   Not able to decay.

Iroquois   North American Indians and their language.

precipitation   Flow, rush, fall.

subside   Ease, dwindle, get weaker.

As a country person, I often feel that I am on the bottom end of the waste problem. I live on the Kentucky River about ten miles from its entrance into the Ohio. The Kentucky, in many ways a lovely river, receives an abundance of pollution from the Eastern Kentucky coal mines and the central Kentucky cities. When the river rises, it carries a continuous raft of cans, bottles, plastic jugs, chunks of styrofoam, and other imperishable trash. After the floods subside, I, like many other farmers, must pick up the trash before I can use my bottomland fields. I have seen the Ohio, whose name (*Oyo* in Iroquois) means "beautiful river," so choked with this manufactured filth that an ant could crawl dry-footed from Kentucky to Indiana. The air of both river valleys is seriously polluted. Our roadsides and roadside fields lie under a constant precipitation of cans, bottles, the plastic-ware of fast food joints, soiled plastic diapers, and sometimes whole bags of garbage. In our county we now have a "sanitary landfill" which daily receives, in addition to our local production, fifty to sixty large truckloads of garbage from Pennsylvania, New Jersey, and New York.

Questions for Discussion

1. What is Berry's topic sentence? What main point does he express in that sentence?
2. How does the sentence beginning "Our roadsides and roadside fields" relate to the topic sentence?

3. Why does telling us that *Oyo* means "beautiful river" help Berry prove his main point?

4. Find examples of words and ideas the author repeats to maintain coherence.

5. What transitional devices does he use to make connections between sentences?

6. Why does Berry put quotation marks around the term *sanitary landfill?*

Suggestions for Journal Entries

1. Use the focused freewriting or listing techniques explained in "Getting Started" to gather information in your journal about pollution in your town. Is it similar to the kind you read about in Berry's paragraph? Do you see trash littering roadsides and fields? What do you find in streams and lakes? Can you describe the sights and smells of smokestacks, buses, trucks, and cars as they foul the air? How about giving examples of noise pollution? Mention as many types of pollution as you can.

2. In Chapter 1 you learned it is a good idea to review your notes and write a preliminary topic sentence or thesis before drafting a paragraph or essay. Read the journal entry you made for item 1 above. Then do the following:

    a. Write a preliminary topic sentence that expresses the central idea for the details you have just gathered.

    b. Underline the main point in that topic sentence.

    c. Read the journal entry for item 1 once more.

    d. Do you find information that doesn't relate to your preliminary topic sentence? If so, cross out that information and keep only what relates directly to the main point in your topic sentence.

Finally, share your two journal entries with other students. Do they think the main point in your topic sentence expresses the general impression they get from reading your journal notes? If not, ask for suggestions about how to revise your topic sentence. Also ask them to provide other examples of pollution. The better your journal entries, the greater your chance of using these details for an assignment described in Suggestions for Writing at the end of this chapter.

Gambling

MICHAEL WITT

Michael Witt wrote "Gambling" in an advanced composition class. When the instructor asked students to interview someone with a unique problem and to write a character sketch, Witt knew whom to call. "Richie Martin" (the name is an alias) provided material to draw this touching portrait of a young man in agony. Witt's essay is a record of "Richie's" battle with an evil as strong and destructive as drug addiction or alcoholism.

Looking Ahead

1. Witt's thesis statement, the first sentence in his essay, contains two parts, each of which helps define his idea of gambling. Read it carefully.
2. One of the reasons for Witt's success is that he did a thorough job of gathering important facts in his interview with "Richie Martin." Another is that he organized the material about his subject in unified and coherent paragraphs, each of which is introduced with a clear, distinct, well-written topic sentence. Examine these topic sentences carefully.
3. Still another reason this essay is so successful is that each of the topic sentences in the body (paragraphs 2 through 7) relates directly to the thesis, keeping the essay unified.

Vocabulary

affliction   Disease, illness, misfortune.

attest   Bear witness to.

doldrums   Depression.

exhilarating   Exciting.

profound   Deep, significant.

rehabilitate   Make healthy, make sound.

suppress   Control.

transcend   Go beyond.

Though most people don't seem to realize it, it's a disease, akin to alcoholism   1
and drug addiction, and it has ruined more families and more relationships than statistics can accurately define. It's gambling—and it's one of the most underrated problems in America today.

Richie Martin can attest to this fact. As he speaks, his eyes tell the story as   2
they transcend the excitement of a racetrack photo finish and the disappointment of losing this month's rent on a solitary basketball game. He's excited, then subtle. His mood changes reflect a man whose very life goes from ecstatic highs to severe doldrums—depending on Sunday's games.

Richie bets on anything, from the World Series to the presidential elec-   3
tion. Hours before his sister delivered her first child, he attempted to bet his brother-in-law thirty dollars it would be a boy. But mainly he gambles on sports and, when playoff time arrives, Richie's money usually departs. "Over

the last five years, I've lost at least twenty-five thousand dollars," he admitted, "and even though it hasn't really broke me, I feel like I'm always chasing what I've lost."

His obsession with gambling has also had a profound effect on several 4
relationships. "I used to bring my ex-girlfriend to the racetrack and Atlantic City all the time," he remembered, "but when I'd lose I'd snap at her all the way home. She couldn't take it any more." His gambling habits started early when, as a young boy, he'd bet nickels with his father on TV bowling tournaments. "We'd bet on every ball that went down the alley," he recalled. "It was just for fun." Though it seemed harmless at the time, it led to a more serious and distressing involvement in gambling. And this, he feels, has thrust upon his father strong feelings of guilt. "I've never blamed him for my problem and he knows it, but I don't think he'll ever be satisfied until I quit."

He freely admits his affliction, which he feels is an important step towards 5
recovery, but the exhilarating world of taking chances is not an easy place to leave. "When I win, it's like everything I touch turns to gold, but when I lose, I wanna dig a hole and crawl right in it," he said. It's these sensations, these extremes of emotion, that give his life a sense of meaning and keep him in constant touch with his bookie.

At times, the stench of losing becomes so unbearable he vows to rehabilitate 6
himself. Every Monday morning, after a weekend of gambling away half of Friday's paycheck, he takes an oath to change his destructive ways—so far without success. "Every time I'm ready to quit, I win a good buck. Then I'm right back where I started."

Lately, however, he has taken some drastic steps towards rehabilitation. He 7
has quit his day job and taken a night one in the hope of isolating himself from the world of racetracks and ballparks, which operate primarily at night. "What I don't know won't hurt me," he says with a sad smile. He also hopes the change in "work friends" will influence his habits.

"It's a no-win situation, just like alcohol and drugs," he concludes. "And 8
I'm tired of it." The world of sports will never go away, nor will the excitement of winning and losing, but with a little luck and a lot of self-control he may suppress his disease—but don't bet on it.

Questions for Discussion

1. In his thesis, Witt says that gambling is "a disease" and that it has "ruined more families and more relationships than statistics can accurately define." In which paragraphs does he describe gambling as a disease? In which does he talk about the relationships it has destroyed?
2. Explain how each topic sentence in paragraphs 2 through 7 relates to Witt's thesis or helps the reader understand his central idea better.
3. Make a list of transitions, linking pronouns, and repeated words and ideas in paragraphs 2 through 7.

4. What transitions and linking pronouns does the author use to create coherence between paragraphs? Does he ever repeat words or ideas to do this?

Suggestions for Journal Entries

1. If you know someone who is suffering from an addiction, write a paragraph that discusses the addiction and its effect on this individual. Start with a topic sentence that names the addiction (such as alcoholism, drug abuse, gambling, or even an addiction to money), and make sure that the topic sentence also explains how the addiction has affected this person's life.

   Both the topic sentence and the paragraph's development must be specific. Limit your discussion to one aspect or part of your subject's life; for instance, you might say that "Martha's drinking problem is affecting her performance on the job." Then provide details that support or prove your topic sentence: explain that Martha has been late three mornings this week because of severe hangovers, that she didn't make it to work the day after a holiday party, and that she never returns to the office if she has a drink with lunch.

   In addition, be sure that your paragraph is unified. Check to see that each detail helps explain how the addiction has affected your subject's life. Finally, maintain coherence throughout the paragraph. Include transitional expressions, repeat words and ideas, and use synonyms and linking pronouns whenever you can to connect one sentence with the next.

2. If you know a person who is suffering from a serious illness, write a paragraph in which you identify the illness and describe *one* and *only* one of the effects it is having on this individual. For instance, your topic sentence might read: "Aunt Clara's diabetes has caused her to make radical changes in her diet." Develop and organize your paragraph by following the advice in item 1.

Exile and Return

JAMES KELLER

As managing editor for his college newspaper, James Keller wrote many news and feature stories. He is now a graduate student in English and plans to become a teacher and professional writer. "Exile and Return" recalls a visit to his high school several years after graduation. This before-and-after portrait reveals as much about the author as it does about his high school.

Looking Ahead

1. Keller's thesis statement appears at the end of his first paragraph. Identify the main point he makes in this essay as you read this sentence.

2. Because the essay provides a before-and-after look, it contains transitional words and expressions having to do with time. However, Keller also uses words and phrases that show his moving from place to place. All help him maintain coherence in and between paragraphs.

3. "Had forked no lightning" (paragraph 5) is from "Do Not Go Gentle into That Good Night," a poem by Dylan Thomas.

Vocabulary

arcane Secret, known only by a few.

asbestos Insulating material now considered a health hazard.

banality Boring quality.

predicting Giving sings of, foretelling.

stifling Suffocating.

It's all different, quiet and grey now, like the sun reflecting on the previous night's darkness or predicting the afternoon's storm. On this stifling summer morning, I scarcely recognize the school I had attended for four years. The life and laughter have died. It is another world.

I walk down the vacant halls, and what light there is shines a path on the mirrored beige floors, leading me past imposing grey lockers that stand erect in columns. At one time, they woke the dead in closing but now remain closed in silence. I remember the faces of people who stood and sometimes slumped before them at day's end. They were friendly faces that looked up and noded or said "Hello" as I galloped past. Now there are other faces, faces of people I never got to know.

The lockers soon give way to the classrooms, cement cells we once lived in, learned in, and often slept in. Steel I-beams I had once hardly noticed now hang like doom over cracked and peeling walls. The architect left them exposed, for want of talent, I assume. From the color scheme of putrid green to the neutral asbestos ceiling and steel rafters, the banality of the classrooms overwhelms me.

The rooms are empty now save the ancient desks. They are yellow clay and steel and much smaller than I remember. I can still read arcane graffiti, its meaning forgotten, on their dull surfaces. The handwriting is my own. I recognize the doodles drawn as every minute ran past like a turtle climbing up a glass wall. Back then, they killed the time. They didn't do much for the furniture either.

Eventually my eyes come to rest on the chalkboards. Old habits die hard. I remember staring at them through teachers whose words "had forked no lightning." My teachers and classmates are gone, but many faces remain. From seats in front and to my side, they turn and stare. They are shadows of the past, bloodless visions, returned from long exile to mock my exile and return. They're looking for me and through me. But they're only memories. They've left, you know—some gone to school, some gone to the world, others gone to their own private hells. Faces that laughed, young and innocent, now cry, worn and haggard. Their expressions hide lives that were true and alive but now are neither.

Out of the building, I walk on grassy playing fields where so many of us 6 found brief insignificant glory. They were greener in another spring. The empty stands play sentinel to the lonely track and football field, and a thousand ghosts applaud a hundred athletes only I can see. I no longer remember who won and lost, only that somehow we all walked away winners and losers to the same heart, veterans of so much happiness and so much pain. It is more than I can bear.

I leave now, maybe forever. I wonder if I ever existed and was ever here at 7 all. To say good-bye is to die a little. And so I do.

Questions for Discussion

1. What is Keller's thesis statement? What words in that thesis express his main point? In short, what is he telling us about his high school?
2. What are the central ideas in paragraphs 2 through 6? Do they relate to Keller's thesis? In what way?
3. In which paragraphs does the topic sentence not appear at the very beginning? Can you find a paragraph in which the central idea is only implied?
4. What transitional words and expressions make connections between sentences and between paragraphs? Which indicate the passage or time? Which show Keller's moving from place to place?
5. Find linking pronouns.
6. Did any part of this essay make you laugh? Was any part especially sad or touching?

Suggestions for Journal Entries

1. Take a mental stroll through the hallways, classrooms, or athletic fields of your high school. What do you remember most about it and about your classmates, your teachers, and yourself? Use focused freewriting or listing to record these memories in your journal.

   Next, read your journal entry. What main impression about your high school experience can you draw from these details? Did you enjoy it? Were you happy and secure around the teachers and students you met each day? Is the opposite true? Or do you have mixed feelings? Put your main impression into a preliminary thesis statement that might get you started on a longer assignment described in the Suggestions for Writing at the end of this chapter.

2. "To say good-bye is to die a little," Keller writes. Recall an incident in which you had to say good-bye to someone, something, or some place. Use focused freewriting to write a brief story about the event. Try to reveal why saying good-bye was so hard.

Vegetable Gardens Are for the Birds

HOWARD SCOTT

Home vegetable gardens have become increasingly popular recently, perhaps because so many of us have the need to "get back to nature." But Howard Scott feels otherwise. In this well-developed, well-organized essay, he humorously explains why he prefers store-bought veggies to those you can grow in the backyard.

"Vegetable Gardens Are for the Birds" first appeared in The New York Times.

Looking Ahead

1. The thesis of this essay is not contained in a single sentence. To understand Scott's central idea, combine the main points in paragraphs 1 and 2.
2. Scott tells us in his opening sentence that in admitting he hates vegetable gardens he runs "the risk of committing heresy." "Heresy" involves advocating ideas that are in opposition to accepted religious beliefs. His use of this word is facetious, of course, designed to make his readers chuckle.
3. In paragraph 3, the "Second Coming" is the Second Coming of Christ predicted in the New Testament.
4. The "Crockett" mentioned in paragraph 4 is *Crockett's Victory Garden,* a book on home gardening.

Vocabulary

consistency   Regularity.
gluttony   Sin of eating to excess.
horrendous   Atrocious, dreadful.
illusion   Fantasy, deception.
induces   Causes, produces.
optimum   Very best.
paraphernalia   Equipment, gear.
tiller   Tool for turning the soil.

At the risk of committing heresy, I want to state my biggest summer gripe: I 1
hate vegetable gardens.

Worse, I scorn gardeners. . . . Even more horrendous, I prefer to eat store- 2
bought veggies instead of newly plucked offerings.

Here are my complaints. Growing plants doesn't take much skill. Every ₃
gardener pridefully displays a ripe tomato or a giant cucumber as though she's
personally carved it out of the earth. "Look at this," she'll say, expecting your
face to look as if it were witnessing the Second Coming. The plain fact is that
any halfwit can grow things. All it takes is doing dumb repetitive tasks with the
plodding consistency of a workhorse.

A garden takes time. Not only is there readying the soil, planting, watering, ₄
weeding, debugging, pruning and harvesting, but also there is the research. A
gardener is constantly checking into Crockett's about snails, reading up on herbs
at the library and phoning fellow planters to arrive at optimum plant dates. So
much so, many of us spouses become earth widows(ers).

A garden costs. First there are the tools. Then the seeds and flats. Next ₅
comes the renting of the tiller. After that comes mulch, manure and prep medication. Next, water followed by insect spraying. Then the experiments with new
irrigation systems and updated equipment. Finally, jars, labels and canning
paraphernalia.

A garden creates waste. At harvest time, 15 heads of lettuce must be picked ₆
within two weeks' time or they'll rot. So you eat three salads a day and bring
bags full to all your friends (most of whom have their own oversupply problems). Needless to say, buying a head or two at the supermarket each week
avoids such cycles of gluttony and famine.

Home-grown vegetables aren't as clean as store-bought produce. You risk ₇
chomping on worms or slugs, breaking a tooth on a pebble, grinding into dirt and
smelling the manure through which the thing prospered. The cellophane wrapping, the official-looking label and the pale, dry coloring of packaged goods
eliminate those possibilities.

Garden vegetables don't taste as mellow as shelved stock. The carrots are ₈
too crispy, the peppers too tangy, the scallions too potent, the celery too stringy.
I prefer my veggies to blend in like a symphony beneath heaping tablespoons of
dressing.

A garden ties its owner down. Taking a week's vacation is impossible ₉
because, what if—God forbid—it doesn't rain. Even a long weekend is tough.
And anybody who lives with a gardener knows the fanaticism of the daily
watering.

A gardener's needs tend to expand. This year it's a 10 by 12 foot plot. Next ₁₀
year, it's a 15 by 20 space and a compost bin. The year after, it's the larger plot,
an experimental patch out front and a shed. The year after, it's a greenhouse.

Gardens make boring conversations. After the umpteenth walk to see little ₁₁
buds popping up, you run out of things to say. Then, as the summer progresses,
it's, "Oh, isn't this salad fresh," and, "I can't get over how succulent these
cantaloupes are." On top of all that, you have to listen to shop talk among
gardeners. Early on, you might make discreet jokes, but after seeing that nobody's listening you just stand around bored.

Gardens offer the illusion of accomplishment. Seeds are planted, and two ₁₂
months later a lush bounty of vegetables emerges from the ground. Amazing,
says the grower. Amazing, nothing. For years, the Government has been paying

farmers billions of dollars for not planting their lands. Warehouses are bursting with excess crops. Face it. The success of this nation is based more on perfect climate and fertile soil than any other condition.

A garden induces contentment. Cultivating the earth makes its owner feel at 13 peace with the world. Fine—but, as with cocaine, medication and booze, it reduces ambition to attempt other challenges. And as inwardly satisfying as the routine might be, there are some things growing vegetables can't solve. But try to tell a gardener that.

Questions for Discussion

1. Scott's thesis is composed of three main points expressed in three different sentences. What are these main points?
2. Identify the topic sentences in paragraphs 3 through 13.
3. A sentence in paragraph 3 makes it easy for the reader to draw a connection between Scott's thesis and the topic sentences in each of the paragraphs that follow. What is this transitional sentence?
4. In which of the paragraphs after Scott's introduction is the topic sentence *not* the first sentence of the paragraph?
5. Paragraph 5 is filled with transitional words that make it easy to follow. What other connectives do you find in the essay's other paragraphs?

Suggestions for Journal Entries

1. Write a paragraph in which you explain why you like or dislike a certain food. In the topic sentence, state one and only one reason for liking or disliking the food. For instance, you might write, ''I hate corn on the cob because it is hard to eat'' or ''I enjoy munching on raw carrots because I know they're very nutritious.''

   Next provide ideas and details that support your topic sentence. Make sure your paragraph is unified by including only details that relate clearly to your topic sentence. For instance, if you hate corn on the cob because it is difficult to eat, you might mention that bits of corn often get caught between your teeth or that the melted butter has a way of dripping all over your clean clothes. However, you probably won't mention that your parents forced you to eat corn on the cob all summer long when you were a child, a piece of information that has nothing do with the fact that the corn is hard to eat.

   Finally, maintain coherence within the paragraph by using transitional devices, linking pronouns, and so forth.
2. Following the advice in item 1, write a paragraph in which you explain why you like or dislike a certain activity. For example, discuss why you enjoy or despise gardening, mowing the lawn, walking the dog, flossing your teeth, going bowling, visiting relatives, or getting up to go to class on a cold morning.

SUGGESTIONS FOR WRITING

1. After reading the paragraph from Norman Cousins' *The Anatomy of an Illness,* you may have used your journal to write about two other interesting paragraphs you found in a textbook or magazine. Reread the journal entries you made and the paragraphs you wrote about.

   Next, rewrite both these paragraphs in your own words. Give each of your versions a topic sentence, and include enough detail in each paragraph to explain the main point of its topic sentence clearly. When you revise and edit your paragraphs, be sure you have maintained coherence by using transitional devices and linking pronouns and by repeating words and ideas.

2. Review the journal entries you made after reading the selections by Farley Mowat or Wendell Berry in this chapter. If you responded to the suggestion after the paragraph from Mowat's *People of the Deer,* you wrote a preliminary topic sentence and gathered details about a painful or uncomfortable experience. If you responded to the suggestions after Berry's "Waste," you wrote a preliminary topic sentence and collected details about pollution in your town. Now, write a paragraph beginning with *one* of these preliminary topic sentences. Develop that paragraph using details from your journal. Keep the paragraph unified; focus your information on the main point of your topic sentence. If you want to refresh your memory about unity, read pages 33–35.

   After completing your first draft, reread the paragraph. Is it coherent? Do you use linking pronouns and repetition to draw logical connections between sentences? Should you add transitional words and expressions? If you are writing about a painful or uncomfortable experience, you can use transitional devices that indicate time, like those you read about on pages 35–36. If you are describing pollution in your town, you can use transitions that introduce examples, that emphasize a point, or that add information, like those you read about on pages 36–37.

   In any event, make several more drafts of your paragraph. Stop revising only when you are satisfied that it is easy to follow and that the information it contains relates to and explains your topic sentence clearly. Then, review your work once more to correct problems with grammar, sentence structure, punctuation, capitalization, and spelling.

3. The Suggestions for Journal Entries following Michael Witt's "Gambling" involve writing about a person who is suffering from an addiction or serious illness. If you responded to either suggestion, you have probably written a unified and coherent paragraph that discusses one of the ways the addiction or illness has affected his or her life.

   Review this paragraph carefully. Then, write several more well-organized paragraphs, each of which explains another way in which the person's life has been changed by this addiction or illness. Next, turn these separate paragraphs into a unified essay by providing an appropriate thesis statement that will appear at the beginning of your essay and serve as its introduction. Then, check to see that you have maintained coherence in and between paragraphs by using techniques explained in the introduction to this chapter. As with other writing assignments, remember that the best papers are those that are revised thoroughly and edited carefully.

4. After you read Keller's "Exile and Return," you might have used your journal to take a "mental stroll" through your high school and to write a preliminary thesis statement for an essay explaining your main impression or opinion of the time you spent there. If so, you might also have begun collecting memories that explain that impression.

Read your journal notes carefully. Add information if you can. Then, use your preliminary thesis as the beginning of an essay on your high school experience. Express your main impression or opinion of the experience through the thesis statement's main point.

Next, write three or four paragraphs that explain or support your thesis. Give each paragraph a topic sentence about one aspect of your experience. Make sure the topic sentence expresses a main point, and focus the information in your paragraph on that point. At the same time, make sure that point relates to your thesis and supports *its* main point. For example, if your thesis states that you loved high school, don't write a paragraph explaining how much you "enjoyed working at Montoya's Drug Store after school." Similarly, don't include a paragraph whose main point is that you hated geometry class. Neither relates to your thesis.

Here's what an outline of such essay might look like; the main points in each sentence are shown in italics:

Thesis
   (in Paragraph 1)   Attending Valley High *helped build my confidence.*
Topic Sentences
Paragraph 2   My classmates *were supportive.*
Paragraph 3   My teachers *taught me how to study for tests.*
Paragraph 4   The math lab tutors *helped me overcome my fear of algebra.*
Paragraph 5   Participating in clubs and sports *showed me I can work well with others.*

After completing the first draft, check your essay for unity and coherence by asking:

- Do all topic sentences relate to the thesis, or should the thesis be revised?
- Is each paragraph unified? Does it contain only details that relate to the main point in the topic sentence?
- Have I maintained coherence in and between paragraphs? Should I add linking pronouns or transitional words and phrases? Can I rephrase sentences so they refer to material that has come before?

Keep the answers to these questions in mind as you revise and then edit your work. Doing so will help you put together a final draft that is well organized and easy to follow.

5. Howard Scott's "Vegetable Gardens Are for the Birds" may have inspired you to discuss your feelings (negative or positive) about a certain food or activity. Reread the journal entry you made after reading this selection.

Then, expand your discussion. Write at least two other paragraphs, *each of which* contains yet another reason you "like walking the dog" or "despise eating cauliflower." Once again, be careful. For the sake of unity, make sure that each paragraph you write explains *one and only one reason.* Tie these paragraphs together into an essay with a thesis statement to which each of the topic sentences you've written relates clearly and logically. Finally, be certain that you maintain coherence in and between paragraphs.

In the process of revising the completed first draft of your essay, make certain that you have maintained coherence in and between paragraphs. If not, use techniques explained in this chapter to strengthen the essay's organization. Then, as always, edit your work to remove distracting errors.

CHAPTER 3

DEVELOPMENT

By now you know from practice that you use the central idea to focus your writing on a main point and to keep it unified. You do so by making sure that all the information in your paragraphs and essays relates clearly to the central idea. This chapter explains how the central idea also controls *development*—how much information a piece of writing contains and how this information is organized.

A paragraph or essay is well developed if it contains all the details it needs to prove, support, or illustrate its central idea. You should provide enough details to make your point clearly and convincingly. You should also arrange these details in a way that fits your purpose and that allows readers to follow your train of thought easily.

DETERMINING HOW MUCH A PARAGRAPH OR ESSAY SHOULD CONTAIN

It is not always easy to determine how much detail is enough to develop a particular point, and there is no simple rule to tell how long a piece of writing should be. Depending upon your thesis, you might be able to develop an essay in only a few paragraphs. But in some cases, your central idea will require that you write several paragraphs of explanation and support.

Something similar is true for paragraphs. In some, you will have to supply many concrete details, illustrations, and other information important to your topic sentence. In other paragraphs, you will be able to make your point clearly with only one or two supportive details. In a *few,* you might find that one sentence is all you need to achieve your purpose. (Keep in mind, however, that using too many one-sentence paragraphs can make your writing seem choppy and incomplete.)

In any event, it is a good idea to rely on your central idea as a guide for development. After all, the central idea contains the main point you want to make. Therefore, it can give you a good clue about the kinds and amount of detail you should use to develop that point effectively.

Let's say you want to explain that there are *several* career opportunities for people majoring in biology. To develop your paragraph adequately, you might start by discussing teaching and medicine. But you will also have to include other fields (such as laboratory research, environmental management, and forestry) if you want your reader to understand all of what you meant when, in your topic sentence or thesis, you wrote, ''Majoring in biology can provide a good foundation for *several* careers.''

You already know that in order to come up with a good central idea, you need to focus on the main point you want to make about your subject. The subject in the sentence above is ''Majoring in biology.'' The main point you want to make about this subject is that it can lead to *''several* careers.'' In order to write a paragraph or essay that develops this point fully, therefore, you will have to discuss *several*—at least three—careers.

In short, you can think of the central idea as a promise you make to your readers at the beginning of a paragraph or essay—a promise to discuss your main point in as much detail as is appropriate. If you start off by writing that ''Three types of birds visit your backyard regularly during the winter,'' make sure to discuss all *three* birds. If you set out to explain that ''There are many ways to decrease cholesterol in the bloodstream,'' discuss *many* ways, not just one or two. If you want to prove that your brother is not neat, don't be content to describe his closet and leave it at that. Talk about the mess of papers and books he often leaves scattered across the floor, and mention the jumble of sporting equipment and dirty clothes on the back seat of his car.

As you have learned, deciding how many details are enough to develop a paragraph or essay fully is not always easy. However, the more experienced you become, the easier it will be to determine how much to include. For now, remember that providing too much detail is better than not providing enough. Too much information might bore your readers, but too little might leave them unconvinced or even confused. The first of these sins is forgivable; the second is not.

Just how much detail to include is what physician Lewis Thomas had to decide when he wrote a paragraph illustrating (giving examples of) the idea that computer errors have become commonplace:

> Everyone must have had at least one personal experience with a computer error by this time. Bank balances are suddenly reported to have jumped from $379 into the millions, appeals for charitable contributions are mailed over and over to people with crazy-sounding names at your address, department stores send the wrong bills, utility companies write that they're turning everything off, that sort of thing. If you manage to get in touch with someone and complain, you then get instantaneously typed, guilty letters from the same computer, saying, ''Our computer was in error, and an adjustment is being made in your account.'' (''To Err Is Human'')

Obviously, Thomas could not include an example of every computer error he had ever heard of. So, he limited himself to those that he thought would make his point most effectively and that his readers would recognize. His decision to include a specific number of examples—four in this case—is not important. We know without counting that Thomas has provided enough information to get his point across. We also know that he might not have made his point as clearly and convincingly had he used fewer examples.

CHOOSING THE BEST METHOD OF DEVELOPMENT

You can develop an idea in many ways. The method you choose depends on your purpose—the point you wish to make and the effect you want your writing to have on your readers. Your purpose can be descriptive, narrative, explanatory, persuasive, or any combination of these.

Description

If your purpose is to introduce your reader to a person, place, or thing, you might *describe* your subject in concrete detail. The easiest way to gather detail for this kind of paragraph or essay is to use your five physical senses. Sight, smell, hearing, taste, and touch provide details that make writing vivid and effective. Description is also discussed in Chapters 8 and 9.

Narration

If you want tell a story—to explain what happened—you will likely *narrate* a series of events as they occurred in time, explaining each event or part of an event in the order it took place. Narration is also discussed in Chapters 10, 11, and 12.

Explanation and Persuasion

If your purpose is to *explain* an idea (expository writing) or to *persuade* your reader that an opinion or belief is correct (persuasive writing), you can choose from several methods to develop your ideas. Among these, of course, are narration and description, as well as the simple method called "conclusion and support," which allows you to defend an opinion or explain an idea by using concrete and specific details that relate to it directly. However, you may want *to explain* or *to persuade* by choosing from seven other methods:

- Illustration: develop an idea with examples
- Definition: explain a term or concept
- Classification: distinguish between types or classes
- Comparison and contrast: point out similarities and differences
- Analogy: compare an abstract or difficult idea to something that is concrete and that the reader knows; usually, the subjects being compared seem unrelated at first
- Cause and effect: explain why something happens
- Process analysis: explain how something happens or how to do something

Deciding which method of development is best for your purpose depends on the idea you are explaining or the point you are making. Let's say you want to persuade your readers that the best way to clean up the rivers in your town is to fine polluters. The cause-and-effect method might work well. If you decide to explain that the daily routine you followed in high school is quite different from the one you follow in college, you might choose contrast. If want to prove how serious a student you are, you can support your opinion with specific details that show how often you visit the library, how infrequently you miss class, or how seldom you go to parties on nights before important tests.

Various methods of development appear in the sample paragraphs and essays that follow in this chapter. You will learn even more about exposition and persuasion in Section Five of this book. There you will find separate chapters on three very common and useful methods of development: illustration, comparison and contrast, and process analysis. Section Five also contains a chapter on techniques useful in persuasive writing. For now, just remember that any method of development can be used by itself or in combination with others to develop paragraphs and essays that explain, that persuade, or that do both.

DECIDING HOW TO ARRANGE THE IDEAS AND DETAILS IN A PARAGRAPH

For Narrative and Descriptive Writing

Often, the best way to organize narration or description is simply to recall details naturally—just as you saw or experienced them. When *narrating,* you can arrange events in the order they happened, from beginning to end; this is called "chronological order," or order of time. In the following narrative paragraph by William Carlos Williams, a doctor recalls what he had to do to examine a young patient. Words that relate to time or that show action are in italics:

> *Then* I *grasped* the child's head with my left hand and *tried to get* the wooden tongue depressor between her teeth. She *fought,* with clenched teeth, desperately! But *now* I also *had grown furious*—at a child. I *tried to hold* myself down but I couldn't. I know how to expose a throat for inspection. And I *did* my best. *When finally* I *got* the wooden spatula behind the last teeth and just the point of it into the mouth cavity, she *opened up* for an instant but *before* I *could see* anything she *came down again* and *gripping* the wooden blade between her molars she *reduced* it to splinters *before* I *could get it out again.* ("The Use of Force")

When *describing,* you can put concrete details into a *spatial* pattern, according to any arrangement you think best. For example, you might describe a place from east to west or from left to right; an object from top to bottom or from inside to outside; and a person from head to toe. In the following paragraph, John Steinbeck introduces a character from his short story "The Chrysanthemums" by telling us about both her facial and physical characteristics and then by describing what she wore:

Elisa watched [the men] for a moment and then went back to her work. She was thirty-five. Her face was lean and strong and her eyes were as clear as water. Her figure looked blocked and heavy in her gardening costume, a man's black hat pulled low down over her eyes, clodhopper shoes, a figured print dress almost completely covered by a big corduroy apron with four big pockets to hold the snips, the trowel and scratcher, the seeds and the knife she worked with. She wore heavy leather gloves to protect her hands while she worked.

For Expository and Persuasive Writing

Again, several choices are available when trying your hand at exposition—writing that explains—and at persuasion—writing that proves a point or defends an opinion. Here are a few patterns of arrangement you can use.

From General to Specific   Starting with a general statement and supporting it with specific details or ideas is a common way to organize a paragraph. Each of the following paragraphs has a different purpose and uses a different method of development. However, all begin with a general statement (the topic sentence) that is followed and developed by specific information.

Illustration: Develop an Idea with Examples

Bizarre [strange], sometimes tragic events checker [mark] the history of aviation in New Jersey. Charles and Anne Lindbergh built their estate at Somerville to be near a test facility; their son's kidnapping and murder exiled [drove] them from America for years. The *Hindenburg,* largest rigid airship ever built, crashed and burned at Lakehurst; that ended the use of dirigibles for passenger service. In his radio version of *War of the Worlds,* Orson Wells landed ''Martians'' at Grover's Mill—a hamlet just south of Princeton—and panicked thousands of listeners into fleeing the imaginary spacecraft. (William Howarth, *The John McPhee Reader*)

Comparison and Contrast: Point Out Similarities and Differences

Grant and Lee were in complete contrast, representing two diametrically opposed elements in American life. Grant was the modern man emerging: behind him, ready to come on the stage, was the great age of steel and machinery, of crowded cities and a restless, burgeoning [blossoming] vitality. Lee might have ridden down from the old age of chivalry, lance in hand, silken banner fluttering over his head. Each man was the perfect champion of his cause, drawing both his strengths and his weaknesses from the people he led. (Bruce Catton, ''Grant and Lee: A Study in Contrasts'')

Classification: Distinguish Between Types or Classes

In general, there are seven basic signals that get communicated from the [baseball] manager . . . to the players. The batter may be ordered to take a pitch on a three-and-zero count, or to hit away. He may be asked to protect a base runner on a hit-and-run by trying to slug the ball on the ground. On a run-and-hit, the batter is ordered to swing at a pitch only if it is in the strike zone; however, on the bunt-and-run, the batter must try to bunt to protect the breaking runner. . . . The batter can be told to sacrifice bunt, which means he should try for the ball only if it is in the strike zone. There are signs for squeeze bunts, and finally, there is the sign to steal a base. (Rockwell Stensrud, ''Who's on Third?'')

Cause and Effect: Explain Why Something Happens

Many lower-income families of the barrio manage to maintain a comfortable standard of living through the communal action of family members who contribute their wages to the head of the family. Economic need creates interdependence and closeness. Small barefoot boys sell papers on cool, dark Sunday mornings, deny themselves pleasantries, and give their earnings to *mamá*. The older the child, the greater the responsibility to help the head of the household provide for the rest of the family. (Robert Ramirez, ''The Woolen Sarape'')

Definition: Explain a Term or Concept

It's hard to imagine what under-development means until you have experienced it. Last year we had to queue [line up] on the road from Medellin to Barranquilla because a landslide had swept part of it away. The road, the only link between Colombia's main industrial city and its principal port, had been closed all weekend. Now it was open again, but only just. We sat in the Jeep, dwarfed by the huge *tractomulas* [tractor trailers] that haul Colombia's freight. . . . Three hours it took, inching forward through the rain, before we came to what they had managed to rebuild of the road; a single lorry's [truck's] width of gravel and mud, shelving precariously [dangerously] on a steep hillside. (Roger Garfitt, ''Bogotá, Colombia'')

From Specific to General   Beginning with specific details and moving toward a general conclusion (the topic sentence) that relates to these details is another way to arrange information. Although the following paragraphs use different methods of development, all move from specific to general.

Conclusion and Support: Use Details That Explain or Prove

A New York taxi driver . . . is licensed to operate, and thereby earn his living, by the city. One of the rules in the taxi code stipulates that the cabdriver must take his customer to any point within the city limits that the rider requests. Never mind that the driver makes more money operating in Manhattan; is lost when he enters the precincts of Brooklyn; is frightened by the prospect of a trip to Harlem at night. The rules are clear. He must go where the customer asks. (Willard Gaylin, *The Rage Within*)

Comparison and Contrast: Point Out Similarities and Differences

Just today I talked to a big blond bruiser of a football player who wants to learn the basics of grammar. I didn't tell him it was too late. You see, he was a very,

very good football player, so good that he never failed a course in high school. He had written on a weekly theme [essay], ''I wants to go to the prose and come fames.'' He may become a pro, may even become famous, but he will probably never read a good book, write a coherent letter or read a story to his children. I will, however, flunk him if he does not learn the material in the course. My job means too much to me to sacrifice my standards and turn soft. Suppose that every time my student played football badly, the coach said it was ''just a game.'' Suppose the coach allowed him to drink booze, stay up all night, eat poorly and play sloppily. My student would be summarily [quickly] dismissed from the team or the team would lose the game. So it goes with academic courses. (Suzanne Britt, ''I Wants to Go to the Prose'')

(You learned earlier that various methods of development can be used together. The paragraph you just read uses both comparison and narration. Britt begins with an anecdote, a very brief story that makes a point. She then compares the standards she demands of a student with those a coach expects of football players.)

I had always thought of stingrays, with their broad wings and graceful movements, as almost mythological [legendary] beasts: part bird, part fish. These creatures have long been feared for their whiplike tails bearing a spine that can deliver an excruciatingly painful wound. Now, as a crystalline [clear] wave washes over my camera—half in, half out of the water—I watch in fascination as two stingrays cruise the shallows of North Sound off Grand Cayman [Island]. I have come to join divers who, amazingly, have been feeding large groups of southern stingrays . . . in waters protected by a barrier reef. As they gather around me, the rays lose their fearsome [frightening] reputation. I find them to be gentle, wondrous birds of the sea. (David Doubilet, ''Ballet with Stingrays'')

(The paragraph above uses both contrast and description.)

Cause and Effect: Explain Why Something Happens

I am tired of fighting. Our chiefs are killed. Looking Glass is dead. Toohulsote is dead. The old men are all dead. It is the young men who say no and yes. He who led the young men is dead. It is cold and we have no blankets. The little children are freezing to death. My people, some of them, have run away to the hills and have no blankets, no food. No one knows where they are—perhaps they are freezing to death. I want to have time to look for my children and see how many of them I can find. Maybe I shall find them among the dead. Hear me, my chiefs, I am tired. My heart is sad and sick. From where the sun stands I will fight no more forever. (Chief Joseph of the Nez Percé, Surrender Speech)

Analogy: Compare an Abstract or Difficult Idea to Something That Is Concrete and That the Reader Knows

. . . imagine a loaf of raisin bread baking in the oven. Each raisin is a galaxy [group of millions of stars]. As the dough rises in the oven, the interior of the loaf expands, and all the raisins move apart from one another. The loaf of bread is like our expanding Universe. Every raisin sees its neighbors receding [moving away] from it; every raisin seems to be at the center of the expansion; but there is no center [to the Universe]. (Robert Jastrow, *Journey to the Stars*)

From Question to Answer   A good way to begin a paragraph is with an interesting question. You can then devote the rest of your paragraph to details that develop an effective answer to that question.

Definition: Explain a Term or Concept

"What is a kike?" Disraeli once asked a small group of fellow politicians. Then, as his audience shifted nervously, Queen Victoria's great Jewish Prime Minister supplied the answer himself. "A kike" he observed, "is a Jewish gentleman who has just left the room." (Charles F. Berlitz, "The Etymology of the International Insult")

Analogy: Compare an Abstract or Difficult Idea to Something That Is Concrete and That the Reader Knows

How can a telescope provide information about the beginning of the Universe? The answer is that when we look out into space, we look into the past. If a galaxy is five billion light-years away, it takes five billion years for the light from this galaxy to reach the earth. Consequently, our telescopes show the galaxy not as it is today, but as it was five billion years ago, when the light we are receiving now had just left that galaxy on its way to the earth. A telescope is a time machine; it carries us back to the past. (Robert Jastrow, *Journey to the Stars*)

(The paragraph above is another that uses more than one method of development. Here, analogy combines with process analysis.)

Cause and Effect: Explain Why Something Happens

Why are youngsters rediscovering booze? One reason is pressure from other kids to be one of the gang. Another is the ever-present urge to act grown-up. For some, it eases the burden of problems at home or at school. And it's cheaper. You can buy a couple of six-packs of beer for the price of three joints of pot. (Carl Rowan, *Just between Us Blacks*)

From Problem to Solution   Organizing a paragraph by stating a problem and explaining how to solve it in the sentences that follow is much like asking a question and answering it. It is especially effective when you are explaining a process or analyzing causes and effects. But it can be used with other methods of development as well:

Process Analysis: Explain How to Do Something

If you are tempted to do something that you know is academically dishonest—such as copy another student's results or lift an idea for a paper without crediting the source or, worse, cheat on an exam—then you are already in the clutches of grade frenzy. Take a break; discuss your situation with an adviser or a friend. Relax. (Thomas C. Hayden, *Handbook for College Admissions*)

Cause and Effect: Explain Why Something Happens

Human beings are . . . always in search of new experiences and sensations, seldom content with the familiar. It is this, I think, that accounts for people wanting to have a taste of your [ice cream] cone, and wanting you to have a taste of theirs. "*Do* have a taste of this fresh peach—it's delicious," my wife used to say to me. . . . An insinuating [suggestive] look of calculating [planned] curiosity would film my wife's eyes. . . . "How's *yours?*" she would say. For this reason, I always order chocolate chip now. Down through the years, all those close enough to me to feel entitled to ask for a taste of my cone—namely my wife and children—have learned what chocolate chip tastes like, so they have no legitimate reason to ask me for a taste. (L. Rust Hills, *How to Do Things Right*)

By Order of Importance   Writers of fiction often place the most important bit of information last. This makes their work suspenseful and creates a more effective climax. If arranged in this pattern, an expository or persuasive paragraph can help you create emphasis by guiding your readers to the details and ideas you believe are most important. In the first of the two paragraphs that follow, for example, Anthony Lewis waits until the end of the paragraph to mention the right to vote—the most important of all rights—which had been denied black people in the South before 1954.

Illustration: Develop an Idea with Examples

It is hard to remember, now, what this country was like before May 17, 1954 [the day the U.S. Supreme Court outlawed racial segregation in public schools]. More than a third of America's public schools were segregated by law. And not just schools: In the Southern and Border states, black men and women and children were kept out of "white" hospitals, and parks, and beaches, and restaurants. Interracial marriage was forbidden. In the deep South, law and brutal force kept blacks from voting. (Anthony Lewis, "The System Worked")

Comparison and Contrast: Point Out Similarities and Differences

We know very little about pain and what we don't know makes it hurt all the more. Indeed, no form of illiteracy in the United States is so widespread or costly as ignorance about pain—what it is, what causes it, how to deal with it without panic. Almost everyone can rattle off the names of at least a dozen drugs that can deaden pain from every conceivable cause—all the way from headaches to hemorrhoids. There is far less knowledge about the fact that about 90 percent of pain is self-limiting, that it is not always an indication of poor health, and that most frequently, it is the result of tension, stress, worry, idleness, boredom, frustration, suppressed rage, insufficient sleep, overeating, poorly balanced diet, smoking, excessive drinking, inadequate exercise, stale air, or any of the other abuses encountered by the human body in modern society. (Norman Cousins, from *The Anatomy of an Illness*)

As you read the following selections, remember what you've just learned about (1) the methods that writers use to develop their ideas and (2) the patterns they use to organize their paragraphs. Approach each selection carefully, and devote as much effort to determining *how* the author has organized and developed the material as you do to understanding what the essay means. Doing so will help you develop your own writing more effectively.

Condolences, It's a Girl

SANDRA BURTON

Written while Burton was in Beijing, capital of the People's Republic of China, this article appeared in a special edition of Time *magazine devoted to issues facing women in the 1990s. Because of its large population, China has a "one-child-per-couple" policy, which, as Burton explains, "has inflamed age-old prejudices against females."*

Looking Ahead

1. Burton's title is a twist on what we expect to hear at the birth of a child: "Congratulations, it's a . . ."
2. The paragraphs in this selection use some methods of development you just read about. Look for contrast, cause and effect, and illustration.
3. In paragraph 3, we learn that the "Communists sought to change" the status of women in China in 1949. That was the year the Communist revolution led by Mao Tse-tung took control of the country.
4. Burton uses "feudal" to explain traditional Chinese thinking about having children. Feudalism was a male-dominated political and economic system in medieval Europe.

Vocabulary

amniocentesis   Medical procedure to determine the health of a fetus.
bastion   Stronghold.
cadre   Group, association.
condolences   Expressions of sympathy.
draconian   Tyrannical, rigid, strict.
enlightened   Well-educated, forward-thinking, progressive.

infanticide   Murder of a baby.
inflamed   Aroused, made stronger.
scion   Offspring, child.
wistful   Sad, melancholic.

The letter from a Chinese woman to her American friend reflected her torment   1
and tears. "I told you I wish a baby girl, because nothing can compare with one's
love of a baby, especially mother and daughter," she wrote in broken English.
Instead of bringing joy, however, the birth of a daughter was destroying her
family. "My husband wants to divorce me," she continued. "When he knew the
baby was a girl, he left quickly." Reluctant to blame only her husband, she
pointed to her in-laws. "He is the only boy, so his having a son is more important
for his parents," she explained. "Although he had been hoping for a boy, I never
thought he would act like this."

Old attitudes die hard in a society that has been a bastion of male chauvinism   2
for 22 centuries. Until a few decades ago, the drowning of infant girls was
tolerated in poor rural areas as an economic necessity. A girl was just another
mouth to feed, another dowry to pay, a temporary family member who would
eventually leave to serve her husband's kin. A boy, on the other hand, meant
more muscle for the farm work, someone to care for aged parents and burn
offerings to ancestors.

The Communists sought to change all that in 1949 by freeing women from   3
the household, putting them to work in fields and factories and giving them the
right to inherit property. Suddenly a girl could have positive economic value.
Still, feudal tradition has resisted change in many regions, and the government's
draconian one-child-per-couple population policy, begun in 1979, has inflamed
age-old prejudices against females. Rural and minority families routinely lie,
cheat or pay fines in order to try a second pregnancy in the hope of having a son.
And female infanticide—plus its modern variation, the misuse of amniocentesis
to identify female fetuses in order to abort them—continues. The problem is so
extensive that government campaigns urge parents to "Love your daughter" and
allow girl babies to live.

Even in enlightened circles, condolences are in order for a couple whose   4
new-born is a girl. Over dinner in the Beijing apartment of a liberal-party cadre,
a young guest proudly passes around color photos of her infant son, lying
spread-eagled on a blanket, his genitals prominently displayed. Seated beside
her, the new mother of a baby girl looks on in wistful silence. She carries no
pictures. Jiang Junsheng, a senior engineer in a Beijing auto-parts factory, says
he wasn't upset when his only child, a daughter, was born, but "my mother did
not like it." That's an understatement, says his wife Chen Yiyun, 50, a well-
known sociologist. "His mother would not take care of our daughter," she says.
"Yet when my husband's brother had a boy, she showered him with attention."

Social observers believe a daughter's lot will improve as women become   5
more valuable to China's growing economy and as the one-child policy eventu-

ally makes every scion—male and female—precious to parents. Chen's own daughter Jiang Xu, 19, reflects changing attitudes when she expresses her preference for a daughter: ''To have a boy means happiness for a moment. To have a girl means a lifetime of good fortune.''

Questions for Discussion

1. What is Burton's thesis statement?
2. Contrasting a mother's and father's reactions to the birth of their daughter (paragraph 1) is a good way to arouse the reader's interest. Where else does Burton use contrast to develop her ideas?
3. In what paragraph is the cause-and-effect method used?
4. What is the central idea in the last paragraph? What method that you learned about earlier does Burton use to develop this idea?
5. Which paragraphs are arranged according to the general-to-specific pattern? Does Burton ever use the specific-to-general pattern? Where?

Suggestions for Journal Entries

1. Use the focused freewriting method you learned about in ''Getting Started'' to describe your reaction to the birth of a sister, brother, niece, nephew, cousin, or child of your own. Did the sex of the child matter to you or to anyone else?
2. Does your family treat boys and girls differently? If you are female, think of ways in which your parents, grandparents, aunts, uncles, and other family members have treated your brother(s) or male cousins. If you are male, think of ways they have treated your sister(s) or female cousins. Were they different from the ways they treated you? If so, list as many of these differences as you can.

The Hibernation of the Woodchuck

ALAN DEVOE

Alan Devoe (1909–1955) was a naturalist who wrote several delightful books and hundreds of articles about the animals he observed on his 100-acre wildlife sanctuary in New York State. He was a staff writer for The American Mercury, The Audubon Magazine, The Atlantic Monthly, *and* Nature.

According to Devoe, the best way to learn about animals is to live near them. He could often be seen walking the grounds of his estate as he observed, talked to, and even fed the many creatures who made it their home. ''The Hibernation of the Woodchuck'' appeared in Lives around Us, *a book on animal behavior that was based on such experiences.*

Looking Ahead

1. In some of Devoe's paragraphs, the central idea is stated clearly and explicitly in a topic sentence; in others, it is only implied.
2. Look for ways Devoe maintains coherence in and between paragraphs: linking pronouns, transitions, and the repetition of words and ideas.
3. Although Devoe's main purpose is to explain a process (how something happens), he uses other methods of development as well. These include comparison and contrast, cause and effect, and conclusion and support. Watch for them as you read ''The Hibernation of the Woodchuck.''

Vocabulary

ascends Rises.
axils Places at which the legs are joined to the body.
dormancy Inactivity, sleep.
fluctuant Unstable, fluctuating.
foraging Searching for food.
gait Walk.
lethargic Sluggish.
oblivion Unconsciousness.

The woodchuck's hibernation usually starts about the middle of September. For weeks he has been foraging with increased appetite among the clover blossoms and has grown heavy and slow-moving. Now, with the coming of mid-September, apples and corn and yarrow tops have become less plentiful, and the nights are cool. The woodchuck moves with slower gait, and emerges less and less frequently for feeding trips. Layers of fat have accumulated around his chest and shoulders, and there is thick fat in the axils of his legs. He has extended his summer burrow to a length of nearly thirty feet, and has fashioned a deep nest-chamber at the end of it, far below the level of frost. He has carried in, usually, a little hay. He is ready for the Long Sleep.

When the temperature of the September days falls below 50 degrees or so, the woodchuck becomes too drowsy to come forth from his burrow in the chilly dusk to forage. He remains in the deep nest-chamber, lethargic, hardly moving. Gradually, with the passing of hours or days, his coarse-furred body curls into a semicircle, like a foetus, nose-tip touching tail. The small legs are tucked in, the handlike clawed forefeet folded. The woodchuck has become a compact ball. Presently the temperature of his body begins to fall.

In normal life the woodchuck's temperature, though fluctuant, averages about 97 degrees. Now, as he lies tight-curled in a ball with the winter sleep stealing over him, his body heat drops ten degrees, twenty degrees, thirty.

Finally, by the time the snow is on the ground and the woodchuck's winter dormancy has become complete, his temperature is only 38 or 40. With the falling of the body heat there is a slowing of his heartbeat and his respiration. In normal life he breathes thirty or forty times each minute; when he is excited, as many as a hundred times. Now he breathes slow and slower—ten times a minute, once a minute, and at last only ten or twelve times in an hour. His heartbeat is a twentieth of normal. He has entered fully into the oblivion of hibernation.

The Long Sleep lasts, on an average, about six months. For half a year the   4 woodchuck remains unmoving, hardly breathing. His pituitary gland is inactive; his blood is so sluggishly circulated that there is an unequal distribution in the chilled body; his sensory awareness has wholly ceased. It is almost true to say that he has altered from a warm-blooded to a cold-blooded animal.

Then, in the middle of March, he wakes. The waking is not a slow and   5 gradual thing, as was the drifting into sleep, but takes place quickly, often in an hour. The body temperature ascends to normal, or rather higher for a while; glandular functions instantly resume: the respiration quickens and steadies at a normal rate. The woodchuck has become himself again, save only that he is a little thinner, and is ready at once to fare forth into the pale spring sunlight and look for grass and berries.

Such is the performance each fall and winter, with varying detail, of bats and   6 worms and bears, and a hundred other kinds of creature. It is a marvel less spectacular than the migration flight of hummingbirds or the flash of shooting stars, but it is not much less remarkable.

Questions for Discussion

1. What is the central idea—stated or implied—in each paragraph?
2. What causes and effects are explained in paragraph 2?
3. Paragraphs 4 and 5 are arranged in the general-to-specific pattern. What methods of development does the author use in these paragraphs?
4. Both process analysis and contrast can be seen in paragraph 3. Which details in this paragraph help explain how something happens? Which explain differences between the woodchuck in hibernation and in "normal life"?
5. Where else in this essay does Devoe use contrast? What is being contrasted in this paragraph?
6. What methods does the author use to maintain coherence in and between paragraphs? Find transitions, linking pronouns, and words or ideas that have been repeated.

Suggestions for Journal Entries

1. Think about an animal you know well—your Siamese cat, the neighbor's German shepherd, a bird that visits your backyard feeder often, or the wood-

chuck that's been eating up your vegetable garden. List important things you know about this creature—anything that would provide clues about its behavior, lifestyle, character, or personality.

Then ask yourself what this information tells you. Draw three or more general conclusions about this animal from the details you've listed, and write out these conclusions in the form of topic sentences for paragraphs that you might later develop about the animal.

2. Devoe uses comparison and contrast to help us understand the woodchuck's hibernation. This is especially true in paragraph 3, in which he contrasts the animal's "normal life" with his "winter dormancy." But animals aren't the only creatures that need to adapt to different conditions.

Think about the way you dress for a date and the way you dress for work or school, the way you act with friends and the way you act among strangers, the schedule you keep during the week and the schedule you follow on weekends, or the foods you eat when you're on a diet and when you're not. Then list as many details as you can to show how your behavior changes under different circumstances.

The Thick and Thin of It

BLYTHE HAMER

"The Thick and Thin of It" first appeared as a column in Science, *a magazine that publishes a variety of informative scientific articles and studies. In this essay Hamer probes the reasons that some areas of the world are so crowded while others are sparsely populated.*

Looking Ahead

1. Hamer doesn't express her central idea in a formal thesis statement, so don't look for one. Instead, draw your own conclusion about her main point in "The Thick and Thin of It."
2. In addition to being well developed, her essay is both unified and coherent. Look for signs of unity and coherence as you read it.
3. Hamer develops this expository (or explanatory) essay in several ways. Comparison and contrast is the primary method of development in at least two paragraphs, while illustration, cause and effect, and conclusion and support are used in others.
4. The Falkland Islands, mentioned in paragraph 2, are a colony of Great Britain located in the South Atlantic Ocean off Argentina. Several years ago these countries fought a brief war over the Falklands, which Britain retained.

Vocabulary

arable   Usable for farming.

compensate   Make up for.

demographer   Expert on population trends.

hinterlands   Wilderness, back country.

impenetrable   Not capable of being penetrated or broken through.

perceptions   Opinions, beliefs.

socioeconomic   Having to do with the kind of society that people live in and/or the economic conditions in which they earn their livings.

subsistence   Bare minimum required to live.

I f every person in Macau were given equal portions of land, each would live   1
in a space a quarter the size of a tennis court. If you take into account the room
necessary for streets, stores, and offices, people living in Macau (like people
living in Manhattan) are more likely to end up with an apartment the size of a
Ping-Pong table. With more than 63,000 people per square mile, Macau, a tiny
city-state off the coast of China, is the most densely populated place in the world.

Every Falkland Islander, by contrast, could roam over two and a half square   2
miles without ever seeing another human. But he'd better watch where he steps;
sheep outnumber people by more than 300 to one.

No single cause explains why some areas of the world are so much more   3
thickly settled than others. But high population density can be an accident of
political history, as it is in city-states such as Macau. And it is often the result
of geography: the three most densely populated countries in the world—Macau,
Hong Kong and Singapore—are all islands. Many larger island countries, such
as Malta, Taiwan, and Barbados, also rank among the most densely settled parts
of the world.

Density can also be the result of the economy of an area. "The Falkland   4
Islands are so thinly settled because they have no resources other than sheep,"
says Tom Merrick of the Population Reference Bureau in Washington, D.C.
"The population doesn't grow because so many people emigrate."

The countries that are least densely populated often have obvious climatic   5
or geographical flaws, like Mongolia (three people per square mile). Australia
has a population density of five per square mile, and Canada has only seven,
demonstrating the effect of huge hinterlands. The United States is not very
crowded, despite perceptions to the contrary, with 65 people per square mile. "A
lot of our land is uninhabitable," says Ken Hill, a demographer at the National
Academy of Sciences in Washington, D.C. "The Rockies, the desert, and the
rangeland are not places people want to live, so they crowd together in pleasanter
surroundings."

If high population density were a measure of pleasantness, then Bangladesh   6
would be pleasant indeed. With 1,800 people per square mile, it the most densely

settled nonisland nation in the world. Nearly 100 million people live in an area the size of Arkansas. All of Bangladesh is arable, and that explains its density. "There are no deserts, mountains, or impenetrable forests," says Hill. "There's plenty of rainfall, so most fields yield two crops a year."

Socioeconomic factors also influence population density. In Bangladesh,   7 mothers and fathers see additional children as contributing to the family labor force, not detracting from the family food supply. Children often work 10-hour days on their families' subsistence-level farms. Women usually have seven or eight children, partly to compensate for the high infant mortality rate. Falkland Islanders, in comparison, have only two children per family. "They have a European attitude toward children," says Hill. "They don't see the need for more, even though for years emigration has been causing the country's population to decline."

When is a place too empty or too crowded? That's a judgement everyone has   8 to make for himself. In Manhattan people press together in subways and on street corners without batting an eye. But in America a hundred years ago, the sound of an axe in the next clearing signalled that it was time to move on.

Questions for Discussion

1. What is the essay's central idea? What main point is Hamer explaining?
2. In the introduction to this chapter, you learned that writers use analogy to explain abstract or hard-to-understand ideas by comparing them to things that are concrete or that the reader may be familiar with. What analogies do you find in this essay?
3. What methods of development are used in paragraphs 2 through 8?
4. Paragraph 2 is much shorter than the rest. Is it well developed? Explain.
5. Every paragraph but one uses the general-to-specific pattern of organization. Which one does not? Which pattern does it follow?
6. Is this essay unified? How do you know?
7. At the beginning of paragraph 4, Hamer uses a transitional word to create coherence between this and the preceding paragraph. What is it? What other words, phrases, and techniques does Hamer use to maintain coherence in and between paragraphs?

Suggestions for Journal Entries

1. While Hamer's eight paragraphs show various methods of development, all but one follow the general-to-specific pattern of organization. Choose one of these seven paragraphs, and reorganize it by using the specific-to-general pattern.
2. How densely or sparsely populated is your campus, hometown, or county? List details in your journal that show how crowded or uncrowded your

environment is. Like Hamer, you might list statistics along with illustrations and analogies, or you might simply begin describing your surroundings.

3. Using Hamer's fine analogies as models, think of an analogy that reveals something important about a subject you know well (such as a friend or relative, a place you visit often, your education, or your lifestyle). Then put this analogy into a well-written topic sentence. Here are some sample topic sentences that contain analogies:

After I stay up all night cramming for a big test, my mind becomes an intellectual garbage heap.

Trying to make good grades in Professor Jones's class is like running an obstacle course.

Eating at Mel's Diner is as close as I've come to playing Russian roulette.

The content of some game shows, soap operas, and situation comedies supports the opinion that television has become a moral wasteland.

Finally, think about the kinds of details that will develop your topic sentence clearly, and list these details in your journal.

A Brother's Dreams

PAUL ARONOWITZ

Paul Aronowitz was a medical student at Case Western Reserve University when he wrote this very sensitive essay comparing his dreams, hopes, and ambitions with those of his schizophrenic brother. Schizophrenia is a mental illness characterized by withdrawal from reality.

Aronowitz's love, compassion, and understanding come across clearly as he unfolds the story of how he learned to deal with the fact that his brother's strange, sometimes violent behavior was the symptom of an illness and not a defect in character. This essay is also Aronowitz's admission and unselfish affirmation that, however "elusive" and "trivial," his brother's dreams might be even more meaningful than his own.

"A Brother's Dreams" first appeared in "About Men," a weekly column in The New York Times Magazine.

Looking Ahead

1. Aronowitz's central idea concerns how he came to understand his brother's illness and to accept the fact that his brother's dreams were meaningful and important. However, the author does not begin to reveal this central idea until well near the end of this essay, and he never puts the idea into a formal thesis statement.

2. Many of the paragraphs in this selection are developed through narration and description, but Aronowitz also makes good use of

cause and effect, comparison and contrast, illustration, and conclusion and support.

3. Josef Mengele, whom Aronowitz mentions in paragraph 5, was a Nazi medical researcher who conducted unspeakable experiments in which he tortured and maimed or killed thousands of human beings.

Vocabulary

acrid   Bitter, harsh, sharp.

aimlessly   Without purpose.

alienate   Make enemies of, isolate oneself from.

delusions   Misconceptions, fantasies.

depravity   Immorality, corruption.

elusive   Hard to grasp, intangible.

paranoid   Showing unreasonable or unwarranted suspicion.

prognosis   Prediction about the course or outcome of an illness.

resilient   Able to bounce back.

siblings   Sisters and brothers.

Each time I go home to see my parents at their house near Poughkeepsie, N.Y., my brother, a schizophrenic for almost nine years now, comes to visit from the halfway house where he lives nearby. He owns a car that my parents help him to maintain, and his food and washing are taken care of by the halfway house. Somewhere, somehow along the way, with the support of a good physician, a social worker and my ever-resilient parents, he has managed to carve a niche for himself, to bite off some independence and, with it, elusive dreams that, to any healthy person, might seem trivial.

My brother sits in a chair across from me, chain-smoking cigarettes, trying to take the edge off the medications he'll be on for the rest of his life. Sometimes his tongue hangs loosely from his mouth when he's listening or pops out of his mouth as he speaks—a sign of tardive dyskinesia, an often-irreversible side effect of his medication.

He draws deeply on his cigarette and tells me he can feel his mind healing—cells being replaced, tissue being restored, thought processes returning. He knows this is happening because he dreams of snakes, and hot, acrid places in which he suffocates if he moves too fast. When he wakes, the birds are singing in the trees outside his bedroom window. They imitate people in his halfway house, mocking them and calling their names. The birds are so smart, he tells me, so much smarter than we are.

His face, still handsome despite its puffiness (another side effect of the medications that allow him to function outside the hospital), and warm brown eyes are serious. When I look into his eyes I imagine I can see some of the suffering he has been through. I think of crossed wires, of receptors and neurotransmitters, deficits and surpluses, progress and relapse, and I wonder, once again, what has happened to my brother.

My compassion for him is recent. For many years, holidays, once happy 5 occasions for our family of seven to gather together, were emotional torture sessions. My brother would pace back and forth in the dining room, lecturing us, his voice loud, dominating, crushing all sound but his own, about the end of the world, the depravity of our existences. His speeches were salted with paranoid delusions: our house was bugged by the F.B.I.; my father was Josef Mengele; my mother was selling government secrets to the Russians.

His life was decaying before my eyes, and I couldn't stand to listen to him. 6 My resentment of him grew as his behavior became more disruptive and aggressive. I saw him as being ultimately responsible for his behavior. As my anger increased, I withdrew from him, avoiding him when I came home to visit from college, refusing to discuss the bizarre ideas he brought up over the dinner table. When I talked with my sister or other two brothers about him, our voices always shadowed in whispers, I talked of him as of a young man who had chosen to spend six months of every year in a pleasant, private hospital on the banks of the Hudson River, chosen to alienate his family with threats, chosen to withdraw from the stresses of the world. I hated what he had become. In all those years, I never asked what his diagnosis was.

Around the fifth year of his illness, things finally changed. One hot summer 7 night, he attacked my father. When I came to my father's aid, my brother broke three of my ribs and nearly strangled me. The State Police came and took him away. My father's insurance coverage had run out on my brother, so this time he was taken to a locked ward at the state hospital where heavily sedated patients wandered aimlessly in stockinged feet up and down long hallways. Like awakening from a bad dream, we gradually began talking about his illness. Slowly and painfully, I realized that he wasn't responsible for his disease any more than a cancer patient is for his pain.

As much as I've learned to confront my brother's illness, it frightens me to 8 think that one day, my parents gone from the scene, my siblings and I will be responsible for portions of my brother's emotional and financial support. This element of the future is one we still avoid discussing, much the way we avoided thinking about the nature of his disease and his prognosis. I'm still not capable of thinking about it.

Now I come home and listen to him, trying not to react, trying not to show 9 disapproval. His delusions are harmless and he is, at the very least, communicating. When he asks me about medical school, I answer with a sentence or two—no elaboration, no revelations about the dreams I cradle in my heart.

He talks of his own dreams. He hopes to finish his associate's degree—the 10 same one he has been working on between hospitalizations for almost eight years now—at the local community college. Next spring, with luck, he'll get a job. His boss will be understanding, he tells me, cutting him a little slack when he has his "bad days," letting him have a day off here or there when things aren't going well. He puts out his cigarette and lights another one.

Time stands still. This could be last year, or the year before, or the year 11 before that. I'm within range of becoming a physician, of realizing something I've been working toward for almost five years, while my brother still dreams of having a small job, living in his own apartment and of being well. As the smoke flows from his nose and mouth, I recall an evening some time ago when I drove upstate from Manhattan to tell my parents and my brother that I was getting married (an engagement later severed). My brother's eyes lit up at the news, and then a darkness fell over them.

"What's wrong?" I asked him.

"It's funny," he answered matter-of-factly. "You're getting married, and I've never even had a girlfriend." My mother's eyes filled with tears, and she turned away. She was trying her best to be happy for me, for the dreams I had—for the dreams so many of us take for granted.

"You still have us," I stammered, reaching toward him and touching his arm. All of a sudden my dreams meant nothing; I didn't deserve them and they weren't worth talking about. My brother shrugged his shoulders, smiled and shook my hand, his large, tobacco-stained fingers wrapping around my hand, dwarfing my hand.

Questions for Discussion

1. If you wanted to write a formal thesis statement for this essay, what would it be?

2. "A Brother's Dreams" contains at least two paragraphs that are developed through description. Identify one of them. What important idea does this paragraph communicate?

3. The purpose of paragraph 6 is to explain a cause and an effect. What is the paragraph's topic sentence (cause)? What details (effect) does Aronowitz provide to develop the paragraph fully?

4. Which paragraphs use narration?

5. Aronowitz gets specific about his brother's dreams in paragraph 10, which he develops by stating a conclusion and then supporting this conclusion with details. Identify these details.

6. Paragraph 11 contrasts some of Aronowitz's dreams to some of his brother's. In what other paragraph do we see their dreams contrasted?

7. Most paragraphs in this essay are organized in the general-to-specific pattern. However, paragraphs 11 and 13 are organized according to order of importance. What is the most important idea in each of these paragraphs?

8. This is a powerful essay. Which paragraph affects you most strongly? What do the details in this paragraph tell you about the author or his brother or both?

Suggestions for Journal Entries

1. Aronowitz writes about a person whose lifestyle and dreams are very different from those of most other people. Do you know someone like this? If so,

write a paragraph showing how this person's lifestyle or dreams differ from those of most others. Use one major method of development; for instance, you might *describe* what this individual looks like (much in the way Aronowitz describes his brother in paragraphs 2 and 4), or you might use *narration* to tell a story about the kind of behavior you have come to expect from the person (as Aronowitz does in paragraphs 3, 5, and 7). You might even want to try your hand at the cause-and-effect method by telling your reader how you normally react to or deal with this person and then explaining what causes you to react in this way.

2. Aronowitz's essay contrasts his brother's dreams to his own. Write a paragraph in which you show how different you are from your brother, sister, or other close relative by contrasting a major goal in your life to one of his or hers.

    Clearly identify the two different goals in your topic sentence, and fill the rest of your paragraph with details showing how different they are; that is, develop the paragraph by contrast. Your topic sentence might go something like this: "My sister Janet intends to move to the city and find a high-paying job, even if she hates every minute of it; I'll be happy earning the modest income that comes with managing our family farm."

SUGGESTIONS FOR WRITING

1. Review your journal notes after Burton's "Condolences, It's a Girl." You may have described important differences in the ways your family treated boys and girls. Focus on one such difference based upon personal experience, and express it in a topic sentence. Here are two examples of what that sentence might say:

   In my house, I spent Saturdays doing housework while my brother played baseball or went fishing.

   When I was a boy, Saturdays meant getting up early to wash the car, mow the lawn, or clean up the basement while my sisters slept until noon!

   Now provide specific examples of what your family expected of you. Talk about having to scrub the bathroom sink or vacuum the rug as you saw your brother stroll out of the house with a baseball bat over his shoulder. Or explain how hard it was to lug garbage up the cellar steps while your sister was still in dreamland. Then talk about the other things you had to do while your brother(s) or sister(s) relaxed! You should wind up with a paragraph developed through both comparison and contrast and illustration. As always, revise and edit your work carefully as you learned in "Getting Started." In the process, check for unity and coherence.

2. If you responded to the first of the Suggestions for Journal Entries after Devoe's "The Hibernation of the Woodchuck," you have already begun to gather details and to draw some general conclusions about an animal with which you are quite familiar. Your list should include a number of specific details, as well as more general ideas or conclusions, that may provide important clues about this animal's habits, lifestyle, behavior, character, or "personality."

   Use one of the conclusions you've come up with as the topic sentence of a paragraph that will tell your reader something important about the animal you've chosen to discuss. Develop your paragraph with details from your journal, but make sure that the details you use relate directly to your topic sentence. If you need to, try to recall additional *appropriate* details to develop your paragraph more fully. In any case, make sure your paragraph is unified!

   Incidentally, you can use a variety of patterns to organize this paragraph, including the question-and-answer approach. For instance, you might start off with a sentence like, "Are domestic cats as intelligent as they seem?" "Do beavers really work as hard as everyone thinks?" or "Are German shepherds as ferocious as they look?"

   However you choose to begin, develop your paragraph well and make it easy to follow. When you revise, add transitions where they are needed. Then, give your work a special polish by editing for sentence structure, punctuation, spelling, grammar, and other important considerations.

3. Item 2 of the Suggestions for Journal Entries after Devoe's essay asks you to list details about the way you change your behavior in order to adapt to

various situations, needs, or circumstances. If you listed details about this topic in your journal, you might have mentioned differences between how you dress for a date and how you dress for school or work, or perhaps you began explaining how different your normal eating habits are from those you follow when on a diet.

Explain such differences in a paragraph developed through contrast. You might arrange your details according to the general-to-specific pattern by beginning with a topic sentence and following it with appropriate details. Then again, the specific-to-general pattern might suit you better. If so, begin with specific details that lead to a topic sentence at the paragraph's end. Either way, make sure your paragraph is well developed, unified, and coherent by revising it carefully. If necessary, include more information, make sure all your details relate to the topic sentence, and add transitions or linking pronouns. Finally, edit for mechanical errors.

4. Write a paragraph that uses the cause-and-effect method to explain why you do something habitually. For instance, explain why you are late for work every day, why you take the same road home, why you frequent a particular restaurant or bar, or why you study in the same place every night.

Arrange the paragraph in a general-to-specific or specific-to-general pattern, provide enough details to develop your central idea clearly and convincingly, and check for unity and coherence. You will find examples of effective cause-and-effect paragraphs in "The Hibernation of the Woodchuck," "The Thick and Thin of It," and "A Brother's Dreams."

As with other assignments, revise your work as necessary; never be satisfied with an early draft! Add or remove detail as appropriate, and insert transitions that will make your ideas easy to follow. Then edit carefully for mechanical errors that might reduce your writing's effectiveness.

5. Look over the notes you made in your journal after reading Blythe Hamer's "The Thick and Thin of It." If you responded to item 2 in the Suggestions for Journal Entries, turn your notes into a paragraph that explains how densely or sparsely populated your campus, your hometown, or your county is. Use either illustration or conclusion and support as a method of development. If you need to review other paragraphs that use these methods, turn back to the introduction, or reread paragraphs 4 and 5 in Hamer's essay.

When it comes time to revise your work, make sure that you have a clearly identifiable topic sentence and that you have developed your central idea in as much detail as you can. Also, eliminate weaknesses in unity and coherence, and correct problems in grammar, punctuation, spelling, and other important areas.

6. After completing Paul Aronowitz's "A Brother's Dreams," you might have written a paragraph in your journal explaining how different your goal in life is from that of your brother, sister, or other close relative. If so, the method by which you developed this paragraph was contrast.

Reread this paragraph. What does it tell you about your subject's character? What kind of person is he or she? Turn your answer into the central idea (thesis statement) of an essay in which you continue to discuss this relative. In fact, make the paragraph you've already written the introduction to your essay.

As you plan this essay, consider writing a paragraph or two in which you describe this individual—the way he walks, the way she dresses, and so on. You might also want to include a narrative paragraph, one in which you tell a story that helps support what you say about him or her in your thesis. Finally, think about using additional methods of development—illustration, and conclusion and support, for example—in other paragraphs to develop your thesis further.

Once again, remember that writing is a process. You owe it to yourself and your readers to produce the most effective paper you can through painstaking rewriting and editing.

CHAPTER 4

INTRODUCTIONS AND CONCLUSIONS

In the previous chapters you learned a number of important principles to help you focus on the central idea of a paragraph or essay and to express this central idea in a topic sentence or thesis statement. You also learned how to develop paragraphs adequately and to make sure that each paragraph in an essay clearly develops the essay's thesis.

Most effective essays begin with an interesting and informative introduction—a paragraph or a series of paragraphs that reveals the essay's thesis and captures the reader's attention. Similarly, most successful essays end with a paragraph or a series of paragraphs that brings the writer's discussion of the subject to a timely and logical conclusion. Effective conclusions always leave the reader satisfied that everything the writer set out to discuss from the very beginning has been discussed.

Clearly, then, introductions and conclusions have special uses and are important to the success of an essay. That's why this entire chapter is devoted to explaining how to write them.

WRITING INTRODUCTIONS

Before deciding exactly what to include in an introduction, how to organize it, or even how to begin it, ask yourself whether the essay you're writing actually calls for a formal introduction. If you're writing a narrative, for instance, you might simply want to start with the very first event in your story. Of course, you can always begin with colorful details, exciting vocabulary, or intriguing ideas that will spark your reader's interest. But you need not provide a thesis statement, background information, explanatory details, or other introductory material before getting into the story proper. If you feel the need to express your central idea in a formal thesis statement, you can do so later, at a convenient point in the body of your essay or even in its conclusion.

On the other hand, you might decide that your essay needs a formal introduction. If so, remember that the *most important* function of an introduction is to capture the attention of the readers and make them read on. However, you can also use an introduction to:

- Reveal the essay's central idea as expressed in the thesis.
- Guide readers to important ideas in the body of the essay.

- Provide background or explanatory information to help readers understand the essay's purpose and thesis.

Consider these four objectives when you plan your introduction. But if you are unable to decide how to begin, simply write out a preliminary thesis statement and go directly on to the body of your essay. You can always get back to your introduction later in the writing process. It certainly does not have to be the very first part of the essay you write!

However you choose to get started, remember that an exciting part of writing is deciding *exactly* what you want to say about your subject. You usually won't make this discovery until after you have completed at least one draft—and often more than one draft—of the middle or body paragraphs of your essay. Once you have done that, your chances of going back and drafting a clearer, more substantial thesis will have improved. So will your chances of writing an interesting and effective introduction.

The simplest and sometimes best way to write an introductory paragraph or series of introductory paragraphs is to place your thesis at the very beginning and to follow it with explanatory details that prepare readers for what they will find in the body of the essay. However, depending on your purpose, your thesis, and your audience, this may not always be the best way to begin. In Chapter 3 you learned several methods to develop and organize the middle paragraphs in a piece of writing. Similarly, there are many methods for developing and organizing an introduction. Here are eight:

1. Use a startling remark or statistic.
2. Ask a question or present a problem.
3. Challenge a widely held assumption or opinion.
4. Use a comparison, a contrast, or an analogy.
5. Tell an anecdote or describe a scene.
6. Use a quotation.
7. Define an important term or concept.
8. Address your readers.

Often, beginning writers limit their introductions to one paragraph. Doing so will help you get to the point quickly. On the other hand, you can—and sometimes must—spread your opening remarks over two or three short paragraphs. This may help you increase your readers' interest because it allows you use a variety of methods to write your introduction. Each method is described below and illustrated by one or more sample paragraphs. In some samples, the central idea is expressed in a formal thesis statement (shown in italics); in others, the central idea is only implied, and no formal thesis statement can be identified.

Use a Startling Remark or Statistic

Some pieces of writing begin with statements or statistics (numbers) that, while true to the author's intent, have an effective shock value—one sure to make readers want to continue. Take this lead paragraph from an article by Ellen L. Bassuk in *Scientific American:*

> More Americans were homeless last winter than at any other time since the Great Depression. Estimates of the size of the vagrant population vary widely. The National Coalition for the Homeless puts the figure at 2.5 million for 1983, an increase of 500,000 over the preceding year. The Federal Department of Housing and Urban Development (HUD) estimates that only 250,000 to 350,000 are homeless nationwide. *Whatever the number is, everyone agrees it is growing.* ("The Homelessness Problem")

You might find this technique particularly effective if you have to take an unpopular stand on a well-known subject, as did former Philadelphia Phillies pitcher Robin Roberts in the opening of "Strike Out Little League":

> In 1939, Little League baseball was organized by Bert and George Bebble and Carl Stotz of Williamsport, Pa. What they had in mind in organizing this kids' baseball program, I'll never know. But *I'm sure they never visualized the monster it would grow into.*

A startling statement is often followed by details—some of them statistics—that explain the writer's point. Such is the case with the introduction to "The Nuclear Winter," in which Carl Sagan warns of nuclear destruction:

> *Except for fools and madmen, everyone knows that nuclear war would be an unprecedented [never having happened before] human catastrophe.* A more or less typical strategic warhead has a yield of 2 megatons, the explosive equivalent of 2 million tons of TNT. But 2 million tons of TNT is about the same as all the bombs exploded in World War II—a single bomb with the explosive power of the entire Second World War but compressed into a few seconds of time and an area 30 to 40 miles across.

In *Victims of Vanity,* a book criticizing laboratory tests on animals, Lynda Dickinson decided that spreading startling remarks and statistics over three short paragraphs would be a better way to capture the readers' attention and prepare them for her thesis than using one long unit:

> Lipstick, face cream, anti-perspirant, laundry detergent . . . these products and hundreds of other personal care and household items have one common ingredient: the suffering and death of millions of animals.
>
> An average of 25 million animals die every year in North America for the testing of everything from new cosmetics to new methods of warfare. Five hundred thousand to one million of these animals are sacrificed each year to test new cosmetics alone.
>
> *Of all the pain and suffering caused by animal research, cosmetic and household product testing is among the least justifiable, as it cannot even be argued that [these] tests are done to improve the quality of human life.*

Ask a Question or Present a Problem

If you begin by asking a question or presenting a problem, you can devote the rest of your essay to discussing that question or problem and, perhaps, to providing answers or solutions. In "I Want a Wife," for example, Judy Brady concludes her two-paragraph introduction with a question that the rest of her essay addresses:

> I belong to that classification of people known as wives. I am A Wife. And, not altogether incidentally, I am a mother.
>
> Not too long ago a male friend of mine appeared on the scene fresh from a recent divorce. He had one child, who is, of course, with his ex-wife. He is obviously looking for another wife. As I thought about him while I was ironing one evening, it suddenly occurred to me that I, too, would like to have a wife. Why do I want a wife?

Making reference to a well-known nursery rhyme, Katha Pollit begins an article in *Time* magazine by stating how difficult it is to raise daughters in a world that puts up with sexual violence. This is the problem to which she offers solutions later in her essay.

> My three-year-old daughter is puzzled. Why . . . did Georgie Porgie kiss the girls and make them cry? "Because he's mean," I say, with a sinking feeling, for how can this be the right answer? As the [nursery] rhyme makes all too clear, young Georgie is . . . clever . . . , all pudding and pie; the tearful girls are merely boring. Mother Goose in one hand and a leaky juice box in the other, I begin the sad, infuriating task shared by all modern mothers of daughters: to raise my child to be confident, adventurous and happy in her gender [sex] in a society saturated [filled] with sexual violence and victim blaming. ("Georgie Porgie Is a Bully")

Challenge a Widely Held Assumption or Opinion

This can be a quick, direct way to state your thesis and stir the reader's interest. In most cases it will take only a few sentences for you to deny the assumption or opinion and to state your own views. Notice how smoothly Roger D. McGrath does this in the introduction to "The Myth of Frontier Violence":

> It is commonly assumed that violence is part of our frontier heritage. But *the historical record shows that frontier violence was very different from violence today.* Robbery and burglary, two of our most common crimes, were of no great significance in the frontier towns of the Old West, and rape was seemingly nonexistent.

Use a Comparison, a Contrast, or an Analogy

Comparison points out similarities; contrast points out differences. Both methods can help you provide important information about your subject, clarify or emphasize a point, and catch the readers' attention.

Donald M. Murray offers students good advice by contrasting the way they sometimes complete writing assignments with the more thorough and careful process used by professionals:

When students complete a first draft, they consider the job of writing done—and their teachers too often agree. *When professional writers complete a first draft, they usually feel that they are at the start of the writing process.* When a draft is completed, the job of writing can begin. (''The Maker's Eye'')

In the following paragraph, student Dan Roland uses both comparison and contrast. He begins by likening Kingston, Jamaica, to any city the reader might recognize, only to follow with a stark contrast between the extremes of wealth and poverty found there. The effect is startling and convincing. Roland has prepared his readers well for the thesis at the end of the paragraph.

> From my seat on an American Airlines 727, Kingston, Jamaica, looks like any other large urban center to me: tall buildings dominate the skyline, traffic weaves its way through roadways laid out like long arteries from the heart of the city. But Kingston is not like other cities, for it is here that some of the most extreme poverty in the world exists. The island of Jamaica was founded as a slave colony to help satisfy Europe's great demand for sugar cane, and its inhabitants are the descendants of slaves. Despair and poverty are part of everyday life and have been for centuries. The leading industry is tourism; every year thousands of well-to-do vacationers, mostly Americans and Canadians, come to stay in the multitudes of luxurious hotels and resorts. *Jamaica is one of the most beautiful places on Earth; it is also one of the most destitute [poorest].* (''Which Side of the Fence?'')

Analogy serves the same purposes as comparison or contrast; the most important of these is, once again, to keep the readers' attention. But analogy can also help explain ideas or feelings that are hard to grasp by allowing you to compare them with things the reader can see or understand more easily. Analogy usually points out similarities between subjects that are unrelated. This is what happens in ''The Tapestry'' when student Steven Grundy compares his family to a fine wall hanging:

> *My family is an ancient tapestry,* worn in places, faded by the passage of time, its colors softened by accumulated dust. It has hung there for so long that we rarely stop to appreciate its value. Yet beneath the dusty coating lies a precious masterpiece, a subtle composition of woven thread.

Tell an Anecdote or Describe a Scene

Anecdotes are brief, interesting stories that illustrate or support a point. An anecdote can help you prepare readers for the issues or problems you will be discussing without your having to state the thesis directly. In the first paragraph of ''The Ambivalence of Abortion,'' for example, Linda Bird Francke tells what happened when she announced her fourth pregnancy, a story that gets us ready for her discussion of abortion later in the essay:

> We were sitting in a bar on Lexington Avenue when I told my husband I was pregnant. It is not a memory I like to dwell on. Instead of the champagne and hope which had heralded [announced] the impending [coming] births of the first,

second and third child, the news of this one was greeted with shocked silence and Scotch. ''Jesus,'' my husband kept saying to himself, stirring the ice cubes around and around ''Oh Jesus.''

Another way to prepare readers for what follows is to describe a scene in a way that lets them know your feelings about a subject. Take the introduction to ''A Hanging,'' an essay in which George Orwell reveals his view of capital punishment. Orwell does not express his opinions in a thesis statement; the essay's gloomy setting—its time and place—does that for him:

> It was Burma, a sodden [soggy] morning of the rains. A sickly light, like yellow tinfoil, was slanting over the high walls into the jail yard. We were waiting outside the condemned cells, a row of sheds fronted with double bars, like small animal cages. Each cell measured about ten feet by ten and was quite bare within except for a plank bed and a pot for drinking water. In some of them brown silent men were squatting at the inner bars, with their blankets draped around them. These were the condemned men, due to be hanged within the next week or two.

Use a Quotation

Quoting an expert or simply using an interesting, informative statement from another writer, from someone you've interviewed formally, or even from someone with whom you've only been chatting can lend interest and authority to your introduction. If you use this method, however, remember to quote your source accurately. Also be sure that the quotation relates to the other ideas in your paragraph clearly and logically.

Philip Shabecoff uses a quotation from world-famous scientist and writer Rachel Carson to lead us to his thesis in the introduction to his essay on pesticides:

> ''The most alarming of all man's assaults upon the environment is the contamination of air, earth, rivers, and sea with dangerous and even lethal materials,'' Rachel Carson wrote a quarter of a century ago in her celebrated book *Silent Spring.* Today there is little disagreement with her warnings in regard to such broad-spectrum pesticides as DDT, then widely used, now banned. *But there is still hot debate over how to apply modern pesticides—which are designed to kill specific types of weeds or insects—in ways that do not harm people and their environment.* (''Congress Again Confronts Hazards of Killer Chemicals'')

Define an Important Term or Concept

Defining a term can explain aspects of your subject that will make it easier for readers to understand and agree with your central idea. But try not to use dictionary definitions. Because they are often limited and rigid, they can make the beginning of an essay flat and uninteresting. Instead, rely on your own knowledge and ingenuity to create definitions that are interesting and appropriate to your purpose. This is what student Elena Santayana has done in the introduction to a paper about alcohol addiction:

> Alcoholism is a disease whose horrible consequences go beyond the patient. Families of alcoholics often become dysfunctional; spouses and children are abandoned or endure physical and emotional abuse. Co-workers suffer too. Alcoholics have a high rates of absenteeism, and their work is often unreliable, thereby decreasing office or factory productivity. Indeed, alcoholics endanger the whole community. One in every two automobile fatalities is alcohol-related, and alcoholism is a major cause of violent crime. ("Everybody's Problem")

Address Your Readers

Speaking to your readers directly and mentioning something that is important to them is an excellent way to get their attention. Notice how effectively Carrie Tuhy uses this technique in "So Who Needs College?" which first appeared in *Money* magazine in 1982:

> Career seekers, the want ads are trying to tell you something. Despite the highest unemployment rate since 1941, Sunday papers . . . are thick with job postings for specialized skills. Employers seem unable to find enough qualified people for such positions as bank teller, commercial artist, computer programmer, data processor, electronics technician, medical technologist, nurse, office manager, salesperson and secretary. *Fewer and fewer classified ads stipulate college as a requirement.*

Another effective way to address your readers is to ask or direct them to place themselves in the setting or situation you are discussing so that they can understand your point better. In the first paragraph of "Who's on Third?" Rockwell Stensrud invites us to imagine ourselves in the grandstand of a ballpark:

> During the next baseball game you see, watch the man standing in the coach's box behind third base. He rubs his stomach, crosses his chest first with his left arm, then with his right. He touches the top of his cap, holds his right elbow with his left hand, then repeats the motion. A second later, he reverses the motion. . . . This all may appear as a random symptom of nervousness, but in fact, *the third base coach is signaling to his team what he wants them to do.*

In "What Is Poverty?" Jo Goodwin Parker has also chosen to address readers directly, but she begins with a question. Notice how much more urgent and emphatic her introduction is than Stensrud's:

> You ask me what is poverty? Listen to me. Here I am, dirty, smelly, and with no "proper" underwear on and with the stench of my rotting teeth near you. I will tell you. Listen to me. Listen without pity. I cannot use your pity. Listen with understanding. Put yourself in my dirty, worn out, ill-fitting shoes, and hear me.

WRITING CONCLUSIONS

Make sure your essay has an effective conclusion. Sometimes, it is on the basis of your conclusion alone that your readers respond to your essay and remember the point it tries to make.

The conclusion's length depends on the essay's length and purpose. For a very short essay, you can simply end the last paragraph with a concluding sentence, which might itself contain details important to developing your thesis. Such is the case in Kenneth Jon Rose's ''2001 Space Shuttle.'' Rose's last paragraph, a description of the shuttle's landing on its return to Earth, also contains his conclusion (shown in italics):

> . . . the sky turns lighter and layers of clouds pass you like cars on a highway. Minutes later, still sitting upright, you will see the gray runway in the distance. Then the shuttle slows to 300 mph and drops its landing gear. Finally, with its nose slightly up like the Concorde SST and at a speed of about 225 mph, the shuttle will land on the asphalt runway and slowly come to a halt. *The trip into space will be over.*

While one-sentence conclusions are fine for short essays, you will often need to close with at least one full paragraph. Either way, a conclusion should bring your discussion of the thesis to a timely and logical end. Try not to conclude abruptly; always give a signal that you are about to wrap things up. And never use your conclusion to introduce new ideas—ideas for which you did not prepare your readers earlier in the essay.

There are many ways to write conclusions. Here are just eight:

1. Rephrase or make reference to your thesis.
2. Summarize or rephrase your main points.
3. Offer advice; make a call to action.
4. Look to the future.
5. Explain how a problem was resolved.
6. Ask a rhetorical question.
7. Close with a statement or quotation readers will remember.
8. Tell an anecdote.

Rephrase or Make Reference to Your Thesis

In Chapter 1 you learned that it can be appropriate to place the thesis statement not in the introduction, but in a later paragraph or even in the conclusion. As a beginning writer, however, you might want to use the more traditional pattern of organization, which is to place your thesis at the beginning of the essay. Of course, this doesn't mean that you shouldn't rephrase or refer to the thesis in your conclusion. Doing so can be an excellent way to emphasize your central idea.

Notice how well the conclusion to Donald M. Murray's ''The Maker's Eye'' recalls the central idea in this essay's introduction (see pages 85–86):

A piece of writing is never finished. It is delivered to a deadline, torn out of typewriter on demand, sent off with a sense of accomplishment and shame and pride and frustration. If only there were a couple of more days, time for just another run at it, perhaps then. . . .

Summarize or Rephrase Your Main Points

For long essays, restating your thesis can be combined with summarizing or rephrasing each of the main points you have made in the body paragraphs. Doing so will help you write an effective summary of the entire essay and emphasize important ideas. This is exactly what Robin Roberts has done in his two concluding paragraphs of "Strike Out Little League" (see his introduction on page 84):

> I still don't know what those three gentlemen in Williamsport had in mind when they organized Little League baseball. I'm sure they didn't want parents arguing with their children about kids' games. I'm sure they didn't want young athletes hurting their arms pitching under pressure. . . . I'm sure they didn't want young boys . . . made to feel that something is wrong with them because they can't play baseball. I'm sure they didn't want a group of coaches drafting the players each year for different teams. I'm sure they didn't want unqualified men working with the young players. I'm sure they didn't realize how normal it is for an 8-year-old boy to be scared of a thrown or batted baseball.
>
> For the life of me, I can't figure out what they had in mind.

Offer Advice; Make a Call to Action

An example of a conclusion that offers advice appears in Elena Santayana's "Everybody's Problem," the introduction to which appears on page 88:

> If you have alcoholic friends, relatives, or co-workers, the worst thing you can do is to look the other way. This disease and its effects are simply not theirs to deal with alone. Try persuading them to seek counseling. Describe the extent to which their illness is hurting their families, co-workers, and neighbors. Explain that their alcoholism endangers the entire community. Above all, don't pretend not to notice! Alcoholism is everybody's problem.

Along the same lines, a good way to end an essay that discusses a problem is to call for a solution, as in the conclusion to "The Nuclear Winter," an essay Carl Sagan wrote in 1983. As you read these two paragraphs you may hear some echoes of the essay's introduction, which appears on page 84:

> It is now almost 40 years since the invention of nuclear weapons. We have not yet experienced thermonuclear war—although . . . we have come tremulously [fearfully] close. I do not think our luck can hold on forever. Men and machines are fallible. . . . Fools and madmen do exist and sometimes rise to power. Concentrating on the near future, we have ignored the long-term consequences of our actions. We have placed our civilization and our species in jeopardy [danger].

Fortunately, it is not yet too late. We can safeguard civilization and the human family if we so choose. There is no more important or more urgent issue.

Sagan fears that "fools and madmen," if in positions of power, could cause a nuclear war. The words "fools and madmen" also appear in his introduction. Repeating words at the end of an essay is similar to summarizing your essay's main points; it reminds readers of important ideas you brought up earlier and helps tie the essay together.

Look to the Future

If you believe the future will bring significant changes or new developments regarding topics discussed in the body of your essay, you might conclude by describing these changes or developments. This is what Gina Kolata does at the end of an article about our increased concern over cholesterol:

> [Doctors] believe that [new] guidelines [regarding cholesterol problems]— combined with better diagnostic devices and ever more effective drugs— may mark the beginning of a new era in public health. The hope . . . is that cholesterol will become like high blood pressure—easily and frequently measured, and usually controlled. ("Advice about Cholesterol Is Finding an Eager Market")

Explain How a Problem Was Resolved

In "The Ambivalence of Abortion" (see pages 86–87 for the introduction to this essay), Linda Bird Francke writes about the difficulty she and her husband had in deciding whether to have or abort their fourth child. Francke's conclusion tells us how they resolved the question and, like many effective endings, reveals the author's feelings:

> My husband and I are back to planning our summer vacation and his career switch. And it certainly does make sense not to be having a baby right now—we say to each other all the time. But I have this ghost now. A very little ghost that only appears when I'm seeing something beautiful, like the full moon on the ocean last weekend. And the baby waves to me. And I wave at the baby. "Of course, we have room," I cry to the ghost. "Of course, we do."

Ask a Rhetorical Question

A rhetorical question (a question whose answer is obvious) asks your readers to participate in your essay's conclusion by answering the question. If you judge that the essay has made the answer so obvious that all readers will indeed respond to the question as you want them to, ending with a rhetorical question can be a fine way to make your essay memorable. As a reader, it's hard to forget an essay when you've answered its question in your own words.

For example, Judy Brady ends "I Want a Wife" by asking, "Who wouldn't want a wife?'' Because her essay showed numerous important ways in which wives contribute to their husbands' comfort, security, and happiness, the question's answer is obvious: ''No one.'' Furthermore, note that the question circles back to the one she asked at the end of her introduction (see page 85), giving her essay a strong sense of unity and emphasis.

Not all rhetorical questions need to be as snappy as Brady's, of course. Jo Goodwin Parker uses this device to emphasize the seriousness of the problem she describes in ''What Is Poverty?'' (see her introduction on page 88):

> I have come out of my despair to tell you this. Remember I did not come from another place to another time. Others like me are all around you. Look at us with an angry heart, anger that will help you help me. Anger that will let you tell of me. The poor are always silent. Can you be silent too?

Close with a Statement or Quotation Readers Will Remember

Deciding whether a statement or quotation will stick in readers' memories isn't easy. Just trust your instincts. If a particular remark has made a strong impression on you, it may work for others. As always, however, make your conclusion relate directly to your essay's contents. In ''A Visit to Belfast,'' Mary Manning closes her discussion of the tragic civil turmoil in Northern Ireland with both a statement and a quotation; it is an image of sorrow and devastation we will not soon forget:

> We drove down the familiar route to the station, and I craned my neck to have a last look at the winter cherry tree. Alas and alas, a car had been bombed beside it during the night, and [it] was now a dirty black umbrella. The streets were empty, but bells were already tolling, calling all good Christians to prayer. The skies were gray and somber, and already a few flakes of snow were falling. All I could think of as I sat in the train on the way to Dublin was the shortest verse in the Bible: ''Jesus wept.'' And I didn't know then that thirteen people were to die in Derry that day.

Tell an Anecdote

Brief stories that show the essence of the central idea can be used to conclude an essay as well as to introduce it. Using an anecdote to conclude will help you summarize or highlight important points you've made earlier. A good example of such an anecdote appears at the end of Suzanne Britt's ''Fun, Oh Boy. Fun. You Could Die from It,'' the first reading selection in this chapter.

Read the introductions and conclusions to the following four essays carefully, and take some time to respond to the Questions for Discussion and the Suggestions for Journal Entries that follow each selection. As always, you will want to try your hand at the Suggestions for Writing at the end of the chapter. Doing so will help you develop the skills needed to write good introductions and conclusions of your own—the kind that will capture your readers' attention and make them look forward to more and more of your writing.

Fun, Oh Boy. Fun. You Could Die from It.

SUZANNE BRITT

Britt's introduction and conclusion play with definitions of "fun," nicely catching the reader's attention and highlighting her purpose throughout the essay, which is to define and humorously evaluate the "fun" side of American culture. Her essay first appeared in The New York Times.

Looking Ahead

1. In her five-paragraph introduction, Britt states her thesis in two short sentences at the very beginning. Spreading the thesis over two sentences is unusual, but here it works well.
2. As you read paragraphs 3 through 5, try to identify one or more of the other techniques discussed earlier in this chapter that you find Britt using in her introduction.
3. You've learned that an anecdote is a brief story that can be used in the beginning, middle, or end of an essay to illustrate or summarize a particular point. Pay special attention to the anecdote that Britt uses to conclude her essay.

Vocabulary

blaspheme   Speak disrespectfully of.
by Jove   Exclamation or expression used to emphasize a point. Jove was the king of the gods in Roman mythology.
epitome   Ultimate form of or embodiment of.
fetish   Unreasonable preoccupation with or regard for something.
licentiousness   Sexual immorality.
mirth   Fun, gaiety.
puritans   Followers of a strict moral code who regarded many types of pleasure as sinful.
reverently   Devoutly, religiously, respectfully.

Fun is hard to have.
  Fun is a rare jewel.   1
  Somewhere along the line people got the modern idea that fun was there for   2
                                                                                          3

the asking, that people deserved fun, that if we didn't have a little fun every day we would turn into (sakes alive!) puritans.

"Was it fun?" became the question that overshadowed all other questions: 4
good questions like: Was it moral? Was it kind? Was it honest? Was it beneficial? Was it generous? Was it necessary? And (my favorite) was it selfless?

When the pleasure got to be the main thing, the fun fetish was sure to follow.   5
Everything was supposed to be fun. If it wasn't fun, then by Jove, we were going to make it fun, or else.

Think of all the things that got the reputation of being fun. Family outings   6
were supposed to be fun. Sex was supposed to be fun. Education was supposed to be fun. Work was supposed to be fun. Walt Disney was supposed to be fun. Church was supposed to be fun. Staying fit was supposed to be fun.

Just to make sure that everybody knew how much fun we were having, we   7
put happy faces on flunking test papers, dirty bumpers, sticky refrigerator doors, bathroom mirrors.

If a kid, looking at his very happy parents traipsing through that very happy   8
Disney World, said, "This ain't fun, ma," his ma's heart sank. She wondered where she had gone wrong. Everybody told her what fun family outings to Disney World would be. Golly gee, what was the matter?

Fun got to be such a big thing that everybody started to look for more and   9
more thrilling ways to supply it. One way was to step up the level of danger or licentiousness or alcohol or drug consumption so that you could be sure that, no matter what, you would manage to have a little fun.

Television commercials brought a lot of fun and fun-loving folks into the   10
picture. Everything that people in those commercials did looked like fun: taking Polaroid snapshots, swilling beer, buying insurance, mopping the floor, bowling, taking aspirin. We all wished, I'm sure, that we could have half as much fun as those rough-and-ready guys around the locker room, flicking each other with towels and pouring champagne. The more commercials people watched, the more they wondered when the fun would start in their own lives. It was pretty depressing.

Big occasions were supposed to be fun. Christmas, Thanksgiving and Easter   11
were obviously supposed to be fun. Your wedding day was supposed to be fun. Your wedding night was supposed to be a whole lot of fun. Your honeymoon was supposed to be the epitome of fundom. And so we ended up going through every Big Event we ever celebrated, waiting for the fun to start.

It occurred to me, while I was sitting around waiting for the fun to start, that   12
not much is, and that I should tell you just in case you're worried about your fun capacity.

I don't mean to put a damper on things. I just mean we ought to treat fun   13
reverently. It is a mystery. It cannot be caught like a virus. It cannot be trapped like an animal. The god of mirth is paying us back for all those years of thinking fun was everywhere by refusing to come to our party. I don't want to blaspheme fun anymore. When fun comes in on little dancing feet, you probably won't be expecting it. In fact, I bet it comes when you're doing your duty, your job, or your work. It may even come on a Tuesday.

I remember one day, long ago, on which I had an especially good time. Pam **14** Davis and I walked to the College Village drug store one Saturday morning to buy some candy. We were about 12 years old (fun ages). She got her Bit-O-Honey. I got my malted milk balls, chocolate stars, Chunkys, and a small bag of M & M's. We started back to her house. I was going to spend the night. We had the whole day to look forward to. We had plenty of candy. It was a long way to Pam's house but every time we got weary Pam would put her hand over her eyes, scan the horizon like a sailor and say, ''Oughta reach home by nightfall,'' at which point the two of us would laugh until we thought we couldn't stand it another minute. Then after we got calm, she'd say it again. You should have been there. It was the kind of day and friendship and occasion that made me deeply regretful that I had to grow up.

It was fun.

15

Questions for Discussion

1. Explain the essay's thesis in your own words.
2. Which of the techniques for writing introductions discussed earlier in this chapter does Britt use in the first two sentences of her essay?
3. Britt makes use of a startling remark and a series of questions in other parts of her introduction. In which paragraphs do we find these techniques?
4. In which paragraph of the essay does Britt address readers directly?
5. In which paragraphs does she use illustration to develop the topic sentence? (For a review of illustration as a method of development, see Chapter 3.)
6. In paragraph 13, Britt tells us that fun ''is a mystery,'' that ''It cannot be caught like a virus,'' and that ''It cannot be trapped like an animal.'' What method of development is she using in this paragraph? (For a review of paragraph development, see Chapter 3.)
7. Britt concludes her essay with an anecdote. Summarize this anecdote in your own words. Does it make for a good conclusion? Does it support the idea that ''fun is a rare jewel''?

Suggestions for Journal Entries

1. Britt's purpose is to define and evaluate fun. What do *you* think fun is? Write a short introductory paragraph or series of introductory paragraphs in which you explain your definition. Use one or more of the techniques discussed earlier in this chapter; for instance, try an analogy, a comparison or contrast, a definition, a startling fact or opinion, or a question.
2. Write an introductory paragraph or series of introductory paragraphs that you might use to explain your notion of friendship, pain, courage, devotion, honesty, unselfishness, poverty, wealth, comfort, health, or any other idea that is as abstract as Britt's fun. Use one or more of the techniques for writing introductions discussed in this chapter.

How to Keep Air Clean

SYDNEY HARRIS

Sydney Harris was born in London in 1917 and began writing as a regular columnist for the Chicago Daily News *in 1941. Models of interesting and effective prose, Harris's newspaper columns, like "How to Keep Air Clean," have proved him to be an important American essayist and earned him thousands of devoted readers over the years. Many of these columns have been used in college textbooks and gathered in book-length collections of his work.*

Looking Ahead

1. The essay's introduction consists of the first three paragraphs. Read these paragraphs carefully, and try to determine what technique Harris relies on most to open this essay.

2. Harris uses two terms from meteorology, the study of the earth's atmosphere. The *troposphere* (paragraph 4) is the bottom layer of the atmosphere, where clouds, rain, snow, and other weather phenomena occur. Directly above the troposphere is the *stratosphere* (paragraph 2), which extends to about 30 miles up.

3. In his conclusion (paragraph 9), Harris calls our attention to the Industrial Revolution, which occurred in the eighteenth and nineteenth centuries in Europe and North America. Not an armed conflict, the Industrial Revolution was a series of technological developments that led to the modern factory system, mass production, and automation.

Vocabulary

infinitely   Without end.

irreversible   Not reversible or repairable.

noxious   Toxic, dangerous, harmful.

particulates   Small particles.

Some months ago, while doing research on the general subject of pollution, I   1
learned how dumb I had been all my life about something as common and familiar—and essential—as air.

In my ignorance, I had always thought that "fresh air" was infinitely   2
available to us. I had imagined that the dirty air around us somehow escaped into the stratosphere, and that new air kept coming in—much as it does when we open a window after a party.

This, of course, is not true, and you would imagine that a grown man with   3 a decent education would know this as a matter of course. What is true is that we live in a kind of spaceship called the earth, and only a limited amount of air is *forever* available to us.

The "walls" of our spaceship enclose what is called the "troposphere," which extends about seven miles up. This is all the air that is available to us. We must use it over and over again for infinity, just as if we were in a sealed room for the lifetime of the earth. 4

No fresh air comes in, and no polluted air escapes. Moreover, no dirt or poisons are ever "destroyed"—they remain in the air, in different forms, or settle on the earth as "particulates." And the more we burn, the more we replace good air with bad. 5

Once contaminated, this thin layer of air surrounding the earth cannot be cleansed again. We can clean materials, we can even clean water, but we cannot clean the air. There is nowhere else for the dirt and poisons to go—we cannot open a window in the troposphere and clear out the stale and noxious atmosphere we are creating. 6

Perhaps every child in sixth grade and above knows this, but I doubt that one adult in a hundred is aware of this basic physical fact. Most of us imagine, as I did, that winds sweep away the gases and debris in the air, taking them far out into the solar system and replacing them with new air. 7

The United States alone is discharging *130 million tons of pollutants a year* into the atmosphere, from factories, heating systems, incinerators, automobiles and airplanes, power plants and public buildings. What is frightening is not so much the death and illness, corrosion and decay they are responsible for—as the fact that this is an *irreversible process.* The air will never be cleaner than it is now. 8

And this is why *prevention*—immediate, drastic and far-reaching—is our only hope for the future. We cannot undo what we have done. We cannot restore the atmosphere to the purity it had before the Industrial Revolution. But we can, and must, halt the contamination before our spaceship suffocates from its own foul discharges. 9

Questions for Discussion

1. What technique discussed earlier in this chapter does Harris rely upon most to open his essay?
2. In paragraph 3, Harris also makes use of an analogy, another of the techniques for beginning an essay discussed earlier. What is this interesting analogy? In what other paragraph does Harris make reference to it?
3. Reread paragraph 3 of "How to Keep Air Clean." What is Harris's thesis?
4. What techniques does he use to conclude this essay?
5. The title suggests that Harris has used process analysis to develop his ideas. Identify one paragraph in which he uses this method of development. (Process analysis was discussed in Chapter 3.)

6. The essay is very well developed and organized. What techniques does the author use to maintain coherence in and between paragraphs? (For ways to maintain coherence, see Chapter 2.)

Suggestions for Journal Entries

1. Summarize in a paragraph of your own the three paragraphs Harris uses to introduce his essay. Make sure to use your own words throughout.

2. To introduce his essay, Harris challenges a widely held opinion or assumption. Think of a widely held opinion or assumption that you believe is incorrect. In a sentence or two, write this idea in your journal. Then, using one of the prewriting techniques described in ''Getting Started,'' write down your major reasons for disagreeing. Here are a few examples of the kinds of opinions or assumptions you might want to correct:

    Someone who has had only one or two drinks shouldn't be prevented from driving a car.
    Breaking an alcohol or drug addiction is relatively easy.
    Women have no aptitude for math.
    Reading poetry, listening to opera, and going to the ballet aren't things that ''real'' men do.

I Was Just Wondering

ROBERT FULGHUM

Robert Fulghum wrote All I Really Need to Know I Learned in Kindergarten, *the best-selling collection of essays from which this one is taken. The contents of this funny book are summed up by its subtitle:* Uncommon Thoughts on Common Things. *Fulghum has worked as a cowboy, IBM sales representative, bartender, teacher, artist, and minister. Judging from this selection, he has a curiosity and love for life that make it easy to understand why his writing is so popular.*

Looking Ahead

1. As you read this essay, ask yourself why Fulghum's introduction and conclusion are effective. Identify methods for writing beginnings and endings you learned earlier in this chapter.

2. In paragraphs 1, 5, and 8, Fulghum intentionally uses incomplete sentences, known as fragments, to create emphasis and establish a conversational tone. They are part of a carefully considered style that this experienced writer chose for his essay. As a rule, however, developing writers should avoid fragments.

Vocabulary

curry   Groom.

epidemic   Widespread occurrence.

meditate   Think, ponder, contemplate.

oracle   Advisor, prophet. (Here, "oracle" is used figuratively; Fulghum describes the habit some folks have of questioning themselves as they look in the mirror.)

Ph.D.   Advanced academic degree, also known as a doctorate.

potions   Liquid medicines, remedies.

preen   Make ready, prepare.

unguents   Salves, ointments.

spelunking   Cave exploring.

I was just wondering. Did you ever go to somebody's house for dinner or a   1
party or something and then use the bathroom? And while you were in there, did
you ever take a look around in the medicine cabinet? Just to kind of compare
notes, you know? Didn't you ever—just look around a little?

I have a friend who does it all the time. He's doing research for a Ph.D. in   2
sociology. He says lots of other people do it, too. And they aren't working on
a Ph.D. in sociology, either. It's not something people talk about much—because
you think you might be the only one who is doing it, and you don't want people
to think you're strange, right?

My friend says if you want to know the truth about people, it's the place to   3
go. All you have to do is look in the drawers and shelves and cabinets in the
bathroom. And take a look at the robes and pajamas and nightgowns hanging on
the hook behind the door. You'll get the picture. He says all their habits and
hopes and dreams and sorrows, illnesses and hangups, and even their sex life—
all stand revealed in that one small room.

He says most people are secret slobs. He says the deepest mysteries of the   4
race are tucked into the nooks and crannies of the bathroom, where we go to be
alone, to confront ourselves in the mirror, to comb and curry and scrape and
preen our hides, to coax our aging and ailing bodies into one more day, to clean
ourselves and relieve ourselves, to paint and deodorize our surfaces, to meditate
and consult our oracle and attempt to improve our lot.

He says it's all there. In cans and bottles and tubes and boxes and vials.   5
Potions and oils and unguents and sprays and tools and lotions and perfumes and
appliances and soaps and pastes and pills and creams and pads and powders and
medicines and devices beyond description—some electric and some not. The
wonders of the ages.

He says he finds most bathrooms are about the same, and it gives him a sense   6
of the wondrous unity of the human race.

I don't intend to start an epidemic of spelunking in people's bathrooms. But   7

I did just go in and take a look in my own. I get the picture. I don't know whether to laugh or cry.

Take a look. In your own. And from now on, please go to the bathroom   8
before you visit me. Mine is closed to the public.

Questions for Discussion

1. What two ways of writing introductions discussed in this chapter did you find in paragraph 1?
2. Which of the methods for concluding discussed earlier best describes Fulghum's approach in paragraph 8?
3. What method of development that you learned about in the previous chapter does Fulghum use in paragraph 3?
4. What techniques does Fulghum use to maintain coherence in and between paragraphs?

Suggestions for Journal Entries

1. Are most people "secret slobs"? What about you? Think of a particular place you call your own. Does the way you keep it show how neat or sloppy you are? If so, use focused freewriting to describe what it looks like. A place to write about might be your bedroom, bathroom, car, closet, area in which you study, or location where you spend most of your time at work.
2. Like Fulghum, do some wondering. Focus on someone you know very well. Can you describe or at least imagine what the inside of his or her room, closet, apartment, house, refrigerator, garage, basement, or bathroom looks like? What might you see in such places that would describe this individual's personality?

The Transformation of Maria Fernandez

ANITA DIPASQUALE

Anita DiPasquale had the rare opportunity to visit Nicaragua near the end of the civil war that devastated that Central American country in the 1980s. She went there with a friend to bring news to relatives of a Nicaraguan child who had been adopted by a family in California. When a college writing instructor asked DiPasquale to narrate an unforgettable experience, she had no trouble deciding what to write about.

Looking Ahead

1. The Iran-Contra affair (paragraph 1) involved the sale of arms to Iran as part of an illegal plan to provide American military aid to the

Nicaraguan *Contras,* the group trying to overthrow that country's *Sandinista* government. The "superpowers," mentioned twice in this essay, are the United States and the former Soviet Union.

2. Like the introductions by Suzanne Britt and Sydney Harris, DiPasquale's is longer than one paragraph, and it uses several methods for beginning essays discussed in this chapter.

3. Although her story takes place in the past, DiPasquale writes in the present tense. In paragraph 2, for example, she tells us that Michael and she "meet," not "met" Maria. Using the present tense often adds excitement to a narrative essay and makes it more convincing.

4. The author kept an informal journal of her conversations with Maria by recording what she remembered of their talks from time to time. What we read may not be exactly what she and Maria said, word for word, but it is a fair re-creation of their conversations.

Vocabulary

adversaries   Opponents, enemies.

apathetic   Unconcerned, uninterested.

communal   Having to do with a community.

covert   Secret, hidden.

defiled   Dirtied, violated.

diverse   Various, assorted.

eking out   Struggling to make.

eradicate   Destroy, annihilate.

ironically   Contrary to what is expected.

meager   Poor, little.

mired   Stuck.

parochial   Isolated, provincial.

raven   Black.

repressive   Tyrannical, dictatorial.

synonymous   Similar in meaning.

Maria's story is testimony to the horror of war. Her country is Nicaragua, one of America's greatest embarrassments and yet another battleground in what the superpowers called the "cold" war. In this impoverished, merciless, yet beautiful land, the Reagan Administration became mired in a series of covert operations known as the Iran-Contra fiasco. Ironically, our shame over this dreadful incident may be the only good thing to come from our presence in Nicaragua. Perhaps Americans who were once parochial and apathetic will realize that Kansas is not Central America, that *Sandinista* and "repressive" are not synonymous, that *Contra* may not mean "freedom fighter," and that all wars, no matter who the adversaries, are barbarous!

My friend Michael and I meet Maria on a trip through hell in Nicaragua's 2 capital, Managua. The month is June, the year 1988. Maria is seventeen, no longer a child, no longer a woman. She is a soldier in the FSLN *(Frente Sandinista de Liberacion Nacional),* the national liberation front named in honor of Augusto Sandino, a guerrilla fighter martyred in an earlier war of liberation.

Maria is thin, with shoulder-length raven hair, which she braids and tucks 3 away under her camouflage hat. Her nose is long and straight, her chin prominent and proud. A silky olive complexion and cheekbones straight out of *Vogue* magazine reveal a face that is truly delicate. How, then, has it come to harbor the deadest eyes I have ever seen?

Maria, Michael and I make our way along the gray and blue cobblestone 4 street and sit on a curb so large it would be considered a ledge in the United States. The masonry buildings around us are old, bruised, and defiled. Bullet holes and political graffiti have stained the faces of these tired shelters. Some still lie battered and tormented by the earthquake that devastated Nicaragua on December 23, 1972.

A young woman bathes in rain water that has collected in an old metal drum 5 across the street. No one notices; people walk by as if she were invisible. Maria catches me staring: ''It's a way of life here; so many people are without water, without homes.''

She is safer here on the street than at the river, I am told. ''Listen, haven't 6 you heard the gunfire or seen the blood?'' asks Maria.

''Have my eyes and ears deceived me?'' I wonder. I have seen no blood and 7 heard no shooting. I know there is a war, but not until many days later will I fully realize what she means.

Michael pulls a photograph from his shirt pocket and hands it to Maria. It 8 is a picture of her brother Alberto; he is seated on a bright red Big Wheel. Alberto is seven and lives in Los Angeles with Michael's uncle. The child is smiling; he knows his world is make-believe, like that of most children in countries free from war.

''I remember,'' she proclaims, as she stares at the photo. ''I remember when 9 I was a child; we lived in the north, in Matagalpa.'' Matagalpa is known for its mountains and its hard living. Aside from the small towns every five miles or so, nothing but small shacks dots the landscape. The people of Matagalpa work alone on small plots of land, eking out a meager existence. There are no real communities here as there are in the Pacific culture, which is known for its communal involvement with the land.

Maria lights a cigarette and sighs. ''We were very poor and lived close to 10 the earth. I can still smell Mama's tortillas cooking in the oven. Our house had two rooms, and the roof was made of corrugated tin. The floor was dirt except for a small area which Papa dug out and covered with wood in order to hide us when the soldiers came through.''

Her face grows solemn for a moment. But she lifts her strong chin and 11 continues proudly. ''As a small girl, I would wear pretty dresses that Mama made from spare pieces of cloth. They always had flowers on them, pink and yellow. I never had a pair of shoes; there was no need for them. My job on the land was to spread the fertilizer.'' Maria's nose crinkles as if she can still smell the manure.

''Once we went on a trip to Puerto Cabezas; Alberto was so small he had 12 just learned to walk. There the Miskito Indians were catching giant sea tortoises on the shore. The tortoises were larger than Alberto,'' she chuckles. ''A Miskito woman gave us a ride on her boat. It was made from a hollowed out tree. That was the last family outing I remember.''

''How did Alberto come to live in America?'' I ask. Michael has never told 13 me, and I know by the look on his face that I should not have asked the question. The story Maria tells is more horrifying than any horror film. It makes the ravages of war real to me. I no longer look on them as someone else's problems. It also explains how a happy little girl in flowered dresses could have become a soldier, a killer, how her eyes can be so dead.

''I must go back a few years to help you understand what led to Alberto's 14 departure,'' began Maria. ''In August of 1978, when I was a very small child, before Alberto was born, our world changed forever. The FSLN had seized the National Palace, taking 1,500 hostages. When the attackers and 59 newly freed prisoners drove to the airport to get a flight to Panama, thousands of people lined the streets and cheered their victory. After the Palace assault, there were many attacks on the National Guard throughout Nicaragua—in Matagalpa, Leon, Masaya, Esteli, and Chinandega. The people lifted up arms against President Anastasio Somoza Debayle. So, to stop the rebels, the Guard destroyed our cities from the air. It took about two weeks and left over 4,000 dead. As the Sandinistas withdrew, they took thousands of newly recruited soldiers. My father was one.

''Later, in 1979, Somoza was driven into exile, to America's Miami. We 15 thought there was hope for our country. Your President Carter worked with us, but then Reagan came. He reorganized Somoza's National Guard, which became the Contras. They were given haven in Honduras. The 75,000 Sandinistas had few weapons and little money, so they could not eradicate the 10,000 Contras, who were well equipped with U.S. weapons and money.

''Back to Alberto. The last day I saw my brother started like any other. I was 16 fourteen or so, Alberto about four. We were home alone with my mother. Papa was off fighting in the jungle. It was September, and a wonderful rain had fallen the night before, leaving the air fragrant with a lush tropical scent. However, smoke hovered over the village, casting shadows on houses and streets and plunging the land into a deep, damp calm.

''Suddenly, I heard our neighbor Guillermo run into our house. He was 17 covered with blood. 'Contras,' he screamed before darting into the mist. Mama moved the heavy trunk that covered the hiding place my father had made. She was eight months pregnant, so I helped. First we placed Alberto into the hole, and I climbed on top of him. Mama placed the wood back on top and threw a rug over the floor.

''Just then the soldiers must have arrived. They were yelling and laughing. 18

I covered Alberto's ears and tried to muffle his crying. I heard my mother's screams; I still hear her screams. They were finally silenced by gunfire.

"The soldiers must have stayed about an hour; it felt like an eternity. The 19 house grew quiet. 'I dare not move,' I thought, so we lay there for several hours. Before I climbed out of the hole, I tied a piece of my dress around Alberto's eyes and around his hands so he wouldn't remove the blindfold. When I entered the daylight I was instantly sick. Mama was dead; they had cut my baby sister from her stomach; they lay there in a pool of blood. Both bodies were riddled with bullets.

"The soldiers had stayed there with their dead bodies long enough to eat our 20 breakfast. There was blood everywhere. I don't know how long I stood motionless when a shadow crossed the doorway. It was Chris, a U.S. reporter who often came by to feed his stories and his belly. He buried Mama and the baby, Isabel. That would have been her name.

"Chris told me my father had died the week earlier in a battle in Jinotega. 21 He said he could get Alberto out of Nicaragua, away from the Contras. He knew someone who was smuggling small, light-skinned children into California. He promised he would personally get him a good home as repayment for the help my family had given him. He was crying when he said I was too big to go. I had forgotten how to cry. Right then, at that moment, I was reborn into this world all alone. You do what you have to do in order to survive. I now know the meaning in the smoke. You do what you have to do to survive."

As Maria finishes her story, my stomach grows heavy and sinks to a depth 22 I did not think was possible. Suddenly, a truck pulls onto the street. It is filled with dead Contras on the way to burial. Another truck pulls up behind; this one is filled with Sandinista soldiers, none of whom look over twenty. Most are between ten and fifteen. Some might be eight. They are all toting rifles, passing cigarettes out among the crowd. When I look into the first truck, I become desperate with fear. Piled one on top of another are men, women, and children. They are all dead.

Back at the ledge, I slump against Michael. Maria emerges from the daze of 23 her horrid memory and kisses Michael on the cheek. She points to the trucks. "If he were here, his world would be all too real."

Sometimes it is nearly impossible to tell Contra soldiers and Sandinistas 24 apart. They have a lot in common: their youth, their camaraderie, their mortality. When Salvadoran Archbishop Rivera y Damas spoke of the role of the superpowers in his country's civil war, he could have been describing the tragedy of Nicaragua: "They supply the weapons, and we supply the dead."

Questions for Discussion

1. A transformation is a very significant change. What significant change has Maria experienced? Has the author experienced a change as a result of meeting Maria?

2. What is DiPasquale's thesis? What events in the story support or develop that thesis best?

3. The introduction to the essay includes several startling remarks. Identify two or three.

4. Where in the introduction does DiPasquale challenge widely held assumptions or opinions? How does the question at the end of paragraph 3 help us understand her thesis?

5. This essay closes with quotations and statements that might stick in your mind long after you have read them. Which of these do you think is most memorable?

6. In what way does the scene described in paragraph 22 support the essay's thesis?

7. In paragraph 24, DiPasquale mentions the "superpowers," which we recall from paragraph 1. What is she trying to accomplish by repeating this word at the end of the essay?

Suggestions for Journal Entries

1. Recall a horrifying or dangerous event that showed you the sad or dark side of life. Ask the journalists' questions (you can find these in "Getting Started," pages 3–4 under Brainstorming) to collect as many details about it as you can. Examples of such an incident include military combat; a bad automobile or industrial accident; a building fire; a tornado; a bout with a serious illness; a violent crime; a fall from a ledge or down a stairs; a mishap at sea, in a lake, river, or other body of water; or a fight in which someone was seriously hurt. Whatever event you write about, make sure to show why it was horrifying or dangerous.

2. Do you know someone who experienced a tragic or horrifying event like those mentioned above? If so, interview him or her using the techniques described in "Getting Started" (pages 4–5). Gather as much information as you can about the incident, and determine how it affected the person you interview.

3. Do you have a friend or relative who went through a drastic and sudden personality change as a result of an important event or development in his or her life? Write about this person by making three lists: one that contains details describing your subject before the change; one that describes him or her after the change; and one that explains what caused the change.

SUGGESTIONS FOR WRITING

1. Reread any one of the college papers you've written this semester. Try to pick the one you or your instructor liked best, but don't limit your choice to papers you've completed for English class. Then, rewrite the beginning and ending to that essay by using any of the techniques for writing effective introductions and conclusions discussed in this chapter.

2. If you responded to either of the Suggestions for Journal Entries that followed Suzanne Britt's "Fun, Oh Boy. Fun. You Could Die from It," you may have made a start in defining "fun," "friendship," "pain," "courage," "devotion," or some other abstract idea of your choice. Add details to this journal entry, and then expand it into a short essay that explains your notion of this abstract idea.

   Before you begin, however, read the following suggestions. They might be useful when you plan or write your essay:

   a. Try to open by using one or more of the techniques for writing introductions discussed earlier in this chapter.

   b. Make sure your introduction includes a thesis statement.

   c. Use the principles of unity and coherence you learned about in Chapter 2. In short, make sure each paragraph in the body of your essay relates to your thesis, and provide clear connections between paragraphs.

   d. Try to conclude with an anecdote as Britt does. However, if you find that an anecdote is inappropriate for your essay, use one of the other methods for concluding that was explained earlier.

   e. Make several drafts of your paper. Edit your best version to make sure that spelling, sentence structure, grammar, and punctuation are correct.

3. In one of the Suggestions for Journal Entries after Sydney J. Harris's "How to Keep Air Clean," you were asked to write a number of reasons that have led you to disagree with a widely held assumption or opinion. If you responded to this item, read over what you recorded in your journal. Then, do the following:

   a. Turn your notes into an introductory paragraph—complete with a formal thesis statement—that challenges this assumption and briefly explains your reasons for disagreeing.

   b. Make each of your reasons for disagreeing the topic of a well-developed paragraph. Use these paragraphs to develop the body of your essay.

   c. Write a concluding paragraph that:

      • Rephrases your thesis and summarizes your major points;
      • Uses an anecdote to illustrate those ideas;
      • Makes a call to action, as Harris does at the end of his essay; or
      • Uses one of the other methods for writing effective conclusions discussed in this chapter.

Incidentally, although you follow the steps above, you need not complete them in the same order that they are listed. For example, writing the body paragraphs and the conclusion before you write the introduction might be an easier and more effective way for you to proceed.

In any case, remember that writing is a process of discovery. Often you might have to revise one part of the essay in light of what you said in another. Therefore, if you begin the assignment by drafting your introduction, don't be afraid to rewrite it later if what you put into the body of the paper demands a change—major or minor—in your thesis or other parts of the introduction. Finally, no matter how many times you revise a paper, make sure to edit the final draft carefully.

4. Do you agree with Robert Fulghum that people's bathrooms tell a lot about them? How about their cars, bedrooms, closets, or refrigerators? Write an essay in which you introduce your readers to a close friend or relative by describing his or her room, home, apartment, car, work area, or the like. Include details that focus on one and only one aspect of your subject's personality. For example, to show that this person has expensive tastes, mention the brand names and estimate the costs of clothes you saw in his or her closet. Then talk about the luxurious furniture and expensive stereo equipment in his or her living room, and so on. If you responded to the second suggestion for journal writing after ''I Was Just Wondering,'' you have already gathered useful details for this assignment.

When you write your introduction, you might use a startling statement or, like Fulghum, ask a question that helps reveal your thesis. Here's an example of such a question: ''How do I know Andy has expensive tastes?''

You can conclude by summarizing your main points, offering advice, or looking to the future. For example:

> Andy spends money faster than he can make it. Unless he gets a better-paying job, cuts back on expensive purchases, or inherits money from a rich relative, the finance company will repossess his furniture.

As with any assignment, begin with a rough draft, and revise your work several times. Make sure your essay is well developed, unified, and coherent. Then edit for grammar, spelling, punctuation, and so on.

5. ''The Transformation of Maria Fernandez'' tells of tragic events that Anita DiPasquale witnessed or that she learned about from someone else. If you responded to either of the first two suggestions for journal writing after this essay, you have collected information about a terrifying incident you experienced directly, witnessed, or heard about from another person. Turn these notes into a full-length essay that tells your story in detail. Like the author of ''The Transformation of Maria Fernandez,'' you might quote yourself or others in your story.

DiPasquale opens by making startling statements, challenging popular assumptions, and asking a rhetorical question. Any of these methods is a good way to introduce your essay, but you can also describe a scene, use a quotation, or explain a problem. When concluding, try a memorable quotation from someone in the story, make a call to action, or look to the future.

You can tell from the final product that DiPasquale wrote several drafts of her essay and edited it quite well. Do the same with yours.

6. Have you ever known anyone who, because of a single experience, went through a drastic and sudden change in personality, lifestyle, or attitude like the one you read about in "The Transformation of Maria Fernandez"? Write the story of this transformation by telling your readers about the experience and by explaining how it changed the person you are writing about. First, however, review the notes you made after reading DiPasquale's essay. If you responded to the third journal suggestion, you may have gathered details you can use in this assignment.

A startling statement, an interesting question or analogy, or the vivid description of a place might make an interesting introduction to your story. Quoting your subject, looking to the future, or asking a rhetorical question might make an effective conclusion.

Once again, remember that writing is a process, so draft, revise, and edit!

SECTION **TWO**

WORD CHOICE AND SENTENCE PATTERNS

In Section One you learned how to approach a subject, to focus on a purpose and central idea, and to organize and develop the information you collected. The three chapters in Section Two explain how to use language and sentence structure to make your writing clearer, more interesting, and more emphatic.

What you will learn in Section Two is just as important as what you learned earlier. In most cases, however, the techniques discussed in this section—refining word choice, creating figures of speech, and reworking sentence structure for emphasis and variety—are things you will turn your attention to after having written at least one version of a paper, not while you are focusing on a central idea, organizing details, or writing your very first rough draft.

Keep this in mind as you read the next three chapters. Chapter 5 explains how to choose vocabulary that is concrete, specific, and vivid. You will learn even more about using words effectively in Chapter 6, which explains three types of figurative language: metaphor, simile, and personification. Finally, Chapter 7 will increase your ability to create variety and emphasis through sentence structure.

Enjoy the selections that follow. Reading them carefully and completing the Questions for Discussion, the Suggestions for Journal Entries, and the Suggestions for Writing will not only help you learn more about the writing process but should also inspire you to continue developing as a writer.

CHAPTER 5

WORD CHOICE: USING CONCRETE, SPECIFIC, AND VIVID LANGUAGE

A writer has three ways to communicate a message: by (1) implying it, (2) telling it, or (3) showing it. Of course, all three types of writing serve specific and important purposes. Usually, however, writing that is the clearest and has the greatest impact uses language that shows what you wish to communicate. Words that show are more concrete, specific, and usually more interesting than those that simply tell the reader what you want to say, and they are always more direct than language that only implies or suggests what you mean.

Although the following two paragraphs discuss the same subject, they contain very different kinds of language. Which of the two will have the greatest impact on the reader?

Writing That Tells

Smith's old car is the joke of the neighborhood. He should have gotten rid of it years ago, but he insists on keeping this ''antique'' despite protests from his family and friends. The car is noisy and unsafe. What's more, it pollutes the environment, causes a real disturbance whenever he drives by, and is a real eyesore.

Writing That Shows

Whenever Smith drives his 1957 Dodge down our street, dogs howl, children scream, and old people head inside and shut their windows. Originally, the car was painted emerald green, but the exterior is so covered with scrapes, dents, and patches of rust that it is hard to tell what it looked like when new. His wife, children, and close friends have begged him to junk this corroded patchwork of steel, rubber, and chicken wire, but Smith insists that he can restore his ''antique'' to its former glory. It does no good to point out that its cracked windshield and bald tires qualify it as a road hazard. Nor does it help to complain about the roar and rattle of its cracked muffler, the screech of its well-worn brakes, and the stench of the thick, black smoke that billows from its rusty tail pipe.

As you will learn in the chapters on narration and description, language that shows makes for effective and interesting writing, especially when your purpose

111

is to describe a person or place or to tell a story. But such language is important to many kinds of writing, and learning how to use it is essential to your development as a writer.

There are three important things to remember about language that shows: It is concrete, it is specific, and it is vivid.

MAKING YOUR WRITING CONCRETE

Concrete language points to or identifies something that the reader can experience or has experienced in some way. Things that are concrete are usually material; they can be seen, heard, smelled, felt, or tasted. The opposite of *concrete* is *abstract,* a term that refers to ideas, emotions, or other intangibles that, while very real, exist in our minds and hearts. That's why readers find it harder to grasp the abstract than the concrete.

Compare the nouns in the following list. The ones on the left represent abstract ideas. The ones on the right stand for concrete embodiments of those ideas; that is, they are physical representations, showing us what such ideas as ''affection'' and ''hatred'' really are.

Abstract	Concrete
Affection	Kiss, embrace
Hatred	Sneer, curse
Violence	Punch, shove
Anger	Shout
Fear	Scream, gasp
Joy	Laugh, smile

Here are three ways to make your writing concrete.

Use Your Five Senses to Recreate an Experience

Giving your readers a straightforward, realistic account of how things look, smell, sound, taste, or feel is one of the most effective ways to make your writing concrete. There are several examples in this book of how authors appeal to the five senses, especially in the chapters on description. For now, read the following passage from ''Once More to the Lake,'' in which E. B. White recalls concrete, sensory details about arriving at the camp in Maine where he spent his summer vacations as a boy. The only sense that White does not refer to is taste; see if you can identify details in this paragraph that appeal to the other four:

> The arriving . . . had been so big a business in itself, at the railway station the
> farm wagon drawn up, the first smell of the pine-laden air, the first glimpse of
> the smiling farmer . . . and the feel of the wagon under you for the long
> ten-mile haul, and at the top of the last long hill catching the first view of the
> lake after eleven months of not seeing this cherished body of water. The shouts

and cries of the other campers when they saw you, and the trunks to be unpacked, to give up their rich burden.

Use Your Five Senses to Create a Concrete Image

An *image* is a mental picture that expresses an abstraction in concrete terms and, therefore, helps readers understand that idea more easily. You can create images by packing your writing with details, usually in the form of nouns and adjectives, that show your readers what things look, sound, smell, taste, or feel like.

The word ''image'' is related to the word ''imagine''; a good time to create an image is when you write about something that your readers have never experienced or that they can only imagine from the information you provide. This is what happens in *A Portrait of the Artist as a Young Man,* when novelist James Joyce puts a startling image into the mouth of a priest who wants to describe his personal vision of hell to a group of schoolboys. Like White, Joyce relies on the senses. Notice the many nouns and adjectives used to create an image of what the speaker thinks eternal damnation is like, an idea that would otherwise have remained very abstract:

> Hell is a strait [narrow] and dark and foulsmelling prison, an abode [home] of demons and lost souls, filled with fire and smoke. The straitness of this prisonhouse is expressly designed by God to punish those who refused to be bound by His laws. In earthly prisons the poor captive [prisoner] has at least some liberty of movement, [if] only within the four walls of his cell or in the gloomy yard of his prison. Not so in hell. There, by reason of the great number of the damned, the prisoners are heaped together in their awful prison, the walls of which are said to be four thousand miles thick: and the damned are so utterly bound and helpless that . . . they are not even able to remove from the eye a worm that gnaws it.

The paragraphs by White and Joyce communicate abstract ideas so concretely that we can understand what the writer is explaining even though we haven't actually experienced it. White's recollection of his arrival makes us feel his personal excitement and anticipation, emotions we could not have appreciated fully had he not used details that appeal to our senses. But such information is even more important in Joyce's paragraph. Unlike that earthly camp in Maine, hell is not part of the world we know. To show us what hell looks like, Joyce must rely on concrete details we recognize from other experiences, details that will help us imagine the scene because they appeal to our senses.

Use Examples

Using easily recognizable examples is a very effective way to help your readers grasp abstract ideas, which might otherwise seem vague or unclear. For instance, if you want to explain that your uncle Wendell is eccentric, you can write that ''he has several quirks,'' that ''he is odd,'' or that ''he is strange.'' But such synonyms are as abstract and as hard to grasp as "eccentric." Instead, why not provide examples that your readers are sure to understand? In other words, *show* them what "eccentric" means by explaining that Uncle Wendell never wears the same color socks, that he often cuts his own hair, that he refuses to speak for days at a time, and that he sometimes eats chocolate-covered seaweed for dessert.

In "Less Work for Mother?" Ruth Schwartz Cowan uses a number of examples we are certain to recognize and understand as she explains the idea that technology has transformed the American household:

> During the first half of the twentieth century, the average American household was transformed by the introduction of a group of machines that profoundly altered the daily lives of housewives. . . . Where once there had been a wood- or coal-burning stove there now was a gas or electric range. Clothes that had once been scrubbed on a metal washboard were now tossed into a tub and cleansed by an electrically driven agitator. The dryer replaced the clothesline; the vacuum cleaner replaced the broom; the refrigerator replaced the ice box and the root cellar. . . . No one had to chop or haul wood anymore. No one had to shovel out ashes or beat rugs or carry water; no one even had to toss egg whites with a fork for an hour to make an angel food cake.

MAKING YOUR WRITING SPECIFIC

As you've learned, writing that shows uses details that are both specific and concrete. Writing that lacks specificity often contains language that is general, which makes it difficult for the writer to communicate clearly and completely. One of the best ways to make your language more specific is to use carefully chosen nouns and adjectives. As you probably know, nouns represent persons, places, and things; adjectives modify (or help describe) nouns, thereby making them more exact and distinct. In the following list, compare the words and phrases in each column; notice how much more meaningful the items become as you move from left to right:

General	More Specific	Most Specific
Automobile	Sports coupe	Fuel-injected Ford Mustang
Residence	House	Large three-bedroom ranch
Fruit	Melon	Juicy cantaloupe
School	College	University of Kentucky
Tree	Evergreen	Young Douglas fir
Baked goods	Pastries	Chocolate-filled cream puffs
Airplane	Jetliner	Brand-new Boeing 747

Beverage	Soft drink	Caffeine-free diet cola
Television show	Situation comedy	*The Cosby Show*
Public transportation	Train	*Orient Express*

You probably noticed that several of the "Most Specific" items contain capitalized words. These are proper nouns, which name specific persons, places, and things. Use proper nouns that your readers will recognize whenever you can. Doing so will show how much you know about your subject and will increase the readers' confidence in you. More important, it will help make your ideas more familiar and easier to grasp.

At first, you might have to train yourself to use specifics. After a while, though, you will become skilled at eliminating flat, empty generalizations from your writing and at filling it with details that clarify and focus your ideas.

Notice the differences between the following two paragraphs. The first uses vague, general language; the second uses specific details—nouns and adjectives—that make its meaning sharper and clearer and that hold the readers' interest better.

General

The island prison is covered with flowers now. A large sign that is visible from a long way off warns visitors away. But since the early 1960s, when they took the last prisoners to other institutions, the sign has really served no purpose, for the prison has been abandoned. The place is not unpleasant; in fact, one might enjoy the romance and solitude out there.

Specific

Alcatraz Island is covered with flowers now: orange and yellow nasturtiums, geraniums, sweet grass, blue iris, black-eyed Susans. Candytuft springs up through the cracked concrete in the exercise yard. Ice plant carpets the rusting catwalks. "WARNING! KEEP OFF! U.S. PROPERTY," the sign still reads, big and yellow and visible for perhaps a quarter of a mile, but since March 21, 1963, the day they took the last thirty or so men off the island . . . the warning has been only *pro forma* [serving no real purpose]. It is not an unpleasant place to be, out there on Alcatraz with only the flowers and the wind and the bell buoy moaning and the tide surging through the Golden Gate. (Joan Didion, "Rock of Ages")

The differences between these two paragraphs can be summed up as follows:

- The first calls the place an "island prison." The second gives it a name, "Alcatraz."
- The first claims that the prison is covered with flowers. The second shows us that this is true by naming them: "nasturtiums, geraniums," and so on. It also explains exactly where they grow: "through the cracked concrete" and on "rusting catwalks."

- The first tells us about a sign that can be seen "from a long way off." The second explains that the sign is "visible for perhaps a quarter of a mile" and shows us exactly what it says.
- The first mentions that the last prisoners were removed from Alcatraz in the 1960s. The second explains that they numbered "thirty or so" and that the exact date of their departure was March 21, 1963.
- The first tells us that we might find "romance and solitude" on Alcatraz Island. The second describes the romance and solitude by calling our attention to "the flowers and the wind and the bell buoy moaning and the tide surging through the Golden Gate."

MAKING YOUR WRITING VIVID

Besides using figurative language (the subject of the next chapter), you can make your writing vivid by choosing verbs, adjectives, and adverbs carefully.

1. Verbs express action, condition, or state of being. If you wrote that "Jan *leaped* over the hurdles," you would be using an action verb. If you explained that "Roberta *did not feel* well" or that "Mario *was* delirious," you would be describing a condition or a state of being.
2. Adjectives describe nouns. You would be using adjectives if you wrote that "the *large, two-story white* house that the *young Canadian* couple bought was *old* and *weather-beaten.*"
3. Adverbs modify (tell the reader something about) verbs, adjectives, or other adverbs. You would be using adverbs if you wrote: "The *easily* frightened child sobbed *softly* and hugged his mother *very tightly* as she *gently* wiped away his tears and *tenderly* explained that the knee he had *just* scraped would stop hurting *soon.*"

   Choosing effective verbs, adjectives, and adverbs can turn dull writing into writing that keeps the readers' interest and communicates ideas with greater emphasis and clarity. Notice how much more effective the rewritten version of each of the following sentences becomes when the right verbs, adjectives, and adverbs are used:

1. The old church needed repair.

   The pre-Civil War Baptist church cried out for repairs to its tottering steeple, its crumbling stone foundation, and its cracked stained-glass windows.
2. The kitchen table was a mess. It was covered with the remains of peanut butter and jelly sandwiches.

   The kitchen table was littered with the half-eaten remains of very stale peanut-butter sandwiches and thickly smeared with the crusty residue of strawberry jelly.

3. Her fellow students showed their approval and their support as the old woman graduated.

Her fellow graduates applauded warmly and enthusiastically as the eighty-six-year-old chemistry major rose proudly and strutted across the auditorium stage to accept her college diploma.

Word choice is extremely important to anyone who wants to become an effective writer. Using the right kind of language marks the difference between writing that is flat, vague, and uninteresting and writing that makes a real impact on its readers. The following selections present the work of poets and essayists who have written clear and effective explanations of very abstract ideas, ideas they would have been unable to explain without language that is concrete, specific, and vivid.

From "The Search for Adam and Eve"

NEWSWEEK

The cover story of the January 11, 1988, Newsweek *proclaimed that anthropologists (scientists who study the origins of the human race) may have found our "common ancestor—a woman who lived over 200,000 years ago" and whose genes are "carried by all of mankind." The scientists studied thousands of women living around the world and found that every one of them has this woman's DNA, the material that determines heredity. Therefore, it is possible that everyone's family tree includes this woman as a member and that everyone on earth is somehow related.*

Looking Ahead

1. Scientists call the woman they believe to be our common ancestor "Eve" after the woman in Genesis, the first book of the Old Testament. The Bible says that, after eating of "the tree of knowledge," Adam and Eve were cast out of the Garden of Eden and later became father and mother to the human race.
2. Many Renaissance artists used the story of Adam and Eve in their works. The Renaissance was an age of intellectual and artistic growth in Europe during the fifteenth, sixteenth, and seventeenth centuries. Milton's poem *Paradise Lost* (1667) tells of the archangel Lucifer's revolt against God and of Adam and Eve's loss of innocence.
3. Martina Navratilova is a professional tennis player.

Vocabulary

evokes Suggests.

fruitful Productive, fertile, bearing many offspring.

genes Biological units that carry the characteristics that offspring inherit from their parents. Genes are composed of DNA (deoxyribonucleic acid).

maternal Motherly.

propagating Producing, breeding, generating.

provocative Suggestive, fascinating.

reluctantly Hesitantly, unwillingly.

savanna Flat grassland.

tresses Hair.

voluptuary Pleasure-seeking.

Scientists are calling her Eve, but reluctantly. The name evokes too many wrong images—the weak-willed figure in Genesis, the milk-skinned beauty in Renaissance art, the voluptuary gardener in "Paradise Lost" who was all "softness" and "meek surrender" and waist-length "gold tresses." The scientists' Eve—subject of one of the most provocative anthropological theories in a decade—was more likely a dark-haired, black-skinned woman, roaming a hot savanna in search of food. She was as muscular as Martina Navratilova, maybe stronger; she might have torn animals apart with her hands, although she probably preferred to use stone tools. She was not the only woman on earth, nor necessarily the most attractive or maternal. She was simply the most fruitful, if that is measured by success in propagating a certain set of genes. Hers seem to be in all humans living today: 5 billion blood relatives. She was, by one rough estimate, your 10,000th great-grandmother.

Questions for Discussion

1. Find adjectives that help make this paragraph specific and vivid.
2. What images does the author create in this selection?
3. What proper nouns do you find? What do such nouns help the writer tell us about the woman who is the subject of the paragraph?
4. How is the "scientists' Eve" different from earlier notions of Eve?
5. How does the writer maintain coherence in this selection?

Suggestion for a Journal Entry

Check your library or local newsstand for the current issue of a magazine you read often or would like to read. Read three or four articles in that issue. Then, analyze the one you found most interesting by using what you have learned about language in this chapter. Pick out words, phrases, and images that make the writing specific, concrete, and vivid. List these in your journal. Finally, to make sure you fully understand what you have read, summarize the writer's main points in three or four sentences of your own.

Those Winter Sundays

ROBERT HAYDEN

Robert Hayden (1913–1980) taught English at Fisk University and at the University of Michigan. For years, the work of this talented black writer received far less recognition than it deserved. Recently, however, his reputation has grown, especially since the publication of his complete poems in 1985.

"Those Winter Sundays" uses the author's vivid memories of his father to show us the depth and quality of love that the man had for his family. Unlike much of Hayden's other work, this poem does not deal with the black experience as such, but it demonstrates the same care and skill in choosing effective language that Hayden used in all his poetry.

If you want to read more by Hayden, look for these poetry collections in your college library: A Ballad of Remembrance, Words in Mourning Time, Angle of Ascent, *and* American Journal.

Looking Ahead

1. Hayden's primary purpose is to explain his father's love for his family. Look for details that are physical signs of that love.
2. The author says his father "made/banked fires blaze." Wood and coal fires were "banked" by covering them with ashes to make them burn slowly through the night and continue giving off heat.
3. The word "offices" isn't used in its usual sense in this poem. Here, it means important services or ceremonies.

Vocabulary

austere   Severe, harsh, difficult, without comfort.
chronic   Persistent, unending, constant.
indifferently   Insensitively, without care or concern.

> Sundays too my father got up early
> and put his clothes on in the blueblack cold,
> then with cracked hands that ached
> from labor in the weekday weather made
> banked fires blaze. No one ever thanked him.   5

I'd wake and hear the cold splintering, breaking.
When the rooms were warm, he'd call,
and slowly I would rise and dress,
fearing the chronic angers of that house,

Speaking indifferently to him,   10
who had driven out the cold
and polished my good shoes as well.
What did I know, what did I know
of love's austere and lonely offices?

Questions for Discussion

1. What details in this poem appeal to our senses?
2. In line 2, Hayden uses ''blueblack'' to describe the cold in his house on Sunday mornings. What other effective adjectives do you find in this poem?
3. Hayden shows us his father in action. What were some of the things this good man did to show his love for his family?
4. What was Hayden's reaction to his father's ''austere and lonely offices'' when he was a boy? How did he feel about his father when he wrote this poem?

Suggestions for Journal Entries

1. In Looking Ahead, you read that Hayden describes his father's love by using language that is concrete, specific, and vivid. In your own words, discuss the kind of love that Hayden's father showed his family.
2. Do you know someone who demonstrates love for other people day in and day out, as Hayden's father did? In your journal, list the offices (services, tasks, or activities) that he or she performs to show this love. Include as many concrete and specific terms as you can. Then expand each item in your list to a few short sentences, showing that these activities are clearly signs of love.

The Station

ROBERT J. HASTINGS

Robert Hastings is an ordained Baptist minister and has taught at numerous colleges and seminaries in the United States, Great Britain, and South America. Hastings' short fiction, much of it set in a mythical American village called Tinyburg, has become quite popular. However, his reputation rests on his work as a syndicated religious columnist in Kentucky and Illinois.

Looking Ahead

1. In comparing our journey through life to a trip across the continent by train, Hastings uses analogy as the primary method of development. To review what you learned about analogy, reread pages 59, 63, and 64 in Chapter 3, and see the Glossary near the end of this book.

2. "The Station" was published in Ann Landers's nationally syndicated newspaper column, and it contains many short paragraphs, which are common in journalistic writing.

Vocabulary

idyllic   Lovely, picturesque, charming, romantic.
relish   Enjoy.
vision   Idea, mental picture.

Tucked away in our subconscious minds is an idyllic vision in which we see   1
ourselves on a long journey that spans an entire continent. We're traveling by train and, from the windows, we drink in the passing scenes of cars on nearby highways, of children waving at crossings, of cattle grazing in distant pastures, of smoke pouring from power plants, of row upon row of cotton and corn and wheat, of flatlands and valleys, of city skylines and village halls.

But uppermost in our minds is our final destination—for at a certain hour   2
and on a given day, our train will finally pull into the station with bells ringing, flags waving, and bands playing. And once that day comes, so many wonderful dreams will come true. So restlessly, we pace the aisles and count the miles, peering ahead, waiting, waiting, waiting for the station.

"Yes, when we reach the station, that will be it!" we promise ourselves.   3
"When we're eighteen . . . win that promotion . . . put the last kid through college . . . buy that 450 SL Mercedes Benz . . . pay off the mortgage . . . have a nest egg for retirement."

From that day on we will all live happily ever after.   4

Sooner or later, however, we must realize there is no station in this life, no   5
one earthly place to arrive at once and for all. The journey is the joy. The station is an illusion—it constantly outdistances us. Yesterday's a memory, tomorrow's a dream. Yesterday belongs to history, tomorrow belongs to God. Yesterday's a fading sunset, tomorrow's a faint sunrise. Only today is there light enough to love and live.

So, gently close the door on yesterday and throw the key away. It isn't the   6
burdens of today that drive men mad, but rather the regret over yesterday and the fear of tomorrow.

"Relish the moment" is a good motto, especially when coupled with Psalm   7
118:24, "This is the day which the Lord hath made; we will rejoice and be glad in it."

So stop pacing the aisles and counting the miles. Instead, swim more rivers, ⁸
climb more mountains, kiss more babies, count more stars. Laugh more and cry
less. Go barefoot oftener. Eat more ice cream. Ride more merry-go-rounds.
Watch more sunsets. Life must be lived as we go along.

Questions for Discussion

1. What is Hastings' central idea, and in what paragraph is it most clearly stated?

2. In paragraphs 1 and 2, Hastings creates an image to describe the journey of
   our lives. Identify a few of the concrete details he uses to create this image.
   Which of the five senses does he rely on?

3. In paragraph 2, we read that ''so many wonderful dreams will come true''
   when we get to our life's destination. What examples in paragraph 3 explain
   this abstract idea?

4. In paragraph 7, Hastings advises us to ''Relish the moment.'' What does he
   mean by this? What examples does he use later in the essay to make this idea
   more concrete?

5. This selection contains a number of effective verbs and adjectives. In paragraph 1, for instance, Hastings writes that ''we *drink* in the passing scenes''
   and see ''smoke *pouring* from power plants.'' What other verbs and adjectives does he use to make his writing vivid?

Suggestions for Journal Entries

1. Reread the essay's conclusion. Do you agree that going barefoot, swimming
   rivers, and watching sunsets are good ways to ''relish the moment''? List
   other ways to get more out of life every day.

2. Hastings provides examples of what many people see as the ''destination''
   of life's journey. Write down details or examples to explain the goals you
   have set for yourself over the next five to ten years. A good way to gather
   such information is to answer questions a journalist might ask, like ''What
   kind of work will I be doing?'' ''Where will I live?'' ''Will I be married?''
   ''Who or what kind of people will be my friends?'' ''How will I achieve my
   'destination'?'' ''Will I enjoy the 'journey'?''

Going Home

MAURICE KENNY

*Maurice Kenny is a Native American poet who lives and teaches in rural New
York State. Among his most important publications are* The Mama Poems *and*
Between Two Rivers. *''Going Home'' expresses the writer's sense of loss and
isolation when he comes home after a long absence.*

Looking Ahead

Kenny uses nouns, both common and proper, to create a picture of the land to which he returns. As you know, nouns name persons, places, and things. Proper nouns, like ''Greyhound'' and ''Syracuse,'' name specific persons, places, and things.

Vocabulary

privies   Toilets.

The book lay unread in my lap
snow gathered at the window
from Brooklyn it was a long ride
the Greyhound followed the plow
from Syracuse to Watertown   5
to country cheese and maples
tired rivers and closed paper mills
home to gossipy aunts . . .
their dandelions and pregnant cats . . .
home to cedars and fields of boulders   10
cold graves under willow and pine
home from Brooklyn to the reservation
that was not home
to songs I could not sing
to dances I could not dance   15
from Brooklyn bars and ghetto rats
to steaming horses stomping frozen earth
barns and privies lost in blizzards
home to a Nation, Mohawk
to faces, I did not know   20
and hands which did not recognize me
to names and doors
my father shut

Questions for Discussion

1. ''The book lay unread in my lap,'' the poet says in line 1. What does this tell us about his state of mind?
2. Kenny says he came home to songs he ''could not sing'' and dances he ''could not dance.'' What idea or feeling do these lines reveal?
3. How would you describe the image that closes this poem? What emotion does it show?
4. What do the adjectives ''tired'' and ''closed'' in line 7 tell us about Kenny's home? Find other adjectives that make his writing vivid.

5. What details does the writer use to contrast the two places he has called home?

6. What nouns, common and proper, do we find in "Going Home"? What effect do they have on you?

Suggestions for Journal Entries

1. Kenny does not say exactly how long he has been away or what has happened during that time. What do you imagine happened to him or to the place and people he left since he was home last? Use brainstorming or focused freewriting to make up details that could explain why he feels so separated from the people and land he is returning to.

2. Think of a town, community, or neighborhood in which you once lived and have been away from for a long time. Would you like to live there again? Why or why not? Answer this question by listing concrete details about the place. Rely on your senses; explain what it looked like, smelled like, and so on. Like Kenny, include nouns, both common and proper, to create images that will reveal your feelings about your subject.

The San Francisco Earthquake

JACK LONDON

One of the world's best-known adventure writers, London (1876–1916) held a number of colorful jobs that took him around the world and supplied material for his stories. When only a boy, he left his native San Francisco on a commercial steamer to Japan. Several adventures later, he traveled to the Klondike to prospect for gold. In 1904, he returned to the Orient as a journalist to report on the Russo-Japanese War, and in 1914, he found himself in Mexico to cover that country's revolution. Among his best-known novels are The Call of the Wild, White Fang, *and* The Sea Wolf.

Looking Ahead

1. London makes his writing concrete and specific by choosing nouns carefully. In paragraph 1, he calls the blaze that followed the earthquake a "conflagration," not simply a fire. In paragraph 2, he tells us about the "hotels and palaces of the nabobs" when he could simply have mentioned their "houses."

2. In paragraph 3, London uses the adjective "lurid" to describe the tower of smoke from the burning city. In paragraph 6, he makes use of an interesting adverb when he explains that dynamite was used

''lavishly.'' Pick out other effective adjectives and adverbs as you read this selection.

3. London was a master at creating concrete visual imagery. One of his best can be found in paragraph 3, but there are others in this essay. Identify them.

Vocabulary

colossal   Gigantic.

conflagration   Large and very destructive fire.

contrivances   Inventions.

cunning   Skillful.

debris   Fragments, remains.

enumeration   Listing.

lavishly   Generously, in great amounts.

lurid   Glaring, shocking.

nabobs   People of wealth and power.

vestiges   Traces.

wrought   Caused.

The earthquake shook down in San Francisco hundreds of thousands of dollars   1
worth of walls and chimneys. But the conflagration that followed burned up hundreds of millions of dollars worth of property. There is no estimating within hundreds of millions the actual damage wrought.

Not in history has a modern imperial city been so completely destroyed. San   2
Francisco is gone. Nothing remains of it but memories and a fringe of dwelling houses on its outskirts. Its industrial section is wiped out. Its social and residential section is wiped out. The factories and warehouses, the great stores and newspaper buildings, the hotels and palaces of the nabobs, all are gone. Remains only the fringe of dwelling houses on the outskirts of what was once San Francisco.

Within an hour after the earthquake shock, the smoke of San Francisco's   3
burning was a lurid tower visible a hundred miles away. And for three days and nights this lurid tower swayed in the sky, reddening the sun, darkening the day, and filling the land with smoke.

On Wednesday morning at quarter past five came the earthquake. A minute   4
later the flames were leaping upward. In a dozen different quarters south of Market Street, in the working class ghetto and in the factories, fires started. There was no opposing the flames. There was no organization, no communication. All the cunning adjustments of a twentieth century city had been smashed by the earthquake. The streets were humped into ridges and depressions, and piled with the debris of fallen walls. The steel rails were twisted into perpendicular and

horizontal angles. The telephone and telegraph systems were disrupted. And the great water mains had burst. All the shrewd contrivances and safeguards of man had been thrown out of gear by thirty seconds' twitching of the earth-crust.

By Wednesday afternoon, inside of twelve hours, half the heart of the city 5 was gone. At that time I watched the vast conflagration from out on the bay. It was dead calm. Not a flicker of wind stirred. Yet from every side wind was pouring in upon the city. East, west, north, and south, strong winds were blowing upon the doomed city. The heated air rising made an enormous suck. Thus did the fire of itself build its own colossal chimney through the atmosphere. Day and night this dead calm continued, and yet, near to the flames, the wind was often half a gale, so mighty was the suck.

Wednesday night saw the destruction of the very heart of the city. Dynamite 6 was lavishly used, and many of San Francisco's proudest structures were crumbled by man himself into ruins, but there was no withstanding the onrush of the flames. Time and again successful stands were made by the firefighters, and every time the flames flanked around on either side, or came up from the rear, and turned to defeat the hard won victory.

An enumeration of the buildings destroyed would be a directory of San 7 Francisco. An enumeration of the buildings undestroyed would be a line and several addresses. An enumeration of the deeds of heroism would stock a library and bankrupt the Carnegie medal fund. An enumeration of the dead—will never be made. All vestiges of them were destroyed by the flames. The number of the victims of the earthquake will never be known.

Questions for Discussion

1. Pick out a few examples of the effective nouns that make the writing in this essay concrete.
2. One reason London's works are still popular is that they are filled with interesting adjectives. Identify those you find especially vivid.
3. London is famous for creating brilliant visual images like the one in paragraph 3. What other effective images do you find in this selection?
4. In paragraph 4, we read ''All the cunning adjustments of a twentieth century city had been smashed by the earthquake.'' What were these ''cunning adjustments''? What examples does London use to explain this idea?
5. What caused the strong wind described in paragraph 5?
6. This essay is well organized. Discuss a few techniques London uses to maintain coherence in and between paragraphs. (Such techniques are explained in Chapter 2.)
7. Did you read about, view on television, or experience firsthand the results of the earthquake that struck San Francisco in October 1989? What ''cunning adjustments'' of a modern city did that earthquake destroy? In what ways were its effects different from what London describes?

Suggestions for Journal Entries

1. Have you ever seen the results of a great natural disaster (a flood, an earth-quake, a forest fire, a tornado, or a hurricane)? If so, write down as many concrete, specific, and vivid details about the scene as you remember. Use the focused-freewriting method, discussed in ''Getting Started.''
2. Take your journal with you as you walk along one of the main streets of a town or city near your college or your home. Spend a half hour or so gathering details about what you see, hear, feel, smell, and even taste. Don't bother listing these sensory details in any specific order; just jot them down as you walk along, journal in hand. When you complete your short outing, find a quiet place to read your notes. Then write a paragraph or two explaining your impression of and reaction to what you just experienced.

Sinnit Cave

HENRY STICKELL

Henry Stickell grew up in the Baltimore area, not a great distance from the mountains of West Virginia, where his fascinating story of spelunking (cave exploration) takes place. Actually, the essay uses details from several expeditions that Stickell and his wife, Betty, have made to Sinnit Cave.

Stickell is now head of circulation at the Levy Library of Mt. Sinai Medical Center in New York City. He wrote ''Sinnit Cave'' for a college writing course.

Looking Ahead

1. One of Stickell's greatest strengths is his ability to choose verbs. In paragraph 4, he writes that ''the miles slid by as we sped over the well-paved expressways.'' Find other examples of verbs that make this essay lively and interesting.
2. Stickell is careful to use nouns that are concrete and specific. To make his writing even more realistic, he tells us about the geologic formations he observed, and he makes mention of such special equipment as ''carbide lamps'' and ''belay lines.''

Vocabulary

dumb   Speechless.
inventory   List.
negotiated   Dealt with successfully.
precipice   Cliff, top of a steep hill.

predicament   Problem, emergency.
rappelled   Descended with the aid of a rope.
welled up   Rose up.

We were struck dumb as we gazed upward from the bottom of the pit. Eighty 1
feet above, we could see debris clogging the entrance that we had used only eight
hours earlier to enter the cave. With the light from our carbide lamps and
flashlights, we probed every crack and crevasse of the shaft in search of an
opening we could squeeze through, that is, if one of us could climb the sheer
walls of the shaft to lower a rope for the rest of us to climb up on. The rappelling
rope that we had left in place had been washed to the bottom of the pit along with
the tree it was attached to. My gut tightened into a painful knot, and panic welled
up inside of me as the realization of our predicament struck home. Why was I
here? It had all started several days ago when a close friend, Dick, telephoned.

"I'm going cave crawling this weekend. Are you and Betty interested?" He 2
continued to tell us, "There's a cave in Pendleton County, West Virginia, called
Sinnit Cave. I've been there once before and want to return to explore a different
section."

I sealed our fate with an enthusiastic, "When do we leave?" Friday evening 3
we loaded the car and drove to Dick's house. As we pulled up in front, we
spotted Roger, Beverly, and Larry waiting in an overloaded blue 1959 Chevy
station wagon. We shifted the load in our vehicle to accommodate Dick and his
mountain of equipment and pulled out of the driveway as the sun was disappear-
ing over the horizon.

The drive from the Baltimore/Washington area started easily, and the miles 4
slid by as we sped over the well-paved expressways. However, once into central
Virginia, the highway pinched down to two lanes and eventually changed into
a narrow country road winding up and down the lush mountains of West Virginia.

It was nearly midnight when we pulled off the road. There was a steep 5
mountain on one side and a stream with an old rickety bridge on the other. We
got out of our cars and paused to savor the cool mountain solitude. The stars were
blazing above, and the Milky Way, usually obscure in the sky over Baltimore,
was plainly visible. We soon had our tents pitched and sleeping bags unfurled
on a level, grassy area near the stream. Larry gathered kindling and fallen
branches while Betty and Beverly broke out the coffee and ham sandwiches.
Soon, we were huddled around a roaring campfire making plans for the next
day's assault on Sinnit Cave.

After supper, Betty and I crawled into our sleeping bags, zipped up the tent, 6
and passed out. In what seemed like only a few moments, however, I heard Larry
saying, "Rise and shine, you all. It's 7:00 A.M. Let's move it!"

The early morning sun bathed the campsite in a hazy glow as we gulped 7
down a hasty breakfast of rolls and coffee. We assembled our gear and, before
long, began the long trek up the steep mountainside in search of the cave's

entrance. By 9:30, we had found the entrance shaft in a meadow near the summit. We rigged a rappelling rope and a belay line, checked our harnesses, and lit the carbide lamps.

"I'll go first," Dick said. He clipped his carbiners to the rappelling rope, 8 stood on the brink of the precipice, and disappeared over the edge, glancing over his shoulder to see his way down. I controlled the belay line as he descended.

Soon the downward tug on the line ceased and I heard Dick holler, "I'm at 9 the bottom! Let up on the belay!"

The rest of us quickly rappelled down the entrance shaft. The world of light 10 disappeared as we penetrated into the dark, damp underground. The next seven hours flowed easily as we explored deeper and deeper into the cavern. There was a variety of speleothemes throughout the cave—beautiful stalactites, stalagmites, and walls of quartz crystal. We even discovered colonies of bats suspended upside down waiting for night to fall in the world above before venturing out in search of supper.

For a time, it seemed as if we were climbing through a fantasy world. 11 Eventually, however, diminishing carbide in the lamps, fatigue, and a ravenous desire for hot food drew us back toward the entrance. That's when we made the frightening discovery that a small avalanche had sealed the cave entrance with earth and rock. Betty squeezed my arm tightly, and suddenly I was jolted from my daydream and into the reality of our predicament.

"Is there another way out?" I asked.

Dick answered, "I remember that there was an article in the latest *Grotto* 13 *News* about a group from Washington, D.C., who found a connection between the upper and lower cave." 12

He pulled out his map and we all gathered around. With a muddy finger, he 14 poked at the approximate location on the map. We took an inventory of our equipment and supplies, and we decided to continue to use up our carbide to the bitter end. We would then rely on candles as our major light source and save the flashlights for illuminating the more difficult sections of the cave.

We searched frantically for more than an hour for the entrance to the 15 connection. It was Beverly who finally found the small squeeze hole under a low ledge. We were sure this was the way. The limestone of the squeeze hole was worn smooth, and there were scratched areas where equipment attached to belts could have scraped the walls of the opening. After two hours of squirming on our bellies through mud, we realized that the squeeze hole was starting to expand. The connection gradually became larger and finally opened into a long chamber with a high ceiling.

"I know this room," Dick exclaimed. "It's called the Big Room on the map. 16 I was in here on my last trip."

Beverly asked, "Do you know the way out?" 17

"Yes. We'll need about another hour or two," Dick answered. 18

As we set out on the last leg of our adventure, our carbide lamps sputtered 19 out one by one. As our lamps failed we lit candles and kept moving. On the way out we negotiated a steep area, called the Silo, that dropped down into the mountain. Then came a long, deep crevasse in the last section of the cave. Up ahead I could see several small points of light. Suddenly, I realized I was looking out the cave entrance at the stars.

The closer I came to the entrance, the more the tension eased from my body.   20 We soon stumbled into the safety of our campsite. The lower cave entrance was only a short distance away. We collapsed into our sleeping bags, and some of us said prayers of thanks before slipping into unconsciousness. I know I did.

Questions for Discussion

1. In Looking Ahead, you learned that Stickell's writing is vivid because of the verbs he chooses. Identify verbs that make his writing lively.
2. Do you agree that the language in this essay is concrete and specific? Pick out two or three paragraphs that you find especially well written, and underline the words that make them so effective. Concentrate on nouns, but also look for well-chosen adjectives and adverbs.
3. What visual images does Stickell create to show us the seriousness of his predicament?
4. What techniques does he use to maintain coherence?
5. "Sinnit Cave" begins in the middle of things, with Stickell's party returning to the cave entrance only to find that it has been blocked. Does starting at this point help the author capture the reader's interest better than starting with Dick's invitation to go spelunking? Explain why it does or doesn't.

Suggestions for Journal Entries

1. Recall a frightening or exciting experience like surfing, boating, or swimming in rough water; getting into a fight or an auto accident; being attacked by an animal; walking outdoors during a thunderstorm; flying in a small plane; hang gliding; skin diving; or riding the roller coaster at an amusement park. Use focused freewriting or listing to record concrete details about this experience. Include as many concrete nouns and vivid adjectives as possible. Like Stickell, also include proper nouns. Whenever possible, use details from one or more of your senses.
2. As you know, Stickell uses visual images to show us his experiences in Sinnit Cave. Use visual details to put together one or two paragraphs that concretely and vividly describe a natural setting you have visited recently. For example, write about a meadow, a mountain, a river, a beach, or even a cave.
3. Think back to a special or memorable outing. List all the details you will need to show your readers how special or memorable a trip it was.

SUGGESTIONS FOR WRITING

1. Hayden's ''Those Winter Sundays'' praises a man who demonstrates his love for others. If you responded to the second journal suggestion after this poem, you have probably made a list of the offices (activities, tasks, or services) that someone you know performs to show his or her love.

   Focus on at least three offices that mean the most to you, and expand your discussion into an essay in which you show how much this individual does for others. Begin with a preliminary thesis that expresses your feelings about your subject, but remember once again that you will probably want to revise this statement after you write your first draft.

   Limit each of the body paragraphs to only one of the offices in your list. Try developing these paragraphs by using methods described in Chapter 3; narration, description, conclusion and support, illustration, and process analysis might work well in such an assignment. Whatever you decide, follow Hayden's lead and use language that is concrete and specific.

   Express your revised thesis in an effective introduction that uses one or more of the techniques for effective openings explained in Chapter 4. Close with a conclusion like one you read about in that chapter. As usual, write several drafts of your paper and edit it carefully.

2. Item 2 of the Suggestions for Journal Entries after Hastings' ''The Station'' invited you to list some of your life's goals in your journal. Add to your notes, trying to focus on goals that you think you will be able to attain within five to ten years. Then, expand your discussion of at least three of these goals into a well-developed essay.

   Limit each of the paragraphs in the body of your essay to only one goal. Give each of these paragraphs a topic sentence that controls its content and that relates to the central idea of your essay. Appropriate methods to develop these paragraphs are illustration, cause and effect, narration, and description, as explained in Chapter 3.

   Whichever method(s) you use, express your ideas by including nouns and adjectives that make your writing concrete and specific. Proper nouns— words that name specific places, persons, and things—might work well in this assignment. A good time to insert such details is during the revision process, as you write your second and third drafts. Another is when you edit your paper.

   There are many ways to introduce your essay. One is to describe a scene that will give your readers clues about your interests, the place in which you hope to live or work, and the kind of job or career you plan to pursue. You might conclude by giving yourself advice or by summarizing ways to achieve your goals.

3. After reading Kenny's ''Going Home,'' you might have made a journal entry about a town, neighborhood, or community that you once lived in and that you may or may not wish to return to. Use your notes and any other important

information you can remember about the place to write an essay that describes it in language that is concrete, specific, and vivid.

Begin with a preliminary thesis statement that clearly expresses your fondness or distaste for the place, your intention to return or to stay away. Use the rest of the essay to explain what about the place makes you feel this way.

If you have trouble deciding how to introduce or conclude your essay, try one or more of the methods for beginning and ending explained in Chapter 3. As with all assignments, remember that you might have to rewrite your thesis after you draft and revise your paper. As a last step in the process, edit your work for mechanical errors that might reduce your essay's effectiveness.

4. If you responded to the first of the Suggestions for Journal Entries after Jack London's ''The San Francisco Earthquake,'' you have already begun gathering details to describe the results of a natural disaster you witnessed recently. Use your notes as the starting point of an essay about the effects of this fire, tornado, earthquake, flood, or the like. Like London, rely on your senses to create effective images, and use verbs and adjectives to make the experience come alive for your readers.

You can add excitement to your essay by beginning with specific details about the disaster itself. In any case, be sure your introduction explains where and when it occurred. Also, try fitting your thesis into your first or second paragraph as London does.

Most important, take your time as you go through the process of describing the effects of this terrible event. Revise the early drafts of your paper by adding important details and improving word choice. Check to see that you have included appropriate transitions to maintain coherence and that you have organized your information well. Finally, edit your paper to remove errors that might detract from the fine work you have produced!

5. Have you ever had a frightening, dangerous, or exciting experience like the one in Stickell's ''Sinnit Cave''? If you made journal notes about such an experience after reading the selection, review that entry and add information that you have since remembered.

Turn your notes into an essay that demonstrates your fear or excitement over that experience. As you learned in Chapter 3, narration is a good way to develop and organize such an essay. Start by writing a preliminary thesis statement that explains how excited or scared you were. Then, simply begin at the beginning of your story. Tell what happened along the way, focusing on and emphasizing details that show your reader the fear or excitement mentioned in your thesis. But don't just explain what happened; include details about what you saw, heard, felt, smelled, and/or tasted.

As you go through the process of rewriting the early drafts of your paper, revise your preliminary thesis statement to make it clearer, and put it into an opening paragraph that relies on a method for writing introductions like those discussed in Chapter 4. Try using a startling statement, describing a scene, or asking your readers a question. End your essay by offering your readers advice, looking to the future, closing with a memorable statement or quotation, or using another type of conclusion you have learned about.

Before you hand in the final version, edit your paper for correctness. As you do, check that you have included language to make the fear or excitement you felt seem real to your readers.

CHAPTER 6

WORD CHOICE: USING FIGURATIVE LANGUAGE

In Chapter 5 you learned that you can clarify abstract ideas by using concrete language. One way to do this is to fill your writing with specific details or to create verbal images (pictures in words) that appeal to the reader's senses. You also learned that using effective verbs, adjectives, and adverbs can help make your writing vivid. All of these techniques will help you *show*—and not simply tell—your reader what you mean.

Another way to make your writing clearer and more vivid is to use figurative language. Such language is called "figurative" because it does not explain or represent a subject directly. A figure of speech works by creating a comparison or other relationship between the abstract idea you want to explain and something concrete that readers will recognize easily. In that way, it can help you explain an idea more clearly and emphatically than if you used literal language alone.

In fact, figures of speech provide a way to create images, mental pictures that allow readers to *see* what you mean. Notice how effective your description of a "clumsy" friend becomes when you compare him to a "bull in a china shop." The concrete image of a "bull in a china shop"—complete with shattered teacups, bowls, and plates—is sharper and more dramatic than an abstaction like "clumsy" can ever be.

The most common figures of speech take the form of comparisons. The three discussed in this chapter are simile, metaphor, and personification.

SIMILE

A simile creates a comparison between two things by using the word "like" or "as." For example, say that you're writing your sweetheart a letter in which you want to explain how much you need him or her. You can express your feelings literally and directly by writing "I need you very much." Then again, you can *show* how strongly you feel by writing that you need him or her "as a great oak needs sunlight," "as an eagle needs the open sky," or "as the dry earth needs spring rain."

Read the following list carefully. Notice how much more concrete, exciting, and rich the ideas on the left become when they are expressed in similes:

134

Literal Expression	Simile
Harry has gained a lot of weight.	Harry has gotten as heavy as a horse.
Eugene is a fancy dresser.	Eugene dresses like a peacock.
The children's bedroom was a mess.	The children's bedroom looked like the town dump.
The old dog moves slowly.	The old dog moved as slowly as corn syrup in winter.

Finally, look at a passage from "Java Jive," an essay in which Al Young recalls a hot Mississippi afternoon from his childhood. Pick out the two effective similes Young uses in this passage:

The sun—like a hot, luminous magnet—happened to be shining powerfully that antique afternoon. My father was busy being his auto mechanic self, and I could see him through the dusty window screen out there in the grass and dirt and clay of the sideyard driveway, fixing on our dark blue Chevy coupe, grease all over his face and forearms; black on black. Pious as a minister or metaphysician [philosopher], he was bent on fixing that car.

METAPHOR

A metaphor also uses comparison to show the relationship between things in order to make the explanation of one of these things clearer and livelier. In fact, a metaphor works just like a simile except that it does not make use of "like" or "as." For instance, you can turn the simile "Eugene dresses like a peacock" into a metaphor by writing "Eugene is a peacock." In neither case, of course, do you actually mean that Eugene is a bird; you're simply pointing out similarities between the way he dresses and the showiness we associate with a peacock.

The important thing to remember is that, like all figures of speech, similes and metaphors turn abstract ideas (like "Eugene is a fancy dresser") into vivid, concrete images. In other words, they communicate more emphatically and clearly than if the writer had used literal language alone. Study the following list of similes and metaphors carefully. What effect do they have on you, especially when compared with the literal expressions on the left?

Literal Expression	Simile	Metaphor
The two young men battled through the night.	The two young men battled like gladiators through the night.	The two young gladiators battled through the night.
In spring, the meadow is beautiful.	In spring, the meadow looks like a painting by Renoir.	In spring, the meadow is a painting by Renoir.
My old car is hard to drive.	My old car drives like a tank.	My old car is a tank!

Literal Expression	Simile	Metaphor
During holidays, shopping malls are crowded and noisy.	During holidays, shopping malls are so crowded and noisy that they seem like madhouses.	During holidays, shopping malls are so crowded and noisy that they become madhouses.
The hayloft was hot.	The hayloft was as hot as a blast furnace.	The hayloft was a blast furnace.

Finally, read the following excerpt from Martin Luther King's "I Have a Dream," a speech he delivered at the Lincoln Memorial during the 1963 march on Washington. Identify the metaphors and similes that Dr. King used to captivate the thousands in his audience and to make his message more concrete, vivid, and effective:

> Five score years ago, a great American, in whose symbolic shadow we stand today, signed the Emancipation Proclamation. This momentous decree came as a great beacon light of hope to millions of Negro slaves who had been seared in the flames of withering injustice. It came as a joyous daybreak to end the long night of their captivity.
>
> But one hundred years later, the Negro still is not free. One hundred years later, the life of the Negro is still sadly crippled by the manacles of segregation and the chains of discrimination.

PERSONIFICATION

Personification is the description of animals, plants, or inanimate objects by using terms ordinarily associated with human beings. Like metaphor and simile, personification is an effective way to turn abstract ideas into vivid and concrete realities that readers will grasp easily and quickly.

One common example of personification is Father Time, the figure of an old man trailing a white beard and carrying a scythe and hourglass. Another is the Grim Reaper, the representation of death pictured as a skeleton holding a scythe. Shakespeare often used personification to enrich the language of his poems and plays. In "Sonnet 18," for example, he described the sun as "the eye of heaven." William Least Heat Moon does something similar when, in *Blue Highways,* he describes the saguaro cactus of the southwestern U.S.:

> Standing on the friable slopes . . . saguaros mimic men as they salute, bow, dance, raise arms to wave, and grin with faces carved in by woodpeckers. Older plants, having survived odds against their reaching maturity of sixty million to one, have every right to smile.

The following selections demonstrate very careful uses of language, both literal and figurative. As you read them, identify their similes, metaphors, and personifications and ask yourself if these figures of speech have made the selections clearer, more vivid, and more effective than if their authors had relied on literal language alone.

From "A Visit to Belfast"

MARY MANNING

This selection is the introduction to an article Manning published in The Atlantic *magazine of May 1972. Belfast is the capital of Northern Ireland, the site of civil strife between Protestants and Catholics that has lasted for many years.*

Looking Ahead

Manning uses both figures of speech and the kinds of nouns and adjectives you learned about in Chapter 5 to make her writing concrete and vivid.

Vocabulary

discothèques   Nightclubs where people dance to recorded music.

It is a dying city, a broken city, a city almost without hope, for where do we go from here? The heart still beats faintly in the University, in beautiful outlying suburbs, in the brave little Lyric Theater, in the few discothèques where the students, girls and boys, line up for hours in the wintry nights just to get in—to have a drink, to listen to the music of the outside world. The few visitors must stay in guesthouses. Hotels, because of the bombings, are increasingly dangerous. But the heart is still beating faintly. Like a patient in intensive care, Belfast, having survived several heart attacks, may survive, for Belfast has a tough Northern heart; it may just make it.

Questions for Discussion

1. Where in this paragraph does Manning use personification? What about simile?
2. Explain one of the images that the author creates in this selection. What details make that image effective?
3. What does Manning see in Belfast to make her believe this city "may just make it"?

Suggestions for Journal Entries

1. A writer personifies an inanimate object by giving it human qualities. Manning has done this with an entire city. Think about a town or city you have

lived in or visited recently. Use focused freewriting to collect details that make the place seem human in one way or another. For example, describe the activity at the center of town as the beating of a heart, the flow of traffic as the flow of blood through veins (streets) or arteries (highways); compare the community to a healthy young child or to a sick old person; or give the place a distinct personality based on your opinion of the kind of people who live there.

2. Cities can be wonderful places to live in, filled with opportunities to work, play, and grow. But they can also be nightmarish and bleak. What image comes to mind when you think about the city you know best? Use listing or answer the journalists' questions to gather concrete details about this place. As you learned in Chapter 5, rely on your five senses. At the same time, try your hand at creating figures of speech—metaphor, simile, and personification—that will show why you would or would not choose to live there permanently.

January Wind

HAL BORLAND

Journalist, nature writer, playwright, novelist, and poet, Hal Borland (1900–1978) was trained as an engineer, an experience which may account for the precision and concreteness of his writing. "January Wind" is one of hundreds of articles on the outdoors he wrote for The New York Times.

Looking Ahead

Borland uses personification to describe the wind. To do this, he makes good use of vivid adjectives and verbs like those you learned about in Chapter 5. He also includes nouns that are concrete and specific.

Vocabulary

lichen   Fungus found on rocks and tree trunks.
hieroglyphics   Ancient Egyptian writing that used figures or pictures.

The January wind has a hundred voices. It can scream, it can bellow, it can 1
whisper, and it can sing a lullaby. It can roar through the leafless oaks and shout down the hillside, and it can murmur in the white pines rooted among the granite ledges where lichen makes strange hieroglyphics. It can whistle down a chimney and set the hearth-flames to dancing. On a sunny day it can pause in a sheltered spot and breathe a promise of spring and violets. In the cold of a lonely night

it can rattle the sash and stay there muttering of ice and snowbanks and deep-frozen ponds.

Sometimes the January wind seems to come from the farthest star in the outer darkness, so remote and so impersonal is its voice. That is the wind of a January dawn, in the half-light that trembles between day and night. It is a wind that merely quivers the trees, its force sensed but not seen, a force that might almost hold back the day if it were so directed. Then the east brightens, and the wind relaxes—the stars, its source, grown dim.

And sometimes the January wind is so intimate that you know it came only from the next hill, a little wind that plays with leaves and puffs at chimney smoke and whistles like a little boy with puckered lips. It makes the little cedar trees quiver, as with delight. It shadow-boxes with the weather-vane. It tweaks an ear, and whispers laughing words about crocuses and daffodils, and nips the nose and dances off.

But you never know, until you hear its voice, which wind is here today. Or, more important, which will be here tomorrow.

Questions for Discussion

1. Where in the essay does the author appeal to the senses?
2. Pick out two or three sentences in which verbs picture the wind as a person.
3. Find several examples of nouns and adjectives that make Borland's writing concrete and specific.
4. What does "lichen makes strange hieroglyphics" mean? What other images do you find in this essay?
5. What is the essay's thesis?

Suggestions for Journal Entries

1. Use listing, brainstorming, or focused freewriting to capture the sounds, sights, feel, smell, and/or taste of wind, rain, snow, hail, thunder, lightning, fire, or another natural phenomenon. Try to remember a particularly vivid experience involving this phenomenon, and compare what you saw, heard, smelled, felt, and/or tasted to sights, sounds, smells, and so on that a reader would recognize easily. In other words, explain the experience by relying on metaphor, simile, and personification.
2. "The January wind has a hundred voices," claims Borland. Explain the different ways in which a natural object, place, or phenomenon can be experienced. For example, write about two or three kinds of wind, rain, and snow you've seen, heard, and felt; describe different types of cacti, evergreen trees, mountains, deserts, or seashores; or discuss the kinds of water you swim in—river, lake, ocean, pool. Like Borland, use figures of speech, especially personification, whenever you can to create distinct and effective images of your subject.

"Joy of an Immigrant, a Thanksgiving" and "Old Man Timochenko"

EMANUEL DI PASQUALE

Emanuel di Pasquale immigrated to the United States from Ragusa, Sicily, when he was fourteen. An accomplished poet and a teacher of composition, creative writing, and children's literature, di Pasquale has published in several important periodicals, including The Nation *and* The Sawanee Review. *His work has been anthologized in college textbooks and in several collections of children's poems.* Genesis, *a full-length collection of his poetry, was published in 1989.*

"Joy of an Immigrant, a Thanksgiving" and "Old Man Timochenko" reveal di Pasquale's intense love of nature and his talent for creating powerful figures of speech that make his writing clear and captivating.

Looking Ahead

1. "Joy of an Immigrant, a Thanksgiving" contains an extended metaphor in which di Pasquale compares himself to a wandering bird. It is an "extended" metaphor because the writer develops the comparison *throughout* the poem.
2. "Old Man Timochenko" is a brilliant portrait of an old man the poet spotted regularly during drives along a country road in eastern Pennsylvania. Identify the many similes and metaphors that di Pasquale uses to reveal important things about Timochenko's character.

Vocabulary

lineaments   Lines.

JOY OF AN IMMIGRANT, A THANKSGIVING

Like a bird grown weak in a land
where it always rains
and where all the trees have died,
I have flown long and long
to find sunlight pouring over branches   5
and leaves. I have journeyed, oh God,
to find a land where I can build a dry nest,
a land where my song can echo.

OLD MAN TIMOCHENKO

Winds scratch his hands
and his sharp bones
deeply assert
their lineaments.
He stands like a   5
trembling leaf
on the branch
of an evergreen,
and will not fall.

Careful,   10
by the road's edge,
silent as a sunray,
he waves
as I drive by.
Like birds' wings,   15
loose as they coast
in the high air,
his eyes
soften and expand.

He moves in slow waves,   20
like an ancient snake,
knowing the end can wait.

Questions for Discussion

1. In "Joy of an Immigrant, a Thanksgiving," di Pasquale compares himself to a bird through an extended metaphor. What details does he use to develop this comparison?

2. Why does di Pasquale subtitle the first of these poems "a Thanksgiving"?

3. What do the metaphors "where I can build a dry nest" and "where my song can echo" show us about the poet's feelings for his new "land"?

4. What is your emotional reaction to the words in the first three lines of "Joy of an Immigrant, a Thanksgiving"? What do they tell you about the place the poet has left?

5. What do the metaphors and similes in "Old Man Timochenko" show us about the old man? What is the poet's attitude toward his subject?

6. In Looking Ahead you learned that di Pasquale uses figures of speech to create vivid and effective images. Describe the verbal pictures you see in his poems.

7. Recall what you learned about concrete details in Chapter 5. What concrete details, other than those which appear in the similes and metaphors you have identified, does di Pasquale include in "Old Man Timochenko"?

Suggestions for Journal Entries

1. Have you ever experienced a change—any change—in your life that was as dramatic or as important as the one di Pasquale describes in "Joy of an Immigrant, a Thanksgiving"? It need not involve moving from one country or even from one town to another, but it should be something that has had an effect on the person you have become. Describe how this change affected you by listing as many concrete details about it as you can. Try to create similes and/or metaphors that will help you describe its effects more vividly.

2. Is there some interesting person in your life who, like Timochenko, would make a good subject for a short descriptive paragraph or poem? Begin gathering details that will help show your reader how you feel about this individual.

The Death of Benny Paret

NORMAN MAILER

Norman Mailer established his reputation in 1948, when he published The Naked and the Dead, *a popular and influential novel about World War II. Since then, he has produced a number of important works, both fiction and nonfiction, many of which have been critical of modern American society. Mailer has won Pulitzer prizes for* Armies of the Night, *his account of the 1967 peace march on Washington, D.C., and for* The Executioner's Song, *the story of convicted murderer Gary Gilmore.*

Looking Ahead

1. Mailer was at ringside on the night of March 25, 1962, when Emile Griffith knocked out Benny Paret in the twelfth round of a welterweight championship bout in New York City's Madison Square Garden. The beating that Paret took that night led to his death. He was twenty-four.

2. "The Death of Benny Paret" contains good examples of all three of the figures of speech discussed earlier in this chapter. Look for places in which Mailer uses simile, metaphor, and personification in this frank and vivid account of one of the most brutal episodes in sports history.

Vocabulary

irrevocably Irreversibly.
maulings Beatings.
orgy Spree, wild party.
psychic Mental, spiritual.

On the afternoon of the night Emile Griffith and Benny Paret were to fight a 1
third time for the welterweight championship, there was murder in both camps.
"I hate that kind of guy," Paret had said earlier to Pete Hamill about Griffith.
"A fighter's got to look and talk and act like a man." One of the Broadway
gossip columnists had run an item about Griffith a few days before. His girl
friend saw it and said to Griffith, "Emile, I didn't know about you being that
way." So Griffith hit her. So he said. Now at the weigh-in that morning, Paret
had insulted Griffith irrevocably, touching him on the buttocks, while making a
few more remarks about his manhood. They almost had their fight on the scales.

The rage in Emile Griffith was extreme. I was at the fight that night, I had 2
never seen a fight like it. It was scheduled for fifteen rounds, but they fought
without stopping from the bell which began the round to the bell which ended
it, and then they fought after the bell, sometimes for as much as fifteen seconds
before the referee could force them apart.

Paret was a Cuban, a proud club fighter who had become welterweight 3
champion because of his unusual ability to take a punch. His style of fighting was
to take three punches to the head in order to give back two. At the end of ten
rounds, he would still be bouncing, his opponent would have a headache. But in
the last two years, over the fifteen-round fights, he had started to take some bad
maulings.

This fight had its turns. Griffith won most of the early rounds, but Paret 4
knocked Griffith down in the sixth. Griffith had trouble getting up, but made it,
came alive and was dominating Paret again before the round was over. Then
Paret began to wilt. In the middle of the eighth round, after a clubbing punch had
turned his back to Griffith, Paret walked three disgusted steps away, showing his
hindquarters. For a champion, he took much too long to turn back around. It was
the first hint of weakness Paret had ever shown, and it must have inspired a
particular shame, because he fought the rest of the fight as if he were seeking
to demonstrate that he could take more punishment than any man alive. In the
twelfth, Griffith caught him. Paret got trapped in a corner. Trying to duck away,
his left arm and his head became tangled on the wrong side of the top rope.
Griffith was in like a cat ready to rip the life out of a huge boxed rat. He hit him
eighteen right hands in a row, an act which took perhaps three or four seconds,
Griffith making a pent-up whimpering sound all the while he attacked, the right
hand whipping like a piston rod which has broken through the crankcase, or like
a baseball bat demolishing a pumpkin. I was sitting in the second row of that
corner—they were not ten feet away from me, and like everybody else, I was

hypnotized. I had never seen one man hit another so hard and so many times. Over the referee's face came a look of woe as if some spasm had passed its way through him, and then he leaped on Griffith to pull him away. It was the act of a brave man. Griffith was uncontrollable. His trainer leaped into the ring, his manager, his cut man, there were four people holding Griffith, but he was off on an orgy, he had left the Garden, he was back on a hoodlum's street. If he had been able to break loose from his handlers and the referee, he would have jumped Paret to the floor and whaled on him there.

And Paret? Paret died on his feet. As he took those eighteen punches   5 something happened to everyone who was in psychic range of the event. Some part of his death reached out to us. One felt it hover in the air. He was still standing in the ropes, trapped as he had been before, he gave some little half-smile of regret, as if he were saying, ''I didn't know I was going to die just yet,'' and then, his head leaning back but still erect, his death came to breathe about him. He began to pass away. As he passed, so his limbs descended beneath him, and he sank slowly to the floor. He went down more slowly than any fighter had ever gone down, he went down like a large ship which turns on end and slides second by second into its grave. As he went down, the sound of Griffith's punches echoed in the mind like a heavy ax in the distance chopping into a wet log.

Questions for Discussion

1. Powerful similes appear in paragraph 4. Find one or two and explain why they work so well.
2. What metaphors does Mailer use in paragraph 4?
3. What examples of personification can be found in paragraph 5?
4. In paragraph 3, Mailer writes that Paret had ''started to take some bad maulings.'' Is ''maulings'' a more effective noun than ''beatings''? In paragraph 4, he tells us that Paret began ''to wilt.'' Is this verb better than ''to weaken''? What other effective nouns and verbs does Mailer use?
5. This selection begins with an anecdote (brief story) about what passed between Griffith and Paret before the fight. Does this anecdote make for a good introduction? How does it help prepare us for what is to follow?

Suggestions for Journal Entries

1. Think about a serious or significant event you recently witnessed: a car accident, a natural disaster, or perhaps an important ceremony. Use one of the strategies for prewriting discussed in ''Getting Started'' to gather details that will help you describe this incident and discuss its impact on you or on anyone else who may have seen it. Include figures of speech in your list of details.
2. Whether physical or verbal, violence always leaves us shaken and disturbed. Think about a fight you saw or were involved in recently. Do some focused

freewriting for about five or ten minutes in which you explain how you felt
during or after the incident. Include figures of speech that *show* what you
were feeling at the time.

The Gift

LI-YOUNG LEE

*Li-Young Lee is a Chinese-American poet born in Indonesia, where his father
had been imprisoned by the government of Sukarno, that country's dictator.
After his father's escape, the family left Indonesia and eventually made their
home in Pennsylvania. Lee's reputation has grown rapidly over the last several
years. He is the author of* Rose, *a book of poems published in 1986.*

Looking Ahead

1. Lee's title is especially significant. Keep it in mind as you read this
   tender poem.
2. Look for examples of both metaphor and personification in "The
   Gift."

Vocabulary

christen   Give a name to.
shard   Fragment of metal or glass.

> To pull the metal splinter from my palm
> my father recited a story in a low voice.
> I watched his lovely face and not the blade.
> Before the story ended he'd removed
> the iron sliver I thought I'd die from.   5
>
> I can't remember the tale
> but hear his voice still, a well
> of dark water, a prayer.
> And I recall his hands,
> two measures of tenderness   10
> he laid against my face,
> the flames of discipline
> he raised above my head.
>
> Had you entered that afternoon
> you would have thought you saw a man   15
> planting something in a boy's palm,

a silver tear, a tiny flame.
Had you followed that boy
you would have arrived here,
where I bend over my wife's right hand. 20

Look how I shave her thumbnail down
so carefully she feels no pain.
Watch as I lift the splinter out.
I was seven when my father
took my hand like this, 25
and I did not hold that shard
between my fingers and think,
Metal that will bury me,
christen it Little Assassin,
Ore Going Deep for My Heart. 30
And I did not lift up my wound and cry,
Death visited here!
I did what a child does
when he's given something to keep.
I kissed my father. 35

Questions for Discussion

1. What "gift" has Lee received? Is it simply the skill to remove a splinter? Or is there more to it than that?
2. Why does he tell us about removing the shard from his wife's hand? What point does this image help him make about his father? About himself?
3. What other image do you see in this poem?
4. To which of the five senses does Lee appeal?
5. What examples of metaphor do you find in this poem? Of personification?
6. Why does Lee tell us that he didn't "christen" the splinter "Little Assassin" (line 29)? What does *"Death visited here!"* mean (line 32)?

Suggestions for Journal Entries

1. Reread Hayden's "Those Winter Sundays," (pages 119–120), which is also about a father's love. In what ways is it similar to Lee's poem? In what ways is it different? Think about what happens in each poem and about its author's purpose. Use listing or brainstorming to record your answers.
2. What Lee is "given . . . to keep" is not material; it is an attitude, an emotional treasure, made plain in his father's voice and gentle touch. Think about similar gifts that your mother, father, or other relative has given you by example and that you will pass on to others. Your father may have shown you

a love for gardening, your great-aunt may have taught you to love animals, and through her actions your mother may have taught you that all people, regardless of race or sex, deserve respect. Use focused freewriting to describe one or more of these gifts. Include figures of speech to make your ideas concrete and vivid.

A Farewell to Arms

RICHARD B. ELSBERRY

Richard Elsberry, a contemporary American writer, wrote the following essay as a feature article for The New York Times Magazine. *It was published in the fall of 1987.*

Looking Ahead

1. The title of this essay is borrowed from Hemingway's *A Farewell to Arms,* a novel about an American ambulance driver in World War I.

2. Like di Pasquale, Elsberry uses an extended metaphor. He compares his attempts to get rid of a garden mole to full-scale warfare *throughout* the essay. However, his intention is to make us smile. In paragraph 8, for instance, he mimics what ancient gladiators used to shout before going into mortal combat during the Roman games. In paragraph 11, he talks about the "scorched-earth policy" of the Union Army during General Sherman's infamous march through Georgia at the end of the Civil War.

3. Elsberry also refers to popular movies and books in this essay. Among them is Rachel Carson's *Silent Spring,* a book about the harmful effects of pesticides.

Vocabulary

armistice   Peace treaty.
bunkers   Fortified shelters.
genetically   Through birth.
leach   Dissolve.
Lilliputian   Tiny, miniature.
nemesis   Unbeatable opponent or enemy.
ramparts   Barricades, walls used for defense.
reconnaissance   Inspection.

recurring   Happening again.

rogue   Outlaw, villain.

slights   Insults.

sonic   Relating to sound.

The war started with a sneak attack. I was cutting my grass in the summer of   1
1986 when the mower made a strange sound. Looking down, I saw the blade had
cut into and exposed brown soil. It had ripped open the top of a burrow, which
snaked across my yard like the path of some drunken sailor.

There was no doubt about it. I had been invaded by a member of the family   2
Talpidae—a mole.

Switching from Nikes to boots, I proceeded to stomp the maze of surface   3
runs so that I could finish cutting the grass without creating an unsightly gash
across the yard.

The mole had completed a reconnaissance of my yard, staking out my turf.   4
And I had retaliated by putting my foot down.

The battle was joined.   5

The nearly blind burrower struck by night, tunneling his way through my   6
bluegrass with the speed of a Japanese bullet train. By day, I flattened his
ramparts and flooded his bunkers with a garden hose. The mole learned to do the
backstroke.

Reluctantly, I resorted to chemical warfare. Poison gas. Sulfurous-looking   7
chemicals were placed in the runs, the fuse lighted, and the top of the burrow
replaced. Then I stood back to watch blue fumes rise slowly through the leaves
of grass.

"Mole who is about to die, I salute you."   8

A few days later, I stepped on another burrow and twisted an ankle. Like a   9
demon from *Poltergeist,* he was back. The campaign dragged on into the fall.
The mole ranged farther afield—an unstoppable six-inch-long bundle of fur and
claws. Finally, winter arrived, and the mole hibernated. I schemed.

As soon as the grass started turning green last spring, I visited my friendly   10
hardware-store manager. He explained that the mole was harvesting cutworms,
grubs and other insects that make up his diet. Eliminate the food supply, he said,
and you eliminate the problem.

I got out my spreader and put down a double coating of insecticide over all   11
the areas the mole had invaded last year. It was my scorched-earth policy. Any
mole operating in this area—like a crow flying over the path of William Tecum-
seh Sherman's army as it marched through Georgia—was going to have to carry
his own rations.

In late April, while planting onions in the garden, I caught sight of an   12
exploratory burrow leading up from a clump of bushes. A combat patrol probing
into what I had come to refer to as No Mole Land.

As the weeks passed, the mole kept coming, seemingly living on stored fat.   13

"What's the matter with you, you dumb animal," I raged as I flattened burrows. "Why don't you move on to greener pastures? There's nothing here to eat."

Then a thought occurred to me. I bought a can of mole bait—poison pellets—and scattered them throughout the tunnels.   14

"Bon appétit," I murmured.   15

I waited a few days and then flattened all the burrows. They stayed flat.   16
Maybe, just maybe, I'd done it. I kept my fingers crossed. But, perhaps, like a depth-charged submarine, he was simply playing possum back in his nest. Like U-boats, moles can run silent, run deep.

After a week, I figured either the poison pills or the grubless wasteland I had   17
created had done the trick. But as I went out to check the garden, my roving eye spied a ripple moving across the turf, a rogue wave on a sea of green tranquillity.

My god, he was at it in midday!   18

But now I had him pinpointed. I rushed back to the garage and grabbed two   19
shovels. One I rammed into the burrow to block any retreat. Then, gleefully, I began to dig. After a time, I had created a small foxhole, surrounded by sod, rocks and loose dirt. But there was no sign of the mole.

Had he heard my original footfalls—or my little cry of "Aha, gotcha!"—   20
and quickly beat a retreat? Was he able to adopt the camouflage of a clump of dirt? Could he read my mind?

Slowly, I repaired the damage as best I could, tamping the raped earth into   21
place, putting down new grass seed and watering it in. I had given it my best shot, but the mole had countered every move I made. Sightless, defenseless, starved, poisoned, gassed—yet my Lilliputian enemy survived.

There were expensive battery-operated sonic devices I could buy—like the   22
thumpers that called the big sandworms in *Dune*. I was told these would drive the mole away, at least while the batteries lasted. And there were costly chemicals that were said to do the trick, assuring not just a silent spring, but a silent summer and a silent fall as well. But I feared they would eventually leach into the ground water and make their way to our well. As I reviewed my options, it seemed this was a war I was never going to win. And, it suddenly struck me, I no longer really cared about winning it.

This was a devastating thought, considering that American males are   23
brought up with the idea that winning is the only thing that counts. Winning is our national obsession. It's what makes our day. And yet my preoccupation with besting an unseen mole was gnawing at me day and night.

As I've gotten older and have witnessed endlessly recurring shoving   24
matches and fistfights over imagined slights, I've noticed that my genetically inherited combativeness seems to be melting away. I've become more inclined to walk away from human conflict—to hang it up and get on with my life. Why not do that with this animal, as well?

It was time, I decided firmly, to reach an accommodation with my nemesis.   25
To sign an armistice.

I went out and bought a lawn roller.   26

Questions for Discussion

1. Where does the author introduce his extended metaphor?
2. What other references to combat do you find in this piece? Explain what one or two of these mean and how they help develop Elsberry's extended metaphor.
3. In paragraph 9, the author explains that the mole was "Like a demon from *Poltergeist.*" How does mentioning this movie help him make his point? What other similes can you find?
4. Realizing he was never going to win this war was "devastating," the author says in paragraph 23. Why was winning so important to him?
5. If you compare Elsberry's paragraphs with Mailer's, some of them seem short. Are they appropriate to Elsberry's purpose?
6. Unlike the other selections in this chapter, Elsberry's essay seems to have been written as much to entertain us as to explain an idea. What parts of "A Farewell to Arms" did you find humorous?

Suggestions for Journal Entries

1. Think of a difficult problem you have tried to solve at home, work, or school. Like Elsberry, did you feel as if you were fighting a battle? Were your attempts to solve the problem as difficult as rolling a stone up a mountain or running a marathon in tight shoes? Or is there some other extended metaphor you might use to describe this experience?

   List details explaining your problem and your attempts to solve it. Then determine what kind of extended metaphor you might use to discuss this experience later on in a longer piece of writing. However, begin developing this metaphor in a paragraph or two in your journal now.
2. Elsberry compares the mole to figures from two popular movies: *Poltergeist* and *Dune.* Think of a particular animal or person you know well. Can he or she be compared to someone or something you have seen in a current movie or television show or have read about in a book, newspaper, or magazine? If so, list similarities in your journal, and include as many figures of speech as you can.

SUGGESTIONS FOR WRITING

1. After reading the paragraph from "A Visit to Belfast," you may have used your journal to gather concrete details and figures of speech expressing an opinion about the city you know best. Use this information to draft two or three paragraphs, each of which explains *one* reason you would or would not choose to live there permanently. Then, set this work aside.

On another piece of paper, explain the reasons that some people hold an opposing opinion about this city. (Come on; you can do it!) Turn these notes into a unified and coherent paragraph. Then, at the end of the paragraph, add a sentence that denies what these other folks think and that states *your* opinion clearly. For example, if you hate the city, the last sentence might read: "However, despite the wonderful things my friends say about Dismalville, I wouldn't live there for the world." On the other hand, if you like the city, you might write: "However, the nasty things my friends say about Dismalville don't impress me, and I am looking forward to living there for many years." Either way, use this paragraph as the introduction to your essay. Make its last sentence your preliminary thesis statement.

Now turn to the paragraphs you set aside. Each should focus on and fully develop one reason you hate or like "Dismalville." If not, rewrite them by adding, removing, or rearranging detail. Place these paragraphs after your introduction. Next, write a conclusion that explains what "Dismalville's" citizens should do to improve their city or that sums up what you think is good about the place.

Now, revise the entire essay—introduction, body, and conclusion. Ask yourself whether your writing can be improved by adding concrete details and figures of speech like those discussed in this chapter. Finally, make sure to edit your last draft.

2. After reading di Pasquale's "Joy of an Immigrant, a Thanksgiving," you might have made journal notes to begin explaining how a dramatic change in your life affected you. Tell the story of what caused this change. Using "Joy of an Immigrant, a Thanksgiving" as an example, include effective metaphors and similes to help your readers understand the full effect of the change. This is also a good time to continue using concrete nouns—both common and proper—and vivid adjectives like those you read about in Chapter 5. They will help you create powerful images to communicate your feelings.

When you finish your story, write an introductory paragraph, complete with a formal thesis statement that states the importance of this change in your life. Describe a scene, use a startling remark, create a contrast or analogy, or try any other method explained in Chapter 4 to write an introduction that captures the readers' attention. Conclude your paper by making reference to your thesis, looking to the future, or using a memorable statement or quotation.

Now review the completed draft of your essay. Is it the best you can do, or can you add detail, strengthen your focus, and improve your word choice? Write at least one more draft. Then revise and edit this version thoroughly before submitting your work to your instructor.

3. If you have ever seen a fight close up, you know how frightening physical or verbal violence can be. Recall a heated argument or fight you witnessed or were involved in. What important point did this incident reveal about other people, about yourself, or about life in general? Put the answer to this question into a preliminary thesis statement. Then, narrate the events that led up to and that occurred during this incident. Explain what caused the problem, and describe the people who took part.

Before you begin your essay, review the notes you made after reading ''The Death of Benny Paret,'' especially those in response to item 2 of the Suggestions for Journal Entries. When you draft your paper, use the concrete details and figures of speech you have already collected. Try adding more of them as you tell your story.

After you complete this rough draft, turn back to your preliminary thesis. Is it right for the essay you have just written? If not, revise the thesis or make changes in your essay so that your thesis will clearly state your main point and prepare readers for what follows. Put your thesis into an introductory paragraph that captures the readers' attention. Next, write a logical and natural conclusion by using methods explained in Chapter 4.

Once you are satisfied that you have produced a well-organized and well-developed final draft, edit that draft carefully for grammar, punctuation, spelling, and other important considerations.

4. ''The Gift'' by Li Young-Lee explains how the poet received an emotional treasure that enriched his life and that he can pass on to others. If you read this poem, you may have made journal notes about similar gifts your parents or others have passed along to you through example. For instance, seeing your sister work hard at her studies may have motivated you to do the same; watching your aunt tend her roses may have made you love flowers; or noticing how cheerful your father remains on bad days may have inspired you to keep smiling through sorrow or adversity.

Use your journal notes as the basis of an essay that discusses one emotional treasure or gift someone in your family (or your family as a whole) has given you. A good way to begin is to explain what that gift is. You might even compare it to the gift Lee discusses in his poem. Then, in the body of your paper, you can provide three or four examples of how your father, mother, or other relative revealed the gift to you. In any case, be specific. Show what difficulties your father has had to face, or describe the long hours and hard work your sister devotes to studying for an exam or completing a paper. A good way to conclude is to explain how you intend to share your gift with someone else.

Use figures of speech to create images that, like those in Lee's poem, will help readers see what you are trying to explain. As always, write several versions of your paper and edit it carefully. Make sure it is fully developed, easy to follow, and free of distracting errors.

5. The extended metaphor in Elsberry's "A Farewell to Arms" helps show how hard it is to get rid of a garden mole. Item 1 of the Suggestions for Journal Entries following this essay asks you to begin creating an extended metaphor that explains how *you* tried to solve a difficult problem at home, work, or school.

   Like Elsberry, you might have compared your attempt at solving the problem to combat. Then again, you might have explained that it was like climbing a steep mountain, sailing a rough sea in a small boat, or losing your way in a dark forest. Continue developing this idea in three or four paragraphs that show how difficult your problem was to solve. These paragraphs will form the body of your paper.

   Whenever possible, use language that develops the extended metaphor on which you are building your essay. As you recall, figures of speech about warfare can be found almost anywhere in "A Farewell to Arms."

   After completing several drafts of the body paragraphs, think about the introduction you want to write. You might begin by explaining your extended metaphor or, like Elsberry, by making a startling statement. A good way to conclude such a paper is by explaining how, if ever, the problem was solved.

   Of course, before you wrap things up, read the entire essay through at least once, and eliminate mechanical errors that might reduce its effectiveness.

6. In "Joy of an Immigrant, a Thanksgiving" and "Old Man Timochenko," di Pasquale expresses human feelings by comparing himself to a bird. Write an essay in which you create an extended metaphor that compares a person you know well to the animal that person most reminds you of. For example, compare your worst enemy to a snake or a worm by describing that creature's most obvious characteristics and by showing that your subject has similar qualities. Use concrete details, figures of speech, and examples to explain his habit of sneaking behind people's backs or to describe the way she squirms out of taking blame that is rightfully hers.

   Then again, you might try another route and, like Elsberry in "A Farewell to Arms," use personification to describe an animal you think has human qualities. Incidentally, Elsberry compared a mole to an enemy soldier, so don't feel that you have to write only about an animal you like or find friendly.

   Whatever you decide, have some fun with this assignment. It's a good chance to create entertaining images of a subject about which you may have strong feelings. As always, begin by checking your journal notes for information that will help get you started. Revise your work several times, and edit it carefully.

   A word of caution: If your essay criticizes a person, keep his or her real identity secret.

CHAPTER 7

SENTENCE STRUCTURE: CREATING EMPHASIS AND VARIETY

In Chapters 5 and 6 you learned to express your ideas more effectively by using language that is concrete, specific, and vivid. In this chapter you will learn how to use sentence structure to give your writing emphasis and variety, making it even more interesting and effective.

EMPHASIS

Communicating ideas clearly often depends on the ability to emphasize, or stress, one idea over another. By arranging the words in a sentence carefully, you can emphasize certain ideas and direct your readers' attention to the heart of your message.

A good way to emphasize an idea is to express it in a short, simple sentence of its own. But you will never develop your writing skills if you stick to a steady diet of such sentences. Even the shortest writing projects require sentences containing two or more ideas. In some cases, these ideas will be equally important; in others, one idea will need to be emphasized over the other or others.

Create Emphasis Through Coordination

Ideas that are equal in importance can be expressed in the same sentence by using coordination. The sentence below coordinates (makes equal) three words in a series: "found," "pitched," and "started."

> We *found* a clearing, *pitched* the tent, and *started* a small fire.

You can also use coordination to join two or more *main clauses.* A main clause contains a subject and verb and, even when standing by itself, expresses a complete idea. You can join main clauses with a comma and a coordinating conjunction, such as "and," "but," "or," "nor," "for," or "so." Here are some examples; the main clauses are shown in italics:

> *Wild ponies gallop through the surf,* and *eagles soar quietly overhead.*
> *Uncle Harry is not the richest person in town,* but *he is one of the most generous.*

154

The raccoons have not been near our house for three days, nor *have they been missed.*

Mullens will return on the midnight train, or *she will have to spend another day in the city.*

Arnold wants to get all A's, so *he is studying hard.*

I want to ask Professor Garcia whether I can rewrite my paper, for *I just found new information about my topic.*

Another way to coordinate main clauses within a sentence is to join them with a semicolon:

Alice's car is an antique; it was built in 1927.

You can use both a semicolon and a conjunction when you want to make sure your readers see the relationship between the ideas you are emphasizing. This is especially important in long sentences:

Hoping to reach Lake Soggy Bottom by noon, we left our house by 6:00 A.M. and took Interstate 90; but traffic was so heavy that we soon realized we would be lucky to reach the lake before dark.

Create Emphasis Through Subordination

The sentences above contain complete ideas—main clauses—that are equal in importance. But what if you decide that one of your ideas is more important than the other? Sometimes, putting the less important idea into a *phrase* or *subordinate clause* helps emphasize the other. A phrase is a group of words without a subject or predicate; a subordinate clause contains a subject and predicate, but, unlike a main clause, it does not express a complete idea. Say you wrote these sentences:

Ethel turned the corner, and she noticed a large truck in her lane. She was frightened, but she avoided the truck.

When revising, you decide that in each sentence the second idea is more important than the first. Therefore, you *subordinate* the first idea to the second:

Turning the corner, Ethel noticed a large truck in her lane.

(The first idea has been put into a phrase.)

Although she was frightened, she avoided the truck.

(The first idea has been put into a subordinate clause.)

Here are three of many ways to subordinate ideas.

Use Participles   *Participles* are adjectives formed from verbs. They describe nouns and pronouns. Each sentence below has been revised by turning one of its main clauses into a phrase that begins with a participle. Doing so helps put emphasis on the main clause that remains.

Original   Charlotte was visiting her Uncle in Knoxville, and she decided to drive through the Great Smoky Mountains.

(The sentence contains two main clauses of the same importance.)

Revised   Visiting her uncle in Knoxville, Charlotte decided to drive through the Great Smoky Mountains.

(The first idea is expressed in a phrase that begins with the participle "Visiting." It is less important than the second idea, which remains in a main clause, "Charlotte decided" . . .)

Original   We were bored with the movie, so we left after twenty minutes.

(The ideas are equally important.)

Revised   Bored with the movie, we left after twenty minutes.

(The first idea is now less important than the second because it is expressed in a phrase, which begins with the participle "Bored.")

Use Subordinate Conjunctions   You can turn a main clause into a subordinate clause with words like "although," "after," "as," "because," "even though," "if," "since," "unless," "until," and "while."

Original   I am not confident about my math skills, so I attend algebra class regularly.

(The ideas are equally important.)

Revised   Because I am not confident about my math skills, I attend algebra class regularly.

(The second idea, expressed in a main clause, is emphasized. The first idea is now in a subordinate clause, which begins with "Because.")

Use Relative Pronouns   Using pronouns like "who," "whom," "whose," "that," and "which" is another way to subordinate one idea to another. Subordinate clauses beginning with relative pronouns describe nouns in the sentence's main clause.

Original   My friend's parents once lived in Corsica; Corsica is the birthplace of Napoleon.

(The ideas are equally important.)

Revised   My friend's parents once lived in Corsica, which is the birthplace of Napoleon.

(The first idea, expressed in a main clause, is more important than the second idea, which is now in a subordinate clause introduced by "which.")

Original   Audrey Davis has spent two years in the Marine Corps; she was sent to Saudi Arabia.

Revised   Audrey Davis, who has spent two years in the Marine Corps, was sent to Saudi Arabia.

(The subordinate clause, introduced by "who," comes in the middle of the main clause.)

Create Emphasis by Using Periodic Sentences

You can create emphasis by putting the strongest or most important word or idea at the end of the sentence. Such sentences are called "periodic" because the emphasis comes just before the period. Here are three examples:

Mario forgot the tomato sauce's most important ingredient, garlic!

India, where over half a billion people have the right to vote, is the world's largest democracy.

Nora Zeale Hurston is remembered not for her work in anthropology, the field in which she was trained, but for her novels.

Create Emphasis by Using the Active or Passive Voice

Sentences that use the *active voice* contain subjects—persons, places, or things—that perform an action. Sentences that use the *passive voice* contain subjects that are acted upon. Notice how the structure of a sentence changes when it is put into the passive voice.

Active

The enthusiastic listeners applauded the young guitarist.

Passive

The young guitarist was applauded by the enthusiastic listeners.

Generally, using the active voice rather than the passive voice makes it easier to stress the subject of a sentence. For instance, if you wanted to report that the president of your college announced her decision to resign, it wouldn't make much sense to write, "Her decision to resign was announced by President Greenspan." A clearer and more emphatic version would be "President Greenspan announced her decision to resign."

However, there are times when using the passive voice can create emphasis. In some cases, you might decide that the receiver of an action is more important than the person, place, or thing who completes that action. For example,

Ann was elected to the Monroe City Council.

is more emphatic than

The residents of Monroe elected Ann to the City Council.

Sometimes, in fact, you might not know who or what is responsible for an action, and you will have to use the passive voice:

> Doors and windows were left open; books, furniture, and clothing were scattered across the room; and curtains, sheets, and blankets were torn to shreds.

Create Emphasis by Repeating Key Words and Phrases

Repeating important words and phrases, carefully and sparingly, can help you stress important ideas over those that deserve less emphasis. This technique is used in the speeches of President John F. Kennedy and of Reverend Martin Luther King, Jr.

In his inaugural address, Kennedy gave a special meaning to his plans for the nation when he said:

> All this will not be finished in the first one hundred days. Nor will it be finished in the first one thousand days, nor in the life of this administration, nor even perhaps in our lifetime on this planet. But let us begin.

Dr. King used repetition to communicate a sense of urgency about civil rights to a massive audience at the Lincoln Memorial when he delivered the speech now known as "I Have a Dream":

> Now is the time to make real the promises of democracy. Now is the time to rise from the dark and desolate valley of segregation to the sunlit path of racial justice. Now is the time to lift our nation from the quicksands of racial injustice to the solid rock of brotherhood. Now is the time to make justice a reality for all of God's children.

Create Emphasis Through Parallelism

Parallelism is a way to connect facts and ideas of equal importance in the same sentence and thereby give them added emphasis. Sentences that are parallel list items by expressing each of them in the same grammatical form. For instance, Adlai Stevenson's eulogy of Winston Churchill, the great British prime minister, contains several examples of parallelism:

> The voice that led nations, raised armies, inspired victories and blew fresh courage into the hearts of men is silenced. We shall hear no longer the remembered eloquence and wit, the old courage and defiance, the robust serenity of indomitable faith. Our world is thus poorer, our political dialogue is diminished, and the sources of public inspiration run more thinly in all of us. There is a lonesome place against the sky.

In the first sentence, Stevenson placed equal emphasis on Churchill's accomplishments by expressing each through a verb followed by a direct object: "led nations," "raised armies," "inspired victories," and "blew fresh courage into the hearts of men." He created parallelism in the second sentence in a series of adjectives and nouns that describe Churchill's best qualities: "the remembered eloquence and wit,'' ''the old courage and defiance,'' ''the robust serenity of indomitable faith.'' In the third sentence, he explained the effects of Churchill's death in a series of main clauses: ''Our world is thus poorer,'' ''our political dialogue is diminished,'' and ''the sources of public inspiration run more thinly in all of us.''

Here are three other examples of how parallelism creates emphasis:

The child enjoyed *running* through fields, *diving* into lakes, and *climbing* over rocks.

(*The sentence contains* gerunds, *nouns formed from verbs by adding "ing"; gerunds show activity.*)

To educate her children, *to help* her neighbors, and *to live* in peace were her only desires.

(*The sentence contains* infinitives, *which are formed by placing "to" before the present tense of the verb. Infinitives act as nouns, adjectives, or adverbs.*)

We haven't decided whether to spend our vacation *at the lake, in the mountains,* or *on the seashore.*

(*The sentence contains* prepositional phrases; *a preposition is a short word—such as "at," "in," or "on"—that shows the relationship of a noun or pronoun to the rest of the sentence.*)

Consistency is the key to making sentences parallel. Express every idea in a list in the same grammatical form. Without a doubt, the eulogy you just read would have sounded awkward and been less emphatic had Stevenson written that Churchill's voice ''led nations, raised armies, inspired victories, and it blew fresh courage into the hearts of men.'' The first three items are verbs followed by objects; the fourth is a main clause.

VARIETY

One sure way to make your readers lose interest in what you have to say—no matter how important—is to ignore the need for variety. Good writers try not to repeat vocabulary monotonously, and they vary the length and structure of their sentences whenever possible.

Create Variety by Changing Sentence Length

A steady diet of long, complicated sentences is sure to put your readers to sleep. On the other hand, relying solely on short, choppy sentences can make your writing seem disconnected and even childish. Therefore, one of the most important things to remember about the sentences you write is to vary their length. You can do this by combining some of them into longer, more complex units and by leaving others short and to the point.

Reread the passage from President Kennedy's Inaugural Address on page 158. One reason it holds our interest is that it contains sentences of different lengths. The last of these leaves a lasting impression, not simply because it comes at the end but because it is so much shorter than the others and carries a special punch.

You can combine two or three short sentences into a longer unit in three ways: coordination, subordination, or compounding.

Coordination   This method is useful if you want to write a longer sentence in which all the main ideas receive equal emphasis. The easiest way to do this is to combine sentences with a comma and the appropriate coordinating conjunction or to use a semicolon, as explained on pages 154–155.

Subordination   As you know, subordination lets you combine two or more sentences in order to emphasize one idea over another. It also helps you vary sentence length and make your writing more interesting. Say you've just written:

> I had been waiting at the bus stop for twenty minutes. The afternoon air was hot, thick, and humid. I became uncomfortable and soon began to perspire. I wished I were home. I thought about getting under the shower, cooling off, and relaxing. My day at work had been long and hard. I looked up from the newspaper I was reading. I saw a huge truck. It sped by, and it covered me with filthy exhaust. I prayed the bus would come soon.

As you read this paragraph, you realize that you haven't emphasized your most important ideas and that your style is choppy and monotonous. Therefore, you decide to rewrite by combining sentences through subordination (you can review ways to do this by rereading pages 155–157):

> I had been waiting at the bus stop for twenty minutes. Because the afternoon air was hot, thick, and humid, I became uncomfortable and soon began to perspire. Wishing I were home, I thought about getting under the shower, cooling off, and relaxing. My day at work had been long and hard. As I looked up from the newspaper I was reading, I saw a huge truck, which sped by and covered me with exhaust. I prayed the bus would come soon.

In combining some sentences, you've made your writing smoother and more interesting because you've created sentences of different lengths. What's more, some ideas have gained emphasis.

Compounding   This method involves putting subjects, verbs, adjectives, and adverbs together in the same sentence as long as they relate to one another logically.

Sometimes, ideas that are very similar seem awkward and boring if expressed in separate sentences. For example: "Egbert has been transferred to Minneapolis. Rowena has also been transferred to that city." Notice how much more interesting these short sentences become when you combine their subjects to make a compound sentence: "Egbert and Rowena have been transferred to Minneapolis." Here are a few more examples:

Original	The blue jay flew through the open window. It nearly crashed into my computer.
Compound verb	The blue jay flew through the open window and nearly crashed into my computer.
Original	The weather around here is sometimes unpredictable. Sometimes it becomes treacherous.
Compound adjective	The weather around here is sometimes unpredictable and treacherous.
Original	Steven called to his brother loudly. He called repeatedly.
Compound adverb	Steven called to his brother loudly and repeatedly.

Create Variety by Changing Sentence Patterns

As you know, all complete sentences contain a subject, a verb, and a complete idea; many also contain modifiers (adjectives, adverbs, prepositional phrases, and the like) and other elements. However, there is no rule that all sentences must begin with a subject, that a verb must follow the subject immediately, or that everything else must be placed at the end of a sentence. Depending on their purpose, good writers create as many patterns as they need to make their writing interesting and effective. Here are a few ways you can vary the basic patterns of your sentences.

Begin with an Adverb *Adverbs* modify verbs, adjectives, or other adverbs. They help explain *how, when, where,* or *why.* The following examples begin with adverbs or with groups of words that contain and serve as adverbs (shown in italics):

Soon the rain stopped and the clouds disappeared.
Suddenly the lights went out.
Slowly and *confidently,* Maria rose to the speaker's platform.
Near the wreck of an old freighter, the divers found two large chests.
Above hundreds of fascinated spectators, the hot air balloon floated peacefully through the clouds.

Begin with an Infinitive As you learned earlier, an *infinitive* is the present tense of a verb with the word "to" in front of it. Infinitives acting as nouns often make good beginnings for sentences:

To skate in the Olympics was his boyhood dream.
To defend unpopular ideas takes courage.
To call him a coward is unfair and inaccurate.

Begin with a Preposition or Prepositional Phrase   *Prepositions* connect or show relationships between nouns or pronouns and the rest of a sentence. *Prepositional phrases* contain prepositions, a noun or pronoun, and any words that modify that noun or pronoun.

Without love, life is empty.
Around the corner, Peter saw a huge dog.
Between the two mountains ran a bright, clear stream.
Inside the barn, Freda found an old plow.
At the romantic dinner Ari had planned for weeks, he finally asked Felicia to marry him.

Begin or End with a Participle or Participial Phrase   A *participle* is a verb turned into an adjective. Many participles end in "ed" or "ing." But words like "caught," "lost" "found," "brought," and "drawn," which are formed from irregular verbs, can also be participles. A *participial phrase* is a group of words containing a participle.

Screeching, the infant birds told their mother they were hungry.
Exhausted, I fell asleep as soon as my head touched the pillow.
Caught in the act, the thief gave up easily.
I stayed home that night, *having nowhere else to go.*
Suddenly, the old bicycle broke apart, *scattering spokes and bits of chain everywhere.*
Jamie wept openly, *his dream destroyed.*

Ask a Rhetorical Question   You learned in Chapters 3 and 4 that asking a question is a good way to begin a paragraph or an essay. Rhetorical questions—those to which the writer knows the answer or to which no answer is expected—can also emphasize important points and create variety. Take this example from a speech condemning television by Federal Communications Commission head Newton Minnow at a meeting of television executives in 1961:

You will see a procession of game shows, violence, audience participation shows, formula comedies about totally unbelievable families, blood and thunder, mayhem, violence, sadism, murder, Western badmen, Western good men, private eyes, gangsters, more violence and cartoons. And endlessly, commercials—many screaming, cajoling, and offending. And, most of all boredom. . . .
Is there one person in this room who claims that broadcasting can't do better?

Reverse the Position of the Subject and the Verb   Say that you write, "Two small pines grew at the crest of the hill." When you read your rough draft, you realize that this is the kind of pattern you've used in many other sentences. To vary the pattern, simply reverse the position of your subject and verb: ''At the crest of the hill grew two small pines.''

The following selections will help you develop the ability to create sentences that are both varied and emphatic. As you read on, try to apply the techniques you're learning in this chapter to your own writing. Don't hesitate to reread important sections in the introduction to this chapter when you need to.

From *America and Americans*

JOHN STEINBECK

Nobel Prize–winning novelist, short story writer, and essayist, John Steinbeck (1902–1968) wrote The Grapes of Wrath, *an American classic that describes the suffering of an Oklahoma family forced from their land by severe drought during the great depression of the 1930s. All of Steinbeck's work shows a deep respect for nature. However, his concern for the environment and his love for the land are expressed no more eloquently than in these two paragraphs from* America and Americans, *a book he published in 1966.*

Looking Ahead

Although some sentences in this selection are relatively short, the author seems to prefer long sentences. Nevertheless, he holds the readers' interest. Look for ways like those you have just learned by which Steinbeck creates variety and emphasis.

Vocabulary

belching   Erupting, gushing forth.
debris   Litter, junk, rubbish.
exhausted   Used up, consumed.
pillaged   Looted, plundered, robbed.
scythe   Tool with a large blade used for mowing or reaping.
uninhibited   Uncontrolled, indiscriminate.

I have often wondered at the savagery and thoughtlessness with which our early   1
settlers approached this rich continent. They came at it as though it were an enemy, which of course it was. They burned the forests and changed the rainfall; they swept the buffalo from the plains, blasted the streams, set fire to the grass,

and ran a reckless scythe through the virgin and noble timber. Perhaps they felt that it was limitless and could never be exhausted and that a man could move on to new wonders endlessly. Certainly there are many examples to the contrary, but to a large extent the early people pillaged the country as though they hated it, as though they held it temporarily and might be driven off at any time.

This tendency toward irresponsibility persists in very many of us today; our rivers are poisoned by reckless dumping of sewage and toxic industrial wastes, the air of our cities is filthy and dangerous to breathe from the belching of uncontrolled products from combustion of coal, coke, oil, and gasoline. Our towns are girdled with wreckage and the debris of our toys—our automobiles and our packaged pleasures. Through uninhibited spraying against one enemy we have destroyed the natural balances our survival requires. All these evils can and must be overcome if America and Americans are to survive; but many of us still conduct ourselves as our ancestors did, stealing from the future for our clear and present profit.

Questions for Discussion

1. Which sentences place equal emphasis on ideas through coordination? What methods discussed in this chapter does Steinbeck use to coordinate these ideas?
2. Does Steinbeck use subordination? Where?
3. What examples of parallelism do you see? In which sentences does Steinbeck use repetition to create emphasis?
4. What figures of speech has he included?
5. Explain what he means by calling America an ''enemy'' to early settlers.
6. Why will the ''uninhibited spraying'' mentioned in paragraph 2 destroy ''the natural balances our survival requires''?

Suggestions for Journal Entries

1. The two paragraphs you have just read were written in the late 1960s. Have we made progress in protecting our environment since then? List two or three things you do or could do to safeguard the air, water, or land that you will pass on to future generations. Then make two other lists: In the first, explain what your community does or could do; in the second, explain what the nation as a whole is or should be doing to save the environment.
2. Using focused freewriting, describe what you believe is the most urgent environmental problem of our day. Is it air pollution? Water pollution? The dumping of toxic wastes? The destruction of the ozone layer? Global warming? Use examples from your experience, observations, or reading to provide examples of and to explain the causes of this problem.

The Vices of Age*

MALCOLM COWLEY

Poet, critic, historian, and literary editor of The New Republic *magazine, Malcolm Cowley (1898–1989) remained energetic and productive well into old age. He is the author of* Exile's Return, *an important book about the "lost generation" of American writers, such as Hemingway and Fitzgerald, who lived in Paris during the 1920s. The paragraphs that follow are taken from "The View from 80," an article that Cowley wrote for* Life *magazine in 1978 and that he later used in a book of the same title.*

Looking Ahead

One of the people discussed in this selection was an "admiralty lawyer." He practiced law governing naval, shipping, and other maritime matters.

Vocabulary

avarice   Greed.

dismantled   Took apart.

dismaying   Disappointing.

immoderate   Extreme, unreasonable.

intruders   Trespassers.

lethargy   Sluggishness, lack of energy.

Among the vices of age are avarice, untidyness, and vanity. . . .   1

Untidiness we call the Langley Collyer syndrome. To explain, Langley   2
Collyer was a former concert pianist who lived alone with his 70-year-old brother in a brownstone house on upper Fifth Avenue. The once fashionable neighborhood had become part of Harlem. Homer, the brother, had been an admiralty lawyer, but was now blind and partly paralyzed; Langley played for him and fed him on buns and oranges, which he thought would restore Homer's sight. He never threw away a daily paper because Homer, he said, might want to read them all. He saved other things as well and the house became filled with rubbish from roof to basement. The halls were lined on both sides with bundled newspapers, leaving narrow passageways in which Langley had devised booby traps to catch intruders.

On March 21, 1947, some unnamed person telephoned the police to report   3
that there was a dead body in the Collyer house. The police broke down the front

---

* Editor's title

door and found the hall impassable; then they hoisted a ladder to a second-story window. Behind it Homer was lying on the floor in a bathrobe; he had starved to death. Langley had disappeared. After some delay, the police broke into the basement, chopped a hole in the roof, and began throwing junk out of the house, top and bottom. It was 18 days before they found Langley's body, gnawed by rats. Caught in one of his own booby traps, he had died in a hallway just outside Homer's door. By that time the police had collected, and the Department of Sanitation had hauled away, 120 tons of rubbish, including, besides the newspapers, 14 grand pianos and the parts of a dismantled Model T Ford.

Questions for Discussion

1. What sentences in this selection are periodic? Explain the ideas they emphasize.
2. What other methods discussed in this chapter does Cowley use to create emphasis? For instance, find an example of parallelism.
3. These paragraphs illustrate ways to create variety. Where does Cowley use participial phrases? In what other way(s) does he create variety?
4. Identify one or two of the vivid images the author uses to show us the kind of life Langley and Homer Collyer led. What words make these images effective?
5. Is Cowley's attitude toward the aged negative? Explain by making reference to specific words and sentences.

Suggestions for Journal Entries

1. People of all ages have vices. Do you know someone who is particularly greedy, sloppy, vain, lazy, or jealous, or who suffers from another bad quality or habit? What does this person say or do to illustrate this vice? Use brainstorming or focused freewriting to record these details. If possible, recall incidents from your subject's life to show how seriously he or she has been affected by this vice. Incidentally, a good subject for this assignment might be a relative, a close friend, or even yourself.
2. Are all elderly people like those Cowley describes? Think about someone about eighty whom you admire. List details to show that, far from being eccentric or strange, he or she keeps up with the times, is active and alert, or contributes much to the lives of others. Once again, recall an incident or two that explain why you think highly of this person.
3. We're all going to get old. Consider your personality, the people and things with which you surround yourself, the kinds of things you save. Ask the journalists' questions to gather notes describing the kind of old age you predict for yourself. Where will you live? With whom? What will you be doing with your time?

Gettysburg Address

ABRAHAM LINCOLN

Abraham Lincoln is one of the best-loved U.S. Presidents. His Second Inaugural Address and the Gettysburg Address are landmarks in American public speaking.

In November 1863, Lincoln came to Gettysburg, Pennsylvania, to dedicate a cemetery at the site of the Civil War's bloodiest contest. The Battle of Gettysburg, which proved to be the turning point of the war, had raged for four days and killed 50,000 Americans before Confederate forces under General Robert E. Lee withdrew.

Lincoln's Gettysburg Address is an eloquent and powerful statement of his grief over the death of his countrymen on both sides and of his belief "that government of the people, by the people, for the people, shall not perish from the earth."

Looking Ahead

1. In his concluding sentence, Lincoln describes a "great task remaining before us." Read this important section of the speech a few times to make sure you understand it fully.

2. "Four score and seven years" equals eighty-seven years. A "score" is twenty.

3. Throughout this speech, and especially in paragraph 3, Lincoln uses parallelism, a technique that makes his sentences more forceful, emphatic, and memorable.

Vocabulary

conceived   Created.

consecrate   Bless, sanctify.

detract   Take away from, lessen.

hallow   Make holy or sacred.

in vain   For no reason or purpose.

measure   Amount.

proposition   Idea, principle.

resolve   Decide, determine.

Four score and seven years ago our fathers brought forth on this continent a   1
new nation, conceived in Liberty, and dedicated to the proposition that all men are created equal.

Now we are engaged in a great civil war, testing whether that nation, or any   2 nation so conceived and so dedicated, can long endure. We are met on a great battlefield of that war. We have come to dedicate a portion of that field, as a final resting place for those who here gave their lives that that nation might live. It is altogether fitting and proper that we should do this.

But, in a larger sense, we can not dedicate—we can not consecrate—we can   3 not hallow—this ground. The brave men, living and dead, who struggled here, have consecrated it, far above our poor power to add or detract. The world will little note, nor long remember what we say here, but it can never forget what they did here. It is for us the living, rather, to be dedicated here to the unfinished work which they who fought here have thus far so nobly advanced. It is rather for us to be here dedicated to the great task remaining before us—that from these honored dead we take increased devotion to that cause for which they gave the last full measure of devotion—that we here highly resolve that these dead shall not have died in vain—that this nation, under God, shall have a new birth of freedom—and that government of the people, by the people, for the people, shall not perish from the earth.

Questions for Discussion

1. What words and ideas are repeated in paragraph 3? What ideas does this repetition emphasize?
2. What examples of parallelism do you find in the Gettysburg Address?
3. Most sentences in this speech are long, but Lincoln does vary sentence length. Where does he do this?
4. What two participial phrases does Lincoln use at the end of his first sentence? Do they help make this sentence more interesting than if he had put the information they convey into another sentence?
5. Does Lincoln include a participial phrase in paragraph 2? Where?
6. What is Lincoln's central idea? What devices or techniques does he use to maintain coherence?

Suggestions for Journal Entries

1. Many speeches in American history have served as sources of inspiration from decade to decade, from generation to generation. With the help of your instructor or your college librarian, locate a speech that you'd like to read or reread. Then analyze this speech. Pick out examples of parallelism, repetition, and other techniques the writer has used to create emphasis. Here are a few speeches you might choose from:

   Abraham Lincoln, Second Inaugural Address
   Franklin Delano Roosevelt, First Inaugural Address
   Adlai Stevenson, Eulogy for Eleanor Roosevelt
   Dwight D. Eisenhower, Farewell Address
   Martin Luther King, Jr., Speech at the Lincoln Memorial (''I Have a Dream'')

Jesse Jackson, Speech to the 1988 Democratic National Convention
Ronald Reagan, Speech at Moscow State University

2. Using as many paragraphs as you like, rewrite Lincoln's speech in your own words. Make sure that you express his central idea clearly and that you emphasize his other important ideas through parallelism, repetition, or any of the other techniques you've learned for creating emphasis.

A Longing

ALICE WNOROWSKI

"A Longing" is a tender, almost dreamlike recollection of a beautiful childhood experience that continues to haunt the author. Wnorowski wrote this short essay in response to a freshman English assignment designed to help students learn to use concrete detail. However, it also illustrates several important principles about sentence structure discussed earlier in this chapter.

Looking Ahead

1. You've learned that coordination can be used to create sentences in which two or more ideas receive equal emphasis and that subordination can be used to create sentences in which one idea is stressed over others. Look for examples of coordination and subordination in this essay.

2. The author puts variety into her writing by using techniques discussed earlier in this chapter. They include beginning sentences with an adverb and a prepositional phrase and using participles to vary sentence structure and length.

3. Remember what you learned about using details in Chapter 5, especially those that appeal to the five senses. Identify such details in ''A Longing.''

Vocabulary

acknowledge   Recognize.
conceived   Understood.
yearn   Desire, long for.

An easy breeze pushed through the screen door, blowing into my open face   1
and filling my nostrils with the first breath of morning. The sun beamed warm rays of white light onto my lids, demanding they lift and acknowledge the day's arrival.

Perched in the nearby woods, a bobwhite proudly shrieked to the world that   2
he knew who he was. His song stirred deep feelings within me, and I was
overcome by an urge to run barefoot through his woods. I jumped up so abruptly
I startled the dog lying peacefully beside me. His sleepy eyes looked into mine
questioningly, but I could give him no answer. I only left him bewildered,
pushing through the front door and trotting down the grassy decline of the front
lawn.

The morning dew chilled my naked feet, and I stopped on the sandy lane.   3
From out of the corner of my eye, I suddenly caught a movement in the wide,
open hay field that lay before me. In the mist-filled dips of the roller-coaster
landscape grazed five deer: three does and two fawns. I sat down in the damp
earth to watch them and got my white nightdress all brown and wet.

They casually strolled along through the thigh-high grass, stopping every   4
other step to dip their heads into the growth and pop them back up again, with
the long, tender timothy stems dangling from the sides of their mouths.

The fawns were never more than two or three yards behind their mothers,   5
and I knew a buck must not be far off in the woods, keeping lookout for enemies.
Suddenly, a car sped along the adjacent road, disrupting the peace of the moment. The deer jumped up in terror and darted towards the trees. They took leaps,
clearing eight to ten feet in a single bound. I watched their erect, white puffs of
tails bounce up and down, until the darkness of the woods swallowed them up
and I could see them no more.

I don't think that at the simple age of eleven I quite conceived what a rare   6
and beautiful sight I had witnessed. Now, eight years later, I yearn to awaken to
the call of a bobwhite and to run barefoot through wet grass in search of him.

Questions for Discussion

1. Find a few examples of both coordination and subordination in this essay.
2. Identify some of the adverbs, prepositional phrases, and participles that
   Wnorowski uses to give her writing variety.
3. In which sentence are the normal positions of the subject and verb reversed?
4. In paragraph 5, the author varies the length and structure of her sentences to
   make her writing more interesting. What methods discussed in this chapter
   does she use?
5. To which of our five senses do the details in this essay appeal?
6. What is the meaning of Wnorowski's title? Why is it appropriate?
7. What techniques does the writer use to maintain coherence in and between
   her paragraphs?

Suggestions for Journal Entries

1. Think back to an experience you would like to relive. Make a list of the things
   that made this experience memorable and that will explain why you have such
   ''a longing'' to relive it.

2. Use the brainstorming technique discussed in ''Getting Started'' to list details about a natural setting (for example, a meadow, mountain, seashore) that you experienced recently or remember vividly.

Inaugural Address

JOHN FITZGERALD KENNEDY

One of the most popular leaders in American history, JFK took the oath of office as our thirty-fifth President on January 20, 1961. Through more than a quarter of a century, his speeches have served to inspire and to instruct new generations of Americans.

The best-remembered and most frequently quoted of Kennedy's speeches, his Inaugural Address, seems fresh and new even after three decades. Perhaps this has to do with his ability to speak to what is deepest and most universal in the human spirit—the real hopes and problems that all generations and all peoples share.

Looking Ahead

1. Like most Presidents, Kennedy relied on a professional speech writer. Ted Sorenson composed his Inaugural Address.

2. Kennedy begins by recognizing several dignitaries on the platform. Among them are Dwight D. Eisenhower, the thirty-fourth President; Richard Nixon, the outgoing Vice President and later the thirty-seventh President; and the new Vice President, Lyndon B. Johnson, who became President upon Kennedy's death in 1963.

3. Paragraphs 19 and 23 make reference to the Old Testament and especially to the prophet Isaiah, who wrote that someday the armies of the world would ''beat their swords into plowshares and their spears into pruning hooks.''

4. This selection makes especially good use of parallel structure and repetition. Look for examples of these techniques.

5. One reason this speech is so spellbinding is that its language and sentence structure are both powerful and varied. The writer was especially successful at changing the length of its sentences at just the right times. As you read JFK's Inaugural Address, identify some of the other methods you've learned for maintaining variety.

Vocabulary

abolish   Eliminate, do away with.
asunder   Apart.
belaboring   Talking about for an unreasonable length of time.

formulate   Create, make.

invective   Verbal abuse, insult.

invoke   Call upon, use.

prescribed   Recommended, directed, dictated.

symbolizing   Representing.

tribulation   Suffering, trouble.

writ   Authority.

Vice President Johnson, Mr. Speaker, Mr. Chief Justice, President Eisenhower,   1
Vice President Nixon, President Truman, Reverend Clergy, Fellow Citizens: We observe today not a victory of party but a celebration of freedom—symbolizing an end as well as a beginning—signifying renewal as well as change. For I have sworn before you and Almighty God the same solemn oath our forebears prescribed nearly a century and three quarters ago.

The world is very different now. For man holds in his mortal hands the   2
power to abolish all forms of human poverty and all forms of human life. And yet the same revolutionary beliefs for which our forebears fought are still at issue around the globe—the belief that the rights of man come not from the generosity of the state but from the hand of God.

We dare not forget today that we are the heirs of that first revolution. Let   3
the word go forth from this time and place, to friend and foe alike, that the torch has been passed to a new generation of Americans—born in this century, tempered by war, disciplined by a hard and bitter peace, proud of our ancient heritage—and unwilling to witness or permit the slow undoing of those human rights to which this nation has always been committed, and to which we are committed today, at home and around the world.

Let every nation know, whether it wishes us well or ill, that we shall pay any   4
price, bear any burden, meet any hardship, support any friend or oppose any foe to assure the survival and the success of liberty.

This much we pledge—and more.   5

To those old allies whose cultural and spiritual origins we share, we pledge   6
the loyalty of faithful friends. United, there is little we cannot do in a host of cooperative ventures. Divided, there is little we can do—for we dare not meet a powerful challenge at odds and split asunder.

To those new states whom we welcome to the ranks of the free, we pledge   7
our word that one form of colonial control shall not have passed away merely to be replaced by a far more iron tyranny. We shall not always expect to find them supporting our view.

But we shall always hope to find them strongly supporting their own free-   8
dom—and to remember that, in the past, those who foolishly sought power by riding the back of the tiger ended up inside.

To those people in the huts and villages of half the globe struggling to break   9
the bonds of mass misery, we pledge our best efforts to help them help themselves, for whatever period is required—not because the Communists may be

doing it, not because we seek their votes, but because it is right. If a free society cannot help the many who are poor, it cannot save the few who are rich.

To our sister republics south of our border, we offer a special pledge—to 10 convert our good words into good deeds—in a new alliance for progress—to assist free men and free governments in casting off the chains of poverty. But this peaceful revolution of hope cannot become the prey of hostile powers. Let all our neighbors know that we shall join with them to oppose aggression or subversion anywhere in the Americas. And let every other power know that this hemisphere intends to remain the master of its own house.

To that world assembly of sovereign states, the United Nations, our last best 11 hope in an age where the instruments of war have far outpaced the instruments of peace, we renew our pledge of support—to prevent it from becoming merely a forum for invective—to strengthen its shield of the new and the weak—and to enlarge the area in which its writ may run.

Finally, to those nations who would make themselves our adversary, we 12 offer not a pledge but a request: That both sides begin anew the quest for peace, before the dark powers of destruction unleashed by science engulf all humanity in planned or accidental self-destruction.

We dare not tempt them with weakness. For only when our arms are 13 sufficient beyond doubt can we be certain beyond doubt that they will never be employed.

But neither can two great and powerful groups of nations take comfort from 14 our present course—both sides overburdened by the cost of modern weapons, both rightly alarmed by the steady spread of the deadly atom, yet both racing to alter that uncertain balance of terror that stays the hand of mankind's final war.

So let us begin anew—remembering on both sides that civility is not a sign 15 of weakness, and sincerity is always subject to proof. Let us never negotiate out of fear. But let us never fear to negotiate.

Let both sides explore what problems unite us instead of belaboring those 16 problems which divide us.

Let both sides, for the first time, formulate serious and precise proposals for 17 the inspection and control of arms—and bring the absolute power to destroy other nations under the absolute control of all nations.

Let both sides seek to invoke the wonders of science instead of its terrors. 18 Together let us explore the stars, conquer the deserts, eradicate disease, tap the ocean depths and encourage the arts and commerce.

Let both sides unite to heed in all corners of the earth the command of 19 Isaiah—to "undo the heavy burdens . . . [and] let the oppressed go free."

And if a beachhead of cooperation may push back the jungle of suspicion, 20 let both sides join in creating a new endeavor: not a new balance of power, but a new world of law, where the strong are just and the weak secure and the peace preserved.

All this will not be finished in the first one hundred days. Nor will it be 21 finished in the first one thousand days, nor in the life of this administration, nor even perhaps in our lifetime on this planet. But let us begin.

In your hands, my fellow citizens, more than mine, will rest the final success 22 or failure of our course. Since this country was founded, each generation of Americans has been summoned to give testimony to its national loyalty. The graves of young Americans who answered the call to service surround the globe.

Now the trumpet summons us again—not as a call to bear arms, though arms 23 we need—not as a call to battle, though embattled we are—but a call to bear the burden of a long twilight struggle, year in and year out, "rejoicing in hope, patient in tribulation"—a struggle against the common enemies of man: Tyranny, poverty, disease and war itself.

Can we forge against these enemies a grand and global alliance, North and 24 South, East and West, that can assure a more fruitful life for all mankind? Will you join in that historic effort?

In the long history of the world, only a few generations have been granted 25 the role of defending freedom in its hour of maximum danger.

I do not shrink from this responsibility—I welcome it. I do not believe that 26 any of us would exchange places with any other people or any other generation. The energy, the faith, the devotion which we bring to this endeavor will light our country and all who serve it—and the glow from that fire can truly light the world.

And so, my fellow Americans: Ask not what your country can do for 27 you—ask what you can do for your country.

My fellow citizens of the world: Ask not what America will do for you, but 28 what together we can do for the freedom of man.

Finally, whether you are citizens of America or citizens of the world, ask of 29 us here the same high standards of strength and sacrifice which we ask of you. With a good conscience our only sure reward, with history the final judge of our deeds, let us go forth to lead the land we love, asking His blessing and His help, but knowing that here on earth God's work must truly be our own.

Questions for Discussion

1. Reread any three or four paragraphs in this selection, and identify examples of parallel structure that are used to create emphasis.

2. Reread paragraph 21, which illustrates repetition. Then find other passages in which key words and phrases are repeated to create emphasis.

3. Paragraphs 6, 7, 9, 10, and 11 are introduced by phrases that begin with the preposition "to." This repetition helps the speaker draw connections between and emphasize important ideas in each of these paragraphs. In what other section of this speech does he use repetition to begin a series of paragraphs?

4. The speech writer's ability to vary sentence length is evident throughout this selection. In what paragraphs is this skill most apparent?

5. Near the conclusion, JFK asks two rhetorical questions that add variety and interest to his presentation. What are they?

6. The speech writer often creates coherence between sentences and paragraphs by beginning with a coordinating conjunction: "And," "But," and "For." Find places in which he does so.

Suggestions for Journal Entries

1. Pick out one or two paragraphs in Kennedy's Inaugural Address that you find particularly moving and effective. Put the ideas he expresses into your own words. Vary sentence length and structure by using the techniques for creating variety explained earlier in this chapter and found in this selection.

2. Kennedy's speech seems fresh and current because it touches something universal in the human spirit, the hopes and the problems of all generations and all peoples. In your journal, list the issues (or problems) mentioned in Kennedy's Inaugural Address that you believe are still important today. Begin discussing details that, in a later assignment, might help show your readers how current these problems still are. Draw these details from your own experiences and/or from what you know about current events.

The Measure of Eratosthenes

CARL SAGAN

A professor of astronomy at Cornell University, Carl Sagan has worked on a number of NASA projects and has completed extensive research on the possibility of life on other planets. He has done much to popularize the study of science and is especially well known as a result of having hosted the public television series Cosmos. *Among his most widely read books are* The Dragons of Eden, *for which he won the Pulitzer Prize in 1977,* Broca's Brain, *and* Cosmos.

Sagan published "The Measure of Eratosthenes" (er-uh-TAHS-thuh-neez) to honor an ancient Greek thinker who, seventeen centuries before Columbus, accurately measured the Earth and proved that it was round.

Looking Ahead

1. In paragraph 4, Sagan claims that "in almost everything, Eratosthenes was 'alpha.'" Alpha is the first letter of the Greek alphabet.

2. Papyrus, mentioned in paragraph 5, is a plant from which paper was made in ancient times.

3. One reason that this selection holds our interest so well is that Sagan succeeds in varying the structure and length of his sentences. Find places where he does this.

Vocabulary

cataract   Large waterfall.
circumference   Distance around a circle or globe.
compelling   Difficult to ignore.
inclined   Slanted.

intergalactic   Between galaxies.

intersect   Cross.

musings   Thoughts.

pronounced   Significant.

randomly   By chance.

The earth is a place. It is by no means the only place. It is not even a typical   1
place. No planet or star or galaxy can be typical, because the cosmos is mostly
empty. The only typical place is within the vast, cold, universal vacuum, the
everlasting night of intergalactic space, a place so strange and desolate that, by
comparison, planets and stars and galaxies seem achingly rare and lovely.

If we were randomly inserted into the cosmos, the chance that we would find   2
ourselves on or near a planet would be less than one in a billion trillion trillion
(10^{33}, a one followed by 33 zeros). In everyday life, such odds are called
compelling. Worlds are precious.

The discovery that the earth is a *little* world was made, as so many important   3
human discoveries were, in the ancient Near East, in a time some humans call
the third century B.C., in the greatest metropolis of the age, the Egyptian city of
Alexandria.

Here there lived a man named Eratosthenes. One of his envious contempo-   4
raries called him ''beta,'' the second letter of the Greek alphabet, because, he
said, Eratosthenes was the world's second best in everything. But it seems clear
that, in almost everything, Eratosthenes was ''alpha.''

He was an astronomer, historian, geographer, philosopher, poet, theater   5
critic, and mathematician. His writings ranged from ''Astronomy'' to ''On
Freedom from Pain.'' He was also the director of the great library of Alexandria,
where one day he read, in a papyrus book, that in the southern frontier outpost
of Syene (now Aswan), near the first cataract of the Nile, at noon on June 21
vertical sticks cast no shadows. On the summer solstice, the longest day of the
year, as the hours crept toward midday, the shadows of the temple columns grew
shorter. At noon, they were gone. A reflection of the sun could then be seen in
the water at the bottom of a deep well. The sun was directly overhead.

It was an observation that someone else might easily have ignored. Sticks,   6
shadows, reflections in wells, the position of the sun—of what possible importance could such simple, everyday matters be? But Eratosthenes was a scientist,
and his musings on these commonplaces changed the world: in a way, they made
the world.

Eratosthenes had the presence of mind to do an experiment—actually to   7
observe whether *in Alexandria* vertical sticks cast shadows near noon on June
21. And, he discovered, sticks do.

Eratosthenes asked himself how, at the same moment, a stick in Syene could   8
cast no shadow and a stick in Alexandria, far to the north, could cast a pronounced shadow.

Consider a map of ancient Egypt with two vertical sticks of equal length, one   9 stuck in Alexandria, the other in Syene. Suppose that, at a certain moment, neither stick casts any shadow at all. This is perfectly easy to understand—provided the earth is flat. The sun would then be directly overhead. If the two sticks cast shadows of equal length, that also would make sense on a flat earth: the sun's rays would then be inclined at the same angle to the two sticks. But how could it be that at the same instant there was no shadow at Syene and a substantial shadow at Alexandria?

The only possible answer, he saw, was that the surface of the earth is 10 curved. Not only that: the greater the curvature, the greater the difference in the shadow lengths. The sun is so far away that its rays are parallel when they reach the earth. Sticks placed at different angles to the sun's rays cast shadows of different lengths. For the observed difference in the shadow lengths, the distance between Alexandria and Syene had to be about seven degrees along the surface of the earth; that is, if you imagine the sticks extending down to the center of the earth, they would intersect there at an angle of seven degrees.

Seven degrees is something like one-fiftieth of 360 degrees, the full circum- 11 ference of the earth. Eratosthenes knew that the distance between Alexandria and Syene was approximately 800 kilometers, because he had hired a man to pace it out.

Eight hundred kilometers times 50 is 40,000 kilometers; so that must be the 12 circumference of the earth. (Or, if you like to measure things in miles, the distance between Alexandria and Syene is about 500 miles, and 500 miles times 50 is 25,000 miles.)

This is the right answer.   13

Eratosthenes' only tools were sticks, eyes, feet, and brains, plus a taste for 14 experiment. With them he deduced the circumference of the earth with an error of only a few percent, a remarkable achievement for 2,200 years ago. He was the first person accurately to measure the size of a planet.

Questions for Discussion

1. Analyze any of the longer paragraphs in this essay: 1, 5, 9, or 10, for example. Explain how Sagan varies the length and structure of the sentences in that paragraph. If necessary, review the techniques for creating variety discussed earlier.

2. Does Sagan make use of rhetorical questions in this selection? What do such questions help him accomplish?

3. Like Kennedy, Sagan sometimes begins a sentence with a coordinating conjunction to create coherence and emphasis. Where in this essay does he do so?

4. Paragraph 3 contains a good example of parallel structure. Identify it.

5. Another way Sagan emphasizes important ideas and creates interest is repetition. Find an example of this practice.

Suggestions for Journal Entries

1. In your own words, summarize the accomplishments of Eratosthenes that Sagan discusses in this selection. Vary your sentence structure as much as you can. If you need to, begin by listing short, simple sentences; then create variety by combining some of these sentences through coordination, subordination, and compounding.

2. Sagan obviously has a great deal of respect for Eratosthenes and what he accomplished. Think about someone you greatly admire. This person need not be an important public servant, artist, athlete, or scientist, and he or she need not hold a prominent place in history. In fact, your grandmother, neighbor, high school chemistry teacher, or close friend might make the best subject. In any case, use your journal to list the qualities or accomplishments that make this person worthy of admiration.

SUGGESTIONS FOR WRITING

1. John Steinbeck may have inspired you to think about what we are doing or should be doing to preserve the natural environment. Read the journal notes you made after reading the selection by Steinbeck. Then, write an essay explaining how well or how poorly we are doing at keeping the environment healthy.

    Focus on a problem you know well: air, land, or water pollution; global warming; and so on. Discuss the causes of the problem first. Then describe its effects. Finally, explain what you and your community are doing or should be doing to solve it.

    Write multiple drafts of your paper and edit them carefully. In the process, use techniques for creating variety and emphasis explained in this chapter.

2. Malcolm Cowley describes the horrible deaths of two old gentlemen as a way to explain one of the "vices" of old age. But we all have vices, whatever our age. Consider someone you care about who suffers from a particular vice, such as laziness, greed, vanity, sloppiness, or even a more serious problem like sexual promiscuity or drug or alcohol abuse. Write this person a letter that recalls two or three startling incidents from his or her life. In other words, show your reader how seriously this vice is affecting him or her.

    You might begin the letter by explaining how much better life could be if your reader overcame the problem. You might conclude by offering your help, advice, and friendship.

    Before you start writing, look at the journal notes you made after reading the Cowley selection; you may have already gathered important information for this assignment. Then, draft the first version of your letter. When you revise this draft, make sure to emphasize important ideas. Like Cowley, for example, use parallelism and include a few periodic sentences. At the same time, try asking your reader a few rhetorical questions.

3. One of the Suggestions for Journal Entries after Alice Wnorowski's "A Longing" asks you to think about an experience you would like to relive. If you responded to this suggestion, you've made a list of effective details that will help explain why you have such a longing to repeat this experience.

    Add to your notes, and expand them into a short essay that shows your readers what made the experience so memorable. Develop your thesis in concrete detail, and don't forget to make your writing unified and coherent by using techniques discussed in Chapter 2.

    After you've written your first draft, read your essay carefully. Should you do more to emphasize important ideas or to maintain your readers' interest? If so, revise your paper by using some of the techniques for creating emphasis and variety explained in the introduction to this chapter. As usual, edit the final draft of your paper carefully.

4. The second item in Suggestions for Journal Entries after "A Longing" invites you to begin listing details about a natural setting—a forest, meadow, seashore, mountain, river—that you visited recently or remember vividly.

Follow the advice in item #3 of Suggestions for Writing, and turn these notes into a short essay.

5. President Kennedy's Inaugural Address mentions serious social and political problems that are still with us. The most obvious of these are poverty and hunger, but there are many others. In fact, you may have already begun writing about such problems in your journal. Focus on the one problem you know most about, either through personal experience or through what you have learned about it from newspapers, television, or other sources. Continue adding details about this problem to your journal.

Then, turn your journal notes into an essay that states the problem in your thesis and explains its effects in the essay's body paragraphs. Your thesis might go something like this: "More than three decades after President Kennedy took office, extreme poverty still plagues even our richest cities."

Take time to revise your rough drafts and to give your sentences both variety and emphasis. Techniques for creating emphasis that might work well in this assignment are parallelism and the repetition of key words and phrases. This is also a good time to use startling images and figures of speech like those discussed in Chapters 5 and 6. Finally, check your writing to make certain it is organized, developed, and edited well.

6. Suggestions for Journal Entries after both Cowley's "The Vices of Age" and Sagan's "The Measure of Eratosthenes" ask you to gather information about someone you admire. If you responded to either or both of these items, read your notes carefully and add to them.

Next, organize what you've written into the paragraphs of an essay. Place your thesis in an introductory paragraph that compares or contrasts your subject with others, that begins with a startling remark, or that uses another technique for writing introductions discussed in Chapter 4. Make sure your thesis states why you admire your subject. Explain that you respect this individual because of his or her accomplishments, or simply name particular character traits you find most admirable. Then, in *each* of the paragraphs that follow, discuss one accomplishment or character trait in detail.

Like Cowley and Sagan, vary the length and structure of your sentences, use rhetorical questions, and practice parallel structure. Don't forget to revise your paper and to edit it carefully.

SECTION **THREE**

DESCRIPTION

This section's two chapters show how to develop verbal portraits—pictures in words—of people, places, and things you know well. The more specific you make any piece of writing, the more interesting, exciting, and effective it will be. And this is especially true of descriptive writing. Successful descriptions require a lot of specific details.

KNOWING YOUR SUBJECT

Gathering descriptive details becomes easier when you know the person, place, or thing you're describing. If you need to learn more about your subject, spend some time observing it. Use your five senses—sight, hearing, touch, taste, and smell—to gather important information. And don't be afraid to take notes. Write your observations, reactions, and impressions in your journal, on note cards, or at least on scratch paper. They will come in handy as you sit down to put together your verbal portrait.

USING LANGUAGE THAT SHOWS

As you learned in Chapter 5, using language that shows makes any writing you do far more *concrete, specific,* and *vivid* than simply telling your readers what you mean. Such language is vital to description.

For instance, it's one thing to say that your mother ''came home from work looking very tired.'' It's quite another to describe ''the dark shadows under her eyes and the slowness of her walk as she entered the house.''

In the first version, the writer uses a weak abstraction to get the point across. But ''looking very tired'' can mean different things to different people. It doesn't show the reader exactly what the writer sees. It doesn't point to things about the subject—the dark shadows under her eyes, the slowness of her walk—that *show* she is tired.

Use Concrete Nouns and Adjectives

The next thing to remember is to make your details as concrete as possible. For example, if you're describing a friend, don't just say that ''He's not a neat

181

dresser'' or that his ''wardrobe could be improved.'' Include concrete nouns and adjectives that will enable your readers to come to the same conclusion. Talk about ''the red dirt along the sides of his scuffed, torn shoes; the large rips in the knees of his faded blue jeans; and the many jelly spots on his shirt.''

The same is true when describing objects and places. It's not enough to claim that your 1969 convertible is ''a real eyesore.'' You've got to *show* it! Describe the scrapes, scratches, dents, and rust spots; mention the cracked headlights, the corroded bumpers, and the bald tires; talk about the fact that the top is faded.

Include Specific Details

After you've chosen a number of important details that are concrete—details that show rather than tell something about your subject—make your description more specific. For instance, revise the description of your friend's attire to ''Red clay was caked along the sides of his scuffed, torn loafers; his knees bulged from the large rips in his faded Levi's; and strawberry jelly was smeared on the collar of his white Oxford shirt.''

When describing that 1969 convertible, don't be content simply to mention ''the scratches and scrapes on the paint job.'' Go on to specify that ''some of them are more than an inch wide and a half inch deep.'' Make sure your readers know that those ''corroded bumpers'' are made of ''chrome'' and ''are scarred with thousands of tiny pockmarks and rusty blemishes.'' Finally, don't say that the top is ''faded''; explain that ''the canvas top, which was once sparkling white, has turned dirty gray with age.''

Create Figures of Speech

In Chapter 6 you learned that one of the best ways to make your writing clear and vivid is to use figures of speech, expressions that convey a meaning beyond their literal sense. Writers rely heavily on figures of speech when they need to explain or clarify abstract, complex, or unfamiliar ideas. Metaphors and similes are the most useful figures of speech for description because they can be used to compare an aspect of the person, place, or thing being described to something else with which the reader may already be familiar. Gilbert Highet makes excellent use of a simile when, in ''Subway Station'' (Chapter 8), he tells us that the paint is peeling off the station walls ''like scabs from an old wound.''

In addition, figures of speech make it possible for writers to dramatize or make vivid feelings, concepts, or ideas that would otherwise have remained abstract and difficult to understand. If you read Emanuel di Pasquale's ''Joy of an Immigrant, a Thanksgiving'' (Chapter 6), you might remember that the poet compares his journey to America to the flight of a bird to a land where he ''can build a dry nest'' and where his ''song can echo.''

Rely on Your Five Senses

Earlier you read that a good way to gather information about any subject is through observation. Observation is often thought of as seeing, and the most common details found in description are visual. However, observing can also include information from the other four senses. Of course, explaining what something sounds, feels, smells, or tastes like can be harder than showing what it looks like. But the extra effort is worthwhile. In fact, whether you describe people, places, or things, the greater the variety of details you include, the more realistic and convincing your description will be.

Next to sight, hearing is perhaps the sense writers rely on most. There are many ways to describe sound. In Chapter 9, for example, Carl Sandburg claims that Lincoln's voice had "a log-cabin smack" and that he pronounced "the word 'really' more like a drawled Kentucky 'ra-a-ly'." In Chapter 8, John Ciardi uses a simile to compare "tires humming" to "the sound of a brook a half mile down in the crease of a mountain." And Annie Dillard relies on her readers' knowing "Old MacDonald Had a Farm," a tune with which she serenades a group of children in Ecuador. "I thought they might recognize the animal sounds," she tells us.

When writers describe rain-covered sidewalks as "slick," scraped elbows as "raw" or "tender," or the surfaces of bricks as "coarse" or "abrasive," they appeal to the sense of touch. Another example appears in Mary Ann Gwinn's "A Deathly Call of the Wild," in Chapter 8, when she writes that some of the oil spilled onto the shores of Alaska had the "consistency of chocolate syrup."

Tastes and smells are perhaps the most difficult things to describe. Nonetheless, you should include them in your writing when appropriate. Notice how well Mary Taylor Simeti does this when describing the Easter picnic she and her family make of take-out food from a hillside restaurant in Sicily:

> . . . [our] obliging host produces [brings out] three foil-covered plates, a bottle
> of mineral water, and a round kilo loaf of fragrant, crusty bread. We drive back
> along the road a little way to a curve that offers space to park and some rocks to
> sit on. Our plates turn out to hold spicy olives, some slices of *prosciutto crudo*
> [cold ham] and of a peppery local salami, and two kinds of pecorino [sheep's
> milk] cheese, one fresh and mild, the other aged and sharper. With a bag of
> oranges from the car, the sun warm on our backs, the mountains rolling down at
> our feet to the southern coast and the sea beyond, where the heat haze clouds the
> horizon and hides Africa from view, we have as fine an Easter dinner as I have
> ever eaten. *(On Persephone's Island)*

BEING OBJECTIVE OR SUBJECTIVE

Describing something objectively requires the writer to report what he or she sees, hears, and so on as accurately and as thoroughly as possible. Subjective description allows the writer to communicate his or her personal feelings or reactions to the subject as well. Both types of description serve important purposes.

Most journalists and historians try to remain objective by communicating facts, not opinions about those facts. In other words, they try to give us the kind of information we'll need to make up our own minds about the subject.

This is what student Meg Potter does when she describes one of the thousands of homeless living on the streets of our cities:

> This particular [woman] had no shoes on, but her feet were bound in plastic bags that were tied with filthy rags. It was hard to tell exactly what she was wearing. She had on . . . a conglomeration of tattered material that I can only say . . . were rags. I couldn't say how old she was, but I'd guess in her late fifties. The woman's hair was grey and silver, and she was beginning to go bald.
>
> As I watched for a while, I realized she was sorting out her bags. She had six of them, each stuffed and overflowing. . . . I caught a glimpse of ancient magazines, empty bottles, filthy pieces of clothing, an inside-out umbrella, and several mismatched shoes. The lady seemed to be taking the things out of one bag and putting them into another. All the time she was muttering to herself. (''The Shopping Bag Ladies'')

Potter never reveals her feelings about her subject. She simply explains what the shopping bag lady looks like and what she does. Even words like ''conglomeration'' and ''filthy,'' while vivid, tell us more about what the writer sees than how she feels about her subject. As a result, we are left to make up our own minds about what we read.

In some cases, however, writers find it useful to reveal their feelings about the person, place, or thing they are describing, so they take a subjective approach. Doing so often adds depth and interest to their work. In ''The Temptress,'' for example, student Dan Roland includes details from his senses and creates figures of speech to communicate various feelings about a golf course he visits:

> A friendly sun peeks out from behind the green hills, revealing a giant coat of glistening frost on a silent land. At this hour, even the birds still sleep. The howling wind's savage teeth bite deeply, and the cold air grips me by the throat. The steaming coffee goes down easily, warming my insides and making the frigid environment almost bearable. I peer over an elegant landscape. As far as I can see, all is calm. Manicured fairways reach out across the land, and ponds of glass reflect the sun's red glow. There are trees everywhere, from delicate symmetrical pines that line the fairways to majestic, spiteful oaks that eat my golf balls for breakfast, lunch, and dinner.

Watch for examples of objective and subjective description as you read the poems and essays in Chapters 8 and 9. At the same time, identify concrete and specific details and figures of speech, which will help you better appreciate and understand what goes into the writing of a vivid, interesting, and well-written piece of description.

CHAPTER 8

DESCRIBING PLACES AND THINGS

The introduction to Section Three explained several ways to increase your powers of description regardless of the subject. This chapter presents several selections that describe places and things. It also explains two techniques, introduced earlier, that will help you make your subjects as interesting and as vivid to your readers as they are to you: using proper nouns and effective verbs.

USING PROPER NOUNS

In addition to filling your writing with concrete details and figures of speech, you might also want to include a number of *proper nouns,* which, as you know, are the names of particular persons, places, and things. Here are some examples: Arizona, University of Tennessee, Lake Michigan, Farmers and Merchants' Savings and Loan, First Baptist Church, Spanish, Chinese, Belmont Avenue, Singer Sewing Machine Company, Harold Smith, San Francisco Opera House, *Business Week* magazine, and Minnesota Vikings.

Including proper nouns that readers recognize easily can make what you are describing more familiar to them. At the very least, it makes your writing more believable. Notice how Alfred Kazin's recollection of his childhood home is enriched by the names of places and things (shown in italics) he uses in this passage from ''My Mother in Her Kitchen'':

> In the corner next to the toilet was the sink at which we washed, and the square tub in which my mother did our clothes. Above it, tacked to the shelf on which were pleasantly arranged square, blue-bordered white sugar and spice jars, hung calendars from the *Public National Bank* on *Pitkin Avenue* and the *Minsker Progressive Branch* of the *Workman's Circle;* receipts for the payment of insurance premiums and household bills on a spindle; two little boxes engraved with *Hebrew* letters. One of these was for the poor, the other to buy back the *Land of Israel.*

USING EFFECTIVE VERBS

We know how important verbs are to narration, but effective verbs can also add much to a piece of description. Writers use verbs to make descriptions more specific, accurate, and interesting. For instance, ''the wind had chiseled deep grooves into the sides of the cliffs'' is more specific than ''the wind had made deep grooves.'' The verb ''chiseled'' also gives the reader a more accurate picture of the wind's action than ''made'' does.

In the introduction to Section Three, you learned how to enrich the description of a friend's clothing by adding specific details. Notice that lively verbs (in italics) make as much of a difference in that sentence as do concrete nouns and adjectives:

> Red clay *was caked* along the sides of his scuffed, torn loafers; his knees *bulged* from the large rips in his faded Levi's; and strawberry jelly *was smeared* on the collar of his white Oxford shirt.''

Something similar can be said about the verbs Robert K. Massey uses in a portrait of the Russian countryside that opens his biography of Peter the Great:

> Around Moscow, the country *rolls* gently up from the rivers *winding* in silvery loops across the pleasant landscape. Small lakes and patches of woods *are sprinkled* among the meadowlands. Here and there, a village *appears, topped* by the onion dome of its church. People *are walking* through the fields on dirt paths *lined* with weeds. Along the riverbanks they *are fishing, swimming* and *lying* in the sun. It is a familiar Russian scene, *rooted* in centuries. *(Peter the Great)*

USING ACTION TO ENRICH THE DESCRIPTION OF A PLACE

As you have learned, narration and description are closely related, and they often appear in the same piece of writing. For example, storytellers make it a point to describe the places where their narratives take place. Writers of description often reveal the character or atmosphere of a place by telling us what happens there.

Take the following paragraph from Annie Dillard's ''In the Jungle,'' which appears in this chapter. Effective verbs, like those we associate with narrative writing—and like the ones discussed earlier—reveal something about the jungle's character by telling us about natural processes and events that occur there.

> Green fireflies *spattered* lights across the air and *illumined* for seconds, now here, now there, the pale trunks of enormous, solitary trees. Beneath us the brown Napo River *was rising,* in all silence; it *coiled* up the sandy bank and *tangled* its foam in vines that *trailed* from the forest and roots that *looped* the shore.

Clearly, the jungle is a place of energy, activity, and excitement. Knowing that is as important as learning about the shapes and sizes of its trees or about the strange sounds of birds flying overhead.

Before you go on to read the essays and poems in this chapter, read another paragraph from ''In the Jungle.'' This one shows how recalling the actions of people you see can reveal the character of a place:

. . . [I wished] I knew some Spanish or some Quechua so I could speak with the ring of little girls who were alternately staring at me and smiling at their toes. I spoke anyway, and fooled with my hair, which they were obviously dying to get their hands on, and laughed, and soon they were all braiding my hair, all five of them, all fifty fingers, all my hair, even my bangs. And then they took it apart and did it again, laughing, and teaching me Spanish nouns, and meeting my eyes and each other's with open delight, while their small brothers in blue jeans climbed down from the trees and began kicking a volleyball around with one of the North American men.

The Eagle

ALFRED, LORD TENNYSON

One of the most famous poets in English, Tennyson (1809–1892) is remembered chiefly as a spokesperson for the Victorian age. In 1850 he was named poet laureate of Great Britain, a position of great distinction, and in this capacity he wrote numerous poems commemorating state occasions and special events. His most famous works include "The Lady of Shalott," "The Lotus-Eaters," and "Ulysses."

In "The Eagle," Tennyson captures the majesty and strength of this magnificent bird in six short but very powerful verses (lines). Like many of his poems, it shows his masterful use of concrete details and figurative language in creating a lifelike portrait.

Looking Ahead

1. As you read the poem, don't expect much descriptive detail about the eagle itself; instead, Tennyson tells us more about the "lonely" world it inhabits. To learn more about the eagle, ask yourself how it interacts with that world.
2. The verbs in the first three lines seem appropriate to a still life; the ones in the second stanza convey action. This two-part view of the eagle helps Tennyson give us a far more complete portrait than if he had simply relied only on physical description and talked about size, shape, color, and the like.

Vocabulary

azure   Deep blue.
crag   Rocky cliff.

He clasps the crag with crooked hands;
Close to the sun in lonely lands,
Ring'd with the azure world, he stands.

The wrinkled sea beneath him crawls;
He watches from his mountain walls,
And like a thunderbolt he falls.

Questions for Discussion

1. Tennyson makes excellent use of adjectives in this poem. What are they? What nouns does he use to describe the eagle?
2. The poem includes more detail about the eagle's world than about the eagle itself. What kind of land is it? What does it tell us about the eagle?
3. Tennyson divides his poem into two three-line sections, called ''triplets.'' How does *each* of these triplets picture the eagle for the reader?
4. Most readers see the eagle as courageous, majestic, and powerful. What details in the poem support this view?
5. What figures of speech does Tennyson use in this poem?

Suggestions for Journal Entries

1. Continue Tennyson's description of the eagle's environment by writing down several of your own impressions that might help other readers see this world even more clearly. Then make your description more concrete; put it into paragraph form and include as many effective adjectives and nouns as you can.
2. Write your own short description of an animal (perhaps a family pet) or type of animal about which you have strong feelings (negative or positive). Start by listing characteristics you associate with this animal. Is it intelligent, swift, and elegant? Is it ferocious and menacing? Is it clumsy, awkward, or humorous to watch? Then focus sharply on *one* of these characteristics. Use concrete nouns and adjectives to develop your description and, if possible, include some figures of speech to make your writing more exciting.

From ''The Ones Who Walk Away from Omelas''

URSULA LE GUIN

Born in Berkeley, California, Le Guin writes short stories, novels, poems, essays, and children's books. She is best known for her works of science fiction and fantasy, types of writing she uses to discuss important human concerns. Her best-known works include The Dispossessed *and* The Lathe of Heaven *as well as* The Farthest Shore, *for which she won a National Book Award in 1973. The selection you will read is the introductory paragraph to a short story.*

Looking Ahead

You know that explaining what happens in a place can reveal a lot about its character or atmosphere. Look for vivid verbs that tell us as much about what Le Guin is describing as do nouns and adjectives.

Vocabulary

decorous   Dignified, mannerly, refined.
grave   Serious, staid.
lithe   Flexible, limber.
mauve   Shade of deep violet or purple.
restive   Restless, impatient.

With a clamor of bells that set the swallows soaring, the Festival of Summer came to the city Omelas, bright-towered by the sea. The rigging of the boats in harbor sparkled with flags. In the streets between houses with red roofs and painted walls, between old moss-grown gardens and under avenues of trees, past great parks and public buildings, processions moved. Some were decorous: old people in long stiff robes of mauve and gray, grave master workmen, quiet, merry women carrying their babies and chatting as they walked. In other streets the music beat faster, a shimmering of gong and tambourine, and the people went dancing, the procession was a dance. Children dodged in and out, their high calls rising like the swallows' crossing flights over the music and the singing. All the processions wound towards the north side of the city, where on the great water-meadow called the Green Fields boys and girls, naked in the bright air, with mud-stained feet and ankles and long, lithe arms, exercised their restive horses before the race. The horses wore no gear at all but a halter without bit. Their manes were braided with streamers of silver, gold, and green. They flared their nostrils and pranced and boasted to one another; they were vastly excited, the horse being the only animal who has adopted our ceremonies as his own. Far off to the north and west the mountains stood up half circling Omelas on her bay. The air of morning was so clear that the snow still crowning the Eighteen Peaks burned with white-gold fire across the miles of sunlit air, under the dark blue of the sky. There was just enough wind to make the banners that marked the racecourse snap and flutter now and then. In the silence of the broad green meadows one could hear the music winding though the city streets, farther and nearer and ever approaching, a cheerful faint sweetness of the air that from time

to time trembled and gathered together and broke out into the great joyous
clanging of the bells.

Questions for Discussion

1. This passage contains many visual details, but Le Guin describes sounds as
   well. What words does she use to convey sound?
2. Pick out examples of concrete and specific language (nouns and adjectives)
   that make her writing crisp and clear.
3. This is as much the description of the ''Festival of Summer,'' an event, as it
   is of ''Omelas,'' a city. What verbs in this passage help Le Guin capture the
   atmosphere of the festival?
4. Does the author use figurative language? Where? What types?
5. What does she mean by explaining that the horse is ''the only animal who has
   adopted our ceremonies as his own''?

Suggestions for Journal Entries

1. Focus on a festival, fair, parade, or other large gathering you have been to
   recently where people came to celebrate an occasion or just to have a good
   time. List details from your senses that would describe both the event and the
   place in which it was held. Then, make a second list about the variety of
   people and activities you observed there.
2. Le Guin's paragraph describes sounds and colors well. Think of a place in
   which you spend a lot of time: for example, the store, office, or factory in
   which you work; the student center or union; a classroom building; a shopping mall; a park. Use listing or focused freewriting to gather information
   about what you might see *and* hear on a typical visit to this place.

Subway Station

GILBERT HIGHET

*Gilbert Highet (1906–1978) came to the United States from Scotland in 1937 to
teach Greek and Latin at Columbia University in New York City. A witty and
urbane writer and speaker, he served as editor of the Book-of-the-Month Club
and was chief book reviewer for* Harper's Magazine. *He also hosted* People,
Places, and Books, *a weekly radio talk show, and published hundreds of essays
on life in New York City. What Highest describes in ''Subway Station'' is typical
of the thousands of stations in New York's vast underground rail system.*

Looking Ahead

1. The most important thing "Subway Station" shows us is Highet's ability to create a photograph in words by piling detail upon detail. For instance, he makes it a point to tell us that the "electric bulbs" were "meager"; then he adds that they were "unscreened, yellow, and coated with filth." Look for other examples of his ability to do this.

2. Highet is also famous for using figurative language, especially metaphors and similes. As you learned in the introduction to Section Three, one of the most startling of these comes about midway in this selection, when he describes the "gloomy vaulting from which dingy paint was peeling off like scabs from an old wound." Look for and mark other examples of figurative language as you read this piece.

3. "Subway Station" mixes objective with subjective description. When Highet recalls various "advertisement posters on the walls," he remains objective. He does not explain whether he approves or disapproves of them, whether he finds them attractive or distasteful. When he tells us that "the floor was a nauseating dark brown," on the other hand, he is being subjective. Look for other places in which Highet is particularly subjective or objective.

Vocabulary

abominable   Disgusting, abhorrent.

congealed   Clotted.

defilement   Filth, dirt, object of disgust.

dubious   Unknown.

encrusted   Covered over, encased with a crusty layer.

laden   Covered with.

leprous   Relating to leprosy, a disease in which parts of the body begin to decay and the skin exhibits sores and severe scaling.

meager   Sparse, skimpy.

nauseating   Sickening.

obscenities   Indecent or offensive language.

perfunctory   Apathetic, without care.

relish   Enjoy.

vaulting   Arched or rounded ceiling.

Standing in a subway station, I began to appreciate the place—almost to enjoy it. First of all, I looked at the lighting: a row of meager electric bulbs, unscreened, yellow, and coated with filth, stretched toward the black mouth of the tunnel, as though it were a bolt hole in an abandoned coal mine. Then I lingered, with zest, on the walls and ceiling: lavatory tiles which had been white about fifty years ago, and were now encrusted with soot, coated with the remains of a dirty liquid which might be either atmospheric humidity mingled with smog or the result of a perfunctory attempt to clean them with cold water; and, above them, gloomy vaulting from which dingy paint was peeling off like scabs from an old wound, sick black paint leaving a leprous white undersurface. Beneath my feet, the floor was a nauseating dark brown with black stains upon it which might be stale oil or dry chewing gum or some worse defilement; it looked like the hallway of a condemned slum building. Then my eye traveled to the tracks, where two lines of glittering steel—the only positively clean object in the whole place—ran out of darkness into darkness about an unspeakable mass of congealed oil, puddles of dubious liquid, and a mishmash of old cigarette packets, mutilated and filthy newspapers, and the debris that filtered down from the street above through a barred grating in the roof. As I looked up toward the sunlight, I could see more debris sifting slowly downward, and making an abominable pattern in the slanting beam of dirt-laden sunlight. I was going on to relish more features of this unique scene: such as the advertisement posters on the walls—here a text from the Bible, there a half-naked girl, here a woman wearing a hat consisting of a hen sitting on a nest full of eggs, and there a pair of girl's legs walking up the keys of a cash register—all scribbled over with unknown names and well-known obscenities in black crayon and red lipstick; but then my train came in at last, I boarded it, and began to read. The experience was over for the time.

Questions for Discussion

1. In Looking Ahead you were asked to find examples of Highet's ability to pile detail upon detail to create a verbal picture—a photograph in words—of the scene. What examples did you find?

2. What examples of figurative language, other than those mentioned in Looking Ahead, did you find?

3. Do you believe Highet succeeds in conveying an accurate picture? What overall feeling or impression of the station does he communicate?

4. Which of his concrete details contribute to this impression the most? Which nouns and adjectives have the strongest effect on you?

5. As you know, "Subway Station" contains both subjective and objective description. Where does Highet use subjective description (showing his personal feelings or emotional reactions)?

Suggestions for Journal Entries

1. Review your responses to item 1 of the Questions for Discussion. Then write a one-sentence description of a familiar object or place by gathering details

(adjectives and nouns) that give the reader a verbal portrait of your subject. For instance, start with an ordinary piece of furniture—perhaps the desk or table you're working on right now—and then begin adding details until you have a list that looks something like this:

The desk

The wooden desk

The large wooden desk

The large brown wooden desk

The large brown wooden desk covered with junk

The large brown wooden desk covered with junk, which squats in the corner of my room

The large brown wooden desk covered with junk, books, and papers, which squats in the corner of my room

Repeat this process, adding as many items as you can, until you've exhausted your mind's supply of nouns and adjectives. Then review your list. Can you make your description even more specific and concrete? For instance, the above example might be revised to read:

The four-foot-long dark brown oak desk was covered with my math book, an old dictionary with the cover ripped off, two chemistry test papers, today's French notes, a half-eaten bologna sandwich, and a can of diet cola.

2. Choose an object or place you know quite well and can describe easily. Start with a totally objective description; then write down your subjective reactions to it in a sentence or two. Repeat the process with three or four other places or things.

Whenever possible, use a simile, metaphor, or other figure of speech to get your feelings across. For instance, describe the bedroom your brother has failed to clean out in two years as "his private garbage scow," or compare your home computer to an "electronic maze."

In the Jungle

ANNIE DILLARD

Born in Pittsburgh in 1945, Annie Dillard worked at Harper's Magazine *from 1973 to 1981 as a contributing editor. Before she was thirty, she won a Pulitzer Prize for* Pilgrim at Tinker Creek, *a narrative about the Roanoke Valley of Virginia, where she once lived. She has also written a book of poetry entitled* Tickets for a Prayer Wheel.

In 1982 she published Teaching a Stone to Talk, *an anthology of essays, which includes "In the Jungle." In this essay, Dillard describes a jungle village she visited while traveling in Ecuador, South America.*

Looking Ahead

1. Paragraph 3, some of which is quoted in the introduction to this chapter, shows that Dillard enriches her description of the jungle by using verbs that show action. Look for such verbs in other parts of the essay as well.

2. Ecuador is located on the western coast of South America between Colombia and Peru. The Andes Mountains dominate the landscape of Ecuador, but in the eastern portion are jungles through which flow tributaries of the Amazon, the world's second-longest river. The Napo is one of these tributaries, or "headwaters."

3. The official language of Ecuador is Spanish, but the Indians speak Quechua or Jarva. The predominant religion is Roman Catholicism.

4. In paragraph 3, Dillard writes: "It was February, the middle of summer." That's not a misprint. When North America is experiencing winter, it's summer in South America.

Vocabulary

canopies   Coverings or kinds of roofs.

goiters   Swellings of the thyroid, a gland found in the neck.

illumined   Lit up.

impaled   Stuck upon.

Jesuit   Order of Roman Catholic priests.

muted   Quieted, muffled.

nightjar   Jungle bird that is active at night.

opaque   Not reflecting light, dull.

Orion   Constellation.

recorder   Musical instrument resembling a flute.

roil   Stir and become muddy.

swath   Patch.

thatch   Leaves, grasses, reeds, or other natural building materials used as roofing and sometimes as siding.

uncanny   Strange, unexplainable.

wistful   Sweetly sad, melancholic.

Like any out-of-the-way place, the Napo River in the Ecuadorian jungle seems   1
real enough when you are there, even central. Out of the way of *what?* I was sitting on a stump at the edge of a bankside palm-thatch village, in the middle of the night, on the headwaters of the Amazon. Out of the way of human life, tenderness, or the glance of heaven?

A nightjar in deep-leaved shadow called three long notes, and hushed. The   2 men with me talked softly in clumps: three North Americans, four Ecuadorians who were showing us the jungle. We were holding cool drinks and idly watching a hand-sized tarantula seize moths that came to the lone bulb on the generator shed beside us.

It was February, the middle of summer. Green fireflies spattered lights   3
across the air and illumined for seconds, now here, now there, the pale trunks of enormous, solitary trees. Beneath us the brown Napo River was rising, in all silence; it coiled up the sandy bank and tangled its foam in vines that trailed from the forest and roots that looped the shore.

Each breath of night smelled sweet, more moistened and sweet than any   4
kitchen, or garden, or cradle. Each star in Orion seemed to tremble and stir with my breath. All at once, in the thatch house across the clearing behind us, one of the village's Jesuit priests began playing an alto recorder, playing a wordless song, lyric, in a minor key, that twined over the village clearing, that caught in the big trees' canopies, muted our talk on the bankside, and wandered over the river, dissolving downstream.

This will do, I thought. This will do, for a weekend, or a season, or a home.   5

Later that night I loosed my hair from its braids and combed it smooth—not   6
for myself, but so the village girls could play with it in the morning.

We had disembarked at the village that afternoon, and I had slumped on   7
some shaded steps, wishing I knew some Spanish or some Quechua so I could speak with the ring of little girls who were alternately staring at me and smiling at their toes. I spoke anyway, and fooled with my hair, which they were obviously dying to get their hands on, and laughed, and soon they were all braiding my hair, all five of them, all fifty fingers, all my hair, even my bangs. And then they took it apart and did it again, laughing, and teaching me Spanish nouns, and meeting my eyes and each other's with open delight, while their small brothers in blue jeans climbed down from the trees and began kicking a volleyball around with one of the North American men.

Now, as I combed my hair in the little tent, another of the men, a freelance   8
writer from Manhattan, was talking quietly. He was telling us the tale of his life, describing his work in Hollywood, his apartment in Manhattan, his house in Paris. . . . ''It makes me wonder,'' he said, ''what I'm doing in a tent under a tree in the village of Pompeya, on the Napo River, in the jungle of Ecuador.'' After a pause he added, ''It makes me wonder why I'm going *back.*''

The point of going somewhere like the Napo River in Ecuador is not to see   9
the most spectacular anything. It is simply to see what is there.

What is there is interesting. The Napo River itself is wide (I mean wider than   10
the Mississippi at Davenport) and brown, opaque and smeared with floating foam and logs and branches from the jungle. White egrets hunch on shoreline deadfalls and parrots in flocks dart in and out of the light. Under the water in the river, unseen, are anacondas—which are reputed to take a few village toddlers every year—and water boas, stingrays, crocodiles, manatees, and sweet-meated fish.

Low water bares gray strips of sandbar on which the natives build tiny   11 palm-thatch shelters, arched, the size of pup tents, for overnight fishing trips. You see these extraordinarily clean people (who bathe twice a day in the river, and whose straight black hair is always freshly washed) paddling down the river in dugout canoes, hugging the banks.

Some of the Indians of this region, earlier in the century, used to sleep naked   12
in hammocks. The nights are cold. Gordon MacCreach, an American explorer in these Amazon tributaries, reported that he was startled to hear the Indians get up at three in the morning. He was even more startled, night after night, to hear them walk down to the river slowly, half asleep, and bathe in the water. Only later did he learn what they were doing: they were getting warm. The cold woke them; they warmed their skins in the river, which was always ninety degrees; then they returned to their hammocks and slept through the rest of the night.

The riverbanks are low, and from the river you see an unbroken wall of dark   13
forest in every direction, from the Andes to the Atlantic. You get a taste for looking at trees: trees hung with the swinging nests of yellow troupials, trees from which ant nests the size of grain sacks hang like black goiters, trees from which seven-colored tanagers flutter, coral trees, teak, balsa and breadfruit, enormous emergent silk-cotton trees, and the pale-barked *samona* palms.

When you are inside the jungle, away from the river, the trees vault out of   14
sight. It is hard to remember to look up the long trunks and see the fans, strips, fronds, and sprays of glossy leaves. . . . Butterflies, iridescent blue, striped, or clear-winged, thread the jungle paths at eye level. And at your feet is a swath of ants bearing triangular bits of green leaf. The ants with their leaves look like a wide fleet of sailing dinghies—but they don't quit. In either direction they wobble over the jungle floor as far as the eye can see.

Long lakes shine in the jungle. We traveled one of these in dugout canoes,   15
canoes with two inches of freeboard, canoes paddled with machete-hewn oars chopped from buttresses of silk-cotton trees, or poled in the shallows with peeled cane or bamboo. Our part-Indian guide had cleared the path to the lake the day before; when we walked the path we saw where he had impaled the lopped head of a boa, open-mouthed, on a pointed stick by the canoes, for decoration.

The lake and river waters are as opaque as rain-forest leaves; they are veils,   16
blinds, painted screens. You see things only by their effects. I saw the shoreline water roil and the sawgrass heave above a thrashing *paichi,* an enormous black fish of these waters; one had been caught the previous week weighing 430 pounds. Piranha fish live in the lakes, and electric eels. I dangled my fingers in the water, figuring it would be worth it.

We would eat chicken that night in the village, and rice, yucca, onions, beets   17
and heaps of fruit. The sun would ring down, pulling darkness after it like a curtain. Twilight is short, and the unseen birds of twilight wistful, uncanny, catching the heart. The two nuns in their dazzling white habits—the beautiful-boned young nun and the warm-faced old—would glide to the open cane-and-thatch schoolroom in darkness, and start the children singing. The children would sing in piping Spanish, high-pitched and pure; they would sing ''Nearer My God to Thee'' in Quechua, very fast. (To reciprocate, we sang for them ''Old

MacDonald Had a Farm''; I thought they might recognize the animal sounds. Of course they thought we were out of our minds.) As the children became excited by their own singing, they left their log benches and swarmed around the nuns, hopping, smiling at us, everyone smiling, the nuns' faces bursting in their cowls, and the clear-voiced children still singing, and the palm-leafed roofing stirred.

The Napo River: it is not out of the way. It is in the way, catching sunlight 18 the way a cup catches poured water; it is a bowl of sweet air, a basin of greenness, and of grace, and, it would seem, of peace.

Questions for Discussion

1. Dillard mentions some terms that may be unfamiliar to you. From the way she uses them, take a guess at the meaning of ''egrets,'' ''anacondas,'' ''manatees,'' ''troupials,'' ''tanagers,'' and ''machete.''
2. The author says little about how the Indians looked, but she does explain what they did. In what paragraphs does she tell us about the natives of Pompeya, and what do these anecdotes reveal about them?
3. Why does Dillard bother to mention in paragraph 12 that ''the Indians get up at three in the morning'' to bathe in the river? Does this help her describe the jungle?
4. Besides the Indians, what inhabitants of the village does Dillard mention? What is her opinion of these other people?
5. Which paragraph in this selection do you find most descriptive? Identify nouns, adjectives, and figures of speech that make it work so well.
6. Where in the essay does Dillard use proper nouns? Pick out a few examples of such words and explain why their inclusion makes ''In the Jungle'' more effective.
7. As noted earlier, Dillard makes excellent use of descriptive verbs in paragraph 3. Where else do you find such verbs?
8. Overall, the author sees the jungle as a very beautiful and pleasant place, but she also includes details that might lead us to the opposite conclusion. Identify such details, and explain what they reveal.
9. Dillard begins with a question. Where does she answer this question? What is her central idea?

Suggestions for Journal Entries

1. Think of a natural setting (for example, a park, forest, garden, seashore) that you visited recently, and list its most pleasant (or unpleasant) aspects. Then, in one or two sentences, sum up your overall reaction to (or impression of) the place.
2. Dillard isn't very specific about what the Indians of Pompeya look like, but she gives us enough details to infer certain things about them. Given the

climate, for instance, they probably wear little clothing. Try to describe what these people look like from what the author tells us about them. If you run into trouble, use your imagination and make up details that you think might apply.

Dawn Watch

JOHN CIARDI

A splendid poet, critic, scholar, and translator of Dante's Divine Comedy, *John Ciardi (1916–1986) was one of the warmest and most personable of all contemporary American writers. Ciardi's subjects are taken from everyday life, and his works, like their author, are down-to-earth and easy to approach. His poems and essays are rich with the kinds of detail we see around us all the time, but they give us a clearer, deeper, and more beautiful vision of the world than we had before we read them.*

"Dawn Watch" is a richly detailed account of one of the most common events we know: sunrise.

Looking Ahead

1. One reason Ciardi finds dawn special is that certain sights and sounds can be experienced only at this time of day. One of these is mentioned in paragraph 2. Find others.
2. Like Dillard and Le Guin, Ciardi uses narration. He tells us what happens in his yard at dawn. Doing so helps him capture the special quality of this part of the day.
3. Ciardi's thesis appears at the very beginning: "Unless a man is up for the dawn and for the half hour or so of first light, he has missed the best of the day." As you read "Dawn Watch," notice how almost every detail helps prove this statement.

Vocabulary

bedraggled   Limp, tired.
braggarts   People who enjoy boasting about themselves.
exhalation   Breath, vapor, exhaling.
foliage   Leaves of a plant.
grackles   Kind of blackbird.
inured   Hardened.
pincer   Pinch.
thickets   Thick bushes or shrubs.

wire services Organizations that provide world and national news to newspapers and broadcasting stations.

Unless a man is up for the dawn and for the half hour or so of first light, he   1
has missed the best of the day.

The traffic has just started, not yet a roar and a stink. One car at a time goes   2
by, the tires humming almost like the sound of a brook a half mile down in the
crease of a mountain I know—a sound that carries not because it is loud but
because everything else is still.

It isn't exactly a mist that hangs in the thickets but more nearly the ghost of   3
a mist—a phenomenon like side vision. Look hard and it isn't there, but glance
without focusing and something registers, an exhalation that will be gone three
minutes after the sun comes over the treetops.

The lawns shine with a dew not exactly dew. There is a rabbit bobbing about   4
on the lawn and then freezing. If it were truly a dew, his tracks would shine black
on the grass, and he leaves no visible track. Yet, there is something on the grass
that makes it glow a depth of green it will not show again all day. Or is that
something in the dawn air?

Our cardinals know what time it is. They drop pure tones from the hemlock   5
tops. The black gang of grackles that makes a slum of the pine oak also knows
the time but can only grate at it. They sound like a convention of broken
universal joints grating uphill. The grackles creak and squeak, and the cardinals
form tones that only occasionally sound through the noise. I scatter sunflower
seeds by the birdbath for the cardinals and hope the grackles won't find them.

My neighbor's tomcat comes across the lawn, probably on his way home   6
from passion, or only acting as if he had had a big night. I suspect him of being
one of those poolroom braggarts who can't get next to a girl but who likes to let
on that he is a hot stud. This one is too can-fed and too lazy to hunt for anything.
Here he comes now, ignoring the rabbit. And there he goes.

As soon as he has hopped the fence, I let my dog out. The dog charges the   7
rabbit, watches it jump the fence, shakes himself in a self-satisfied way, then
trots dutifully into the thicket for his morning service, stopping to sniff everything on the way back.

There is an old mountain laurel on the island of the driveway turn-around.   8
From somewhere on the wind a white morning-glory rooted next to it and has
climbed it. Now the laurel is woven full of white bells tinged pink by the first
rays through the not quite mist. Only in earliest morning can they be seen. Come
out two hours from now and there will be no morning-glories.

Dawn, too, is the hour of a weed I know only as a day flower—a bright blue   9
button that closes in full sunlight. I have weeded bales of it out of my flower
beds, its one daytime virtue being the shallowness of its root system that allows
it to be pulled out effortlessly in great handfuls. Yet, now it shines. Had it a few
more hours of such shining in its cycle, I would cultivate it as a ground cover,
but dawn is its one hour, and a garden is for whole days.

There is another blue morning weed whose name I do not know. This one   10
grows from a bulb to pulpy stems and a bedraggled daytime sprawl. Only a
shovel will dig it out. Try weeding it by hand and the stems will break off to be
replaced by new ones and to sprawl over the chosen plants in the flower bed. Yet,
now and for another hour it outshines its betters, its flowers about the size of a
quarter and paler than those of the day flower but somehow more brilliant,
perhaps because of the contrast of its paler foliage.

And now the sun is slanting in full. It is bright enough to make the leaves   11
of the Japanese red maple seem a transparent red bronze when the tree is between
me and the light. There must be others, but this is the only tree I know whose
leaves let the sun through in this way—except, that is, when the fall colors start.
Aspen leaves, when they first yellow and before they dry, are transparent in this
way. I tell myself it must have something to do with the red-yellow range of the
spectrum. Green takes sunlight and holds it, but red and yellow let it through.

The damned crabgrass is wrestling with the zinnias, and I stop to weed it out.   12
The stuff weaves too close to the zinnias to make the iron claw usable. And it
won't do to pull at the stalks. Crabgrass (at least in a mulched bed) can be
weeded only with dirty fingers. Thumb and forefinger have to pincer into the dirt
and grab the root-center. Weeding, of course, is an illusion of hope. Pulling out
the root only stirs the soil and brings new crabgrass seeds into germinating
position. Take a walk around the block and a new clump will have sprouted by
the time you get back. But I am not ready to walk around the block. I fill a small
basket with the plucked clumps, and for the instant I look at them, the zinnias
are weedless.

Don't look back. I dump the weeds in the thicket where they will be   13
smothered by the grass clippings I will pile on at the next cutting. On the way
back I see the cardinals come down for the sunflower seeds, and the jays join
them, and then the grackles start ganging in, gate-crashing the buffet and clatter-
ing all over it. The dog stops chewing his rawhide and makes a dash into the
puddle of birds, which splashes away from him.

I hear a brake-squeak I have been waiting for and know the paper has   14
arrived. As usual, the news turns out to be another disaster count. The function
of the wire services is to bring us tragedies faster than we can pity. In the end
we shall all be inured, numb, and ready for emotionless programming. I sit on
the patio and read until the sun grows too bright on the page. The cardinals have
stopped singing, and the grackles have flown off. It's the end of birdsong again.

Then suddenly—better than song for its instant—a hummingbird the color   15
of green crushed velvet hovers in the throat of my favorite lily, a lovely high-
bloomer I got the bulbs for but not the name. The lily is a crest of white horns
with red dots and red velvet tongues along the insides of the petals and with an
odor that drowns the patio. The hummingbird darts in and out of each horn in
turn, then hovers an instant, and disappears.

Even without the sun, I have had enough of the paper. I'll take that hum-   16
mingbird as my news for this dawn. It is over now. I smoke one more cigarette
too many and decide that, if I go to bed now, no one in the family need know

I have stayed up for it again. Why do they insist on shaking their heads when they find me still up for breakfast, after having scribbled through the dark hours? They always do. They seem compelled to express pity for an old loony who can't find his own way to bed. Why won't they understand that this is the one hour of any day that must not be missed, as it is the one hour I couldn't imagine getting up for, though I can still get to it by staying up? It makes sense to me. There comes a time when the windows lighten and the twittering starts. I look up and know it's time to leave the papers in their mess. I could slip quietly into bed and avoid the family's headshakes, but this stroll-around first hour is too good to miss. Even my dog, still sniffing and circling, knows what hour this is.

Come on, boy. It's time to go in. The rabbit won't come back till tomorrow, 17 and the birds have work to do. The dawn's over. It's time to call it a day.

Questions for Discussion

1. Ciardi makes it a point to record the sounds as well as the sights of dawn. What are some of these sounds?
2. What does Ciardi mean by ''There is a rabbit bobbing about on the lawn and then *freezing*''?
3. ''Weeding . . . is an illusion of hope,'' the author tells us. What details does he use to explain this remark?
4. Ciardi is a master at using nouns and adjectives that are concrete and specific. Which paragraph(s) in this essay contain(s) the most descriptive details?
5. In paragraph 15, we are treated to a brilliant snapshot: ''better than song for its instant—a hummingbird the color of green crushed velvet hovers in the throat of my favorite lily.'' Analyze this image; explain what makes it so effective.
6. Find a paragraph—other than 15—in which Ciardi's language is especially effective in revealing his feelings about the place or creatures he describes.
7. What is his family's attitude toward his staying up to meet the dawn? Explain what he means when he suggests that he and his dog ''call it a day.''

Suggestions for Journal Entries

1. Describe the sounds of morning, afternoon, or evening in a park, on campus, in your backyard, in your kitchen, or anywhere else you choose. Focus on three or four of the sounds you like best and recreate them for your reader. In doing so, you might want to use figures of speech—metaphors and similes. An excellent example of a simile can be found in paragraph 5, where the grackles ''sound like a convention of broken universal joints grating uphill.''
2. What is the best part of the day for you—dawn, sundown, late afternoon? Like Ciardi, describe the things that make it special by recalling what this time is like at a place you enjoy: the seashore, a mountain lake, or even your

own backyard, for example. Then, write a paragraph that shows why you think this is your favorite time.

A Deathly Call of the Wild

MARY ANN GWINN

Mary Ann Gwinn was among several reporters at the Seattle Times *who wrote about the effects of the Exxon Valdez oil spill on Prince William Sound in 1989. Their stories were so penetrating that they won a Pulitzer Prize in journalism.*

Gwinn's article shows that, in the right hands, description has uses beyond pure observation. In some ways, "A Deathly Call of the Wild" is the kind of writing scientists do: it explains a serious problem by carefully recording the effects of that problem. At the same time, Gwinn uses what she saw to persuade us that we have a lot to learn from nature. However we look at it, she proves that description is a powerful tool for many purposes.

Looking Ahead

1. "A Deathly Call of the Wild" is an example of narration and description working together. Gwinn tells us what she observed on a trip to Prince William Sound. An expert reporter, she also includes a great many direct quotes from people she spoke with. You will learn more about using quoted material and other narrative techniques in Section Four.

2. Although writing straight news stories demands objectivity, journalists are permitted a more subjective approach in columns, human-interest stories, or feature articles like this one.

Vocabulary

cause célèbre   Important cause or issue.
compelling   Urgent, demanding.
compulsively   Involuntarily, as if being forced or compelled.
havoc   Ruin, destruction.
intermittently   Now and again.
lacerated   Cut, torn, scraped.
mournful   Sad, heartbreaking.
plumage   Feathers.
provoke   Cause, bring about, induce.
pruned   Trimmed, clipped.

rationality   Reason, intelligence.

sinuous   Curved.

vain   Useless, futile.

vengeance   Revenge.

wreaked   Caused.

V ALDEZ, Alaska—I had tried to prepare myself for Green Island, but nothing   1
can prepare you for the havoc wreaked on the creatures of Prince William Sound.

From the helicopter that took me there, the 987-foot tanker Exxon Valdez,   2
stuck like a toy boat on Bligh Reef, was dwarfed by the immensity of the sound.
It was hard to believe that we could fly 60 miles, land and walk right into the
ruination of a landscape, so far from that broken boat.

The helicopter landed on the beach of Green Island. Its beaches are broad   3
and slope gently, in contrast to the rocky, vertical shores of many of the other
islands in the sound. For that reason, Green Island is favored by wildlife. Now
the oil has turned the gentle beach into a death trap.

No sooner had the Alaska National Guard helicopter roared away than a   4
black lump detached itself from three or four others bobbing in the oil-streaked
water. It was an old squaw, a sea bird normally recognizable by its stark
black-and-white plumage. The tuxedo plumage had turned a muddy brown and
orange.

It staggered up the beach, its head compulsively jerking back and forth, as   5
if trying to escape the thing that was strangling it. Tony Dawson, a photographer
for Audubon magazine, and I watched it climb a snowbank and flap into the still
center of the woods. ''They move up into the grass, along the creek beds and into
the woods, where they die,'' Dawson said. ''It's like they're fleeing an invisible
enemy.''

Dawson used to be a veterinarian. He said documenting the oil spill makes   6
him feel like a photographer in Vietnam: ''Every day, a new body count.'' As
in that war, helicopters drone across the sky, boats beach on shore, men land, size
up the situation and depart.

Eleven days into the spill, scientists are trying to decide which beaches to   7
clean and which to leave alone, reasoning that disruption would hurt some more
than it would help. Very little actual beach cleanup is taking place. Most of the
animals are going to die, a few dozen or hundred every day, by degrees.

I walked along the beach, which in some places was glutted with oil like   8
brown pudding; in others, streaked and puddled with oil the consistency of
chocolate syrup. The only sounds came from a few gulls and the old squaw's
mate, which drifted down the polluted channel toward its fate. Far away, a
cormorant spread its wings and stretched in a vain attempt to fluff its oil-soaked
feathers. A bald eagle passed overhead.

It was then that I heard a sound so strange, for a brief moment all my 20th   9
century rationality dropped away.

Something was crying in the vicinity of the woods, a sound not quite human.   10
I looked into the trees.

Whooooooh. Whooooh. Whoooh. Up and down a mournful scale. Some-   11
thing is coming out of those woods, I thought, and is going to take vengeance
for this horror on the first human being it sees.

Then I saw a movement in the grass at the end of the beach. It was a loon.   12

Loons have become something of a cause célèbre to bird lovers. They are   13
beautiful birds, almost as large as geese, with long, sharp beaks, striking black-
and-white striped wings and a graceful, streamlined head. They are a threatened
species in the United States because they need large bodies of water to fish in
and undeveloped, marshy shorelines to nest on, and most shoreline in this
country has been landscaped and pruned.

The most compelling thing about the loon is its call—something between a   14
cry, a whistle and a sob, a sound so mournful and chilling it provoked the word
"loony," a term for someone wild with sorrow, out of their head.

This was an artic loon in its winter plumage, brown instead of the striking   15
black and white of summer. It had ruby-red eyes, which blinked in terror because
it could barely move. It was lightly oiled all over—breast, feet, wings, head—
destroying its power of flight. Its sinuous head darted here and there as we
approached. It flapped and stumbled trying to avoid us, and then it came to rest
between two large rocks.

As Dawson photographed it, it intermittently called its mournful call. Its   16
mate swam back and forth, calling back, a few yards offshore.

I could see it tremble, a sign that the bird was freezing. Most oiled birds die   17
because the oil destroys their insulation.

"It's like someone with a down coat falling into a lake," Dawson explained.   18
The breeze ruffled its stiffening feathers. As Dawson moved closer with the
camera, it uttered a low quivering cry.

After 10 minutes or so, I just couldn't watch anymore. It was so beautiful,   19
and so helpless and so doomed. We had nothing like a bag, sack or cloth to hold
it in. I walked around the point.

Then I heard Dawson calling. He walked into view holding the furious,   20
flapping loon by its upper wings, set it down on the grass and said, "Come here
and help me. He won't hurt you."

I was stunned by the rough handling of such a wild thing, but it developed   21
that Dawson, the former veterinarian, knew his birds. He had grasped the loon
exactly in the place where his wings would not break. He would tell me later that
most bird rescuers are too tender-hearted or frightened of birds to contain them,
and let a lot of salvageable birds get away.

We had to wait for the helicopter, and Dawson had to take more pictures,   22
so I grasped the loon behind the upper wings, pinning them together, and took
up the loon watch. The bird rose, struggled and fell back to earth, then was still.

I was as afraid of the loon as it was of me in a way that touching a totally   23
wild thing can provoke. But I began to feel its strength. It was warm, it had

energy, and it could still struggle. I could hear it breathing, and could feel its pulse. It turned its red eye steadily on me. We breathed, and waited, together.

Dawson returned, took a black cord from a lens case and neatly looped it 24 around the bird's wings. The helicopter dropped out of the sky and settled on the beach. I held the string as the loon, unblinking, faced the terrific wind kicked up by the machine. Then Dawson neatly scooped up the bird and settled into the helicopter. The loon lashed out with its needle beak until David Grimes, a fisherman working with the state on the spill, enveloped it in a wool knit bag he carried with him. The bird stilled.

Dawson and I were both streaked with oil and blood from the loon's feet, 25 lacerated by barnacles on the beach. He gave me a small black and white feather that had fallen from the bird's wing.

We took the loon to the bird-rescue center in Valdez. I don't know if it will 26 live. Dawson thought it had a good chance. I thought of the mate we had left behind in the water.

Afterward, we talked about whom bird rescues help more, the rescued or the 27 rescuer. Most rescued birds don't make it. And tens of thousands more from the Valdez spill will die before they even get a chance.

I know only that the loon told me something that no one other thing about 28 this tragedy could. If only we could learn to value such stubborn, determined life. If only we could hold safe in our hands the heart of the loon.

Questions for Discussion

1. What makes Gwinn's description of the loon's call disturbing? Why does she say it is ''not quite human'' (paragraph 10)? Why does she bother to define the word ''loony'' (paragraph 14)?

2. What is it about the loon's appearance that makes its cry even more ''mournful''?

3. To which sense besides sight and hearing does Gwinn appeal?

4. Identify effective verbs she uses to reveal the tragedy in Prince William Sound. Why does she explain how she and her companion reacted; why doesn't she simply focus on the birds?

5. What examples of analogy do you find? How about comparison or contrast?

6. If the article is about the loon, why does Gwinn talk about the ''old squaw,'' the cormorant, and other birds?

7. What is she getting at when she wonders ''whom bird rescues help more, the rescued or the rescuer'' (paragraph 27)?

8. Does the image in paragraph 23 prepare us for the conclusion of this essay? In what way?

9. The loon has told the author ''something that no one other thing about this tragedy could'' (paragraph 28). What has she learned from the bird?

Suggestions for Journal Entries

1. We don't need to fly to Prince William Sound to see pollution, nor can we say that protecting nature is the responsibility of big oil companies alone. Focus on a natural scene near your home or campus—a hillside, forest, lake, park, seashore—whose beauty is diminished because of what careless individuals have done. Are there beer bottles, paper bags, and cigarette wrappers around? Have people carved their initials in trees or spray-painted large rocks? Does the water contain old tires or other junk instead of fish, birds, and other wildlife? Can you hear car horns and loud radios? Brainstorm about this place, if possible with someone else who has been there. Gather details that show the effects of human irresponsibility on the environment you are describing.

2. Have you ever had to help an animal in trouble? Think about a lost dog or cat, an injured bird, or even a larger animal like a cow, sheep, or horse that needed assistance. Use listing or focused freewriting to gather details that (1) describe the animal; (2) explain where, when, and how you tried to help it; and (3) reveal how both you and it reacted to the problem. For inspiration, reread some of the more moving paragraphs in Gwinn's article, especially paragraph 23.

3. The essay's title is particularly effective. Think back to a time when you found yourself in a wilderness: a forest, mountain range, desert, large state or national park. How did you react to what you saw, heard, felt, and so on? What word best describes your reaction to being there: "excitement," "uneasiness," "fear," "terror," "contentment," "peacefulness," "happiness," "boredom," "discomfort"? Use any method for gathering information discussed in "Getting Started" to begin describing this "wild" place and to explain how you felt about being there.

SUGGESTIONS FOR WRITING

1. After reading Tennyson's "The Eagle" you might have gathered information in your journal on a particular characteristic of an animal or type of animal about which you have strong feelings (positive or negative). Continue discussing the animal in an essay. Describe its appearance, but concentrate on the one characteristic that comes to mind whenever you think of this creature: for example, its loyalty, intelligence, stupidity, gracefulness, clumsiness, bravery, timidity, or friendliness.

   Begin with a preliminary thesis statement that explains both how you feel about your subject and why you feel that way. Here's an example: "I've always loved cats because of their intelligence." Develop your essay by discussing your own cat or other cats you know well or have observed; include details that show how *intelligent* they are!

   After writing a first draft, decide whether you have included enough information to support your thesis. If not, describe the animal's movements or behavior to give readers a better picture of the particular characteristic you are discussing. As you continue revising, add details that appeal to the senses or create figures of speech that will make your writing vivid and concrete. Then, review your best draft. Correct distracting errors and make certain it is easy to read.

2. Ursula Le Guin describes Omelas by telling us what happens in that city during the Festival of Summer. Write a letter inviting out-of-town friends to a fair, festival, parade, carnival, picnic, or other celebration in your town or school. Persuade them to visit by mentioning the exciting sights, sounds, smells, tastes of the affair. But don't forget to enrich your description with action; describe events they might want to watch or take part in. If you are writing about a Fourth of July celebration, for example, recall the fun of a softball game at last year's picnic or describe the fireworks that ended the day.

   Begin this assignment by looking over the journal notes you made after reading Le Guin's paragraph. You might be able to use this information in your first draft. To make your writing vivid and convincing, add details and figures of speech as you develop ideas from one draft to the next. When deciding how to open or close your letter, consider methods for writing introductions or conclusions discussed in Chapter 4.

   In any case, edit your letter well. If you respect your friends, you will send them something that is clear, correct, and easy to read.

3. Highet describes a subway station both objectively and subjectively. Think of a public place you visit often, such as a bus or train station, the post office, your church or temple, a ball park, a movie theater, a gymnasium, or a shopping mall. Perhaps you have collected information about this place in your journal. Now, write an essay that describes it fully and explains how you feel about it.

   In your first draft, use details that will give readers an objective picture of your subject: talk about its size and shape, the colors of the walls, the furniture it contains, the people who frequent it. In your next draft(s), add other information about what it looks, sounds, smells, and, if possible, feels like. As you do this, begin revealing your subjective reactions. Like Highet, use concrete details, vivid verbs, adjectives and adverbs, and figures of speech to let readers know whether you enjoy the place, find it attractive, and like the people you meet there—or whether the opposite is true.

After completing your second or third draft, write a thesis statement expressing your overall opinion. Put that thesis into an introductory paragraph that captures the readers' attention. Close your essay with a memorable statement or with a summary of the reasons you are or are not looking forward to visiting this place again. Finally, edit your work by checking grammar, spelling, word choice, and other important considerations.

4. Ciardi's essay is unique among those in this chapter; it describes a time as well as a place or object. In response to item 2 of Suggestions for Journal Entries following ''Dawn Watch,'' you may have begun describing a place during your favorite time of day. Add to this short paragraph in your journal by recording more information that appeals to the senses. Focus on a short period in a particular place, say the two or three hours after dawn or before sunset at a lake. Then, use these details in an essay that explains why you enjoy this time and place.

If this assignment doesn't interest you, write about a place at a time of day or night when you don't want to be there. Start by gathering details in your journal or on scrap paper about what you dislike or fear most about this place and time. Rely on your senses as you do this. Once you think you have enough information, develop your notes into a descriptive essay.

With either assignment, explain how being in a place at a particular time affects you. Do you find it exciting, tiring, soothing, nerve-wracking, invigorating? To get your point across, try to include sounds in your writing. Paragraphs 2 and 5 in Ciardi's essay contain good examples of language that appeals to hearing. You can find other passages that describe sound in the selections by Le Guin, Dillard (paragraphs 4 and 17), and Gwinn (paragraphs 10, 11, and 14).

As always, complete the process of writing carefully; rewrite and revise your work as many times as necessary to make it clear, well developed, and polished.

5. The three journal suggestions following Gwinn's ''A Deathly Call of the Wild'' provide good starts for longer assignments.

If you responded to item 1, turn your notes into an essay about the effects of pollution on a natural setting you know well. Explain how civilization has marred or destroyed its beauty, and don't be afraid to give your subjective reaction to what you see, hear, and so on. A good way to begin is to use a startling remark or to contrast what *is* with what *should be*. A good way to conclude is to make a call to action.

If you responded to item 2 in the Suggestions for Journal Entries after Gwinn's essay, use this information to write about an incident in which you had to help an animal in trouble. Explain what happened, describing the animal and the scene vividly and concretely. Like Gwinn, however, focus on one thing: what you learned about the animal, about yourself, *or* about your relationship with nature. In fact, summarize what the experience taught you in your thesis statement.

If you responded to suggestion 3, continue the description of a "wild" place by explaining how you reacted to being there. Again, express the central idea that all of your essay's details will support in a thesis statement. In other words, use your thesis to tell readers how you felt about the experience. Then, in the rest of the essay, include information about the place that will show why you felt that way.

Good luck. Any of these suggestions can lead to an exciting essay. Whichever one you choose, follow a careful process of revising and editing to produce a paper that is well developed, vivid, and free of errors.

6. Annie Dillard, John Ciardi, and Mary Ann Gwinn draw inspiration from nature. Review the journal notes you made after reading their essays. You have probably put down details and ideas that you can use in a paper describing an outdoor setting like a beach, park, garden or backyard, wood, desert, mountainside, or jungle. Add to these notes by doing more prewriting in your journal. Then turn them into an essay that explains your subjective reaction to the place.

Begin by writing a preliminary thesis statement that sums up that reaction clearly. Here are two examples:

I never felt more frightened than when I camped overnight at Willow Creek. What we saw and heard while hiking in the Cascade Mountains showed us how exciting nature can be.

In the body of your essay, use techniques you learned in this chapter to describe the place and to reveal your reaction to it. But remember to focus on the main point in your thesis. If you want to show how *frightened* you were, describe sights, sounds, and the like; tell of events; and create figures of speech that express your fear. Don't include details about how expensive your trip was or how much fun you had swimming in a cold stream on a hot afternoon.

After completing your first draft, revise the thesis if necessary. Next, write an introduction—if you haven't done so already—in which to place the thesis. Then, decide on a conclusion.

Again, remember that writing is a process. Don't hand in a final version until you have completed several drafts, each one building on, adding to, and refining the one that came before.

CHAPTER 9

DESCRIBING PEOPLE

In Chapter 8, you learned that writers often go beyond physical appearance when describing a place or thing; they reveal its character as well. This is even more true when people are the subjects of description. Writers describe gardens at dawn, summer festivals, or dirty subway stations because they are impressed by what that they see, hear, and so on. More often than not, they describe human beings because they are fascinated by their personalities, values, and motivations as well as by their looks and the sounds of their voices. Of course, many writers start by describing physical appearance—what's on the outside. But they often end up talking about their subjects' characters—what's on the inside.

All the authors represented in this chapter use concrete and specific details (nouns and adjectives) to describe the physical characteristics of their subjects. This is always a good way to begin. You can start off by explaining something about your subjects' physical appearance, the clothes they wear, the sound of their voices, the language they use, or simply the way they walk. Such description might also help you introduce your subjects' personalities to your readers, for someone's physical appearance can reveal a great deal about what he or she is like inside.

You can also communicate a great deal about the people you're describing by telling your reader what you've heard about them from others and even what you've heard them say about themselves; such information is usually conveyed through dialogue (quoted material). Recalling anecdotes about your subjects is still another good way to convey important information about them. Finally, some authors comment directly on their subjects' personalities or use figurative language to make their descriptions more lively and appealing. Remember such techniques when you gather and communicate important information about your subjects.

DESCRIBING YOUR SUBJECT'S APPEARANCE AND SPEECH

Physical appearance can show a great deal about a person's character, and writers don't hesitate to use outward details as signs or symbols of what's inside. For instance, how often have you heard people mention deep-set, shifty eyes or a sinister smile when describing a villain? Aren't heavy people often described as jolly? And often, aren't the clothes people wear or the way they comb their hair seen (fairly or unfairly) as a sign of their character?

Carl Sandburg uses physical appearance to reveal the complexity and depth of Abraham Lincoln's character. Here's just one example you will find when you read Sandburg's portrait of the sixteenth President later in this chapter:

> In his eyes as nowhere else was registered the shifting light of his moods; their language ran from rapid twinkles of darting hazel that won the hearts of children on to a fixed baffling gray that the shrewdest lawyers and politicians could not read, to find there an intention he wanted to hide.

As you will see later, Sandburg does a good job of describing Lincoln's face and body, and he even talks about the kind of clothes he wore and the way he combed his hair. But he doesn't limit himself to the President's looks. He also recreates the sound of his voice. To show that Lincoln was a man of the frontier, for example, Sandburg tells us that he pronounced the word "idea" more like "idee."

Another good way to provide insight into someone's personality is to recall what he or she says. In "Mothers and Fathers," for example, Phyllis Rose quotes her mother directly to show that, despite losing her husband and nearly all her eyesight, this woman retains her spunk and sense of humor. For example, when the author praises her mother on being able to apply lipstick perfectly despite her poor vision, the seventy-five-year-old "beauty" replies: "By now I should know where my mouth is." You will find that several other selections in this chapter use the words of people they describe to reveal important aspects of their personalities. In "Obāchan," Gail Y. Miyasaki even includes a few Japanese and Hawaiian words to give us a more realistic and touching picture of her Japanese-born grandmother.

REVEALING WHAT YOU KNOW ABOUT YOUR SUBJECT

You have learned that narrating events helps capture the character or atmosphere of a place you are describing. Similarly, you can reveal a lot about someone by discussing his or her actions or behavior. One of the best ways to do this is by telling anecdotes, brief stories that highlight or illustrate an important aspect of your subject's personality. For example, Sandburg demonstrates Lincoln's sensitivity and "natural grace" through a story about his open expression of grief at a friend's funeral. Anecdotes like this help us understand how someone reacts to various people, problems, and situations. They say a lot about a person's attitude toward life.

Another good way to reveal character is to tell readers important facts about your subject's life, home, or family. In "Two Gentlemen of the Pines," for example, we learn that Bill's parents abandoned him as a child and that, except for some help from neighbors, he survived alone. This information goes a long way toward accounting for his shyness. In the same selection, we are treated to a good look at the house and yard of Fred Brown, a picture that gives us a more complete understanding of the old man's character than simply learning what he looks or talks like.

REVEALING WHAT OTHERS SAY ABOUT YOUR SUBJECT

One of the quickest ways to learn about someone is to ask people who know this individual to tell you about his or her personality, lifestyle, morals, disposition, and so on. Often, authors use dialogue or quotes from other people to reveal something important about their subject's character. In ''Crazy Mary,'' student Sharon Robertson combines physical description (concrete details) with information she learned from other people (dialogue) to create a memorable and disturbing portrait of an unfortunate woman she once knew:

> She was a middle-aged woman, short and slightly heavy, with jet-black hair and solemn blue eyes that were bloodshot and glassy. She always looked distant, as if her mind were in another place and time, and her face lonely and sad. We called her ''Crazy Mary.''
>
> Mary came to the diner that I worked in twice a week. She would sit at the counter with a scowl on her face and drink her coffee and smoke cigarettes. The only time she looked happy was when an old song would come on the radio. Then Mary would close her eyes, shine a big tobacco-stained smile, and sway back and forth to the music.
>
> One day an elderly couple came in for dinner. They were watching Mary over their menus and whispering. I went over to their table and asked if they knew who she was. The old man replied, ''Aw, dat's just old Mary. She's loonier than a June bug, but she ain't nutten to be afraid of. A few years back, her house caught fire and her old man and her kids got kilt. She ain't been right since.''
>
> After hearing this, it was easy to understand her odd behavior.

Other people can make good sources of information. We know from experience, however, that what others say about a person is often inaccurate. Sometimes, in fact, different people express very different—even contradictory—opinions about the same person. Consider two selections in this chapter. At the end of Edwin Arlington Robinson's poem ''Richard Cory,'' we learn that Cory was certainly not as happy as the townspeople believed, a fact that is important to understanding his character and theirs. And in ''Abraham Lincoln,'' Carl Sandburg tells us that some folks saw Lincoln as a cold and crafty politician, others as a ''sad, odd, awkward man,'' and still others as a ''superb human struggler.''

Enjoy the selections that follow. Each contains examples of the practices discussed above, and each provides additional hints to help you make your writing stronger and more interesting.

Richard Cory

EDWIN ARLINGTON ROBINSON

Born in Gardiner, Maine, Edwin Arlington Robinson (1869–1935) wrote a number of poems that are psychological portraits of people who in some respects resemble characters found in a typical New England, if not typical American, town of his time. Many of his works reveal a pessimistic outlook on life, the result of a troubled family environment.

In 1922 his Collected Poems *won him a Pulitzer Prize, but it is for his earlier work, like "Richard Cory," that Robinson has remained popular. In this poem he created one of the saddest and most memorable characters in literature. The same is true of "Miniver Cheevy," a companion piece with a similar theme. Both poems first appeared in a collection called* Children of the Night *(1897).*

Looking Ahead

Robinson makes sure to draw a distinction between Richard Cory and everyone else in town. Look for this distinction as you read the poem.

Vocabulary

arrayed   Adorned, dressed elegantly.
fluttered   Ruffled.
grace   Pleasing quality, charm, refinement.

> Whenever Richard Cory went down town,
> We people on the pavement looked at him:
> He was a gentleman from sole to crown,
> Clean favored, and imperially slim.
>
> And he was always quietly arrayed,   5
> And he was always human when he talked;
> But still he fluttered pulses when he said,
> "Good-morning," and he glittered when he walked.
>
> And he was rich—yes, richer than a king—
> And admirably schooled in every grace: 10
> In fine, we thought that he was everything
> To make us wish that we were in his place.
>
> So on we worked, and waited for the light,
> And went without the meat, and cursed the bread;
> And Richard Cory, one calm summer night,   15
> Went home and put a bullet through his head.

Questions for Discussion

1. The details used to describe Richard Cory have been chosen carefully. What do words like "crown," "imperially," "arrayed," "glittered," and "grace" tell us about him?

2. What do the townspeople think of Cory? Why do their pulses flutter every time they see him? What do we learn about the townspeople in lines 13 and 14?

3. The townspeople were obviously wrong about Cory. He wasn't "everything/ To make us wish that we were in his place." What was he missing?

4. We can learn a lot about someone from his or her behavior. What do Richard Cory's actions tell us about his personality?

5. One of the themes (or main ideas) in this poem is that appearances are deceiving. How does Robinson make this clear?

Suggestions for Journal Entries

1. Robinson doesn't give us a great deal of detail about Cory's physical appearance, except to say that he was well-dressed and thin. Using your imagination, make up some details that describe how you think Cory looked.

2. Have you ever met anyone you'd consider a tragic figure? Describe this person briefly, and explain why you find the person tragic.

From "Mothers and Fathers"

PHYLLIS ROSE

A biographer, literary critic, and essayist, Phyllis Rose is the author of a life of British novelist Virginia Woolf. She has also published in Vogue, The Atlantic, *and* The Washington Post. *The two paragraphs that make up this selection are taken from an essay Rose wrote for "Hers," a regular column of* The New York Times Magazine.

Looking Ahead

1. Like "Richard Cory," this selection focuses on the subject's personality, not on her appearance. Find techniques for revealing character discussed in the introduction to this chapter as you read Rose's description of her mother.

2. In paragraph 1, the author tells us her mother used the Latin saying "De gustibus non disputandum est." Translated literally, this means that taste is not something to be argued about.

Vocabulary

enhancer   Something that increases, improves, or intensifies something else.

glaucoma   Eye disease that can result in blindness.

My mother has always said: "The daughters come back to you eventually. 1 When the sons go they're gone." She has other favorite sayings—"A father's not a mother," "The beginning is the half of all things," and "De gustibus non disputandum est," which she translated as "That's what makes horse races"— all of which have become increasingly meaningful to me with time. Recently I told her that she was right in a fight we had twenty-seven years ago about which language I should study in high school. This came up because I had just had the same discussion with my son and took the side my mother took then (French). She laughed when I told her that she was right twenty-seven years ago. There have been more and more nice moments like that with my mother as we both grow older.

She is seventy-five, ash blond, blue-eyed, a beauty. When my father died 2 three years ago she suddenly developed glaucoma and lost a lot of her vision. She says she literally "cried her eyes out." She can read only very slowly, with the help of a video enhancer supplied by the Lighthouse for the Blind. Nevertheless, her lipstick is always perfect. She doesn't use a mirror. She raises her hand to her lips and applies it. When I praise her for this, she says, "By now I should know where my mouth is."

Questions for Discussion

1. Other than quoting the subject directly, what technique for revealing character do you see here?

2. These two paragraphs are short; nonetheless Rose tells us a great deal about her subject. What kind of person is her mother? Identify two or three of her personality traits.

3. Why is quoting what Rose's mother says about daughters a good way to begin?

4. The author explains that her mother's sayings "have become increasingly meaningful to [her] with time." What does this tell us about their relationship?

Suggestions for Journal Entries

1. Rose obviously loves and honors her mother for a variety of reasons. Use focused freewriting to write a paragraph or two about a parent, a grandparent, or other older relative whom you love and honor. For now, describe this person by focusing on the one personality trait in him or her that you admire most.

2. Think of a favorite saying your mother, your father, or another relative uses. Explain what it means and what it tells you about the person who uses it.

Miracle*

RICHARD SELZER

Richard Selzer has taught both surgery and writing at the Yale University Medical School. The author of numerous essays and short stories, he contributes regularly to periodicals like Harper's, The American Review, *and* Vanity Fair. *He has also published several collections of essays about his life as a physician, the latest of which is* Taking the World in for Repairs. *"Miracle" is from "A Mask on the Face of Death," an essay published in* Life *magazine in 1988. It recalls Selzer's trip to Haiti to witness the effects of an AIDS epidemic.*

Looking Ahead

1. Like "A Deathly Call of the Wild" (Chapter 8), "Miracle" shows that description is an important tool for scientists. Selzer describes someone's physical appearance and behavior to explain the effects of a terrible disease.

2. In a part of "A Mask on the Face of Death" that doesn't appear here, Selzer attacks a widespread myth by reminding us that "Haitians are no more susceptible to AIDS than anyone else." Saying this helps him emphasize his message to readers in all parts of the world.

Vocabulary

audible   Able to be heard.

cistern   Underground tank containing liquid.

contagion   Spreading of disease from person to person.

emaciated   Abnormally skinny as a result of famine or disease.

icons   Images, pictures.

interspersed   Placed in between, mingled.

labyrinth   Maze.

organism   Living thing; in this case a germ.

stethoscope   Medical instrument used to listen to the heart and lungs.

subdued   Controlled.

telltale   Revealing, giving a sign of.

* Editor's title

I have been invited by Dr. Jean William Pape to attend the AIDS clinic of   1
which he is the director. Nothing from the outside of the low whitewashed
structure would suggest it as a medical facility. Inside, it is divided into many
small cubicles and a labyrinth of corridors. At nine A.M. the hallways are
already full of emaciated silent men and women, some sitting on the few
benches, the rest leaning against the walls. The only sounds are subdued
moans of discomfort interspersed with coughs. How they eat us with their eyes
as we pass.

The room where Pape and I work is perhaps ten feet by ten. It contains a   2
desk, two chairs and a narrow wooden table that is covered with a sheet that will
not be changed during the day. The patients are called in one at a time, asked
how they feel and whether there is any change in their symptoms, then examined
on the table. If the patient is new to the clinic, he or she is questioned about
sexual activities.

A twenty-seven-year-old man whose given name is Miracle enters. He is   3
wobbly, panting, like a groggy boxer who has let down his arms and is waiting
for the last punch. He is neatly dressed and wears, despite the heat, a heavy
woolen cap. When he removes it, I see that his hair is thin, dull reddish and
straight. It is one of the signs of AIDS in Haiti, Pape tells me. The man's skin
is covered with a dry itchy rash. Throughout the interview and examination he
scratches himself slowly, absentmindedly. The rash is called prurigo. It is another symptom of AIDS in Haiti. This man has had diarrhea for six months. The
laboratory reports that the diarrhea is due to an organism called cryptosporidium,
for which there is no treatment. The telltale rattling of the tuberculous moisture
in his chest is audible without a stethoscope. He is like a leaky cistern that
bubbles and froths. And, clearly, exhausted.

"Where do you live?" I ask.   4

"Kenscoff." A village in the hills above Port-au-Prince.   5

"How did you come here today?"   6

"I came on the *tap-tap.*" It is the name given to the small buses that   7
swarm the city, each one extravagantly decorated with religious slogans, icons,
flowers, animals, all painted in psychedelic colors. I have never seen a *tap-tap*
that was not covered with passengers as well, riding outside and hanging on.
The vehicles are little masterpieces of contagion, if not of AIDS then of the
multitude of germs which Haitian flesh is heir to. Miracle is given a prescrip-
tion for a supply of Sera, which is something like Gatorade, and told to return
in a month.

"Mangé kou bêf," says the doctor in farewell. "Eat like an ox." What can   8
he mean? The man has no food or money to buy any. Even had he food, he has
not the appetite to eat or the ability to retain it. To each departing patient the
doctor will say the same words—*"Mangé kou bêf."* I see that it is his way of
offering a hopeful goodbye.

"Will he live until his next appointment?" I ask.   9

"No." Miracle leaves to catch the *tap-tap* for Kenscoff.   10

Questions for Discussion

1. This selection combines the description of place with the description of a person. What do we learn about the clinic that will shed light on Miracle's condition? What does the place tell us about the AIDS epidemic in Haiti?
2. Why does Selzer comment on the other patients in the clinic? Why does he describe the *tap-tap?*
3. To which of our five senses does the author appeal?
4. Where does he use figures of speech?
5. Besides describing the symptoms of an illness, this selection sheds light on other social problems. What are they?
6. In paragraph 8, we learn the Haitian French phrase for "Eat like an ox." If Selzer is writing for an American audience, why doesn't he use the English translation alone?
7. Is Selzer's description purely objective, or does he also hint at an emotional reaction to what he sees?

Suggestions for Journal Entries

1. List the symptoms of a disease or an ailment you or someone you know has suffered from. Here are some examples: diabetes, asthma, high blood pressure, alcoholism, cancer, drug abuse, anemia, anorexia nervosa, AIDS.
2. Selzer describes one of the poorest countries in the world, but you don't need to travel abroad to find poverty. Recall the last time you saw a homeless person. Use focused freewriting or listing to gather details about his or her physical appearance and about the place you saw this individual. You might want to be objective as you jot down your notes; then again, there's no reason not to include your feelings about what you saw, heard, smelled, and so on.

Two Gentlemen of the Pines*

JOHN MCPHEE

A productive writer with a wide range of interests, John McPhee has been a long-time essayist for The New Yorker *magazine. Among his latest books are* Rising from the Plains *(1986) and* The Control of Nature *(1989). One of the things McPhee does best is to describe the human character. His portraits of people he meets on his travels are among the most memorable in contemporary American literature. McPhee ran into two of his most interesting subjects on a trip through New Jersey's Pine Barrens, a wilderness whose name he used as the title of a book from which this selection is taken.*

* Editor's title

Looking Ahead

1. You know that we can learn a lot about people from what they say. This is very true of Fred, the first of McPhee's subjects, but less true of Bill. Nonetheless, the little that Bill lets slip out provides good clues to his personality.

2. Like Selzer, McPhee describes the setting in which he meets his subjects; doing so helps enrich their portraits.

Vocabulary

cathode ray tubes   Television picture tubes.

dismantled   Taken apart.

eyelets   Holes through which laces can pass.

gaunt   Lean, thin, angular.

mallet   Heavy hammer with a short handle.

poacher   Someone who uses another's land to hunt or fish there illegally.

thong   Strip of leather used as a lace.

"turfing it out"   Digging out the top layer of soil and grass.

understory   Underbrush.

undulating   Changing, varying, fluctuating.

vestibule   Small room at the entrance to a building.

visored   Having a long brim that shades the sun.

Fred Brown's house is on an unpaved road that curves along the edge of a wide   1
cranberry bog. What attracted me to it was the pump that stands in his yard. It was something of a wonder that I noticed the pump, because there were, among other things, eight automobiles in the yard, two of them on their sides and one of them upside down, all ten years old or older. Around the cars were old refrigerators, vacuum cleaners, partly dismantled radios, cathode-ray tubes, a short wooden ski, a large wooden mallet, dozens of cranberry picker's boxes, many tires, an orange crate dated 1946, a cord or so of firewood, mandolins, engine heads, and maybe a thousand other things. The house itself, two stories high, was covered with tarpaper that was peeling away in some places, revealing its original shingles, made of Atlantic white cedar from the stream courses of the surrounding forest. I called out to ask if anyone was home, and a voice inside called back, "Come in. Come in. Come on the hell in."

I walked through a vestibule that had a dirt floor, stepped up into a kitchen,   2
and went on into another room that had several overstuffed chairs in it and a porcelain-topped table, where Fred Brown was seated, eating a pork chop. He was dressed in a white sleeveless shirt, ankle-top shoes, and undershorts. He gave me a cheerful greeting and, without asking why I had come or what I

wanted, picked up a pair of khaki trousers that had been tossed onto one of the overstuffed chairs and asked me to sit down. He set the trousers on another chair, and he apologized for being in the middle of his breakfast, explaining that he seldom drank much but the night before he had had a few drinks and this had caused his day to start slowly. "I don't know what's the matter with me, but there's got to be something the matter with me, because drink don't agree with me anymore," he said. He had a raw onion in one hand, and while he talked he shaved slices from the onion and ate them between bites of the chop. He was a muscular and well-built man, with short, bristly white hair, and he had bright, fast-moving eyes in a wide-open face. His legs were trim and strong, with large muscles in the calves. I guessed that he was about sixty, and for a man of sixty he seemed to be in remarkably good shape. He was actually seventy-nine. "My rule is: Never eat except when you're hungry," he said, and he ate another slice of the onion.

In a straight-backed chair near the doorway to the kitchen sat a young man 3 with long black hair, who wore a visored red leather cap that had darkened with age. His shirt was coarse-woven and had eyelets down a V neck that was laced with a thong. His trousers were made of canvas, and he was wearing gum boots. His arms were folded, his legs were stretched out, he had one ankle over the other, and as he sat there he appeared to be sighting carefully past his feet, as if his toes were the outer frame of a gunsight and he could see some sort of target in the floor. When I had entered, I had said hello to him, and he had nodded without looking up. He had a long, straight nose and high cheekbones, in a deeply tanned face that was, somehow, gaunt. I had no idea whether he was shy or hostile. Eventually, when I came to know him, I found him to be as shy a person as I have ever had a chance to know. His name is Bill Wasovwich, and he lives alone in a cabin about half a mile from Fred. First his father, then his mother left him when he was a young boy, and he grew up depending on the help of various people in the pines. One of them, a cranberry grower, employs him and has given him some acreage, in which Bill is building a small cranberry bog of his own, "turfing it out" by hand. When he is not working in the bogs, he goes roaming, as he puts it, setting out cross-country on long, looping journeys, hiking about thirty miles in a typical day, in search of what he calls "events"— surprising a buck, or a gray fox, or perhaps a poacher or a man with a still. Almost no one who is not native to the pines could do this, for the woods have an undulating sameness, and the understory—huckleberries, sheep laurel, sweet fern, high-bush blueberry—is often so dense that a wanderer can walk in a fairly tight circle and think that he is moving in a straight line. State forest rangers spend a good part of their time finding hikers and hunters, some of whom have vanished for days. In his long, pathless journeys, Bill always emerges from the woods near his cabin—and about when he plans to. In the fall, when thousands of hunters come into the pines, he sometimes works as a guide. In the evenings, or in the daytime when he is not working or roaming, he goes to Fred Brown's house and sits there for hours. The old man is a widower whose seven children are long since gone from Hog Wallow, and he is as expansively talkative and worldly as the young one is withdrawn and wild. Although there are fifty-three years between their ages, it is obviously fortunate for each of them to be the other's neighbor.

Questions for Discussion

1. What do details about Fred's and Bill's physical appearances say about them?
2. Think about the way the older man welcomes his visitor. How do such actions reveal his character?
3. The original shingles on Fred's house are made of cedar "from the stream courses of the surrounding forest" (paragraph 1). In what way is this and other information about the house helpful to understanding Fred?
4. Does Fred's claiming there is "something the matter" with him explain the way he views himself?
5. Why is learning about Bill's youth important to understanding his character?
6. Bill says he goes into the woods in search of "events." What are these events? Should the author have used a synonym for this word instead of quoting Bill directly? Why or why not?

Suggestions for Journal Entries

1. As this selection shows, we can learn a lot about people from the places they call home. Use listing to begin describing a place you consider your own: your room, your kitchen, your garage, the inside of your car, for example. You might even describe a place—public or private, indoors or out of doors—that you enjoy visiting. Gather details that show how this place reflects your personality or that explain what draws you to it time and again.
2. Have you ever taken a trip and come upon strangers you found interesting because they were different from most people you know? Use focused freewriting to explain why they captured your attention.
3. McPhee accounts for Bill's shyness by explaining that his parents abandoned him. Do you know someone who experienced an event or set of circumstances that marked his or her personality? Interview this person; learn what in his or her past contributed to a particular characteristic or personality trait. Say your great uncle is thrifty. When you interview him, you find that he was orphaned at age eight, that he lived many years in poverty, and that he is afraid of being poor again. Good subjects for this assignment include anyone with a distinctive personality trait and a willingness to talk about his or her past.

Abraham Lincoln

CARL SANDBURG

One of America's best-loved poets and biographers, Carl Sandburg (1878-1967) had a deep respect for common folk, and he filled his work with images from their simple and sometimes tragic lives. He is remembered chiefly for Corn Huskers *and for* The People, Yes, *a collection of poems published during the Great Depression. He is also known for his six-volume biography of Abraham Lincoln, for which he won one of his three Pulitzer Prizes.*

The following excerpt, from Abraham Lincoln: The Prairie Years, *describes Lincoln at age thirty-seven, about the time he left New Salem, Illinois, and his job as postmaster, lawyer, and storekeeper to enter the U.S. Congress (1847–1849). For a time, Lincoln had served in the Illinois legislature in Springfield, where he certainly would not have won the "best-dressed" award. For Sandburg, however, there's more to a person than his clothing; therefore, he goes well beyond appearances to reveal the inner strength and nobility of our sixteenth President.*

Another selection by Sandburg appears in Chapter 11.

Looking Ahead

1. Sandburg uses a number of interesting anecdotes (brief, sometimes humorous stories) from Lincoln's life to illustrate something about his personality. Look for such anecdotes as you read through this piece.

2. The author also uses specific and concrete details in this early portrait of Lincoln. Many have to do with his physical appearance—his height, the way his eyes looked, the shape of his nose and cheeks, for example. Ask yourself what Lincoln's physical appearance tells you about his character.

3. Sandburg explains in paragraph 1 that by the time Lincoln was thirty-seven, he "had changed with a changing western world." In the 1840s Illinois and Kentucky were still considered the "west" (although this concept was changing fast as the United States pushed its borders toward the Pacific).

   Nonetheless, as the author tells us, there was still a great deal of the simple frontiersman in Lincoln, the *central* idea that ties this essay together and gives it focus. You can review what you've already learned about central ideas by rereading the introduction to Chapter 1.

Vocabulary

angular   Thin and bony.
broadcloth   Plain, tightly woven wool cloth.

buckskin breeches   Pants made of deer hide.

cravat   Necktie.

dejection   Emotional depression.

falsetto   Tone much higher than the normal range of men's voices.

granitic   Hard as granite.

gravity   Seriousness.

melancholy   Sadness.

modulations   Variations.

niche   Nook, place.

pretenses   False shows.

resolve   Steadfastness, determination.

shambled   Shuffled, walked lazily.

The thirty-seven-year-old son of Thomas Lincoln and Nancy Hanks Lincoln   1
had changed with a changing western world. His feet had worn deer-skin moccasins as a boy; they were put into rawhide boots when he was full-grown; now he had them in dressed calf leather. His head-cover was a coonskin cap when he was a boy, and all men and boys wore the raccoon tail as a high headpiece; floating down the Mississippi to New Orleans he wore a black felt hat from an eastern factory and it held the post-office mail of New Salem; now he was a prominent politician and lawyer wearing a tall, stiff, silk hat known as a "stovepipe," also called a "plug hat."

In this "stovepipe" hat he carried letters, newspaper clippings, deeds, mort-   2
gages, checks, receipts. Once he apologized to a client for not replying to a letter; he had bought a new hat and in cleaning out the old hat he missed this particular letter. The silk stovepipe hat was nearly a foot high, with a brim only an inch or so in width; it was a high, lean, longish hat and it made Lincoln look higher, leaner, more longish.

And though Lincoln had begun wearing broadcloth and white shirts with a   3
white collar and black silk cravat, and a suggestion of sideburns coming down three-fourths the length of his ears, he was still known as one of the carelessly dressed men of Springfield. . . .

The loose bones of Lincoln were hard to fit with neat clothes; and, once on,   4
they were hard to keep neat; trousers go baggy at the knees of a story-teller who has the habit, at the end of a story, where the main laugh comes in, of putting his arms around his knees, raising his knees to his chin, and rocking to and fro. Those who spoke of his looks often mentioned his trousers creeping to the ankles and higher; his rumpled hair, his wrinkled vest. When he wasn't away making speeches, electioneering or practicing law on the circuit, he cut kindling wood, tended to the cordwood for the stoves in the house, milked the cow, gave her a few forks of hay, and changed her straw bedding every day.

He looked like a farmer, it was often said; he seemed to have come from   5 prairies and barns rather than city streets and barber shops; and in his own way he admitted and acknowledged it; he told voters from the stump that it was only a few years since he had worn buckskin breeches and they shrank in the rain and crept to his knees leaving the skin blue and bare. The very words that came off his lips in tangled important discussions among lawyers had a wilderness air and a log-cabin smack. The way he pronounced the word ''idea'' was more like ''idee,'' the word ''really'' more like a drawled Kentucky ''ra-a-ly.''

As he strode or shambled into a gathering of men, he stood out as a special 6 figure for men to look at; it was a little as though he had come farther on harder roads and therefore had longer legs for the traveling; and a little as though he had been where life is stripped to its naked facts and it would be useless for him to try to put on certain pretenses of civilization.

The manners of a gentleman and a scholar dropped off him sometimes like 7 a cloak, and his speech was that of a farmer who works his own farm, or a lawyer who pails a cow morning and evening and might refer to it incidentally in polite company or in a public address. He was not embarrassed, and nobody else was embarrassed, when at the Bowling Green funeral he had stood up and, instead of delivering a formal funeral address on the character of the deceased, had shaken with grief and put a handkerchief to his face and wept tears, and motioned to the body-bearers to take his dead friend away. There was a natural grace to it; funerals should be so conducted; a man who loves a dead man should stand up and try to speak and find himself overwhelmed with grief so that instead of speaking he smothers his face in a handkerchief and weeps. This was the eloquence of naked fact beyond which there is no eloquence.

Standing, Lincoln loomed tall with his six feet, four inches of height; sitting 8 in a chair he looked no taller than other men, except that his knees rose higher than the level of the seat of the chair. Seated on a low chair or bench he seemed to be crouching. The shoulders were stooped and rounded, the head bent forward and turned downward; shirt-collars were a loose fit; an Adam's apple stood out on a scrawny neck; his voice was a tenor that carried song-tunes poorly but had clear and appealing modulations in his speeches; in rare moments of excitement it rose to a startling and unforgettable falsetto tone that carried every syllable with unmistakable meaning. In the stoop of his shoulders and the forward bend of his head there was a grace and familiarity so that it was easy for shorter people to look up into his face and talk with him.

The mouth and eyes, and the facial muscles running back from the mouth 9 and eyes, masked a thousand shades of meaning. In hours of melancholy, when poisons of dejection dragged him, the underlip and its muscles drooped. . . . [However,] across the mask of his dark gravity could come a light-ray of the quizzical, the puzzled. This could spread into the beginning of a smile and then spread farther into wrinkles and wreaths of laughter that lit the whole face into a glow; and it was of the quality of his highest laughter that it traveled through his whole frame, currents of it vitalizing his toes.

A fine chiseling of lines on the upper lip seemed to be some continuation 10 of the bridge of the nose, forming a feature that ended in a dimple at the point of the chin. The nose was large; if it had been a trifle larger he would have been called big-nosed; it was a nose for breathing deep sustained breaths of air, a strong shapely nose, granitic with resolve and patience. Two deepening wrinkles started from the sides of the right and left nostrils and ran down the outer rims of the upper lip; farther out on the two cheeks were deepening wrinkles that had been long crude dimples when he was a boy; hours of toil, pain, and laughter were deepening these wrinkles. From the sides of the nose, angular cheek-bones branched right and left toward the large ears, forming a base for magnificently constructed eye-sockets. Bushy black eyebrows shaded the sockets where the eyeballs rested. . . . In his eyes as nowhere else was registered the shifting light of his moods; their language ran from rapid twinkles of darting hazel that won the hearts of children on to a fixed baffling gray that the shrewdest lawyers and politicians could not read, to find there an intention he wanted to hide.

The thatch of coarse hair on the head was black when seen from a distance, 11
but close up it had a brownish, rough, sandy tint. He had been known to comb it, parting it far on the right side, and slicking it down so that it looked groomed by a somewhat particular man; but most of the time it was loose and rumpled. The comb might have parted it either on the far right or on the far left side; he wasn't particular.

It was natural that Abraham Lincoln was many things to many people; some 12
believed him a cunning, designing lawyer and politician who coldly figured all his moves in advance; some believed him a sad, odd, awkward man trying to find a niche in life where his hacked-out frame could have peace and comfort; some believed him a superb human struggler with solemn and comic echoes and values far off and beyond the leashes and bones that held him to earth and law and politics.

Questions for Discussion

1. As noted in Looking Ahead, Sandburg's central idea is that Lincoln had a great deal of the simple frontiersman in him. In any one paragraph, which details develop this central idea?

2. In paragraph 1, Sandburg gives a brief history of Lincoln's footwear. What do his shoes reveal about him?

3. From the physical details Sandburg provides, what do you think Lincoln looked like?

4. Lincoln's trousers were ''baggy at the knees.'' Look back to paragraph 4. What does this physical description reveal about his character?

5. What other details about Lincoln's appearance help us understand his personality?

6. A number of anecdotes in this selection show us things about Lincoln's personality. What does his sobbing at a friend's funeral reveal about him? Pick out two or three other anecdotes that you find especially revealing.

7. In paragraphs 9 and 10, Sandburg indicates that Lincoln could experience a variety of moods. Describe these moods.
8. The public held differing views of Lincoln. What were they?

Suggestions for Journal Entries

1. Use your journal to list details you found in this selection that build a full portrait of Lincoln's physical appearance.
2. How would you describe Lincoln's personality? Use details from Sandburg to write a paragraph about the kind of person he was. Start by listing words that might help you define his character. For instance, you might include "simple," "straightforward," "honest," or "humorous."
3. Lincoln's inner nobility, simplicity, and lack of pretense were reflected in the way he dressed. Do you know people whose outward appearance provides clues to what they are inside? Write a short description of one such person, concentrating on only one or two outward features that reveal what he or she is like inside.

Obāchan

GAIL Y. MIYASAKI

Born in Hawaii, Gail Y. Miyasaki is a Japanese-American who has distinguished herself as a journalist, scholar, and professor of ethnic studies. She is the author of Asian Women *and* Montage: An Ethnic History of Women in Hawaii. *"Obā-chan" means "grandmother" in Japanese.*

Looking Ahead

1. If you read McPhee's "Two Gentlemen of the Pines," you know that someone's past can provide information about the kind of person he or she has become. Such information can be found in this essay as well.
2. Obāchan appears to be just a simple, hardworking old woman, but her character is rich and fascinating. Miyasaki develops her portrait slowly by dropping hints about aspects of her grandmother's personality that are not obvious at first. Read this essay twice to appreciate how carefully it is written.

Vocabulary

admonishings   Warnings.
Bon   Buddhist religious festival.

Caucasian   In this case, the term is being used to describe a white person.

futon   Thin mattress placed on the floor for sleeping.

kimono   Traditional Japanese gown.

pauhana   After work.

ultimatum   Demand.

unwavering   Steadfast, unbending.

Her hands are now rough and gnarled from working in the canefields. But they are still quick and lively as she sews the "futon" cover. And she would sit like that for hours Japanese-style with legs under her, on the floor steadily sewing.   1

She came to Hawaii as a "picture bride." In one of her rare self-reflecting moments, she told me in her broken English-Japanese that her mother had told her that the streets of Honolulu in Hawaii were paved with gold coins, and so encouraged her to go to Hawaii to marry a strange man she had never seen. Shaking her head slowly in amazement, she smiled as she recalled her shocked reaction on seeing "Ojitchan's" (grandfather's) ill-kept room with only lauhula mats as bedding. She grew silent after that, and her eyes had a faraway look.   2

She took her place, along with the other picture brides from Japan, beside her husband on the plantation's canefields along the Hamakua coast on the island of Hawaii. The Hawaiian sun had tanned her deep brown. But the sun had been cruel too. It helped age her. Deep wrinkles lined her face and made her skin look tough, dry, and leathery. Her bright eyes peered out from narrow slits, as if she were constantly squinting into the sun. Her brown arms, though, were strong and firm, like those of a much younger woman, and so different from the soft, white, and plump-dangling arms of so many old teachers I had had. And those arms of hers were always moving—scrubbing clothes on a wooden washboard with neat even strokes, cutting vegetables with the big knife I was never supposed to touch, or pulling the minute weeds of her garden.   3

I remember her best in her working days, coming home from the canefields at "pauhana" time. She wore a pair of faded blue jeans and an equally faded navy-blue and white checked work shirt. A Japanese towel was wrapped carefully around her head, and a large straw "papale" or hat covered that. Her sickle and other tools, and her "bento-bako" or lunch-box, were carried in a khaki bag she had made on her back.   4

I would be sitting, waiting for her, on the back steps of her plantation-owned home, with my elbows on my knees. Upon seeing me, she would smile and say, "Tadaima" (I come home). And I would smile and say in return, "Okaeri" (Welcome home). Somehow I always felt as if she waited for that. Then I would watch her in silent fascination as she scraped the thick red dirt off her heavy black rubber boots. Once, when no one was around, I had put those boots on, and deliberately flopped around in a mud puddle, just so I could scrape off the mud on the back steps too.   5

Having retired from the plantation, she now wore only dresses. She called   6
them "makule-men doresu," Hawaiian for old person's dress. They were always
gray or navy-blue with buttons down the front and a belt at the waistline. Her
hair, which once must have been long and black like mine, was now streaked
with gray and cut short and permanent-waved.

The only time she wore a kimono was for the "Bon" dance. She looked so   7
much older in a kimono and almost foreign. It seemed as if she were going
somewhere, all dressed up. I often felt very far away from her when we all
walked together to the Bon dance, even if I too was wearing a kimono. She
seemed almost a stranger to me, with her bent figure and her short pigeon-toed
steps. She appeared so distantly Japanese. All of a sudden, I would notice her
age; there seemed something so old in being Japanese.

She once surprised me by sending a beautiful "yūkata" or summer kimono   8
for me to wear to represent the Japanese in our school's annual May Day festival.
My mother had taken pictures of me that day to send to her. I have often
wondered, whenever I look at that kimono, whether she had ever worn it when
she was a young girl. I have wondered too what she was thinking when she
looked at those pictures of me.

My mother was the oldest daughter and the second child of the six children   9
Obāchan bore, two boys and four girls. One of her daughters, given the name of
Mary by one of her school teachers, had been disowned by her for marrying a
"haole" or Caucasian. Mary was different from the others, my mother once told
me, much more rebellious and independent. She had refused to attend Honokaa
and Hilo High Schools on the Big Island of Hawaii, but chose instead to go to
Honolulu to attend McKinley High School. She smoked cigarettes and drove a
car, shocking her sisters with such unheard of behavior. And then, after graduation, instead of returning home, Mary took a job in Honolulu. Then she met a
haole sailor. Mary wrote home, telling of her love for this man. She was met with
harsh admonishings from her mother.

"You go with haole, you no come home!" was her mother's ultimatum.   10

Then Mary wrote back, saying that the sailor had gone home to America,   11
and would send her money to join him, and get married. Mary said she was going
to go.

"Soon he leave you alone. He no care," she told her independent daughter.   12
Her other daughters, hearing her say this, turned against her, accusing her of
narrow-minded, prejudiced thinking. She could not understand the words that
her children had learned in the American schools; all she knew was what she felt.
She must have been so terribly alone then.

So Mary left, leaving a silent, unwavering old woman behind. Who could   13
tell if her old heart was broken? It certainly was enough of a shock that Honolulu
did not have gold-paved streets. Then, as now, the emotionless face bore no sign
of the grief she must have felt.

But the haole man did not leave Mary. They got married and had three   14
children. Mary often sends pictures of them to her. Watching her study the
picture of Mary's daughter, her other daughters know she sees the likeness to

Mary. The years and the pictures have softened the emotionless face. She was wrong about this man. She was wrong. But how can she tell herself so, when in her heart, she only feels what is right?

''I was one of the first to condemn her for her treatment of Mary,'' my 15 mother told me. ''I was one of the first to question how she could be so prejudiced and narrow-minded.'' My mother looked at me sadly and turned away.

''But now, being a mother myself, and being a Japanese mother above all, 16 I *know* how she must have felt. I just don't know how to say I'm sorry for those things I said to her.''

Whenever I see an old Oriental woman bent with age and walking with short 17 steps, whenever I hear a child being talked to in broken English-Japanese, I think of her. She is my grandmother. I call her ''Obāchan.''

Questions for Discussion

1. Explain how Miyasaki's description of her grandmother's appearance helps reveal her character.
2. What was Obāchan's reaction when she arrived in America? Why does the author tell us about it?
3. What else do we learn about the old woman's life in the United States that helps us understand the person she has become?
4. Mary was given that name ''by one of her school teachers,'' we learn in paragraph 9. Does this help explain Obāchan's response to her marrying a ''haole''?
5. Reread paragraphs 15 and 16. Why does Miyasaki discuss her mother's regret over condemning Obāchan's treatment of Mary?
6. This is a balanced portrait. The writer honors her grandmother without pretending she is perfect. Find details that support this idea.
7. Sprinkled through the essay are details about the author. Should she have told us about herself? What does such information add to the portrait of her grandmother?
8. Why does Miyasaki include Japanese and Hawaiian words? Should she have used their English translations alone?

Suggestions for Journal Entries

1. This essay stresses a point you learned earlier: be careful when considering the opinions others have about your subject. Have you ever developed an opinion of someone based on what you heard from others? Using listing or focused freewriting, briefly explain what these people told you. Then explain what you learned for yourself to help you change or revise your opinion.
2. In some ways this essay is about the clash of two cultures and the difficulty it causes people. Do you know someone (besides yourself) who came here

from another country and has experienced difficulties and disappointments? Were they like those you read about in "Obāchan"? In preparation for the writing of a full-length character sketch about this person, list details to show how difficult it was for your subject to fit into a new society and how hard he or she tried to build a new life. While your overall impression of this person may be positive, don't be afraid to mention one or two shortcomings among the many virtues you see.

SUGGESTIONS FOR WRITING

1. "Richard Cory" might have inspired you to begin writing in your journal about a "tragic figure" you know. If so, check the notes you made after reading Robinson's poem. Then, write an essay describing this individual.

   One way to begin is to list reasons you think he or she is tragic. Do this in your journal or on a separate piece of paper. Next, write an introduction for your essay that includes a thesis statement defining what you mean by this term. Make sure your definition relates to the list you have just completed.

   In the paper's body paragraphs, develop each item in your list. In other words, explain the reasons the person you are writing about fits your definition of "tragic." Describe what your subject looks like, where he or she lives, or the kind of clothes he or she wears. Also, discuss behavior that shows why you call this person "tragic."

   After you draft the body paragraphs, review your introduction and thesis. Rewrite them if necessary so that they accurately prepare readers for what follows. Then think about an effective closing. One way to conclude your essay is to predict the type of future your subject might expect. Another is to explain how others can avoid what he or she has experienced.

   As with other assignments, your journal entry might provide enough information for a rough draft. Add details that come to mind as you write the second and third drafts, and make sure to edit your best draft carefully before handing your paper to your instructor.

2. Review the journal entry you made after Richard Selzer's "Miracle." Use this information in a descriptive essay that expresses your feelings about someone you know who suffers from a serious illness or is the victim of homelessness.

   Concentrate on what the person looks, smells, and/or sounds like. Describe his or her clothing and the place in which he or she lives, whether it be his or her home, a hospital room, a nursing home, or an alley off a city street. Talk about your subject's day-to-day activities to show how difficult or painful his or her life has become.

   Start with a rough draft. As you revise, include details that appeal to the senses, and create figures of speech—like those you read about in Chapter 6—to make your writing vivid and concrete. Double-check word choice when you edit your paper for grammar, spelling, and other important matters.

   If you have trouble writing an introduction, try a startling remark, describe a scene, or ask a question. As for concluding, explain what you think the future holds for your subject or relate an anecdote about him or her that will stick in your readers' minds.

3. Describe someone you know by focusing on the strongest or most important feature of his or her personality. Here's an example of a preliminary thesis statement for such an essay: "When I think of Millie, what comes to mind first is her faith in people."

   As you draft the body of your essay, tell of something in your subject's past that accounts for this characteristic. For example, explain that Millie has had an unshakable faith in the goodness of people ever since, as a child, she lost her parents and was raised by neighbors. Then, give examples of that faith. Use what you have learned about Millie from personal experience, from people who know her, or from Millie herself. Tell one or two anecdotes (brief, illustrative stories) to convince readers that what you say is true.

A good way to learn more about the person you are describing is to interview him or her. Take accurate notes. When it comes time to write your essay, try quoting your subject directly; use his or her own words to explain how she feels. Examples of how to put direct quotations into your work appear in Rose's ''Mothers and Fathers'' and McPhee's ''Two Gentlemen of the Pines.'' In fact, if you responded to the journal suggestions after these selections, you may already have gotten a fine start on the assignment.

Revise your paper as often as necessary. Make sure it includes enough information and is well organized. As part of the editing process, check that you have used quoted material correctly. If you have doubts, speak with your instructor.

4. If you responded to item 3 of the Suggestions for Journal Entries after Sandburg's ''Abraham Lincoln,'' you have begun writing about a person whose appearance is a clue to his or her character. Turn this short sketch into an essay. Focus on the one aspect (part) of your subject's personality that is most obvious or important. Start off with a preliminary thesis that tells how his or her outward appearance reflects what is on the inside. Here's an example: ''The bags under Nelson's eyes, the tightness in his face, and the droop of his shoulders tell us he is not happy.''

In the first draft, describe what your subject looks and even sounds like. Then, go back and include details about his or her behavior to make the main point in your thesis even clearer. Don't be afraid to describe strange mannerisms you've noticed—perhaps the odd gestures she uses while speaking or the curious way he shuffles down the street.

Once satisfied that you have included enough information, revise your thesis if necessary and make sure your introduction works well. If you haven't written an introduction yet, try a startling remark or an interesting anecdote like the one in paragraph 2 of Sandburg's description of Abraham Lincoln. To conclude, express your personal reaction to the person you have just described or make some predictions about his or her future.

Revise the completed draft once more; check that the details in your paper relate directly to one aspect of your subject's personality—the one mentioned in your thesis. Then, correct punctuation, grammar, spelling, and other types of errors that will reduce the quality of your work.

5. Both Phyllis Rose and Gail Y. Miyasaki write about brave women: one battles an eye disease; the other struggles to make a life in a strange culture. Do you know people who have faced hardship and disappointment? What do their reactions tell you about their characters?

Describe one such person by explaining how he or she reacts to difficulty and disappointment. Tell interesting facts from his or her personal history to help readers understand the strength (or weakness) of your subject's character. In addition, explain what other people think of this individual, quote him or her directly, or use anecdotes to tell readers about the way he or she faces misfortune.

Summarize the information you have gathered in a thesis statement that expresses your feelings about this person. Of course, you don't need to place the thesis at the very beginning of your essay. Put it anywhere it fits, even at the end. In fact, you can open your first draft simply by describing physical appearance. If you do this, however, try to follow Miyasaki's example: choose details that show what your subject looks like and that provide clues to his or her character.

In any case, before you get started, look over the journal entries you made after reading ''From 'Mothers and Fathers' '' and ''Obāchan.'' Then, go through the process of writing systematically. Never remain satisfied with an early draft; for best results, always revise and edit!

6. Most people send friends and relatives store-bought greeting cards on their birthdays. Try something different. Write a birthday letter to a friend or relative whom you love and admire! Begin with a standard birthday greeting if you like. But follow this with four or five well-developed paragraphs that explain the reasons for your love and admiration. Use your knowledge of your reader's past—what you have learned firsthand or heard from others—to recall anecdotes that support your opinion. In other words, show what in his or her character deserves love and admiration.

Not everything you say in this letter has to be flattering. In fact, this is a good chance to do some mild kidding. So, don't hesitate to poke good-natured fun at your reader—and at yourself—as a way of bringing warmth and sincerity to your writing. Just remember that your overall purpose is positive.

This assignment is different from most others. Nonetheless, it demands the same effort and care. In fact, the more you love or admire your reader, the harder you should work at revising and editing this tribute.

SECTION **FOUR**

NARRATION

The selections in the three chapters of this section have a great deal in common. Their most basic and most obvious similarity is that they tell stories. They do this through *narration,* a process by which events or incidents are presented to the reader in a particular order. Usually, this is done in chronological order, or order of time.

The logical arrangement of events in a story is called its "plot." Often, writers begin by telling us about the first event in this series, the event that sets the whole plot in motion. And they usually end their stories with the last bit of action that takes place.

But this is not always the case. Where a writer begins or ends depends on the kind of story he or she is telling and the reason or purpose for telling it. Some stories begin in the middle or even at the end and then use flashbacks to recall what happened earlier. A good example is Henry Stickell's "Sinnit Cave," in Chapter 5. Other stories are preceded or followed by information the author thinks is important. For instance, in "38 Who Saw Murder Didn't Call the Police" (Chapter 11), Martin Gansberg tells us about the police investigation of a crime before narrating the crime itself.

More than 2300 years ago, the Greek philosopher Aristotle taught that a narrative must have a beginning, a middle, and an end. In other words, a successful story must be complete. It must contain all the information a reader will need to learn what has happened and to follow along easily. That's the single most important idea to remember about writing effective narratives, but there are several others you should keep in mind.

DISTINGUISHING FICTION FROM NONFICTION

Narration can be divided into two types: fiction and nonfiction. Works of nonfiction recount events that actually occurred. Works of fiction, though sometimes based on real-life experiences, are born of the author's imagination and do not recreate events exactly as they happened. The short stories that appear in Chapter 12 are examples of fiction.

235

DETERMINING PURPOSE AND THEME

Many nonfiction stories are written to inform people about events or developments that affect or interest them. Newspaper articles, like Martin Gansberg's "38 Who Saw Murder Didn't Call the Police" (Chapter 11), are perfect examples. This type of writing is also used by scientists to explain natural processes as they occur step by step over time. In fact, narration can explain complex ideas or make important points about very real situations. Adrienne Schwartz's "The Colossus in the Kitchen" (Chapter 11), for instance, tells a true story that illustrates the evil and stupidity of apartheid, the political system whose effects Schwartz witnessed in South Africa.

On the other hand, fiction is written to entertain people. As the short stories in Chapter 12 prove, good fiction enriches the emotional, spiritual, and intellectual lives of its readers as well.

Whether fiction or nonfiction, therefore, many narratives are written to dramatize or present an important (central) idea, often called a "theme." They portray life in such a way as to reveal something important about people, human nature, society, or life itself. At times, this theme is stated in a "moral," as in Aesop's fables, the ancient Greek stories that teach lessons about living. More often than not, however, the theme or idea behind a story is unstated or implied. It is revealed only as the plot unfolds. In other words, most stories speak for themselves.

As a developing writer, one of the most important things to remember as you sit down to write a narrative is to ask yourself whether the story you're about to tell is important to you in some way. That *doesn't mean* that you should limit yourself to narrating events from personal experience only, though personal experience can often provide just the kind of information you'll need to spin a good yarn. It *does mean* that the more you know about the people, places, and events you're writing about and the more those people, places, and events mean to you, the better able you'll be to make your writing interesting and meaningful to your readers.

FINDING THE MEANING IN YOUR STORY

As explained above, you won't always have to reveal why you've written your story or what theme it is supposed to present. You can allow the events you're narrating to speak for themselves. Often, in fact, you won't know what the theme of your story is or why you thought it important until you're well into the writing process. Sometimes, you won't know that until after you've finished.

But that's just fine, for writing is a voyage of discovery! It helps you learn things about your subject (and yourself) that you would not have known had you not started the process in the first place. *Just write about something you find interesting and believe is important.* This is the first step in telling a successful story. You can always figure out why your story is important or what theme you want it to demonstrate later in the process, when you write your second or third draft.

DECIDING WHAT TO INCLUDE

In most cases, you won't have much trouble deciding what details to include. You'll be able to put down events as they happened or at least as you remember them. However, in some cases—especially when you are trying to present a particular theme or idea—you'll have to decide which events, people, and so on should be emphasized or talked about in great detail, which should be mentioned only briefly, and which should be excluded from the story altogether.

In "Back Home" (Chapter 11), for example, Langston Hughes's purpose is to explain the racism he encountered on his trip home from Mexico. He could have talked about many of the events on the journey that had nothing to do with racial prejudice. However, he chose to exclude them and to focus only on the two incidents that illustrate his theme.

MAKING YOUR STORIES LIVELY, INTERESTING, AND BELIEVABLE

Once again, good stories dramatize ideas or themes. They do this through actions and characters that seem vivid and interesting, as if they were alive or real.

One of the best ways to keep your readers' interest and to make your writing vivid is to use verbs effectively. More than any other part of speech, verbs convey action! They tell *what happened*. It's important to be accurate when reporting an incident you've experienced or witnessed. You ought to recapture it exactly as you remember and without exaggeration. However, good writing can be both accurate and interesting, both truthful and colorful. You can achieve this balance by choosing verbs carefully.

In "Wanderlust" (Chapter 10), Charles Kuralt chooses to write that his father and he "rolled" along country roads. Of course, words like "traveled" and "drove" would have communicated the same general idea, but "rolled" captures the sensation Kuralt experienced more accurately and it is a far more interesting word.

Similarly, notice how Edgar Lee Masters' verbs and participles—adjectives made from verbs—in "Lucinda Matlock" (Chapter 10) reveal his subject as an energetic, vivacious, and agreeable person. We learn that she *"Rambled* over the fields" and that she could be heard *"Shouting* to the wooded hills, *singing* to the green valleys." How less interesting she would have seemed had we seen her "walking" through the fields and heard her "talking" to the hills.

Using adverbs—words that tell something about verbs, adjectives, and other adverbs—can also add life to your writing and will often make it more specific and accurate to boot. Consider this sentence from E. B. White's "Twins," an essay in Chapter 11 about the birth of deer: "The mother, *mildly* resentful of our presence and dazed from her labor, raised one forefoot and stamped *primly.*" The first adverb modifies the adjective "resentful"; the second adverb modifies the verb "stamped."

A good way to make your writing both more interesting and more believable is to include proper nouns—names of specific persons, places, and things— which will help your readers feel they are experiencing the story as they read it. In "Wanderlust," for example, Charles Kuralt writes that he traveled with his father to towns like *New Bern* and *Swanquarter,* his dad smoking *Tampa Nuggets* and reading *Burma-Shave* signs as they drove along. He also recalls a song from a *Judy Garland* movie *(The Wizard of Oz),* and later he mentions the colorful names of people he met on a baseball road trip.

SHOWING THE PASSAGE OF TIME

Of course, the most important thing in a story is the plot, a series of events occurring in time. Writers must make sure that their plots make sense, that they are easy to follow, and that each event or incident flows into the next logically.

One of the best ways to show time order is to indicate the actual time that an event took place. In "38 Who Saw Murder Didn't Call the Police," for instance, Martin Gansberg introduces the story of Kitty Genovese's murder with "This is what the police say happened beginning at 3:20 A.M." Later on, he tells us that a bus passed the scene at "3:35 A.M." and that an ambulance finally took the body away at "4:25 A.M."

Another way of indicating the passage of time is by using transitions or connectives, the kinds of words and expressions used to create coherence within and between paragraphs. In his popular essay about future trips to outer space, Kenneth Jon Rose uses a number of such transitional devices (in italics) as he explains what it might be like to leave the earth on a tourist shuttle to the stars. Notice how they keep the story moving and make it easy to follow:

> *[While] looking out your window,* you'll see the earth rapidly falling away, and the light blue sky progressively turning blue-black. You'll *now* be about 30 miles up, traveling at about 3000 mph. *Within minutes,* the sky will appear jet black, and only the fuzzy curve of the earth will be visible. *Then,* at perhaps 130 miles above the surface of the earth and traveling at 17,000 mph, engines will shut down and . . . you'll become weightless. ("2001: Space Shuttle")

If you want to refresh your memory about other effective transitional devices to use in your writing, turn back to Chapter 2.

DESCRIBING SETTING AND DEVELOPING CHARACTERS

Establishing the setting of your story involves describing the time and place in which it occurs. You've probably done some of that in response to the assignments in Chapter 8, "Describing Places and Things." Developing characters involves many of the skills you practiced in Chapter 9, "Describing People."

In general, the more you say about the people in your narrative and about the time and place in which it is set, the more realistic and convincing it will seem to your readers. And the more they will appreciate what it has to say! Remember that your purpose in writing a narrative is to tell a story. But the kind of characters who inhabit that story and the kind of world in which it takes place can be as interesting and as important to your readers as the events themselves.

As you probably know, an important narrative element is dialogue, the words a writer allows people in the story to speak. You can use dialogue to help reveal important aspects of someone's personality, to describe setting, and even to relate events that move the plot along. In fact, several authors whose selections follow allow their characters to explain what happened or to comment on the story's action in their own words. Usually, such comments are quoted exactly— complete with grammatical errors and slang expressions. So, whether you are writing fiction or nonfiction, try letting your characters speak for themselves. They may be able to tell your readers a lot about themselves, about other characters, and about the stories in which they appear.

CHAPTER 10

PERSONAL REFLECTION AND AUTOBIOGRAPHY

Though different in style and content, the selections in this chapter are similar because they are written in the *first person*. This is the *point of view* from which the authors have chosen to tell their stories. In first-person narration, the story-teller, also known as the narrator, participates in the action and recalls the events from his or her personal perspective.

When writers reveal things about other people's lives or talk about events in which they were not involved, they often rely on third-person narration and use the pronouns "he," "she," "it," and "they" to explain who did what in the story. Examples of this kind of writing can be found in Chapter 11, "Reporting Events." However, all the selections in Chapter 10 are intended to reveal something important about the lives or personalities of their storytellers. That's why they can be classified as "personal reflection" or "autobiography" and are written from the first-person point of view, using the pronouns "I" or "we."

This is even true of the two poems from *Spoon River Anthology*. To make his poems more believable, Edgar Lee Masters lets his title characters speak for themselves and tell us about their lives in their own words. As such, Lucinda Matlock and Margaret Fuller Slack become the narrators of the poems that bear their names.

Incident

COUNTEE CULLEN

Countee Cullen (1903–1946) played a significant role in the Harlem Renaissance, one of the most influential artistic movements in modern America. As a member of this important group of black poets, novelists, and playwrights in New York's Harlem during the 1920s, he helped create an authentic voice for American blacks and contributed to a tradition that is among the finest in American literature.

During his brief lifetime he authored several volumes of poetry, was the editor of two important black journals, and at age thirty published Caroling Dusk, *a collection of poetry by important black writers.*

Looking Ahead

Although brief, ''Incident'' contains the basic narrative elements: plot, setting, character, and dialogue.

Vocabulary

whit Bit, small amount.

> Once riding in old Baltimore,
> Heart-filled, head-filled with glee,
> I saw a Baltimorean
> Keep looking straight at me.
>
> Now I was eight and very small,
> And he was no whit bigger,
> And so I smiled, but he poked out
> His tongue, and called me, ''Nigger.''
>
> I saw the whole of Baltimore
> From May until December,
> Of all the things that happened there
> That's all that I remember.

5

10

Questions for Discussion

1. What is the narrator's mood as he rides in ''old Baltimore''?
2. What three events make up the plot of ''Incident''?
3. What example of dialogue do we find in this selection? How is it important to the poem?
4. Why does the speaker tell us that the ''Baltimorean'' he met was about his age and size?
5. Cullen does not provide many details about the setting, but he does give us a clue. Where does the poem take place?

Suggestions for Journal Entries

1. Think of an incident from your childhood in which someone insulted you, called you names, or tried to degrade you in some way. Briefly recall what happened and explain your reaction to this incident.
2. In your journal, explain your emotional reaction to ''he poked out/His tongue, and called me, 'Nigger.' ''

Namas-te*

PETER MATTHIESSEN

Peter Matthiessen has explored and written about remote parts of the world like the Amazon River, the Sudan, and New Guinea. Among his best-known works are Far Tortuga, *a novel, and* Blue Meridian, *which tells of the author's search for the great white shark and which was filmed as* Blue Water, White Death. *"Namas-te" is taken from* The Snow Leopard, *a book for which Matthiessen received the National Book Award. It recalls his travels through Nepal, a small country between India and Tibet, where he went to study the blue sheep of the Himalaya Mountains and to find the legendary snow leopard.*

Looking Ahead

1. This piece begins with a sentence fragment. Professional writers create dramatic effects with fragments, but developing writers should avoid them.

2. In paragraph 3, Matthiessen mentions places that he visited and events that happened much earlier in his journey. He even recalls the death of his wife, which took place before he left home. Gorkha and Pokhara are cities in central Nepal, near the site of this story.

3. GS is George Schaller, a zoologist and friend of the author.

Vocabulary

Annapurna   Mountain of the Himalayas.
luminous   Bright, radiant.
mortality   Certainty of death.
pitiable   Sad, deserving pity.
ravines   Gaps, crevasses.
Sanskrit   Ancient language of India.
subdued   Overcome.
tamper with   Interfere with, disturb.

A luminous mountain morning. Mist and fire smoke, sun shafts and dark ravines: a peak of Annapurna poises on soft clouds. In fresh light, to the peeping of baby chickens, we take breakfast in the village tea house, and are under way well before seven. [1]

A child dragging bent useless legs is crawling up the hill outside the village. [2]

* Editor's title

Nose to the stones, goat dung, and muddy trickles, she pulls herself along like a broken cricket. We falter, ashamed of our strong step, and noticing this, she gazes up, clear-eyed, without resentment—it seems much worse that she is pretty. In [parts of the world], GS says stiffly, beggars will break their children's knees to achieve this pitiable effect for business purposes: this is his way of expressing his distress. But the child that lies here at our boots is not a beggar; she is merely a child, staring in curiosity at tall, white strangers. I long to give her something—a new life?—yet am afraid to tamper with such dignity. And so I smile as best I can, and say *"Namas-te!"* "Good morning!" How absurd! And her voice follows as we go away, a small clear smiling voice—*"Namas-te!"*—a Sanskrit word for greeting and parting that means, "I salute you."

We are subdued by this reminder of mortality. I think of the corpse in 3 Gorkha Country, borne on thin shoulders in the mountain rain, the black cloths blowing; I see the ancient dying man outside Pokhara; I hear again my own wife's final breath.

Questions for Discussion

1. What is the story's setting, the time and place in which it occurs?
2. How does Matthiessen describe the child's voice? What does this information tell us about her?
3. What else do we learn about the girl?
4. Matthiessen says GS and he are "subdued" by this experience. What does he mean? What else do we learn about these men as a result of their meeting the child?
5. In what way is meeting her a "reminder of mortality"? Whose mortality?
6. Why does the author include GS's statement about beggars in paragraph 2?

Suggestions for Journal Entries

1. Remember the last time you witnessed a pitiable sight. Use listing to record details about what you saw, heard, smelled, and so forth. Describe the setting of the story by recalling when and where it took place. Like Matthiessen, include names of specific people, places, or things. Most of all, recall as much as you can about the events and people you observed. Finally, sum up your reaction to the experience in a sentence or two.
2. Despite her terrible situation, the young child in Matthiessen's story manages to greet the travelers with joy in her voice. Do you know someone who suffers from a severe handicap? Use focused freewriting to explain this person's attitude toward him- or herself, toward the handicap, toward other people, or toward life in general. Briefly recall incidents from his or her life that will help you explain what you mean.

From *Spoon River Anthology*

EDGAR LEE MASTERS

Spoon River Anthology *is a collection of poems spoken by people buried in the cemetery of a fictional nineteenth-century village that Masters based upon recollections of his hometown. One by one, Spoon River's citizens are made to address us from the grave and to reveal important secrets about their relatives and friends, and, most of all, about themselves.*

Born in Kansas in 1869, Masters eventually settled in Chicago, where he practiced law for several years before taking up writing as a career. When Spoon River Anthology *was published, it became a literary sensation. The idea of unraveling the story of a town through the recollections of people lying in its cemetery was unique, and it attracted the attention of thousands of readers and many imitators. "Lucinda Matlock" and "Margaret Fuller Slack," the two poems in this selection, are taken from* Spoon River Anthology.

Looking Ahead

1. Lucinda's and Margaret's very different outlooks on life reveal a great deal about their personalities. Ask yourself what their attitudes tell you about them.

2. Chandlerville and Winchester, which Lucinda mentions, are towns near Spoon River. By including these place names, Masters makes the poem and Lucinda seem more realistic and believable.

3. Margaret claims that she could have been as good a writer as George Eliot. "George Eliot" was the pen name of the nineteenth-century English novelist Mary Ann Evans, who wrote *The Mill on the Floss, Silas Marner,* and *Middlemarch.*

Vocabulary

celibacy   Life without sex.

degenerate   Not strong in spirit.

ere   Before.

holiday   Vacation.

ironical   Ironic, exactly the opposite of what is expected. Margaret's death as a result of tetanus was "ironical" because one of the disease's first symptoms is lockjaw.

luring   Attracting.

repose   Rest.

unchastity   Sex outside of marriage.

untoward   Unhappy, unlucky.

LUCINDA MATLOCK

I went to the dances at Chandlerville,
And played snap-out at Winchester.
One time we changed partners,
Driving home in the moonlight of middle June,
And then I found Davis. 5
We were married and lived together for seventy years,
Enjoying, working, raising the twelve children,
Eight of whom we lost
Ere I had reached the age of sixty.
I spun, I wove, I kept the house, I nursed the sick, 10
I made the garden, and for holiday
Rambled over the fields where sang the larks,
And by Spoon River gathering many a shell,
And many a flower and medicinal weed—
Shouting to the wooded hills, singing to the green valleys. 15
At ninety-six I had lived enough, that is all,
And passed to a sweet repose.
What is this I hear of sorrow and weariness,
Anger, discontent and drooping hopes?
Degenerate sons and daughters, 20
Life is too strong for you—
It takes life to love Life.

MARGARET FULLER SLACK

I would have been as great as George Eliot
But for an untoward fate.
For look at the photograph of me made by Penniwit,
Chin resting on hand, and deep-set eyes—
Gray, too, and far-searching. 5
But there was the old, old problem:
Should it be celibacy, matrimony or unchastity?
Then John Slack, the rich druggist, wooed me,
Luring me with the promise of leisure for my novel,
And I married him, giving birth to eight children, 10
And had no time to write.
It was all over with me, anyway,
When I ran the needle in my hand
While washing the baby's things,
And died from lock-jaw, an ironical death. 15
Hear me, ambitious souls,
Sex is the curse of life!

Questions for Discussion

1. Lucinda seems to have had a very active and productive life. What events in her poem make this clear?
2. Masters uses a number of interesting verbs to describe Lucinda's life. Identify these verbs in the poem. What do they reveal about her?
3. Lucinda's life hasn't been all joy. Which events in the poem reveal that she has experienced great sorrow too?
4. Why does Lucinda call her sons and daughters ''degenerate''?
5. What does Lucinda mean when she says that ''It takes life to love Life''? What does this tell us about her personality?
6. Margaret Fuller Slack says that she was lured into her marriage ''with the promise of leisure for [her] novel.'' What does this reveal about her attitude toward marriage? How does her attitude differ from Lucinda's, and what does this difference tell us about Margaret's character?
7. What does Margaret mean by ''Sex is the curse of life!''?
8. What verbs does Masters use in ''Margaret Fuller Slack'' to keep the story moving and to maintain the reader's interest?

Suggestions for Journal Entries

1. In a paragraph or two, describe Lucinda's rather healthy attitude toward life and contrast it to Margaret's view.
2. Do you know someone like Lucinda Matlock, who has kept smiling and maintained a courageous attitude even though he or she has had a difficult life? Make a list of the difficulties this person has experienced, and explain how he or she manages to remain hopeful and happy.
3. Do you know someone like Margaret, who is resentful about the way his or her life has unfolded? What events in this person's life have caused him or her to adopt this attitude?

The Boys*

MAYA ANGELOU

Born Marguerita Johnson in 1928, Maya Angelou has had a magnificent career as a writer, dancer, and actress. She has appeared in musical and dramatic productions the world over, including the TV miniseries Roots.

Angelou grew up in Stamps, Arkansas, where her grandmother (known as ''Sister Henderson'' to the neighbors and ''Momma'' to her grandchildren) owned the general store, which was Angelou's home and which serves as the

* Editor's title

setting for "The Boys." She published the first volume of her autobiography, I Know Why the Caged Bird Sings, *in 1970. Taken from this book, "The Boys" recalls a moving childhood experience that both angered and demoralized her.*

Looking Ahead

1. Uncle Willie, who is really the central character in this story, walked with a severe limp. This is the "affliction" Angelou mentions in paragraph 4. Bailey, whom Angelou first mentions in paragraph 2, is her younger brother.

2. Angelou introduces the story by providing a very complete description of the setting. This comes in the first several paragraphs, which describe the "Store" at various times of the day. Read these paragraphs carefully, picking out the various ways in which Angelou indicates the passage of time.

3. The story contains several examples of personification, simile, and metaphor. (To review figurative language, see Chapter 6.)

Vocabulary

abominations   Hateful, disgusting things.

astraddle   Across.

concoctions   Mixtures.

condoned   Excused.

covenant   Agreement, contract.

heinous   Horrible, evil.

nonchalance   Carelessness, ease.

obsession   Preoccupation, constant desire for.

rakishly   In a sexy or suggestive way.

serfs   Slaves, persons bound to land owned by someone else.

squire   Rich landowner, country gentleman.

tedious   Boring, tiresome.

testimony   Witnessing or swearing to.

twang   Nasal sound.

Weighing the half-pounds of flour, excluding the scoop, and depositing them   1 dust-free into the thin paper sacks held a simple kind of adventure for me. I developed an eye for measuring how full a silver-looking ladle of flour, mash, meal, sugar or corn had to be to push the scale indicator over to eight ounces or one pound. When I was absolutely accurate our appreciative customers used to admire: "Sister Henderson sure got some smart grandchildrens." If I was off in the Store's favor, the eagle-eyed women would say, "Put some more in that sack, child. Don't you try to make your profit offa me."

Then I would quietly but persistently punish myself. For every bad judg- 2 ment, the fine was no silver-wrapped Kisses, the sweet chocolate drops that I loved more than anything in the world, except Bailey. And maybe canned pineapples. My obsession with pineapples nearly drove me mad. I dreamt of the days when I would be grown and able to buy a whole carton for myself alone.

Until I was thirteen and left Arkansas for good, the Store was my favorite 3 place to be. Alone and empty in the mornings, it looked like an unopened present from a stranger. Opening the front doors was pulling the ribbon off the unexpected gift. The light would come in softly (we faced north), easing itself over the shelves of mackerel, salmon, tobacco, thread. It fell flat on the big vat of lard and by noontime during the summer the grease had softened to a thick soup. Whenever I walked into the Store in the afternoon, I sensed that it was tired. I alone could hear the slow pulse of its job half done. But just before bedtime, after numerous people had walked in and out, had argued over their bills, or joked about their neighbors, or just dropped in "to give Sister Henderson a 'Hi y'all,'" the promise of magic mornings returned to the Store and spread itself over the family in washed life waves.

Momma opened boxes of crispy crackers and we sat around the meat block 4 at the rear of the Store. I sliced onions, and Bailey opened two or even three cans of sardines and allowed their juice of oil and fishing boats to ooze down and around the sides. That was supper. In the evening, when we were alone like that, Uncle Willie didn't stutter or shake or give any indication that he had an "affliction." It seemed that the peace of a day's ending was an assurance that the covenant God made with children, Negroes and the crippled was still in effect.

Throwing scoops of corn to the chickens and mixing sour dry mash with 5 leftover food and oily dish water for the hogs were among our evening chores. Bailey and I sloshed down twilight trails to the pig pens, and standing on the first fence rungs we poured down the unappealing concoctions to our grateful hogs. They mashed their tender pink snouts down into the slop, and rooted and grunted their satisfaction. We always grunted a reply only half in jest. We were also grateful that we had concluded the dirtiest of chores and had only gotten the evil-smelling swill on our shoes, stockings, feet and hands.

Late one day, as we were attending to the pigs, I heard a horse in the front 6 yard (it really should have been called a driveway, except that there was nothing to drive into it), and ran to find out who had come riding up on a Thursday evening when even Mr. Steward, the quiet, bitter man who owned a riding horse, would be resting by his warm fire until the morning called him out to turn over his field.

The used-to-be sheriff sat rakishly astraddle his horse. His nonchalance was 7 meant to convey his authority and power over even dumb animals. How much more capable he would be with Negroes. It went without saying.

His twang jogged in the brittle air. From the side of the Store, Bailey and 8

I heard him say to Momma, ''Annie, tell Willie he better lay low tonight. A crazy nigger messed with a white lady today. Some of the boys'll be coming over here later.'' Even after the slow drag of years, I remember the sense of fear which filled my mouth with hot, dry air, and made my body light.

The ''boys''? Those cement faces and eyes of hate that burned the clothes   9 off you if they happened to see you lounging on the main street downtown on Saturday. Boys? It seemed that youth had never happened to them. Boys? No, rather men who were covered with graves' dust and age without beauty or learning. The ugliness and rottenness of old abominations.

If on Judgment Day I were summoned by St. Peter to give testimony to the   10 used-to-be sheriff's act of kindness, I would be unable to say anything in his behalf. His confidence that my uncle and every other Black man who heard of the Klan's coming ride would scurry under their houses to hide in chicken droppings was too humiliating to hear. Without waiting for Momma's thanks, he rode out of the yard, sure that things were as they should be and that he was a gentle squire, saving those deserving serfs from the laws of the land, which he condoned.

Immediately, while his horse's hoofs were still loudly thudding the ground,   11 Momma blew out the coal-oil lamps. She had a quiet, hard talk with Uncle Willie and called Bailey and me into the Store.

We were told to take the potatoes and onions out of their bins and knock out   12 the dividing walls that kept them apart. Then with a tedious and fearful slowness Uncle Willie gave me his rubber-tipped cane and bent down to get into the now-enlarged empty bin. It took forever before he lay down flat, and then we covered him with potatoes and onions, layer upon layer, like a casserole. Grandmother knelt praying in the darkened Store.

It was fortunate that the ''boys'' didn't ride into our yard that evening and   13 insist that Momma open the Store. They would have surely found Uncle Willie and just as surely lynched him. He moaned the whole night through as if he had, in fact, been guilty of some heinous crime. The heavy sounds pushed their way up out of the blanket of vegetables and I pictured his mouth pulling down on the right side and his saliva flowing into the eyes of new potatoes and waiting there like dew drops for the warmth of morning.

Questions for Discussion

1. What is the story's central idea, or theme?
2. What point of view does Angelou use?
3. The author establishes the setting of her story by mentioning a number of events or incidents that tell us what a typical day at the ''Store'' was like. What are they?
4. ''Whenever I walked into the Store in the afternoon,'' Angelou writes in paragraph 3, ''I sensed that it was tired.'' What does this personification suggest about her attitude toward this place?

5. Paragraph 5 contains verbs that make Angelou's writing particularly lively and interesting. Pick out a few examples in that paragraph and in at least one other.

6. What is Angelou's reaction to Uncle Willie's having to hide in the vegetable bin? What does this reaction and her description of his suffering reveal about her?

7. Who are the "boys," and what is Angelou's attitude toward them?

Suggestions for Journal Entries

1. Angelou begins by describing the "Store" in detail at different times of the day. Think of a setting you spend a lot of time in, such as the place where you work. Jot down your impressions of this place at different times of the day or night.

2. Recall an incident in which you were forced to do something that demoralized or offended you. Briefly describe what happened, and explain in a sentence or two why you felt demoralized or offended.

3. Angelou's indignation at Uncle Willie's having to hide in the vegetable bin reveals her pride in her family and her race as well as her belief in the dignity of all people. Recall a stressful or emotion-filled incident in your life, and briefly explain what your reaction to this incident says about you.

From *Zen and the Art of Motorcycle Maintenance*

ROBERT PIRSIG

A native of Minneapolis-St. Paul, Robert Pirsig taught composition and rhetoric at the University of Chicago and has worked as a technical writer for several years.

Zen and the Art of Motorcycle Maintenance is one of the most celebrated books of the 1970s. It recreates Pirsig's experiences on cross-country motorcycle trips, through which he learned how to come to grips with important aspects of his own personality and how to care for a highly technical piece of machinery. According to Pirsig: "The real cycle you're working on is a cycle called 'yourself.' Working on a motorcycle, working well, caring, is to become part of a process, to achieve an inner peace of mind."

In the following selection from Zen and the Art of Motorcycle Maintenance, *we meet Pirsig as he and his young son, Chris, encounter some very bad weather while cycling to Canada.*

Looking Ahead

1. The word ''Zen'' comes from ''Zen Buddhism,'' an ancient sect of Buddhism still followed by millions in Japan, China, and other parts of Asia. It stresses personal meditation and individual thinking over a blind adherence to rules. Thinking problems out thoroughly and independently is also an important aspect of Pirsig's work.

2. The author makes excellent use of transitions to indicate the passage of time. In paragraph 4, for instance, he says: ''The cycle slowed down to twenty-five, then twenty. Then it started missing.'' Look for several other transitional words or expressions in this narrative.

3. Each paragraph in this selection covers only one incident in the long series of events. Notice how Pirsig provides only those details necessary to keep the story moving steadily and to maintain the reader's interest.

4. Pirsig waits until the last paragraph to reveal the theme of his story. It tells us what he learned from his experiences, both about motorcycle maintenance and about himself.

Vocabulary

ponchos Large waterproof cloaks used as raincoats.

stopcock Valve that controls the flow of gasoline.

I remember Chris and I were on a trip to Canada a few years ago, got about 130   1
miles and were caught in a warm front of which we had plenty of warning but which we didn't understand. The whole experience was kind of dumb and sad.

We were on a little six-and-one-half-horsepower cycle, way overloaded with   2
luggage and way underloaded with common sense. The machine could do only about forty-five miles per hour wide open against a moderate head wind. It was no touring bike. We reached a large lake in the North Woods the first night and tented amid rainstorms that lasted all night long. I forgot to dig a trench around the tent and at about two in the morning a stream of water came in and soaked both sleeping bags. The next morning we were soggy and depressed and hadn't had much sleep, but I thought that if we just got riding the rain would let up after a while. No such luck. By ten o'clock the sky was so dark all the cars had their headlights on. And then it really came down.

We were wearing the ponchos which had served as a tent the night before.   3
Now they spread out like sails and slowed our speed to thirty miles an hour wide open. The water on the road became two inches deep. Lightning bolts came crashing down all around us. I remember a woman's face looking astonished at us from the window of a passing car, wondering what in earth we were doing on a motorcycle in this weather. I'm sure I couldn't have told her.

The cycle slowed down to twenty-five, then twenty. Then it started missing,   4 coughing and popping and sputtering until, barely moving at five or six miles an hour, we found an old run-down filling station by some cutover timberland and pulled in.

At the time . . . I hadn't bothered to learn much about motorcycle mainte- nance. I remember holding my poncho over my head to keep the rain from the tank and rocking the cycle between my legs. Gas seemed to be sloshing around inside. I looked at the plugs, and looked at the points, and looked at the carbu- retor, and pumped the kick starter until I was exhausted.

We went into the filling station, which was also a combination beer joint and restaurant, and had a meal of burned-up steak. Then I went back out and tried it again. Chris kept asking questions that started to anger me because he didn't see how serious it was. Finally I saw it was no use, gave it up, and my anger at him disappeared. I explained to him as carefully as I could that it was all over. We weren't going anywhere by cycle on this vacation. Chris suggested things to do like check the gas, which I had done, and find a mechanic. But there weren't any mechanics. Just cutover pine trees and brush and rain.

I sat in the grass with him at the shoulder of the road, defeated, staring into the trees and underbrush. I answered all of Chris's questions patiently and in time they became fewer and fewer. And then Chris finally understood that our cycle trip was really over and began to cry. He was eight then, I think.

We hitchhiked back to our own city and rented a trailer and put it on our car and came up and got the cycle, and hauled it back to our own city and then started out all over again by car. But it wasn't the same. And we didn't really enjoy ourselves much.

Two weeks after the vacation was over, one evening after work, I removed the carburetor to see what was wrong but still couldn't find anything. To clean off the grease before replacing it, I turned the stopcock on the tank for a little gas. Nothing came out. The tank was out of gas. I couldn't believe it. I can still hardly believe it.

I have kicked myself mentally a hundred times for that stupidity and don't think I'll ever really, finally get over it. Evidently what I saw sloshing around was gas in the reserve tank which I had never turned on. I didn't check it carefully because I assumed the rain had caused the engine failure. I didn't understand then how foolish quick assumptions like that are. Now we are on a twenty-eight-horse machine and I take the maintenance of it very seriously.

Questions for Discussion

1. As Pirsig finally reveals, he didn't check the gas carefully enough because of a "quick" assumption about the engine. What was this assumption?
2. In what way was Pirsig's experience "dumb"? In what way was it "sad"?
3. As discussed in Looking Ahead, Zen Buddhism stresses the importance of thinking for oneself. How do Pirsig's problems with the cycle relate to this idea?

4. Pirsig includes only those details that relate to the story's central idea, or theme. What is this central idea, or theme, of his story? What has Pirsig learned from his experiences?
5. Do Chris's many questions in paragraphs 6 and 7 relate to the central idea? Why does Pirsig bother to include them?
6. What does the author's relationship with his son reveal about him?
7. What transitional words or expressions do you find in this essay?

Suggestions for Journal Entries

1. Did you ever make a very wrong assumption about someone or something? What happened as a result? In a paragraph or two, sketch out a short narrative about this incident and explain what you learned from it.
2. Have you ever traveled through a heavy or dangerous storm? In your journal, list the details that come to mind about this incident. Then write a short paragraph describing what happened and explaining how you felt as you endured this journey.
3. Recall a long trip you took with someone you are or were close to. In your journal, list the things that the trip revealed about you and/or about your relationship with this person.

Wanderlust

CHARLES KURALT

A native of North Carolina, Charles Kuralt has long been one of America's most respected journalists and has won almost every major award for television journalism. He is the host of CBS's Sunday Morning, *a television magazine that has earned national acclaim. "Wanderlust" is the first chapter of* A Life on the Road, *the story of Kuralt's travels as a reporter. Like Maya Angelou in "The Boys," Kuralt looks back to his childhood to reveal much about himself, both then and now.*

Looking Ahead

1. The Depression was a severe economic downturn in the 1930s; it caused widespread unemployment and poverty. One way President Roosevelt's administration fought these problems was through public-works and social-services programs that created jobs for people. Often referred to by their initials, the offices that ran these programs were known as the "alphabet agencies."

2. The Washington Senators were a major league baseball team. Farm teams are organizations that train young players for the major leagues.

Vocabulary

banter Playful conversation, teasing.

cadre Small group of people who lead a larger organization.

chaperoneship Guidance, direction.

contrived Thought up, imagined.

curfew Time by which one has to be indoors.

detachment Group sent to do a job.

enlistees Ordinary soldiers, nonofficers.

forerunner Predecessor, something that comes before.

indiscriminately Without plan or preference.

pith helmet Light hat that shades the sun.

plug Fishing lure.

rapture Joy, ecstasy.

three-stripers Sergeants.

Before I was born, I went on the road. The road was U.S. 17, south from Jacksonville, North Carolina, through the Holly Shelter Swamp to Wilmington, where the hospital was. My father backed the Chevrolet out of its place in the hay barn next to the farm cart and helped my mother into the front seat on the afternoon of September 9, 1934. He made the trip in little more than an hour, barely slowing down for the stop signs in Dixon, Folkstone and Holly Ridge. I was born the next morning with rambling in my blood and fifty miles already under my belt.

We lived on my grandparents' farm off and on for a while there during the Depression. A sandy road passed in front of the house and a logging path through the pine woods behind it. I always wondered where the roads went, and after I learned that the one in front went to another farm a mile away, I wondered where it went from there. Once, playing in the woods, I surprised a flock of wild turkeys, which went flying down the logging road and out of sight. I remember wanting to go with them. Whenever I hear the Judy Garland lyric ''Birds fly over the rainbow—Why then, oh why can't I?'' it's those turkeys I see flying.

My mother was a schoolteacher and my father was getting started in what seemed to him the right job for the times, helping out poor people. There was no shortage of poor people to help out in the thirties, of course. My father, who had earned a Phi Beta Kappa key at the University of North Carolina and had planned to become a big businessman, became a social worker instead. He found employment in several of President Roosevelt's alphabet agencies, the CCC, the

ERA, the WPA, then went back to the university at Chapel Hill, took some graduate courses in social work, and accepted a job with the state Department of Public Welfare. We moved from one town to another in eastern North Carolina, and I loved every move. I began to find out where the roads went.

My father's job as field supervisor for the state required him to travel to the   4 small-town county seats to visit the local welfare offices. Since my mother was busy teaching school, somebody had to take care of me. The solution—a little troublesome for my father, I imagine, but perfect for me—was for him to take me with him on his trips.

We rolled along the country roads to the old tidewater towns, Edenton and   5 Plymouth and New Bern and Swanquarter, my father smoking Tampa Nuggets and spinning yarns for my amusement. He tried a little history on me, thinking to improve my mind: "The people here didn't like the British governor, and had a fight with the British at this bridge." He filled me with local lore: "At Harkers Island over there, they make wonderful strong boats and go to sea in them." He taught me to read the Burma-Shave signs: " 'Twould Be More Fun . . . to Go by Air . . . but We Couldn't Put . . . These Signs Up There. Burma-Shave." We stopped in the afternoons to fish for a few minutes in roadside creeks turned black by the tannin of cypress trees, my father casting a red-and-white plug expertly with the old bait-casting rod he carried in the trunk, and patiently picking out the backlashes that snarled the reel when I tried it. We stopped for suppers of pork chops, sweet potatoes and collard greens at roadside cafes, and rolled on into the night, bound for some tourist home down the road, my father telling tales and I listening in rapture, just the two of us, rolling on, wrapped in a cloud of companionship and smoke from his five-cent cigar.

I wanted never to go home from these trips, and when we did go home, I   6 contrived longer trips to farther-away places, trips of the mind. In a field within walking distance of our farm, a small detachment of U.S. Marines was setting up a tent camp, forerunner of what was to become Camp LeJeune, the sprawling Marine base that eventually changed Jacksonville forever. On hot summer mornings, I used to walk barefoot down the sandy road to the tent camp towing a red wagon filled with quart jars of milk from our cows and sugar cookies my grandmother had baked and wrapped in wax paper. It never took more than a few minutes to sell out my stock of milk and cookies to the Marines. If they didn't have money, I accepted souvenirs. Somewhere in my folks' attic, there must still be a cigar box containing sharpshooter medals, uniform buttons and globe-and-anchor emblems from the pith helmets of those Marines. Most of them were young enlistees, I suppose, who had never traveled farther than a few miles from home, but the cadre was composed of old sergeants who told me casual tales of service in places I had trouble imagining, places where the people spoke other languages entirely, they told me, places with names like the Philippines and Nicaragua and the Canal Zone. I learned to seek out the three-stripers when I wanted to hear good traveling stories. I learned the words of their song, "From the halls of Montezuma to the shores of Tripoli . . ." More than anything else, I wanted to wear a Marine pith helmet and go to the halls of Montezuma. I asked a jolly fat sergeant named Carpenter if he had ever been there. He always called me "Charlie, my boy." "Charlie, my boy," he said, "I'll tell you the truth. I've never even figured out where Montezuma might be. But if the United States Marines decide to send me there, I'll send you a penny postcard." I asked Sergeant Carpenter how old he was when he joined the Marines. "Charlie, my boy," he said, "I was a grand old man of sixteen." You had to be sixteen, he said. I was only six.

In school, I proved to be a below-average student in all forms of mathematics, and later in such subjects as chemistry and biology, but I was good at reading—I had started early on the Burma-Shave signs—and I was fascinated by history and geography, subjects that were still taught in public school in those days. Indiscriminately, I read the works of writers who had traveled, including everything I could find of Richard Halliburton's. I knew the capitals of all the states. The ones I most wanted to go to were Montpelier, Vermont, and Olympia, Washington, for they were the ones that sounded most distant and wondrous.   7

I entered contests that promised travel as a prize. In 1947, when I was twelve, to my surprise, I won one of these competitions—or rather, finished second for the second straight year, which proved to be just as good as winning. We lived in Charlotte, North Carolina, then, where my father had become the county welfare superintendent. *The Charlotte News* sponsored an annual baseball writing contest for students on the subject "My Favorite Hornet." The prize was a road trip with the Charlotte Hornets, our Washington Senators' farm team. Baseball was my passion and regularly I spent my Saturdays in the old green grandstand watching the Hornets play, but it was the trip I was after. My essay on "bouncing" Bobby Beal, the third baseman, was judged good enough that I was invited to accompany the winner, an older boy named Buddy Carrier. We were to ride in the bus with the team and take turns covering six games in Asheville, North Carolina, and Knoxville, Tennessee. I loved it. I loved the easy chaperoneship of manager Cal Ermer, who assigned Buddy and me the same curfew that applied to the team—one A.M.! I loved listening to the banter of the players on the bus, sitting in the dugout during the games and hanging around the hotel lobbies with my heroes. I loved being away from home, in places I had only heard about. Asheville! Knoxville! A good-natured country pitcher named Sonny Dixon played catch with me on the field before each game began and took to introducing me to players on the other teams as "Flash Kuralt, our traveling big-time sports writer." I loved that, too. But best of all was climbing up to the press box as the game was about to end and pecking out my story on the battered portable typewriter I had borrowed for the trip from a caseworker in my father's office, then, downtown after the game, swaggering into the Western Union office, tossing the copy across the counter and saying to the clerk the words I had been instructed to say by Ray Howe, the *Charlotte News* sports editor. They are words that still give me a little thrill of importance all these years later. I did my twelve-year-old best to growl them like a veteran.   8

The words were:

"The Charlotte News. Press rate collect."   9
10

Questions for Discussion

1. Which type(s) of introduction discussed in Chapter 4 does this essay use?
2. Where in this selection do we learn about the setting, the story's time and place?
3. What techniques does Kuralt use to describe the people in his story? How does telling us about them help him move the plot along?
4. Why does he bother to include so many proper names?
5. Selling milk and cookies to the Marines didn't take young Charles far from home. Should the author have spent as much time as he did recalling this experience?
6. In the introduction to Section Four you read examples of language that makes Kuralt's writing lively and believable. Find other examples of effective verbs, adjectives, and nouns.
7. This is a story about visiting new places, meeting new people, and discovering new realities. What does all this exploration reveal about the character of the boy who did the exploring? Would he be fun to know, to grow up with?
8. What does the story reveal about Kuralt the adult?

Suggestions for Journal Entries

1. To illustrate his passion for traveling, the author tells us about rambling over country roads, selling milk and cookies to Marines, and going on a trip with the Hornets. Think about a passion you had as a child: raising tropical fish, collecting stamps, dancing, playing video games, playing and/or watching a sport, for example. Use focused freewriting to recall an incident like one of those in Kuralt's essay. Make sure the incident you narrate shows how ''passionately'' you felt about this activity.
2. Is there someone in your life who inspired a special interest or talent in you much like Kuralt's father encouraged his interest in travel? Use any method for collecting information discussed in ''Getting Started'' to recall what this person did to inspire or encourage you.

SUGGESTIONS FOR WRITING

1. Use narration to explain what someone did to influence you either positively or negatively. Show how this person encouraged or discouraged you to develop a particular interest or talent; explain what he or she taught you about yourself; or discuss ways he or she strengthened or weakened your self-esteem.

   You need not express yourself in an essay. Consider writing a letter instead. Address it to the person who influenced you, and explain your appreciation or resentment of that influence. Either way, put your thesis—a statement of just how positively or negatively he or she affected you—in the introduction to your essay or letter.

   Before you begin, check the journal entries you made after reading Cullen or Kuralt. Then, write one or two stories from personal experience that show how the person in question affected you. After completing your first draft, try adding dialogue to your stories. Reveal your subject's attitude toward you by recalling words he or she used when answering your questions, giving you advice or instructions, or commenting on your efforts.

   As you revise your work further, make sure you have explained the results of this person's influence on you thoroughly. Add details as you move from draft to draft. Then, edit for grammar, punctuation, spelling, and other problems that can make your writing less effective.

2. In "Namas-te," Peter Matthiessen explains that the sight of a crippled child dragging herself through the mud was a "reminder of mortality." If you have seen human suffering up close, you know that it can affect people in different ways. Write an essay or a letter to a friend in which you recall a "pitiable" sight or event you recently witnessed.

   Narrate what happened from beginning to end. Include vivid descriptions of the setting and of the people involved. Tell what you and they did and said during this experience; use dialogue when appropriate. Most important, as you conclude, explain how this experience affected you personally. For example, express anger, sadness, or disappointment that human beings are allowed to suffer, or give thanks that life has not been as cruel to you as it has been to the person(s) you are describing. Like Matthiessen, you might even explain why this incident was a "reminder of mortality."

   As you revise and edit, make sure the information you include and the vocabulary you choose clearly reflect your reaction to the incident. A good place to find such details might be the journal entries you made after reading "Namas-te," but also check your journal notes on Angelou's "The Boys."

3. How we face life's hardships, fears, or emergencies says a lot about the people we are. We can see this clearly in Masters' "Lucinda Matlock." Tell the story of how you, a close friend, neighbor, or relative has dealt with a serious personal problem or concern. As you draft your essay, make sure that the events of your narrative reveal the strength or lack of strength in your subject's character.

Begin by reviewing the journal notes you made after reading Masters' poems. Your responses to Matthiessen's "Namas-te" might also come in handy.

A general overview of your subject's character can make a good introduction to this essay. If you are writing about someone other than yourself, explain how well you know each other or how close you are. Make sure the introduction also includes a statement that clearly expresses the way your subject handles hardship, stress, or adversity. This will be your thesis, the idea that the rest of your essay will illustrate or prove through narration.

After you have completed the second or third draft, read your story carefully and decide whether you have included enough detail to make it convincing. Add information if necessary. At the same time, check that transitions between sentences and paragraphs are clear and logical. As always, polish the final version to catch errors in grammar, spelling, and so on.

4. Cullen, Angelou, and Kuralt tell stories about childhood experiences that had a significant effect on their visions of the world and even on the persons they were to become. What one event in your childhood do you remember most clearly?

Recall this experience in an essay that also explains why it is important to you even today. First, however, review what you wrote in your journal after reading the selections by the authors mentioned above. Your notes might provide both inspiration and information for this assignment. Whether the experience you write about is positive or negative, tell your story vividly by using verbs, adjectives, and adverbs like those in this chapter's poems and essays. Also, include the exact names of places, people, and things to help make your story believable.

After you have written two or three drafts and are convinced your essay is well developed, write a concluding paragraph that explains how the event you have just narrated continues to touch your life today. In other words, explain how it has helped make you the person you are, how it affects the way you view yourself or others, or how it influences the way you now live.

Finally, review the paper as a whole. Have you included enough information, maintained coherence in and between paragraphs, and eliminated distracting errors in spelling, grammar, and the like?

5. Like Robert Pirsig, tell the story of a long trip you took with a relative, friend, or someone you love or loved. If you made a journal entry in response to Pirsig's essay, you may have gotten a good jump on this assignment already.

Spend time describing the setting: talk about the weather; describe the car, bus, train, or other vehicle you traveled in; and give readers concrete details about the place(s) you visited. Like Pirsig, use transitional words and expressions to keep your story moving. If possible, recreate bits of the conversations you had with your companion to help describe him or her, to make your story believable, or simply to explain what happened. At the same time, mention the names—proper nouns—of the places, people, and things you came upon along the way. Of course, you don't have to put all of this information into your first draft. There is always time to add important details as you go through the process of rewriting and editing your work.

A good way to introduce this essay is to discuss your relationship with your traveling partner in a paragraph or two. Make sure your readers know how you felt about each other before you set out on your trip. After completing the story, conclude your essay by explaining what new things the trip taught you about your companion, about yourself, or about your relationship.

6. ''Wanderlust'' traces Charles Kuralt's passion for travel by recalling incidents in his youth, all the way back to the afternoon *before* he was born! Think back to a time in your childhood or teen years when you seemed to focus your attention on one activity: flying kites, playing basketball, making model airplanes, playing with dolls, collecting baseball cards, teasing a brother or sister, playing video or board games, for example.

If you responded to the journal entries after Kuralt's essay, you might have done some freewriting about an incident that shows how ''passionate'' you were about this activity. Turn your journal entry into a full-length essay by narrating two or three more incidents to develop this idea. Try following Kuralt's example by opening your paper with a startling remark, and include a thesis statement that clearly explains how strong your interest was.

As you revise early drafts, make sure your essay contains enough details to support your thesis, to show how passionate you were about the activity you are discussing. Then, before you begin editing your final version for grammar, spelling, and punctuation, review the language you have used. Is your writing concrete, vivid, and convincing? Will your paper hold the readers' interest as firmly as the passion you are describing held yours?

CHAPTER 11

REPORTING EVENTS

The poems and essays in the preceding chapter are autobiographical; they look inward and explain something important about the narrator, the person telling the story. As you recall, each of them is told from the first-person point of view, using the pronoun "I" or "we."

The poems and essays you will read in this chapter, on the other hand, look outward. Some may reveal important facts and insights about their storytellers. Nevertheless, they tell us more about the worlds their narrators live in than about the narrators themselves.

Several of these selections recreate incidents from personal experience and show their writers involved in the action in some way. As a result, they, too, are written in first person. An example is Adrienne Schwartz's "The Colossus in the Kitchen," a story about racism in South Africa, told from the perspective of its young narrator.

In Gansberg's "38 Who Saw Murder Didn't Call the Police," on the other hand, the storyteller is not part of the action. He learns of the murder only secondhand, after talking with eyewitnesses and police. As such, he tells the story from a third-person point of view, using "he," "she," and "they" to explain who did what. As you can see, then, a story's point of view depends upon whether the narrator is a participant or is an outsider—someone who is actually involved in the action or someone who observes it from a distance or learns about it secondhand.

Whichever point of view the selections in this chapter use, they provide a sometimes touching, sometimes terrifying, and always interesting account of their authors' reactions to the world around them. In the introduction to Section Four, you read that narration can be used for a variety of purposes. The poems and essays that follow prove that reporting events is one way to make a point about the nature of human beings and the worlds in which they live. Indeed, if you have ever taken a course in psychology or sociology, you know how important narration can be to explaining human and social behaviors.

Though not always expressed in a formal thesis statement, the main point in each of these selections comes across clearly and forcefully because of the writer's powerful command of language and of other techniques important to telling a story. Use these poems and essays as sources of inspiration for your own work. Reporting events you have heard about, witnessed, or even taken part in is an excellent way to continue growing as a writer. It can also help you discover a clearer and more perceptive vision of the world, at least the world you are writing about.

Child of the Romans

CARL SANDBURG

In the introduction to "Abraham Lincoln" (Chapter 9), you learned that Sandburg is one of America's best-loved poets and biographers. His respect for the common people and his support for labor are evident in "Child of the Romans," a sketch of an Italian immigrant railroad worker. For Sandburg, this "dago shovelman" was typical of the immigrant laborers who built America's factories and railroads.

Looking Ahead

1. "Dago" is an insulting term for an Italian. The poem's title refers to the fact that 2000 years ago Italy was the center of the powerful Roman Empire.
2. Sandburg contrasts the life of the shovelman with those of the people on the train. It is this comparison that serves as the theme of the poem.
3. Verbs and adjectives create a sense of reality in this poem and keep it interesting. Look for them as you read "Child of the Romans."

Vocabulary

eclairs   Rich, custard-filled pastries topped with chocolate.
jonquils   Garden plants of the narcissus family with lovely yellow or white flowers.

> The dago shovelman sits by the railroad track
> Eating a noon meal of bread and bologna.
> A train whirls by, and men and women at tables
> Alive with red roses and yellow jonquils,
> Eat steaks running with brown gravy,
> Strawberries and cream, eclairs and coffee.   5
> The dago shovelman finishes the dry bread and bologna,
> Washes it down with a dipper from the water-boy,
> And goes back to the second half of a ten-hour day's work
> Keeping the road-bed so the roses and jonquils
> Shake hardly at all in the cut glass vases   10
> Standing slender on the tables in the dining cars.

Questions for Discussion

1. The poem's plot is very simple. What events take place during the shovelman's lunch?

2. Sandburg gets very detailed in listing the various items that the railroad passengers are dining on. How do these contrast with what the shovelman is eating?

3. Why does Sandburg make sure to tell us that the train ''whirls'' by as the man eats his lunch? How does his description of the movement of the train contrast with what you read in the last three lines of this poem?

4. How long is the shovelman's day? In what way does his work, ''keeping the road-bed,'' affect the passengers?

5. The poem has two very different settings. What are they, and how does the contrast between the two help Sandburg get his point across?

Suggestions for Journal Entries

1. If you know a hardworking immigrant who has come here in search of a better life, write a story about this person's typical workday.

2. If you have ever had a job in which you provided a service for other people (perhaps as a housepainter, waitress, or salesclerk), narrate one or two events from a typical workday.

3. After reading Sandburg's story of the shovelman's difficult life, many readers are inclined to count their blessings. List some things in your life that make it easier and more hopeful than that of the shovelman.

Back Home

LANGSTON HUGHES

In Chapter 10 you met Countee Cullen, a member of the Harlem Renaissance. Another important figure of this 1920s literary movement was Langston Hughes (1902–1967). One of the best-known black American writers, Hughes relied heavily on personal experience in his work. ''Back Home'' first appeared in The Big Sea, *an autobiography about his early years. In the selection that follows, Hughes tells of the racial discrimination he experienced during his return to the United States from Mexico. In many respects, the theme of this story is similar to what we read in Cullen's ''Incident.'' The difference is that Cullen looks inward; he explains how racism affected him personally. Hughes looks outward; he tells his story as a way to comment upon American society.*

Looking Ahead

1. Until the Civil Rights Act of 1964, ''Jim Crow'' laws prevented blacks from using waiting rooms, restaurants, and other public facilities reserved for whites.

2. Hughes includes excellent examples of dialogue in this essay. Ask yourself how they help make his writing more interesting and realistic.

Vocabulary

pomade   Perfumed hairdressing.

Pullman berth   Small sleeping compartment on a train.

On the way back to Cleveland an amusing thing happened. During the trip to   1
the border, several American whites on the train mistook me for a Mexican, and some of them even spoke to me in Spanish, since I am of a copper-brown complexion, with black hair that can be made quite slick and shiny if it has enough pomade on it in the Mexican fashion. But I made no pretense of passing for a Mexican, or anything else, since there was no need for it—except in changing trains at San Antonio in Texas, where colored people had to use Jim Crow waiting rooms, and could not purchase a Pullman berth. There, I simply went in the main waiting room, as any Mexican would do, and made my sleeping-car reservations in Spanish.

But that evening, crossing Texas, I was sitting alone at a small table in the   2
diner, when a white man came in and took the seat just across the table from mine. Shortly, I noticed him staring at me intently, as if trying to puzzle out something. He stared at me a long time. Then, suddenly, with a loud cry, the white man jumped up and shouted: "You're a nigger, ain't you?" And rushed out of the car as if pursued by a plague.

I grinned. I had heard before that white Southerners never sat down to table   3
with a Negro, but I didn't know until then that we frightened them that badly.

Something rather less amusing happened at St. Louis. The train pulled into   4
the station on a blazing-hot September afternoon, after a sticky, dusty trip, for there were no air-cooled coaches in those days. I had a short wait between trains. In the center of the station platform there was a news stand and soda fountain where cool drinks were being served. I went up to the counter and asked for an ice cream soda.

The clerk said: "Are you a Mexican or a Negro?"   5
I said: "Why?"   6
"Because if you're a Mexican, I'll serve you," he said. "If you're colored,   7
I won't."

"I'm colored," I replied. The clerk turned to wait on someone else. I knew   8
I was home in the U.S.A.

Questions for Discussion

1. What similarities are there between the two episodes (or stories within a story) in "Back Home"? What is the point Hughes is trying to make in them?

2. Why does he bother to say that he could have passed for a Mexican if he had wanted to?
3. In Looking Ahead, you read that Hughes makes excellent use of dialogue. In what way does the dialogue in ''Back Home'' make it more interesting and more realistic?
4. Hughes uses transitional words and phrases to show the passage of time and maintain coherence. What are some of these words and phrases?

Suggestion for a Journal Entry

Hughes says that he ''made no pretense of passing for a Mexican, or anything else, since there was no need for it'' (paragraph 1). If you've ever been insulted or looked down upon because of who or what you are, write a summary of this incident and explain how you felt.

What the Gossips Saw

LEO ROMERO

A native of New Mexico, Leo Romero is among a growing number of contemporary southwestern writers whose poetry and fiction are becoming popular across the country. Romero studied at the University of New Mexico, where he took a degree in English. His poems have appeared in several recent collections of poetry and prose. ''What the Gossips Saw'' was first published in 1981 in a periodical called Agua Negra.

Looking Ahead

1. This is the story of a community's response to a woman who had her leg amputated. What it says about the way society sometimes reacts to those who are who ''different'' can be compared with what we learn from two other pieces in this chapter: Schwartz's ''The Colossus in the Kitchen'' and Hughes's ''Back Home.''
2. Romero chooses to leave out periods and other end marks. Doing so sometimes helps poets create dramatic effects. Nevertheless, developing writers should always include appropriate punctuation.

Vocabulary

alluring   Appealing, tempting.
conjecture   Guessing, speculation.
hobble   Limp.

in cohorts   In league with, cooperating with.
murmur   Mumble discontentedly.

Everyone pitied Escolastica, her leg
had swollen like a watermelon in the summer
It had practically happened over night
She was seventeen, beautiful and soon
to be married to Guillermo who was working   5
in the mines at Terreros, eighty miles away
far up in the mountains, in the wilderness
Poor Escolastica, the old women would say
on seeing her hobble to the well with a bucket
carrying her leg as if it were the weight   10
of the devil, surely it was a curse from heaven
for some misdeed, the young women who were
jealous would murmur, yet they were grieved too
having heard that the doctor might cut
her leg, one of a pair of the most perfect legs   15
in the valley, and it was a topic of great
interest and conjecture among the villagers
whether Guillermo would still marry her
if she were crippled, a one-legged woman—
as if life weren't hard enough for a woman   20
with two legs—how could she manage

Guillermo returned and married Escolastica
even though she had but one leg, the sound
of her wooden leg pounding down the wooden aisle
stayed in everyone's memory for as long   25
as they lived, women cried at the sight
of her beauty, black hair so dark
that the night could get lost in it, a face
more alluring than a full moon

Escolastica went to the dances with her husband   30
and watched and laughed but never danced
though once she had been the best dancer
and could wear holes in a pair of shoes
in a matter of a night, and her waist had been
as light to the touch as a hummingbird's flight   35
And Escolastica bore five children, only half
what most women bore, yet they were healthy
In Escolastica's presence, no one would mention
the absence of her leg, though she walked heavily
And it was not long before the gossips   40

> spread their poison, that she must be in cohorts
> with the devil, had given him her leg
> for the power to bewitch Guillermo's heart
> and cloud his eyes so that he could not see
> what was so clear to them all   45

Questions for Discussion

1. Escolastica's neighbors both pitied and envied her. What does this say about them?
2. How do the gossips explain the fact that Guillermo marries Escolastica despite her misfortune? What does their explanation say about the way they think?
3. What can we conclude about the villagers' opinion of Guillermo and of men in general?
4. The gossips believe Guillermo ''could not see/what was so clear to them all.'' Is this true, or does Guillermo see something they can't?
5. Is the theme of Langston Hughes's ''Back Home'' like the theme of this poem? Explain.
6. Schwartz's ''The Colossus in the Kitchen,'' which comes next in this chapter, shows that a person's bad luck can be mistaken by small-minded people as a sign of sinfulness and of God's punishment. Where does this theme appear in Romero's poem?
7. Pick out words and phrases the author uses to show time passing in this story.
8. What figures of speech does he include?

Suggestions for Journal Entries

1. Think of a person or an event that was the subject of gossip in your school or community. Use listing or another method for gathering details discussed in ''Getting Started'' to explain how much the gossips exaggerated, twisted, or lied about the facts. Try to show how they changed the truth in order to make it seem more sensational, startling, racy, or horrible than it was.
2. Not all communities react badly to people who are different. Do you agree? If so, provide evidence from personal experience, from newspapers, or from other sources to support this idea. For example, talk about how quickly people in your city responded when they heard a neighbor needed expensive medical care, or explain how well students at your school accept newcomers from other cultures.
3. The gossips would have us believe that Escolastica lost her leg because she made a pact with the devil. In Schwartz's ''The Colossus in the Kitchen'' (page 269), the death of an infant is blamed on the fact that its mother and father were not married. Do you know of a case in which people tried to

explain away a tragedy in someone else's life by claiming it was a kind
of punishment? Use focused freewriting to record all you can about this
case.

The Colossus in the Kitchen

ADRIENNE SCHWARTZ

*Adrienne Schwartz was born in Johannesburg in the Republic of South Africa,
where she lived until 1978. Now a U.S. citizen, she is completing her studies in
English to become a professional writer.*

*"The Colossus in the Kitchen" is about the tragedy of apartheid. Tandi, the
black woman Schwartz makes the centerpiece of her story, was her nursemaid
for several years and occupied a special place in her home and her heart.*

Looking Ahead

1. The "Group Areas Act," which Schwartz refers to in paragraph 7,
   required blacks to seek work *only* in those areas of the country for
   which the government had granted them a permit. Unfortunately,
   Tandi's legal husband was not allowed to work in the same region
   as she.
2. The "Colossus" was the giant bronze statue of a male figure straddling the inlet to the ancient Greek city of Rhodes. It was known as
   one of the seven wonders of the ancient world. More generally, this
   term refers to anything that is very large, impressive, and very
   powerful. As you read this essay, ask yourself what made Tandi a
   colossus in the eyes of young Schwartz.

Vocabulary

apoplectic   Characterized by a sudden loss of muscle control or ability
to move.

ashen   Gray.

bestriding   Straddling, standing with legs spread widely.

cavernous   Like a cave or cavern.

confections   Sweets.

cowered   Lowered in defeat.

dauntless   Fearless.

deviants   Moral degenerates.

disenfranchised   Without rights or power.

entailed   Involved.

flaying   Whipping.

gangrenous   Characterized by decay of the flesh.

nebulous   Without a definite shape or form.

prerogative   Privilege.

sage   Wise.

I remember when I first discovered the extraordinary harshness of daily life for   1
black South Africans. It was in the carefree, tumbling days of childhood that I
first sensed apartheid was not merely the impoverishing of the landless and all
that that entailed, but a flaying of the innermost spirit.

The house seemed so huge in those days, and the adults were giants bestrid-   2
ing the world with surety and purpose. Tandi, the cook, reigned with the authori-
tarian discipline of a Caesar. She held audience in the kitchen, an enormous room
filled with half-lights and well-scrubbed tiles, cool stone floors and a cavernous
black stove. Its ceilings were high, and during the heat of midday I would often
drowse in the corner, listening to Tandi sing, in a lilting voice, of the hardships
of black women as aliens in their own country. From half-closed eyes I would
watch her broad hands coax, from a nebulous lump of dough, a bounty of
confections, filled with yellow cream and new-picked apricots.

She was a peasant woman and almost illiterate, yet she spoke five languages   3
quite competently; moreover, she was always there, sturdy, domineering and
quick to laugh.

Our neighbors, in conformity with established thinking, had long branded   4
my mother, and therefore all of us, as deviants, agitators, and no less than second
cousins to Satan himself. The cause of this dishonorable labeling was founded
in the fact that we had been taught to believe in the equality and dignity of man.

''Never take a person's dignity away from him,'' my mother had said, ''no   5
matter how angry or hurt you might be because in the end you only diminish
your own worth.''

That was why I could not understand the apoplectic reaction of the neighbors   6
to my excited news that Tandi was going to have a baby. After all, this was not
politics; this was new life.

Tandi's common-law husband lived illegally with her in the quarters as-   7
signed to them; complying with the law on this and many other petty issues was
not considered appropriate in our household. It was the Group Areas Act that had
been responsible for the breakup of Tandi's marriage in the first place. Her
lawful husband, who was not born in the same area as she, had been refused a
permit to work in the Transvaal, and like others placed in such a burdensome
situation, suffered the continuous degradation of being dragged from his wife's
bed in the middle of the night and of being jobless more often than he could
tolerate. Eventually, he simply melted away, wordlessly, never to be seen or
heard from again, making legal divorce impossible.

The paradox of South Africa is complex in the extreme. It is like a rare and   8 precious stone, set amid the barren wastes, and yet close up it is a gangrenous growth that feeds off its own flesh.

The days passed and Tandi's waist swelled, and pride glowed in her dauntless eyes.   9

And then the child was born, and he lived for a day, and then he died.   10

I could not look at Tandi. I did not know that the young could die. I thought   11 death was the prerogative of the elderly. I could not bear to see her cowered shoulders or ashen face.

I fled to the farthest corner of the yard. One of the neighbors was out picking   12 off dead buds from the rose bushes. She looked over the hedge in concern.

"Why! You look terrible . . . are you ill, dear?" she said.   13

"It's Tandi, Mrs. Green. She lost her baby last night," I replied.   14

Mrs. Green sighed thoughtfully and pulled off her gardening gloves. "It's   15 really not surprising," she said, not unkindly, but as if she were imparting as sage a piece of advice as she could. "These people (a term reserved for the disenfranchised) have to learn that the punishment always fits the crime."

Questions for Discussion

1. Schwartz's reference to Tandi as a colossus is obviously complimentary. What details does she use to show that Tandi is impressive and powerful?
2. The author uses dialogue to emphasize major ideas. What does the quote from Mrs. Green reveal about the world Schwartz grew up in?
3. What was the Schwartz family's attitude toward apartheid, and what did their neighbors think of them because of their political opinions?
4. Why did Tandi's lawful husband leave her? Is it important for Schwartz to explain the reasons for his departure?
5. Schwartz describes the kind of life that Tandi was forced to live by recounting several events about her (in paragraphs 2, 7, 9, and 10). Which event made the greatest impression on you?
6. The death of Tandi's baby and the reactions of her neighbors convinced Schwartz of how harsh a life black South Africans endured. She writes in paragraph 1 that apartheid was not "merely the impoverishing of the landless" but also "a flaying of the innermost spirit." What does she mean by this? In what way do the events at the end of the story dramatize this "flaying"?
7. Earlier in this chapter, you might have read Leo Romero's "What the Gossips Saw." In what way is the theme of that poem similar to the theme of "Colossus in the Kitchen"?

Suggestions for Journal Entries

1. Have you or anyone you know well ever witnessed or been involved in a case of intolerance based on race, color, creed, or sex? List the important events that made up this incident and, if appropriate, use the focused-freewriting

method explained in "Getting Started" to write short descriptions of the characters involved.

2. Schwartz's essay is a startling account of her learning some new and very painful things about life. Using any of the prewriting methods discussed in "Getting Started," make notes about an incident from your childhood that opened your eyes to some new and perhaps unpleasant reality.

3. Were you ever as close to an older person as Schwartz was to Tandi? Examine your relationship with the individual by briefly narrating one or two experiences you shared with him or her.

Twins

E. B. WHITE

E. B. White (1899–1985) was born in Mount Vernon, a suburb of New York City just above the Bronx, where "Twins" takes place. A regular contributor to The New Yorker *magazine and to* Harper's Magazine, *he remains one of the best-known and most highly respected of American essayists of this century. White also wrote several children's books, including* Charlotte's Web *and* Stuart Little, *and, with William Strunk, Jr., he co-authored* Elements of Style, *a classic little book on language usage.*

Looking Ahead

1. The Bronx Zoo, in New York City, is one of the largest municipal animal parks in the world.

2. The setting of "Twins" is very important. Look for the details that describe it.

Vocabulary

captious   Complaining, hard to please.

fastnesses   Enclosed areas.

ingenuity   Skill, cleverness.

Mittel Bronx   The middle of the Bronx.

primate   Member of the family of mammals that includes monkeys, apes, and human beings.

primly   Stiffly.

reducing glass   Lens that makes things look smaller.

resentful   Displeased.

sullenly   With a gloomy or dull expression.

sylvan   Forestlike.
trinket   Tiny ornament or toy.
twinning   Giving birth to twins.
withered   Dried out, dead.

On a warm, miserable morning last week we went up to the Bronx Zoo to see   1
the moose calf and to break in a new pair of black shoes. We encountered better
luck than we had bargained for. The cow moose and her young one were
standing near the wall of the deer park below the monkey house, and in order
to get a better view we strolled down to the lower end of the park, by the brook.
The path there is not much travelled. As we approached the corner where the
brook trickles under the wire fence, we noticed a red deer getting to her feet.
Beside her, on legs that were just learning their business, was a spotted fawn, as
small and perfect as a trinket seen through a reducing glass. They stood there,
mother and child, under a gray beech whose trunk was engraved with dozens of
hearts and initials. Stretched on the ground was another fawn, and we realized
that the doe had just finished twinning. The second fawn was still wet, still
unrisen. Here was a scene of rare sylvan splendor, in one of our five favorite
boroughs, and we couldn't have asked for more. Even our new shoes seemed to
be working out all right and weren't hurting much.

The doe was only a couple of feet from the wire, and we sat down on a rock   2
at the edge of the footpath to see what sort of start young fawns get in the deep
fastnesses of Mittel Bronx. The mother, mildly resentful of our presence and
dazed from her labor, raised one forefoot and stamped primly. Then she lowered
her head, picked up the afterbirth, and began dutifully to eat it, allowing it to
swing crazily from her mouth, as though it were a bunch of withered beet greens.
From the monkey house came the loud, insane hooting of some captious primate,
filling the whole woodland with a wild hooroar. As we watched, the sun broke
weakly through, brightened the rich red of the fawns, and kindled their white
spots. Occasionally a sightseer would appear and wander aimlessly by, but of all
who passed none was aware that anything extraordinary had occurred. ''Looka
the kangaroos!'' a child cried. And he and his mother stared sullenly at the deer
and then walked on.

In a few moments the second twin gathered all his legs and all his ingenuity   3
and arose, to stand for the first time sniffing the mysteries of a park for captive
deer. The doe, in recognition of his achievement, quit her other work and began
to dry him, running her tongue against the grain and paying particular attention
to the key points. Meanwhile the first fawn tiptoed toward the shallow brook, in
little stops and goes, and started across. He paused midstream to make a slight
contribution, as a child does in bathing. Then, while his mother watched, he
continued across, gained the other side, selected a hiding place, and lay down
under a skunk-cabbage leaf next to the fence, in perfect concealment, his legs
folded neatly under him. Without actually going out of sight, he had managed
to disappear completely in the shifting light and shade. From somewhere a long

way off a twelve-o'clock whistle sounded. We hung around awhile, but he never budged. Before we left, we crossed the brook ourself, just outside the fence, knelt, reached through the wire, and tested the truth of what we had once heard: that you can scratch a new fawn between the ears without starting him. You can indeed.

Questions for Discussion

1. How has White described the setting of "Twins"? Why is it important for us to know about the surroundings into which the two deer have been born?
2. The story's plot is rather simple. What are its most significant events?
3. Some of the natural processes that White reports, such as the doe's disposing of the afterbirth, might startle some readers. Should he have left such details out?
4. The author mentions the "insane hooting of some captious primate." What do such details add to the story?
5. White has captured the beauty of the fawns and doe by describing their movements. What verbs, adjectives, and adverbs communicate this beauty to us? Look especially at paragraph 3.
6. Compared to monkeys and kangaroos, deer are not very exotic animals. What qualities in the deer have evidently moved White to write this simple, lovely story about them?
7. Earlier you read that the selections in this chapter reveal something about the nature of human beings and of the worlds in which they live. What does this essay tell us about human nature?

Suggestions for Journal Entries

1. If you've ever been present at the birth of any creature, list in your journal the event's most important and startling details. How did the birth you witnessed compare with what is described in "Twins"?
2. List details that capture your memories of a recent trip through a park, zoo, or other natural place. Then, in a paragraph or two, describe the most memorable of the sights and events you observed.

38 Who Saw Murder Didn't Call the Police

MARTIN GANSBERG

Martin Gansberg was a reporter and editor at The New York Times *when he wrote "38 Who Saw Murder Didn't Call the Police" for that newspaper in 1964. This story about the murder of a young woman is doubly terrifying, for the thirty-eight witnesses to the crime might very well have saved her life if only they had had the courage to become involved.*

Looking Ahead

1. The setting is Kew Gardens, a well-to-do neighborhood in Queens, New York. One reason Gansberg describes it in great detail is to make his story realistic. Another is to show his readers that the neighbors had a clear view of the crime from their windows. But there are other reasons as well. Pay close attention to the details used to describe the setting.

2. Gansberg begins the story by using dialogue to report an interview he had with the police. He ends it similarly, including dialogue from interviews with several witnesses. Read these two parts of the narrative as carefully as the story of the murder itself. They contain important information about Gansberg's reaction to the incident and his purpose in writing this piece.

3. The story of Kitty Genovese is a comment about the fact that people sometimes ignore their responsibilities to neighbors and lose that important sense of community which binds us together. Identify this central idea, or theme, as you read ''38 Who Saw Murder Didn't Call the Police.''

Vocabulary

deliberation   Thinking.

distraught   Very upset, nervous.

punctuated   Were clearly heard (literally ''made a mark in'').

recitation   Speech, lecture.

Tudor   Type of architecture in which the beams are exposed.

For more than half an hour 38 respectable, law-abiding citizens in Queens 1
watched a killer stalk and stab a woman in three separate attacks in Kew Gardens.

Twice their chatter and the sudden glow of their bedroom lights interrupted 2
him and frightened him off. Each time he returned, sought her out, and stabbed her again. Not one person telephoned the police during the assault; one witness called after the woman was dead.

That was two weeks ago today. 3

Still shocked is Assistant Chief Inspector Frederick M. Lussen, in charge of 4
the borough's detectives and a veteran of 25 years of homicide investigations. He can give a matter-of-fact recitation on many murders. But the Kew Gardens slaying baffles him—not because it is a murder, but because the ''good people'' failed to call the police.

"As we have reconstructed the crime," he said, "the assailant had three 5
chances to kill this woman during a 35-minute period. He returned twice to
complete the job. If we had been called when he first attacked, the woman might
not be dead now."

This is what the police say happened beginning at 3:20 A.M. in the staid, 6
middle-class, tree-lined Austin Street area:

Twenty-eight-year-old Catherine Genovese, who was called Kitty by almost 7
everyone in the neighborhood, was returning home from her job as manager of
a bar in Hollis. She parked her red Fiat in a lot adjacent to the Kew Gardens Long
Island Rail Road Station, facing Mowbray Place. Like many residents of the
neighborhood, she had parked there day after day since her arrival from Connect-
icut a year ago, although the railroad frowns on the practice.

She turned off the lights of her car, locked the door, and started to walk the 8
100 feet to the entrance of her apartment at 82-70 Austin Street, which is in a
Tudor building, with stores in the first floor and apartments on the second.

The entrance to the apartment is in the rear of the building because the front 9
is rented to retail stores. At night the quiet neighborhood is shrouded in the
slumbering darkness that marks most residential areas.

Miss Genovese noticed a man at the far end of the lot, near a seven-story 10
apartment house at 82-40 Austin Street. She halted. Then, nervously, she headed
up Austin Street toward Lefferts Boulevard, where there is a call box to the
102nd Police Precinct in nearby Richmond Hill.

She got as far as a street light in front of a bookstore before the man grabbed 11
her. She screamed. Lights went on in the 10-story apartment house at 82-67
Austin Street, which faces the bookstore. Windows slid open and voices punctuated the early-morning stillness.

Miss Genovese screamed: "Oh, my God, he stabbed me! Please help me! 12
Please help me!"

From one of the upper windows in the apartment house, a man called down: 13
"Let that girl alone!"

The assailant looked up at him, shrugged and walked down Austin Street 14
toward a white sedan parked a short distance away. Miss Genovese struggled to
her feet.

Lights went out. The killer returned to Miss Genovese, now trying to make 15
her way around the side of the building by the parking lot to get to her apartment.
The assailant stabbed her again.

"I'm dying!" She shrieked. "I'm dying!" 16

Windows were opened again, and lights went on in many apartments. The 17
assailant got into his car and drove away. Miss Genovese staggered to her feet.
A city bus, Q-10, the Lefferts Boulevard line to Kennedy International Airport,
passed. It was 3:35 A.M.

The assailant returned. By then, Miss Genovese had crawled to the back of 18
the building, where the freshly painted brown doors to the apartment house held
out hope for safety. The killer tried the first door; she wasn't there. At the second
door, 82-62 Austin Street, he saw her slumped on the floor at the foot of the
stairs. He stabbed her a third time—fatally.

It was 3:50 by the time the police received their first call, from a man who 19
was a neighbor of Miss Genovese. In two minutes they were at the scene. The
neighbor, a 70-year-old woman, and another woman were the only persons on
the street. Nobody else came forward.

The man explained that he had called the police after much deliberation. He 20
had phoned a friend in Nassau County for advice and then he had crossed the
roof of the building to the apartment of the elderly woman to get her to make
the call.

"I didn't want to get involved," he sheepishly told the police.   21

Six days later, the police arrested Winston Moseley, a 29-year-old business- 22
machine operator, and charged him with homicide. Moseley had no previous
record. He is married, has two children and owns a home at 133-19 Sutter
Avenue, South Ozone Park, Queens. On Wednesday, a court committed him to
Kings County Hospital for psychiatric observation.

When questioned by the police, Moseley also said that he had slain Mrs. 23
Annie May Johnson, 24, of 146-12 133rd Avenue, Jamaica, on Feb. 29 and
Barbara Kralik, 15, of 174-17 140th Avenue, Springfield Gardens, last July. In
the Kralik case, the police are holding Alvin L. Mitchell, who is said to have
confessed to that slaying.

The police stressed how simple it would have been to have gotten in touch 24
with them. "A phone call," said one of the detectives, "would have done it."
The police may be reached by dialing "O" for operator or SPring 7-3100.

Today witnesses from the neighborhood, which is made up of one-family 25
homes in the $35,000 to $60,000 range with the exception of the two apartment
houses near the railroad station, find it difficult to explain why they didn't call
the police.

A housewife, knowingly if quite casually, said, "We thought it was a lover's 26
quarrel." A husband and wife both said, "Frankly, we were afraid." They
seemed aware of the fact that events might have been different. A distraught
woman, wiping her hands on her apron, said, "I didn't want my husband to get
involved."

One couple, now willing to talk about that night, said they heard the first 27
screams. The husband looked thoughtfully at the bookstore where the killer first
grabbed Miss Genovese.

"We went to the window to see what was happening," he said, "but the 28
light from our bedroom made it difficult to see the street." The wife, still
apprehensive, added: "I put out the light and we were able to see better."

Asked why they hadn't called the police, she shrugged and replied: "I don't 29
know."

A man peeked out from the slight opening in the doorway to his apartment 30
and rattled off an account of the killer's second attack. Why hadn't he called the
police at the time? "I was tired," he said without emotion. "I went back to
bed."

It was 4:25 A.M. when the ambulance arrived to take the body of Miss 31
Genovese. It drove off. "Then," a solemn police detective said, "the people
came out."

Questions for Discussion

1. Catherine Genovese "was called Kitty by almost everyone in the neighborhood" (paragraph 7). What does this fact reveal about her relationship with her neighbors?

2. In Looking Ahead, you learned that there are several reasons for Gansberg's including details to describe the setting of this story. In what kind of neighborhood does the murder take place? What kind of people live in it?

3. The story's theme might be that people seem to be losing their sense of community for fear of "getting involved." Using details from the story, explain this idea more fully.

4. In reporting several interviews he had with the police and with witnesses, Gansberg frames the story with dialogue at the beginning and end. What do we learn from this dialogue?

5. The author keeps the story moving by mentioning the times at which various episodes in the attack took place. Where does he mention these times?

6. In addition, what transitional words or expressions does Gansberg use to show the passage of time?

7. The story's verbs demonstrate how brutal and terrifying the murder of Kitty Genovese actually was. Identify a few of these verbs.

Suggestions for Journal Entries

1. Make a list of things you might have done to help Kitty Genovese had you been an eyewitness.

2. This story illustrates what can happen when people lose their sense of community and refuse to "get involved." Use focused freewriting to make notes about one or two incidents from your own experiences that illustrate this idea too.

3. Recall a time when you thought you were in some danger. Briefly describe what it was like. What did you do to try to avoid or escape physical harm?

SUGGESTIONS FOR WRITING

1. Sandburg's "Child of the Romans" contrasts the shovelman's life with those of the railroad passengers. Show how difficult or easy your life seems when contrasted with the life of someone you know. If you made a journal entry after Sandburg's poem, you might have already gathered details for this paper.

   Focus your essay on the other person; recall events that show the kind of life he or she has led. At the same time, remember that setting is important, so include details that reveal where or when these events took place.

   A good way to introduce the essay is to explain how difficult or easy life seems to you. Then, write a thesis statement that contrasts your life with the life of the other person. Put the thesis at the end of your introduction. For example, say you start by complaining about the difficult courses you are taking, the many hours you work as a cashier, or the fact that you drive an old car. The thesis at the end of this introduction might be: "My life may be hard, but I count my blessings when I think about the sacrifices my cousin made to get through college."

   However you begin, make the events you narrate in the body of your essay illustrate or prove your thesis. If they don't, revise the thesis or rewrite the body of the paper to include details that relate to the thesis more directly. Conclude your essay by explaining what this assignment has taught you about yourself or your society.

   Finally, rewrite and edit the finished product. Make sure your information is well organized, your language is vivid and clear, and your grammar, sentence structure, punctuation, and spelling are correct.

2. Several selections in this chapter are about life's painful realities. Hughes's "Back Home" and Schwartz's "The Colossus in the Kitchen" tell of encounters with racism; Gansberg's "38 Who Saw Murder Didn't Call the Police" explains how apathy and fear can paralyze a neighborhood; "What the Gossips Saw" and "The Colossus in the Kitchen" show that people can become mean-spirited toward those who appear different from them.

   Use these selections as inspiration, and write the story of an event that taught you something distressing about human behavior or society. Try to include the journal notes you made after reading the works mentioned above.

   There are several ways to organize this narrative. Perhaps the easiest is to tell the story from beginning to end, just as you remember it. You need not write a formal introduction unless, like Gansberg, you want to share important insights or background information with readers before beginning the story itself. In fact, your central idea can wait until you write a concluding paragraph that summarizes what the events you just narrated taught you.

   As always, write several drafts and provide enough details to make your story believable. This is a good time to include proper nouns and write dialogue that will give readers the feeling they are on the scene. As you edit, make sure the story moves smoothly and remains interesting. If not, include words and expressions that show the passage of time, and add vivid verbs and adjectives.

3. In "What the Gossips Saw," Romero shows that people who gossip can exaggerate or twist a story so badly that, in their mouths, the truth becomes unrecognizable. Look back to the journal notes you made after reading this poem. Then, begin drafting an essay that tells what happened when gossips spread rumors about a person or event in your school or community.

   As with other assignments, there are several ways to organize your thoughts. For example, start by revealing the truth of a story and then explain step-by-step how gossips distorted that truth. On the other hand, you might recall how false rumors began, how they spread, and how they affected people. A good way to end this kind of paper is to tell the truth as you know it.

   Whether you use either of these methods or follow one of your own, make the story persuasive. Write several drafts, each of which develops the plot in greater and more vivid detail. In addition, explain what this experience taught you about gossip and about the people who spread it. The best place to do this is in the paper's introduction or conclusion.

   This assignment is a good chance to use dialogue and to practice other techniques discussed in Chapter 9 for describing people and their personalities. As you revise your work, rely on such techniques to make the characters in your story interesting and believable. When the time comes to edit, double-check any dialogue you have included for correct punctuation.

4. Have you ever been present at the birth of an animal or human being? Write an essay about this event. Before you begin, review the journal notes you made after reading E. B. White's "Twins" for useful details.

   When you write your first draft, include information about the setting of the birth, but, like White, concentrate on the mother, her offspring, and what happened. As you prepare your second and third drafts, make sure your story is being told slowly, carefully, and completely. Capture the wonder, excitement, or other emotion you experienced at the sight of new life. If you want, make this emotion the focus of your story, and express it in a formal thesis statement at the beginning or end of your paper. Once again, the details of your narrative should relate to and develop this idea.

   When you edit the last draft, check that you have provided appropriate transitions to move the plot along smoothly and naturally. Also, add vivid verbs, adverbs, and adjectives as needed to keep the readers' interest.

5. The selections by Hughes, Schwartz, and Romero speak of the unfair treatment people sometimes receive. Have you ever been treated unfairly because of your race, religion, nationality, a physical handicap, a personal belief, or any other reason? Tell your story vividly and completely, and reveal your feelings about what occurred. More important, explain what the experience taught you about other people or about society in general. You can express this idea in a thesis statement somewhere in your essay.

A good example of an essay that uses narration to develop a strong thesis statement is Schwartz's "The Colossus in the Kitchen." In the first paragraph, the author defines apartheid as "a flaying of the innermost spirit." The story she tells in the rest of the essay shows exactly what she means.

Like Schwartz, you may want to focus on one event. On the other hand, like Hughes and Romero, you can narrate two or three events to support your thesis. Either way, remember to include details about the people in your story as you write and revise. Describing their personalities by recalling what they said or did is one way to convey your opinion of the world you live in. Then, as you edit for grammar, punctuation, and the like, pay special attention to the vocabulary you have chosen. Include proper nouns as appropriate, and make sure your language is both specific and vivid.

6. Have you ever witnessed or experienced an automobile accident, a robbery, a mugging, a house fire, serious injury, sudden illness, or other violence or misfortune? Tell what happened during this terrible experience and describe the people involved. However, spend most of your time discussing the reactions of people who looked on as the event took place. Were you one of them? What did they do or say? What didn't they do that they should have done?

You might find inspiration and information for this project in the journal entries you made after reading Romero, Schwartz, and Gansberg. Before you write your first draft, however, think about what the event itself and the onlookers' reactions taught you about human nature. Were you encouraged or disappointed by what you learned? Express your answer in a preliminary thesis statement. Write at least two drafts of your story, and make sure to include details that will support this thesis.

Then revise at least one more time by turning what you have just written into a letter to the editor of your college or community newspaper. Use your letter to explain your approval or disappointment about the way the onlookers reacted, but don't mention their names. If appropriate, offer suggestions about the way your readers might respond if faced with an experience like the one you have narrated. Whether or not you send your letter to a newspaper, edit it carefully, just as if it were going to be published!

CHAPTER 12

THE SHORT STORY

In the introduction to Section Four, you learned the major difference between nonfiction and fiction. The former is based upon fact. The latter is, for the most part, a product of the author's imagination and, as such, does not recreate events as they actually happened.

Whether fiction or nonfiction, the selections in Section Four use important narrative tools like character, setting, dialogue, point of view, and, of course, plot to develop a central idea or theme. In some cases, especially in works of nonfiction, this idea or theme is stated plainly, in a thesis. In fact, writers of nonfiction often use their stories as concrete illustrations or examples of an important principle or idea about themselves, other people, or life in general.

However, in works of fiction, like the selections you will read in this chapter, the theme is rarely stated openly. What the writer wishes to tell his or her readers about life is revealed through plot, character development, and other narrative elements. In most cases, in fact, it is up to the reader to identify the theme for him- or herself after having read and analyzed the story carefully. This process, known as interpretation, can make reading fiction both challenging and exciting for you, and it is sure to make it more enjoyable.

Charles

SHIRLEY JACKSON

Shirley Jackson (1919–1965) launched her career in the 1940s, when she began to publish short stories in periodicals such as The New Republic *and* The New Yorker. *Her most important short story is "The Lottery." Like most of her other work, it uses ordinary people and places—in this case a typical American farm community—to reveal something strange or terrifying about the human character. The people we meet in "Charles" are also quite recognizable. But in this story Jackson explains human nature by poking us with gentle humor, not by scaring the wits out of us.*

Looking Ahead

1. There seem to be two main characters in this selection, Laurie and Charles. Look for similarities in their personalities by comparing what one says and does with what you learn about the other.

282

2. To make the plot realistic, Jackson gives the job of telling the story to Laurie's mother, another important character. She is the narrator. This is similar to what Michael Anthony does in "Sandra Street," a story later in this chapter.

Vocabulary

cynically   Distrustfully, skeptically.
incredulously   Doubtfully, without believing.
insolently   Disrespectfully.
renounced   Rejected.
unsettling   Disturbing.

The day my son Laurie started kindergarten he renounced corduroy overalls   1
with bibs and began wearing blue jeans with a belt; I watched him go off the first morning with the older girl next door, seeing clearly that an era of my life was ended, my sweet-voiced nursery-school tot replaced by a long-trousered, swaggering character who forgot to stop at the corner and wave good-bye to me.

He came home the same way, the front door slamming open, his cap on the   2
floor, and the voice suddenly become raucous shouting, "Isn't anybody *here?*"

At lunch he spoke insolently to his father, spilled his baby sister's milk, and   3
remarked that his teacher said we were not to take the name of the Lord in vain.

"How *was* school today?" I asked, elaborately casual.   4

"All right," he said.   5

"Did you learn anything?" his father asked.   6

Laurie regarded his father coldly. "I didn't learn nothing," he said.   7

"Anything," I said. "Didn't learn anything."   8

"The teacher spanked a boy, though," Laurie said, addressing his bread and   9
butter. "For being fresh," he added, with his mouth full.

"What did he do?" I asked. "Who was it?"   10

Laurie thought. "It was Charles," he said. "He was fresh. The teacher   11
spanked him and made him stand in a corner. He was awfully fresh."

"What did he do?" I asked again, but Laurie slid off his chair, took a cookie,   12
and left, while his father was still saying, "See here, young man."

The next day Laurie remarked at lunch, as soon as he sat down, "Well,   13
Charles was bad again today." He grinned enormously and said, "Today Charles hit the teacher."

"Good heavens," I said, mindful of the Lord's name, "I suppose he got   14
spanked again?"

"He sure did," Laurie said. "Look up," he said to his father.   15

"What?" his father said, looking up.   16

"Look down," Laurie said. "Look at my thumb. Gee, you're dumb." He   17
began to laugh insanely.

"Why did Charles hit the teacher?" I asked quickly.   18

"Because she tried to make him color with red crayons," Laurie said. 19
"Charles wanted to color with green crayons so he hit the teacher and she
spanked him and said nobody play with Charles but everybody did."

The third day—it was Wednesday of the first week—Charles bounced a 20
see-saw onto the head of a little girl and made her bleed, and the teacher made
him stay inside all during recess. Thursday Charles had to stand in a corner
during story-time because he kept pounding his feet on the floor. Friday Charles
was deprived of blackboard privileges because he threw chalk.

On Saturday I remarked to my husband, "Do you think kindergarten is too 21
unsettling for Laurie? All this toughness, and bad grammar, and this Charles boy
sounds like such a bad influence."

"It'll be all right," my husband said reassuringly. "Bound to be people like 22
Charles in the world. Might as well meet them now as later."

On Monday Laurie came home late, full of news. "Charles," he shouted as 23
he came up the hill; I was waiting anxiously on the front steps. "Charles,"
Laurie yelled all the way up the hill, "Charles was bad again."

"Come right in," I said, as soon as he came close enough. "Lunch is 24
waiting."

"You know what Charles did?" he demanded, following me through the 25
door. "Charles yelled so in school they sent a boy in from first grade to tell the
teacher she had to make Charles keep quiet, and so Charles had to stay after
school. And so all the children stayed to watch him."

"What did he do?" I asked. 26

"He just sat there," Laurie said, climbing into his chair at the table. "Hi, 27
Pop, y'old dust mop."

"Charles had to stay after school today," I told my husband. "Everyone 28
stayed with him."

"What does this Charles look like?" my husband asked Laurie. "What's his 29
other name?"

"He's bigger than me," Laurie said. "And he doesn't have any rubbers and 30
he doesn't ever wear a jacket."

Monday night was the first Parent-Teachers meeting, and only the fact that 31
the baby had a cold kept me from going; I wanted passionately to meet Charles's
mother. On Tuesday Laurie remarked suddenly, "Our teacher had a friend come
to see her in school today."

"Charles's mother?" my husband and I asked simultaneously. 32

"Naaah," Laurie said scornfully. "It was a man who came and made us do 33
exercises, we had to touch our toes. Look." He climbed down from his chair and
squatted down and touched his toes. "Like this," he said. He got solemnly back
into his chair and said, picking up his fork, "Charles didn't even *do* exercises."

"That's fine," I said heartily. "Didn't Charles want to do exercises?" 34

"Naaah," Laurie said. "Charles was so fresh to the teacher's friend he 35
wasn't *let* do exercises."

"Fresh again?" I said. 36

"He kicked the teacher's friend," Laurie said. "The teacher's friend told 37
Charles to touch his toes like I just did and Charles kicked him."

"What are they going to do about Charles, do you suppose?" Laurie's father 38
asked him.

Laurie shrugged elaborately. "Throw him out of school, I guess," he said. 39

Wednesday and Thursday were routine; Charles yelled during story hour 40
and hit a boy in the stomach and made him cry. On Friday Charles stayed after
school again and so did all the other children.

With the third week of kindergarten Charles was an institution in our family; 41
the baby was being a Charles when she cried all afternoon; Laurie did a Charles
when he filled his wagon full of mud and pulled it through the kitchen; even my
husband, when he caught his elbow in the telephone cord and pulled telephone,
ashtray, and a bowl of flowers off the table, said, after the first minute, "Looks
like Charles."

During the third and fourth weeks it looked like a reformation in Charles; 42
Laurie reported grimly at lunch on Thursday of the third week, "Charles was so
good today the teacher gave him an apple."

"What?" I said, and my husband added warily, "You mean Charles?" 43

"Charles," Laurie said. "He gave the crayons around and he picked up the 44
books afterward and the teacher said he was her helper."

"What happened?" I asked incredulously. 45

"He was her helper, that's all," Laurie said, and shrugged. 46

"Can this be true, about Charles?" I asked my husband that night. "Can 47
something like this happen?"

"Wait and see," my husband said cynically. "When you've got a Charles 48
to deal with, this may mean he's only plotting."

He seemed to be wrong. For over a week Charles was the teacher's helper; 49
each day he handed things out and he picked things up; no one had to stay after
school.

"The P.T.A. meeting's next week again," I told my husband one evening. 50
"I'm going to find Charles's mother there."

"Ask her what happened to Charles," my husband said. "I'd like to know." 51

"I'd like to know myself," I said. 52

On Friday of that week things were back to normal. "You know what 53
Charles did today?" Laurie demanded at the lunch table, in a voice slightly
awed. "He told a little girl to say a word and she said it and the teacher washed
her mouth out with soap and Charles laughed."

"What word?" his father asked unwisely, and Laurie said, "I'll have to 54
whisper it to you, it's so bad." He got down off his chair and went around to
his father. His father bent his head down and Laurie whispered joyfully. His
father's eyes widened.

"Did Charles tell the little girl to say *that?*" he asked respectfully. 55

"She said it *twice,*" Laurie said. "Charles told her to say it *twice.*" 56

"What happened to Charles?" my husband asked. 57

"Nothing," Laurie said. "He was passing out the crayons."   58

Monday morning Charles abandoned the little girl and said the evil word   59
himself three or four times, getting his mouth washed out with soap each time.
He also threw chalk.

My husband came to the door with me that evening as I set out for the P.T.A.   60
meeting. "Invite her over for a cup of tea after the meeting," he said. "I want
to get a look at her."

"If only she's there," I said prayerfully.   61

"She'll be there," my husband said. "I don't see how they could hold a   62
P.T.A. meeting without Charles's mother."

At the meeting I sat restlessly, scanning each comfortable matronly face,   63
trying to determine which one hid the secret of Charles. None of them looked
to me haggard enough. No one stood up in the meeting and apologized for the
way her son had been acting. No one mentioned Charles.

After the meeting I identified and sought out Laurie's kindergarten teacher.   64
She had a plate with a cup of tea and a piece of chocolate cake; I had a plate with
a cup of tea and a piece of marshmallow cake. We maneuvered up to one another
cautiously, and smiled.

"I've been so anxious to meet you," I said. "I'm Laurie's mother."   65

"We're all so interested in Laurie," she said.   66

"Well, he certainly likes kindergarten," I said. "He talks about it all the   67
time."

"We had a little trouble adjusting, the first week or so," she said primly,   68
"but now he's a fine little helper. With occasional lapses, of course."

"Laurie usually adjusts very quickly," I said. "I suppose this time it's   69
Charles's influence."

"Charles?"   70

"Yes," I said, laughing, "you must have your hands full in that kindergar-   71
ten, with Charles."

"Charles?" she said. "We don't have any Charles in the kindergarten."   72

Questions for Discussion

1. Although the truth may come as a shock, there are indications throughout the
   story that Charles is none other than Laurie. What things does Laurie do at
   home that are similar to what Charles does in school?

2. How would you describe Laurie's personality? Is the fact that he has created
   an imaginary friend unusual?

3. What changes do we see in Laurie's personality as the story progresses?

4. There are many things about Laurie's family life that seem quite ordinary.
   Are there others that strike you as strange?

5. What kind of parents are Laurie's mother and father? Does the fact that they
   can't see through Laurie's lies seem believable to you? Would you have been
   able to see through Laurie's lies if you were his parents?

6. Think about your answer to question 5. What is the theme of this story? What does it tell us about human nature?

Suggestions for Journal Entries

1. Write a short character sketch of Laurie. Compare him to children you've known who like to pretend a lot.

2. Sometimes we have difficulty recognizing the truth even when it is right under our noses. Recall an incident from your own experience or from something you've read recently (Pirsig's essay in Chapter 10 might be an excellent choice) that illustrates this theme. In a brief journal entry, explain in what ways the incident is similar to Shirley Jackson's "Charles."

3. Did you ever have an imaginary friend or classmate as a child? Use the focused-freewriting method explained in "Getting Started" to recall one or two experiences you had with this companion. If you can, explain why you created this person in the first place.

The Son from America

ISAAC BASHEVIS SINGER

One of the most popular short story writers in America, Isaac Bashevis Singer (1904–1991) composed his works in Yiddish, his first language, then translated them into English. Born in Poland, the country in which this story takes place, Singer immigrated to the United States in 1935. He wrote regularly for the Jewish Daily Forward *and* The New Yorker *magazine. In 1978, he won the Nobel Prize in literature.*

Like many of Singer's other works, "The Son from America" deals with the isolation and the nobility of old age. It appears in A Crown of Feathers, *a collection of short stories that received the National Book Award.*

Looking Ahead

1. The story takes place at about the turn of the century, a time when Russia controlled part of Poland. The characters in this story were driven out of their homes in Russia and forced to settle in Poland as a result of the "pogroms," the severe persecution of Jews by the government of the czar (the Russian emperor). Warsaw, mentioned in paragraph 5, is Poland's capital.

2. The story's setting reveals a great deal about its characters and theme. Keep a sharp lookout for details about Lentshin, the town in which the story takes place, and about the home of Berl and Berlcha, the main characters.

3. The story's theme can be seen most clearly in the differences between the two worlds: the old world of Europe and the new world of America.

Vocabulary

circumcision Religious ceremony in which the foreskin of a male infant's penis is surgically removed.

contours Outline.

Gentile Non-Jewish person.

hinterland Remote region.

Kaddish Prayer for the dead.

Messiah Deliverer or savior of the Jewish people sent by God as promised in the scriptures.

squiresses Women squires or wealthy landowners.

synagogue Temple, house of worship.

Talmud Collection of sacred writings.

Torah Body of Jewish literature, both written and oral, that contains the sacred laws and teachings of the religion.

Yiddish Language spoken by Jews in eastern Europe.

The village of Lentshin was tiny—a sandy marketplace where the peasants of 1 the area met once a week. It was surrounded by little huts with thatched roofs or shingles green with moss. The chimneys looked like pots. Between the huts there were fields, where the owners planted vegetables or pastured their goats.

In the smallest of these huts lived old Berl, a man in his eighties, and his 2 wife, who was called Berlcha (wife of Berl). Old Berl was one of the Jews who had been driven from their villages in Russia and had settled in Poland. In Lentshin, they mocked the mistakes he made while praying aloud. He spoke with a sharp ''r.'' He was short, broad-shouldered, and had a small white beard, and summer and winter he wore a sheepskin hat, a padded cotton jacket, and stout boots. He walked slowly, shuffling his feet. He had a half acre of field, a cow, a goat, and chickens.

The couple had a son, Samuel, who had gone to America forty years ago. 3 It was said in Lentshin that he became a millionaire there. Every month, the Lentshin letter carrier brought old Berl a money order and a letter that no one could read because many of the words were English. How much money Samuel sent his parents remained a secret. Three times a year, Berl and his wife went on foot to Zakroczym and cashed the money orders there. But they never seemed to use the money. What for? The garden, the cow, and the goat provided most of their needs. Besides, Berlcha sold chickens and eggs, and from these there was enough to buy flour for bread.

No one cared to know where Berl kept the money that his son sent him. There were no thieves in Lentshin. The hut consisted of one room, which contained all their belongings: the table, the shelf for meat, the shelf for milk foods, the two beds, and the clay oven. Sometimes the chickens roosted in the woodshed and sometimes, when it was cold, in a coop near the oven. The goat, too, found shelter inside when the weather was bad. The more prosperous villagers had kerosene lamps, but Berl and his wife did not believe in newfangled gadgets. What was wrong with a wick in a dish of oil? Only for the Sabbath would Berlcha buy three tallow candles at the store. In summer, the couple got up at sunrise and retired with the chickens. In the long winter evenings, Berlcha spun flax at her spinning wheel and Berl sat beside her in the silence of those who enjoy their rest.

Once in a while when Berl came home from the synagogue after evening prayers, he brought news to his wife. In Warsaw there were strikers who demanded that the czar abdicate. A heretic by the name of Dr. Herzl had come up with the idea that Jews should settle again in Palestine. Berlcha listened and shook her bonneted head. Her face was yellowish and wrinkled like a cabbage leaf. There were bluish sacks under her eyes. She was half deaf. Berl had to repeat each word he said to her. She would say, ''The things that happen in the big cities!''

Here in Lentshin nothing happened except usual events: a cow gave birth to a calf, a young couple had a circumcision party, or a girl was born and there was no party. Occasionally, someone died. Lentshin had no cemetery, and the corpse had to be taken to Zakroczym. Actually, Lentshin had become a village with few young people. The young men left for Zakroczym, for Nowy Dwor, for Warsaw, and sometimes for the United States. Like Samuel's, their letters were illegible, the Yiddish mixed with the languages of the countries where they were now living. They sent photographs in which the men wore top hats and the women fancy dresses like squiresses.

Berl and Berlcha also received such photographs. But their eyes were failing and neither he nor she had glasses. They could barely make out the pictures. Samuel had sons and daughters with Gentile names—and grandchildren who had married and had their own offspring. Their names were so strange that Berl and Berlcha could never remember them. But what difference do names make? America was far, far away on the other side of the ocean, at the edge of the world. A Talmud teacher who came to Lentshin had said that Americans walk with their heads down and their feet up. Berl and Berlcha could not grasp this. How was it possible? But since the teacher said so it must be true. Berlcha pondered for some time and then she said, ''One can get accustomed to everything.''

And so it remained. From too much thinking—God forbid—one may lose one's wits.

One Friday morning, when Berlcha was kneading the dough for the Sabbath   9
loaves, the door opened and a nobleman entered. He was so tall that he had to
bend down to get through the door. He wore a beaver hat and a cloak bordered
with fur. He was followed by Chazkel, the coachman from Zakroczym, who
carried two leather valises with brass locks. In astonishment Berlcha raised her
eyes.

The nobleman looked around and said to the coachman in Yiddish, "Here   10
it is." He took out a silver ruble and paid him. The coachman tried to hand him
change but he said, "You can go now."

When the coachman closed the door, the nobleman said, "Mother, it's me,   11
your son Samuel—Sam."

Berlcha heard the words and her legs grew numb. Her hands, to which pieces   12
of dough were sticking, lost their power. The nobleman hugged her, kissed her
forehead, both her cheeks. Berlcha began to cackle like a hen, "My son!" At
that moment Berl came in from the woodshed, his arms piled with logs. The goat
followed him. When he saw a nobleman kissing his wife, Berl dropped the wood
and exclaimed, "What is this?"

The nobleman let go of Berlcha and embraced Berl. "Father!"   13

For a long time Berl was unable to utter a sound. He wanted to recite holy   14
words that he had read in the Yiddish Bible, but he could remember nothing.
Then he asked, "Are you Samuel?"

"Yes, Father, I am Samuel."   15

"Well, peace be with you." Berl grasped his son's hand. He was still not   16
sure that he was not being fooled. Samuel wasn't as tall and heavy as this man,
but then Berl reminded himself that Samuel was only fifteen years old when he
had left home. He must have grown in that faraway country. Berl asked, "Why
didn't you let us know you were coming?"

"Didn't you receive my cable?" Samuel asked.   17

Berl did not know what a cable was.   18

Berlcha had scraped the dough from her hands and enfolded her son. He   19
kissed her again and asked, "Mother, didn't you receive a cable?"

"What? If I lived to see this, I am happy to die," Berlcha said, amazed by   20
her own words. Berl, too, was amazed. These were just the words he would have
said earlier if he had been able to remember. After a while Berl came to himself
and said, "Pescha, you will have to make a double Sabbath pudding in addition
to the stew."

It was years since Berl had called Berlcha by her given name. When he   21
wanted to address her, he would say, "Listen," or "Say." It is the young or
those from the big cities who call a wife by her name. Only now did Berlcha
begin to cry. Yellow tears ran from her eyes, and everything became dim. Then
she called out, "It's Friday—I have to prepare for the Sabbath." Yes, she had
to knead the dough and braid the loaves. With such a guest, she had to make a
larger Sabbath stew. The winter day is short and she must hurry.

Her son understood what was worrying her, because he said, "Mother, I will   22
help you."

Berlcha wanted to laugh, but a choked sob came out. "What are you saying? 23 God forbid."

The nobleman took off his cloak and jacket and remained in his vest, on 24 which hung a solid-gold watch chain. He rolled up his sleeves and came to the trough. "Mother, I was a baker for many years in New York," he said, and he began to knead the dough.

"What! You are my darling son who will say Kaddish for me." She wept 25 raspingly. Her strength left her, and she slumped onto the bed.

Berl said, "Women will always be women." And he went to the shed to get 26 more wood. The goat sat down near the oven; she gazed with surprise at this strange man—his height and his bizarre clothes.

The neighbors had heard the good news that Berl's son had arrived from 27 America and they came to greet him. The women began to help Berlcha prepare for the Sabbath. Some laughed, some cried. The room was full of people, as at a wedding. They asked Berl's son, "What is new in America?" And Berl's son answered, "America is all right."

"Do Jews make a living?"

"One eats white bread there on weekdays." 28

"Do they remain Jews?" 29

"I am not a Gentile." 30

31

After Berlcha blessed the candles, father and son went to the little synagogue 32 across the street. A new snow had fallen. The son took large steps, but Berl warned him, "Slow down."

In the synagogue the Jews recited "Let Us Exult" and "Come, My 33 Groom." All the time, the snow outside kept falling. After prayers, when Berl and Samuel left the Holy Place, the village was unrecognizable. Everything was covered with snow. One could see only the contours of the roofs and the candles in the windows. Samuel said, "Nothing has changed here."

Berlcha had prepared gefilte fish, chicken soup with rice, meat, carrot stew. 34 Berl recited the benediction over a glass of ritual wine. The family ate and drank, and when it grew quiet for a while one could hear the chirping of the house cricket. The son talked a lot, but Berl and Berlcha understood little. His Yiddish was different and contained foreign words.

After the final blessing Samuel asked, "Father, what did you do with all the 35 money I sent you?"

Berl raised his white brows. "It's here."

"Didn't you put it in a bank?" 36

"There is no bank in Lentshin." 37

"Where do you keep it?" 38

39

Berl hesitated. "One is not allowed to touch money on the Sabbath, but I 40 will show you." He crouched beside the bed and began to shove something heavy. A boot appeared. Its top was stuffed with straw. Berl removed the straw and the son saw that the boot was full of gold coins. He lifted it.

"Father, this is a treasure!" he called out.

"Well." 41

42

"Why didn't you spend it?"   43

"On what? Thank God, we have everything."   44

"Why didn't you travel somewhere?"   45

"Where to? This is our home."   46

The son asked one question after the other, but Berl's answer was always 47
the same: they wanted for nothing. The garden, the cow, the goat, the chickens
provided them with all they needed. The son said, "If thieves knew about this,
your lives wouldn't be safe."

"There are no thieves here."   48

"What will happen to the money?"   49

"You take it."   50

Slowly, Berl and Berlcha grew accustomed to their son and his American 51
Yiddish. Berlcha could hear him better now. She even recognized his voice. He
was saying, "Perhaps we should build a larger synagogue."

"The synagogue is big enough," Berl replied.   52

"Perhaps a home for old people."   53

"No one sleeps in the street."   54

The next day after the Sabbath meal was eaten, a Gentile from Zakroczym 55
brought a paper—it was the cable. Berl and Berlcha lay down for a nap. They
soon began to snore. The goat, too, dozed off. The son put on his cloak and his
hat and went for a walk. He strode with his long legs across the marketplace. He
stretched out a hand and touched a roof. He wanted to smoke a cigar, but he
remembered it was forbidden on the Sabbath. He had a desire to talk to someone,
but it seemed that the whole of Lentshin was asleep. He entered the synagogue.
An old man was sitting there, reciting psalms. Samuel asked, "Are you praying?"

"What else is there to do when one gets old?"   56

"Do you make a living?"   57

The old man did not understand the meaning of these words. He smiled, 58
showing his empty gums, and then he said, "If God gives health, one keeps on
living."

Samuel returned home. Dusk had fallen. Berl went to the synagogue for the 59
evening prayers and the son remained with his mother. The room was filled with
shadows.

Berlcha began to recite in a solemn singsong, "God of Abraham, Isaac, and 60
Jacob, defend the poor people of Israel and Thy name. The Holy Sabbath is
departing; the welcome week is coming to us. Let it be one of health, wealth and
good deeds."

"Mother, you don't need to pray for wealth," Samuel said. "You are 61
wealthy already."

Berlcha did not hear—or pretended not to. Her face had turned into a cluster 62
of shadows.

In the twilight Samuel put his hand into his jacket pocket and touched his 63
passport, his checkbook, his letters of credit. He had come here with big plans.
He had a valise filled with presents for his parents. He wanted to bestow gifts

on the village. He brought not only his own money but funds from the Lentshin Society in New York, which had organized a ball for the benefit of the village. But this village in the hinterland needed nothing. From the synagogue one could hear hoarse chanting. The cricket, silent all day, started again its chirping. Berlcha began to sway and utter holy rhymes inherited from mothers and grand-mothers:

> Thy holy sheep
> In mercy keep,
> In Torah and good deeds;
> Provide for all their needs,
> Shoes, clothes, and bread
> And the Messiah's tread.

Questions for Discussion

1. What does the story's setting reveal about Berl and Berlcha and about their standard of living?
2. Why didn't they learn about the coming of their son until after he arrived? What does this tell you about their village?
3. Singer includes details about the kind of life the son leads in America. What are these details, and what do they show us about the son?
4. There are indications that Berl and Berlcha have led very hard lives. What are some of these indications?
5. Despite all his wealth, the son from America worries about certain things. What is the source of his worry?
6. Despite their problems, Berl and Berlcha seem content; in fact, they refuse to spend the money their son has sent them over the years. What is the source of their contentment?
7. What is the theme of this story?

Suggestions for Journal Entries

1. Berl and Berlcha are set on finding happiness (or contentment) despite the hardships of life. In Chapter 10, Edgar Lee Masters' Lucinda Matlock also possessed this positive attitude. If you've ever known or read about anyone else like this, write a brief journal entry about a memorable event in this person's life that illustrates how courageous he or she is.
2. The story's setting reveals a lot about its major characters. Do you know someone whose home, office, or backyard shows something about the kind

of life that he or she has lived? Describe this setting in as much detail as you can.

3. Explain your personal reaction to the characters in Singer's story. How do you feel about Berl, Berlcha, and their son?

4. This is a story in which religious principles and a belief in God are extremely important. Recall an incident in which your belief in a moral, ethical, or religious principle had a significant effect on you or on someone you know well. Sketch out a few details about the story and explain why the principle in question was important.

Sandra Street

MICHAEL ANTHONY

Michael Anthony was born and has spent most of his life in Trinidad, the setting for much of his work. Like "Sandra Street," many of his other short stories are about growing up on this island, and they reflect a deep appreciation for Caribbean culture. Anthony is also known for his novels, among which are Streets of Conflict *and* All That Glitters.

Looking Ahead

In "Sandra Street," the person telling the story is not the author but one of the major characters. This *speaker* or *narrator,* whom the author calls "Steve," tells the story in the first person ("I"). As such, he reveals as much about himself as about Sandra Street or about Mr. Blades, the other major character.

Vocabulary

appease   Satisfy, make peaceful.

cricket   Outdoor sport developed in Great Britain and similar to base-ball in some ways.

cumbersomely   In an awkward or clumsy way.

exultantly   Happily, jubilantly, triumphantly.

fiendish   Devilish.

laden   Full of, heavy with.

profuse   Abundant.

savannah   Flat, open grassland without trees.

self-conscious   Overly aware of one's self or actions, ill at ease.

sombre   Sad, gloomy.

Mr Blades, the new teacher, was delighted with the compositions we wrote   1
about Sandra Street. He read some aloud to the class. He seemed particularly
pleased when he read what was written by one of the boys from the other side
of the town.

"Sandra Street is dull and uninteresting," the boy wrote. "For one half of   2
its length there are a few houses and a private school (which we go to) but the
other half is nothing but a wilderness of big trees." Mr Blades smiled from the
corners of his mouth and looked at those of us who belonged to Sandra Street.
"In fact," the boy wrote, *"it* is the only street in our town that has big trees, and
I do not think it is a part of our town at all because it is so far and so different
from our other streets."

The boy went on to speak of the gay attractions on the other side of the town,   3
some of which, he said, Sandra Street could never dream to have. In his street,
for instance, there was the savannah where they played football and cricket, but
the boys of Sandra Street had to play their cricket in the road. And to the
amusement of Mr Blades, who also came from the other side of the town, he
described Sandra Street as a silly little girl who ran away to the bushes to hide
herself.

Everyone laughed except the few of us from Sandra Street, and I knew what   4
was going to happen when school was dismissed, although Mr Blades said it was
all a joke and in fact Sandra Street was very fine. I did not know whether he
meant this or not, for he seemed very much amused and I felt this was because
he came from the other side of the town.

He read out a few more of the compositions. Some of them said very nice   5
things about Sandra Street, but those were the ones written by ourselves. Mr
Blades seemed delighted about these, too, and I felt he was trying to appease us
when he said that they showed up new aspects of the beauty of Sandra Street.
There were only a few of us who were appeased, though, and he noticed this and
said all right, next Tuesday we'll write about the other side of the town. This
brought fiendish laughter from some of us from Sandra Street, and judging from
the looks on the faces of those from the other side of the town, I knew what
would happen next Tuesday, too, when school was dismissed. And I felt that
whatever happened it wasn't going to make any difference to our side or to the
other side of the town.

Yet the boy's composition was very truthful. Sandra Street was so different   6
from the other streets beyond. Indeed, it came from the very quiet fringes and
ran straight up to the forests. As it left the town there were a few houses and
shops along it, and then the school, and after that there were not many more
houses, and the big trees started from there until the road trailed off to the river
that bordered the forests. During the day all would be very quiet except perhaps
for the voice of one neighbour calling to another, and if some evenings brought
excitement to the schoolyard, these did very little to disturb the calmness of
Sandra Street.

Nor did the steel band gently humming from the other side of the town. I   7 had to remember the steel band because although I liked to hear it I had to put into my composition that it was very bad. We had no steel bands in Sandra Street, and I thought I could say that this was because we were decent, cultured folk, and did not like the horrible noises of steel bands.

I sat in class recalling the boy's composition again. Outside the window I **8** could see the women coming out of the shops. They hardly passed each other without stopping to talk, and this made me laugh. For that was exactly what the boy had written—that they could not pass without stopping to talk, as if they had something to talk about.

I wondered what they talked about. I did not know. What I did know was **9** that they never seemed to leave Sandra Street to go into the town. Maybe they were independent of the town! I chuckled a triumphant little chuckle because this, too, would be good to put into my composition next Tuesday.

Dreamingly I gazed out of the window. I noticed how Sandra Street stood **10** away from the profusion of houses. Indeed, it did not seem to belong to the town at all. It stood off, not proudly, but sadly, as if it wanted peace and rest. I felt all filled up inside. Not because of the town in the distance but because of this strange little road. It was funny, the things the boy had written; he had written in anger what I thought of now in joy. He had spoken of the pleasures and palaces on the other side of the town. He had said why they were his home sweet home. As I looked at Sandra Street, I, too, knew why it was my home sweet home. It was dull and uninteresting to him but it meant so much to me. It was . . .

"Oh!" I started, as the hand rested on my shoulder. **11**

"It's recess," said Mr Blades. **12**

"Oh! . . . yes, sir." The class was surging out to the playground. I didn't **13** seem to have heard a sound before.

Mr Blades looked at me and smiled. "What are you thinking of?" he said. **14**

He seemed to be looking inside me. Inside my very mind. I stammered out **15** a few words which, even if they were clear, would not have meant anything. I stopped. He was still smiling quietly at me. "You are the boy from Sandra Street?" he said.

"Yes, sir." **16**

"I thought so," he said. **17**

What happened on the following Tuesday after school was a lot worse than **18** what had ever happened before, and it was a mystery how the neighbours did not complain or Mr Blades did not get to hear of it. We turned out to school the next morning as if all had been peaceful, and truly, there was no sign of the battle, save the little bruises which were easy to explain away.

We kept getting compositions to write. Mr Blades was always anxious to **19** judge what we wrote but none gave him as much delight as those we had written about Sandra Street. He had said that he knew the other side of the town very well and no one could fool him about that, but if any boy wrote anything about Sandra Street he would have to prove it. And when he had said that, he had looked at me and I was very embarrassed. I had turned my eyes away, and he had said that when the mango season came he would see the boy who didn't speak the truth about Sandra Street.

Since that day I was very shy of Mr Blades, and whenever I saw him walking 20 towards me I turned in another direction. At such times there would always be a faint smile at the corners of his mouth.

I stood looking out of the school window one day thinking about this and 21 about the compositions when again I felt a light touch and jumped.

"Looking out?" Mr Blades said.

"Yes, sir." 22

23

He stood there over me and I did not know if he was looking down at me 24 or looking outside, and presently he spoke; "Hot, eh?"

"Yes," I said.

25

He moved in beside me and we both stood there looking out of the window. 26 It was just about noon and the sun was blazing down on Sandra Street. The houses stood there tall and rather sombre-looking, and there seemed to be no movement about save for the fowls lying in the shadows of the houses. As I watched this a certain sadness came over me and I looked over the houses across to the hills. Suddenly my heart leapt and I turned to Mr Blades, but I changed my mind and did not speak. He had hardly noticed that I looked up at him. I saw his face looking sad as his eyes wandered about the houses. I felt self-conscious as he looked at the houses for they no longer were new and the paint had been washed off them by the rains and they had not been repainted. Then, too, there were no gates and no fences around them as there were in the towns, and sometimes, with a great flurry, a hen would scamper from under one house to another leaving dust behind in the hot sun.

I looked at Mr Blades. He was smiling faintly. He saw me looking at him. 27 "Fowls," he said.

"There are no gates," I apologized.

28

"No, there are no gates." And he laughed softly to himself. 29

"Because . . ." I had to stop. I did not know why there were no gates. 30

"Because you did not notice that before." 31

"I noticed that before," I said. 32

Looking sharply at me he raised his brows and said slowly: "You noticed 33 that before. Did you put that in your composition? You are the boy from Sandra Street, are you not?"

"There are more from Sandra Street." 34

"Did you notice the cedar grove at the top?" he went on. "You spoke of 35 the steel band at the other side of the town. Did you speak of the river? Did you notice the hills?"

"Yes," 36

"Yes?" His voice was now stern and acid. His eyes seemed to be burning 37 up from within.

"You noticed all this and you wrote about Sandra Street without mentioning 38 it, eh? How many marks did I give you?"

"Forty-five." 39

He looked surprised. "I gave you forty-five for writing about the noises and 40
about the dirty trams of the town? Look!" he pointed, "do you see?"

"Mango blossoms," I said, and I felt like crying out: *"I wanted to show it* 41
to you!"

"Did you write about it?" 42

"No." I just wanted to break out and run away from him. He bent down to 43
me. His face looked harder now, though kind, but I could see there was fury
inside him.

"There is something like observation, Steve," he said. *"Observation.* You 44
live in Sandra Street, yet Kenneth writes a composition on your own place better
than you."

"He said Sandra Street was soppy," I cried. 45

"Of course he said it was soppy. It was to his purpose. He comes from the 46
other side of the town. What's he got to write on—gaudy houses with gates like
prisons around them? High walls cramping the imagination? The milling crowd
with faces impersonal as stone, hurrying on buses, hurrying off trams? Could he
write about that? He said Sandra Street was soppy. Okay, did you prove it wasn't
so? Where is your school and his, for instance?"

I was a little alarmed. Funny how I did not think of that point before. 47
"Here," I said. "In Sandra Street."

"Did you mention that?" 48

Mercifully, as he was talking, the school bell sounded. The fowls, startled, 49
ran out into the hot sun across the road. The dust rose, and above the dust, above
the houses, the yellow of mango blossom caught my eye.

"The bell, sir." 50

"Yes, the bell's gone. What's it now—Geography?" 51

"Yes, sir," I said. And as I turned away he was still standing there, looking 52
out into the road.

It was long before any such thing happened again. Though often when it was 53
dry and hot I stood at the window looking out. I watched the freedom of the
fowls among the tall houses, and sometimes the women talked to each other
through the windows and smiled. I noticed, too, the hills, which were now
streaked with the blossoms of the poui, and exultantly I wondered how many
people observed this and knew it was a sign of the rains. None of the mango
blossoms could be seen now, for they had already turned into fruit, and I knew
how profuse they were because I had been to the hills.

I chuckled to myself. *There is something like observation, Steve.* And how 54
I wished Mr Blades would come to the window again so I could tell him what
lay among the mango trees in the hills.

I knew that he was not angry with me. I realized that he was never angry 55
with any boy because of the parts the boy came from. We grew to like him, for
he was very cheerful, though mostly he seemed dreamy and thoughtful. That is,
except at composition time.

He really came to life then. His eyes would gleam as he read our composi- 56
tions and whenever he came to a word he did not like he would frown and say

any boy was a sissy to use such a word. And if a composition pleased him he would praise the boy and be especially cheerful with him and the boy would be proud and the rest of us would be jealous and hate him.

I was often jealous. Mr Blades had a passion for compositions, and I was 57 anxious to please him to make up for that day at the window. I was anxious to show him how much I observed and often I noted new things and put them into my compositions. And whenever I said something wonderful I knew it because of the way Mr Blades would look at me, and sometimes he would take me aside and talk to me. But many weeks ran out before we spoke at the window again.

I did not start this time because I had been expecting him. I had been 58 watching him from the corners of my eyes.

"The sun's coming out again," he said. 59

"It's cloudy," I said. 60

The rains had ceased but there were still great patches of dark cloud in the 61 sky. When the wind blew they moved slowly and cumbersomely, but if the sun was free of one cloud there would soon be another. The sun was shining brightly now, although there was still a slight drizzle of rain, and I could smell the steam rising from the hot pitch and from the galvanized roofs.

"Rain falling sun shining," Mr Blades said. And I remembered that they 62 said at such times the Devil fought his wife, but when Mr Blades pressed me to tell what I was laughing at I laughed still more and would not say. Then thoughtfully he said, "You think they're all right?"

"What, sir?" 63

"In the 'mortelle root." 64

I was astonished. I put my hands to my mouth. How did he know? 65

He smiled down at me: "You won't be able to jump over now." And the 66 whole thing came back. I could not help laughing. I had put into my composition how I had gone into the hills on a Sunday evening, and how the mango trees were laden with small mangoes, some full, and how there were banana trees among the immortelle and poui. I had written, too, about the bunch of green bananas I had placed to ripen in the immortelle roots and how afterwards I had jumped across the river to the other bank.

"They're all right," I said, and I pretended to be watching the steam rising 67 from the hot pitch.

"I like bananas," said Mr Blades. I was sure that he licked his lips as he 68 looked towards the hills.

I was touched. I felt as one with him. I liked bananas, too, and they always 69 made me lick my lips. I thought now of the whole bunch which must be yellow by now inside the immortelle roots.

"Sir . . ." I said to him, hesitating. Then I took the wild chance. And when 70 he answered, a feeling of extreme happiness swept over me.

I remember that evening as turning out bright, almost blinding. The winds 71 had pushed away the heavy clouds, and the only evidence of the rains was the little puddles along Sandra Street. I remember the hills as being strange in an enchanted sort of way, and I felt that part of the enchantment came from Mr

Blades being with me. We watched the leaves of the cocoa gleaming with the moisture of the rains, and Mr Blades confessed he never thought there was so much cocoa in the hills. We watched the cyp, too, profuse among the laden mango trees, and the redness of their rain-picked flowers was the redness of blood.

We came to the immortelle tree where I had hidden the bananas. I watched 72 to see if Mr Blades licked his lips but he did not. He wasn't even watching.

"Sir," I said in happy surprise, after removing the covering of trash from 73 the bunch. Mr Blades was gazing across the trees. I raised my eyes. Not far below, Sandra Street swept by, bathed in light.

"The bananas, sir," I said. 74

"*Bananas!*" he cried, despairingly. "Bananas are all you see around you, 75 Steve?"

I was puzzled. I thought it was for bananas that we had come to the hills. 76

"Good heavens!" he said with bitterness. "To think that you instead of 77 Kenneth should belong to Sandra Street."

Questions for Discussion

1. How does the narrator react to Kenneth's description of Sandra Street? In what ways is Kenneth's composition fair and accurate? In what ways is it not?

2. In his own paper, Steve writes that the steel band from the other side of town "was very bad" (paragraph 7). What does this statement reveal about his character at this point in the story?

3. How does the narrator view Sandra Street at the beginning of the story? Does his neighborhood differ from the other part of town?

4. Discuss the difference between the ways Steve and Mr. Blades see the world as explained in paragraphs 59 and 60.

5. How does Steve feel about his new teacher? Does their relationship change as we near the end of the story?

6. In paragraph 44, Mr. Blades says, "There is something like observation." What is he trying to teach Steve?

7. Read paragraphs 70 and 71 again. What "wild chance" is Steve taking and what does it tell us about him?

Suggestions for Journal Entries

1. Did you ever have a teacher who inspired you, built your confidence, or helped you see the world in a new and brighter light? Use focused freewriting to record everything you can remember about this individual. Write nonstop for about five minutes; then read what you have put down. Finish your entry by spending another five minutes explaining how this person affected your life.

2. The setting of Anthony's story is obviously important. Use listing or brainstorming to gather details about your street, neighborhood, or hometown. Try to write about various aspects of the place by capturing its sights, sounds, smells, and so on. If your reaction is generally positive, balance that view by also explaining how your community might be improved. By the same token, if your reaction is negative, find something good to say about the place as well.

A Worn Path

EUDORA WELTY

Like all great writers, Pulitzer Prize–winning Eudora Welty relies on her powers of observation to write about what she knows best. Born in Jackson, Mississippi, she sets her stories in the rural South, where she has lived most of her life.

Many of Welty's characters seem eccentric, even bizarre, and they remain stuck in our minds and hearts long after we read about them. Their stories can be comical, disturbing, and touching all at the same time. But often the dignity of the human spirit shines through so brightly that we can't help being inspired by the experience.

Looking Ahead

1. The major character in this story, Phoenix Jackson, gets her first name from a mythical bird that became a symbol of rebirth. According to myth, the phoenix would live for 500 years and then burn itself into a pile of ashes from which another phoenix would arise.

2. We learn a great deal about Phoenix Jackson by what she does in this story. Try to analyze each of her actions as you make your way through the plot.

3. Look closely at the dialogue that old Phoenix uses when she talks to herself, to the animals, and to the other natural objects along the way. Incidentally, you'll notice that Welty has realistically captured the natural rhythm and sound of her speech, complete with regional pronunciation and grammatical errors.

4. As you've learned in Chapter 9, what we come to know about a character from other people in the story may be just as important as what the narrator says. Phoenix meets a few people during the story, each of whom helps reveal something important about her.

Vocabulary

appointed   Assigned.
enduring   Lasting.

frailest   Most delicate.

grave   Somber, sad.

illuminated   Lit up.

limber   Agile, flexible.

meditative   Thoughtful, prayerful.

pullets   Young hens.

ravine   Gorge.

rouse   Awaken, stir up.

It was December—a bright frozen day in the early morning. Far out in the   1
country there was an old Negro woman with her head tied in a red rag, coming
along a path through the pinewoods. Her name was Phoenix Jackson. She was
very old and small and she walked slowly in the dark pine shadows, moving a
little from side to side in her steps, with the balanced heaviness and lightness of
a pendulum in a grandfather clock. She carried a thin, small cane made from an
umbrella, and with this she kept tapping the frozen earth in front of her. This
made a grave and persistent noise in the still air, that seemed meditative like the
chirping of a solitary little bird.

She wore a dark striped dress reaching down to her shoe tops, and an equally   2
long apron of bleached sugar sacks, with a full pocket: all neat and tidy, but
every time she took a step she might have fallen over her shoe-laces, which
dragged from her unlaced shoes. She looked straight ahead. Her eyes were blue
with age. Her skin had a pattern all its own of numberless branching wrinkles
and as though a whole little tree stood in the middle of her forehead, but a golden
color ran underneath, and the two knobs of her cheeks were illuminated by a
yellow burning under the dark. Under the red rag her hair came down on her neck
in the frailest of ringlets, still black, and with an odor like copper.

Now and then there was a quivering in the thicket. Old Phoenix said, "Out   3
of my way, all you foxes, owls, beetles, jack rabbits, coons, and wild animals!
. . . Keep out from under these feet, little bob-whites. . . . Keep the big wild hogs
out of my path. Don't let none of those come running my direction. I got a long
way." Under her small black-freckled hand her cane, limber as a buggy whip,
would switch at the brush as if to rouse up any hiding things.

On she went. The woods were deep and still. The sun made the pine needles   4
almost too bright to look at, up where the wind rocked. The cones dropped as
light as feathers. Down in the hollow was the mourning dove—it was not too late
for him.

The path ran up a hill. "Seem like there is chains about my feet, time I get   5
this far," she said, in the voice of argument old people keep to use with
themselves. "Something always take a hold of me on this hill—pleads I should
stay."

After she got to the top she turned and gave a full, severe look behind her   6
where she had come. "Up through pines," she said at length. "Now down
through oaks."

Her eyes opened their widest, and she started down gently. But before she   7
got to the bottom of the hill a bush caught her dress.

Her fingers were busy and intent, but her skirts were full and long, so that   8
before she could pull them free in one place they were caught in another. It was
not possible to allow the dress to tear. "I in the thorny bush," she said. "Thorns,
you doing your appointed work. Never want to let folks pass—no sir. Old eyes
thought you was a pretty little *green* bush."

Finally, trembling all over, she stood free, and after a moment dared to stoop   9
for her cane.

"Sun so high!" she cried, leaning back and looking, while the thick tears   10
went over her eyes. "The time getting all gone here."

At the foot of this hill was a place where a log was laid across the creek.   11
"Now comes the trial," said Phoenix.
                                                                                  12
Putting her right foot out, she mounted the log and shut her eyes. Lifting her   13
skirt, leveling her cane fiercely before her, like a festival figure in some parade,
she began to march across. Then she opened her eyes and she was safe on the
other side.

"I wasn't as old as I thought," she said.
                                                                                  14
But she sat down to rest. She spread her skirts on the bank around her and   15
folded her hands over her knees. Up above her was a tree in a pearly cloud of
mistletoe. She did not dare to close her eyes, and when a little boy brought her
a little plate with a slice of marble-cake on it she spoke to him. "That would be
acceptable," she said. But when she went to take it there was just her own hand
in the air.

So she left that tree, and had to go through a barbed-wire fence. There she   16
had to creep and crawl, spreading her knees and stretching her fingers like a baby
trying to climb the steps. But she talked loudly to herself: she could not let her
dress be torn now, so late in the day, and she could not pay for having her arm
or her leg sawed off if she got caught fast where she was.

At last she was safe through the fence and risen up out in the clearing. Big   17
dead trees, like black men with one arm, were standing in the purple stalks of
the withered cotton field. There sat a buzzard.

"Who you watching?"
                                                                                  18
In the furrow she made her way along.
                                                                                  19
"Glad this not the season for bulls," she said, looking sideways, "and the   20
good Lord made his snakes to curl up and sleep in the winter. A pleasure I don't
see no two-headed snake coming around that tree, where it come once. It took
a while to get by him, back in the summer."

She passed through the old cotton and went into a field of dead corn. It   21
whispered and shook and was taller than her head. "Through the maze now,"
she said, for there was no path.

Then there was something tall, black, and skinny there, moving before   22
her.

At first she took it for a man. It could have been a man dancing in the field.   23
But she stood still and listened, and it did not make a sound. It was as silent as
a ghost.

"Ghost," she said sharply, "who be you the ghost of? For I have heard of   24
nary death close by."

But there was no answer—only the ragged dancing in the wind.   25

She shut her eyes, reached out her hand, and touched a sleeve. She found   26
a coat and inside that an emptiness, cold as ice.

"You scarecrow," she said. Her face lighted. "I ought to be shut up for   27
good," she said with laughter. "My senses is gone. I too old. I the oldest people
I ever know. Dance, old scarecrow," she said, "while I dancing with you."

She kicked her foot over the furrow, and with mouth drawn down, shook her   28
head once or twice in a little strutting way. Some husks blew down and whirled
in streamers about her skirts.

Then she went on, parting her way from side to side with the cane, through   29
the whispering field. At last she came to the end, to a wagon track where the
silver grass blew between the red ruts. The quail were walking around like
pullets, seeming all dainty and unseen.

"Walk pretty," she said. "This the easy place. This the easy going."   30

She followed the track, swaying through the quiet bare fields, through the   31
little strings of trees silver in their dead leaves, past cabins silver from weather,
with the doors and windows boarded shut, all like old women under a spell
sitting there. "I walking in their sleep," she said, nodding her head vigorously.

In a ravine she went where a spring was silently flowing through a hollow   32
log. Old Phoenix bent and drank. "Sweet-gum makes the water sweet," she
said, and drank more. "Nobody know who made this well, for it was here when
I was born."

The track crossed a swampy part where the moss hung as white as lace from   33
every limb. "Sleep on, alligators, and blow you bubbles." Then the track went
into the road.

Deep, deep the road went down between the high green-colored banks.   34
Overhead the live-oaks met, and it was as dark as a cave.

A black dog with a lolling tongue came up out of the weeds by the ditch.   35
She was meditating, and not ready, and when he came at her she only hit him
a little with her cane. Over she went in the ditch, like a little puff of milkweed.

Down there, her senses drifted away. A dream visited her, and she reached   36
her hand up, but nothing reached down and gave her a pull. So she lay there and
presently went to talking. "Old woman," she said to herself, "that black dog
come up out of the weeds to stall you off, and now there he sitting on his fine
tail, smiling at you."

A white man finally came along and found her—a hunter, a young man, with   37
his dog on a chain.

"Well, Granny!" he laughed. "What are you doing there?"   38

"Lying on my back like a June-bug waiting to be turned over, mister," she   39
said, reaching up her hand.

He lifted her up, gave her a swing in the air, and set her down, "Anything   40
broken, Granny?"

"No sir, them old dead weeds is springy enough," said Phoenix, when she   41
had got her breath. "I thank you for your trouble."

"Where do you live, Granny?" he asked, while the two dogs were growling   42
at each other.

"Away back yonder, sir, behind the ridge. You can't even see it from here."   43

"On your way home?"   44

"No, sir, I going to town."   45

"Why, that's too far! That's as far as I walk when I come out myself, and   46
I get something for my trouble." He patted the stuffed bag he carried, and there
hung down a little closed claw. It was one of the bob-whites, with its beak
hooked bitterly to show it was dead. "Now you go on home, Granny!"

"I bound to go to town, mister," said Phoenix. "The time come around."   47

He gave another laugh, filling the whole landscape. "I know you old colored   48
people! Wouldn't miss going to town to see Santa Claus!"

But something held Old Phoenix very still. The deep lines in her face went   49
into a fierce and different radiation. Without warning, she had seen with her own
eyes a flashing nickel fall out of the man's pocket onto the ground.

"How old are you, Granny?" he was saying.   50

"There is no telling, mister," she said, "no telling."   51

Then she gave a little cry and clapped her hands and said, "Git on away   52
from here, dog! Look! Look at that dog!" She laughed as if in admiration. "He
ain't scared of nobody. He a big black dog." She whispered, "Sic him!"

"Watch me get rid of that cur," said the man. "Sic him, Pete! Sic him!"   53

Phoenix heard the dogs fighting, and heard the man running and throwing   54
sticks. She even heard a gunshot. But she was slowly bending forward by that
time, further and further forward, the lids stretched down over her eyes, as if she
were doing this in her sleep. Her chin was lowered almost to her knees. The
yellow palm of her hand came out from the fold of her apron. Her fingers slid
down and along the ground under the piece of money with the grace and care
they would have in lifting an egg from under a sitting hen. Then she slowly
straightened up, she stood erect, and the nickel was in her apron pocket. A bird
flew by. Her lips moved. "God watching me the whole time. I come to stealing."

The man came back, and his own dog panted about them. "Well, I scared   55
him off that time," he said, and then he laughed and lifted his gun and pointed
it at Phoenix.

She stood straight and faced him.   56

"Doesn't the gun scare you?" he said, still pointing it.   57

"No, sir, I seen plenty go off closer by, in my day, and for less than what   58
I done," she said, holding utterly still.

He smiled, and shouldered the gun. "Well, Granny," he said, "you must be   59
a hundred years old, and scared of nothing. I'd give you a dime if I had any
money with me. But you take my advice and stay home, and nothing will happen
to you."

"I bound to go on my way, mister," said Phoenix. She inclined her head in   60
the red rag. Then they went in different directions, but she could hear the gun
shooting again and again over the hill.

She walked on. The shadows hung from the oak trees to the road like   61 curtains. Then she smelled wood-smoke, and smelled the river, and she saw a steeple and the cabins on their steep steps. Dozens of little black children whirled around her. There ahead was Natchez shining. Bells were ringing. She walked on.

In the paved city it was Christmas time. There were red and green electric 62 lights strung and crisscrossed everywhere, and all turned on in the daytime. Old Phoenix would have been lost if she had not distrusted her eyesight and depended on her feet to know where to take her.

She paused quietly on the sidewalk where people were passing by. A lady 63 came along in the crowd, carrying an armful of red-, green-, and silver-wrapped presents; she gave off perfume like the red roses in hot summer, and Phoenix stopped her.

"Please, missy, will you lace up my shoe?" She held up her foot. 64

"What do you want, Grandma?" 65

"See my shoe," said Phoenix. "Do all right for out in the country, but 66 wouldn't look right to go in a big building."

"Stand still then, Grandma," said the lady. She put her packages down on 67 the sidewalk beside her and laced and tied both shoes tightly.

"Can't lace 'em with a cane," said Phoenix. "Thank you, missy. I doesn't 68 mind asking a nice lady to tie up my shoe, when I gets out on the street."

Moving slowly and from side to side, she went into the big building and into 69 a tower of steps, where she walked up and around and around until her feet knew to stop.

She entered a door, and there she saw nailed up on the wall the document 70 that had been stamped with the gold seal and framed in the gold frame, which matched the dream that was hung up in her head.

"Here I be," she said. There was a fixed and ceremonial stiffness over her 71 body.

"A charity case, I suppose," said an attendant who sat at the desk before 72 her.

But Phoenix only looked above her head. There was sweat on her face, the 73 wrinkles in her skin shone like a bright net.

"Speak up, Grandma," the woman said. "What's your name? We must 74 have your history, you know. Have you been here before? What seems to be the trouble with you?"

Old Phoenix only gave a twitch to her face as if a fly were bothering her. 75

"Are you deaf?" cried the attendant. 76

But then the nurse came in. 77

"Oh, that's just old Aunt Phoenix," she said. "She doesn't come for 78 herself—she has a little grandson. She makes these trips just as regular as clockwork. She lives away back off the Old Natchez Trace." She bent down. "Well, Aunt Phoenix, why don't you just take a seat? We won't keep you standing after your long trip." She pointed.

The old woman sat down, bolt upright in the chair. 79

"Now, how is the boy?" asked the nurse. 80

Old Phoenix did not speak.   81

"I said, how is the boy?"   82

But Phoenix only waited and stared straight ahead, her face very solemn and   83
withdrawn into rigidity.

"Is his throat any better?" asked the nurse. "Aunt Phoenix, don't you hear   84
me? Is your grandson's throat any better since the last time you came for the
medicine?"

With her hands on her knees, the old woman waited, silent, erect and   85
motionless, just as if she were in armour.

"You mustn't take up our time this way, Aunt Phoenix," the nurse said.   86
"Tell us quickly about your grandson, and get it over. He isn't dead, is he?"

At last there came a flicker and then a flame of comprehension across her   87
face, and she spoke.

"My grandson. It was my memory had left me. There I sat and forgot why   88
I made my long trip."

"Forgot?" The nurse frowned. "After you came so far?"   89

Then Phoenix was like an old woman begging a dignified forgiveness for   90
waking up frightened in the night. "I never did go to school, I was too old at
the Surrender," she said in a soft voice. "I'm an old woman without an education. It was my memory fail me. My little grandson, he is just the same, and I
forgot it in the coming."

"Throat never heals, does it?" said the nurse, speaking in a loud, sure voice   91
to Old Phoenix. By now she had a card with something written on it, a little list.
"Yes. Swallowed lye. When was it—January—two-three years ago—"

Phoenix spoke unasked now. "No, missy, he not dead, he just the same.   92
Every little while his throat begin to close up again, and he not able to swallow.
He not get his breath. He not able to help himself. So the time come around, and
I go on another trip for the soothing medicine."

"All right. The doctor said as long as you came to get it, you could have it,"   93
said the nurse. "But it's an obstinate case."

"My little grandson, he sit up there in the house all wrapped up, waiting by   94
himself," Phoenix went on. "We is the only two left in the world. He suffer and
it don't seem to put him back at all. He got a sweet look. He going to last. He
wear a little patch quilt and peep out holding his mouth open like a little bird.
I remember so plain now. I not going to forget him again, no, the whole enduring
time. I could tell him from all the others in creation."

"All right." The nurse was trying to hush her now. She brought her a bottle   95
of medicine. "Charity," she said, making a check mark in a book.

Old Phoenix held the bottle close to her eyes and then carefully put it into   96
her pocket.

"I thank you," she said.   97

"It's Christmas time, Grandma," said the attendant. "Could I give you a   98
few pennies out of my purse?"

"Five pennies is a nickel," said Phoenix stiffly.   99

"Here's a nickel," said the attendant.   100

Phoenix rose carefully and held out her hand. She received the nickel and   101
then fished the other nickel out of her pocket and laid it beside the new one. She
stared at her palm closely, with her head on one side.

Then she gave a tap with her cane on the floor.   102

"This is what come to me to do," she said. "I going to the store and buy   103
my child a little windmill they sells, made out of paper. He going to find it hard
to believe there such a thing in the world. I'll march myself back where he
waiting, holding it straight up in this hand."

She lifted her free hand, gave a little nod, turned round, and walked out of   104
the doctor's office. Then her slow step began on the stairs, going down.

Questions for Discussion

1. Welty provides numerous vivid and exciting details to establish the story's
   setting. Why does she spend so much time describing the country through
   which Phoenix has to travel?
2. Phoenix's comments to the animals, trees, and other natural objects on her
   journey might be an indication that she is going mad or that she is a very
   colorful character with a vivid imagination. What do you think?
3. One thing is for sure: Phoenix is a survivor. What in the story shows us that
   she is persistent? What signs are there that Phoenix is, in fact, quite clever?
4. What do the people whom she encounters reveal about Phoenix through their
   conversations with her?
5. Is Phoenix appropriately named? Are there times in the story when she seems
   to be defeated, only to rise again?
6. What events in the story demonstrate the nobility of Phoenix Jackson? How
   does the story's title contribute to this idea?

Suggestions for Journal Entries

1. "A Worn Path" dramatizes the strength, courage, and selflessness of Phoenix Jackson. Do you know someone who displays similar qualities? Use the
   focused-freewriting method to recall an incident from his or her life that
   illustrates nobility of character.
2. Discuss the emotions you felt when you learned the reason for Phoenix's long
   journey.
3. If you saw Phoenix on the street corner, you might take her for a poor, lonely
   eccentric to be pitied by those who lead more fortunate lives. In what ways
   would "A Worn Path" disprove your theory?

SUGGESTIONS FOR WRITING

1. Jackson's "Charles" is about boy who creates an imaginary classmate to explain his behavior in school and to get his parents' attention. Have you ever had an imaginary friend? If so, tell the story of one "adventure" in which he or she played an important role and which would help readers understand why you created this companion. Before you begin, look for useful facts, ideas, or insights in the journal notes you made after reading "Charles."

   In the first drafts of your paper, write your story in detail, telling as much as you can about your imaginary friend's actions and personality. Use dialogue if you think it will make your story more interesting or believable. Then, read the best of your rough drafts; ask what the story says about the reason(s) you created this companion. Put your answer into a thesis statement that appears in an introductory paragraph or paragraphs. Follow this introduction with the story you just wrote.

   Then, revise your paper once more; make sure it contains enough details to illustrate or prove your thesis. Add information if it doesn't. By the same token, remove details that don't relate to the thesis, that don't help you explain why you created your imaginary friend. Finally, as with all assignments, edit your work carefully.

2. At special times in our lives, we encounter people who help us learn important things about ourselves or our world. Accepting what they teach us can often be difficult, stressful, and even frightening. At times, however, what they offer comes upon us gently and silently.

   Write the story of an encounter with a person who taught you something that permanently changed the way you look at yourself, at other people, or at the world. In other words, explain how he or she changed your outlook on life. To start, review the journal notes you made after reading Anthony's "Sandra Street."

   Before you begin drafting your paper, however, write a preliminary thesis statement that will make your central idea and purpose clear. Keep this thesis in mind as you develop your paper. You can always revise it near the end of the process, when the time comes to rewrite and edit.

   In any case, make several drafts. Tell your story in detail, and show how what you learned from the experience continues to be important to you. At the same time, reveal enough about the person who influenced you to show how great an effect he or she has had on your life. Use dialogue when you can, and describe the story's setting if doing so will help make your point clearer.

3. Some of the characters you have read about in this chapter demonstrate positive and even courageous outlooks on life. Write a story about a person you know whose outlook is clearly positive. Narrate one or two events from your subject's life to show that you and your readers might draw inspiration from his or her example. If possible, begin by expanding the journal notes you made after reading Singer's "The Son from America," Welty's "A Worn Path," or Anthony's "Sandra Street."

Include enough details in the events you narrate to convince readers that what you are saying about your subject is true. A good way to do this is to write several drafts of your work, adding relevant details as you go along. When you are satisfied that you have enough information, write a statement that, based upon the events you have just recalled, sums up your subject's attitude about life and explains why you find that attitude so admirable. Make this statement your thesis, and include it in a well-written introduction or conclusion. Finally, make sure your paper is well organized, contains vivid and concrete language, and is free of distracting errors.

4. In "A Worn Path," Welty tells the moving story of a woman who might have lived in her hometown. In "Sandra Street," Anthony describes neighborhoods like those in his native Trinidad. Whether these stories are true isn't important. What matters is that the authors rely on knowledge of familiar places—their homes—to make their writing *realistic*.

Write a true or made-up story set in your county, town, or neighborhood, or in any location you know well. Like Welty and Anthony, make your story realistic and vivid by using concrete details to describe its setting and its people.

One way to gather information for this project is to visit the location in which your story will be set. Keep a sharp lookout for details that reveal the character of the place and its people. As you take notes, remember to rely on your senses and to name the things you see so that readers will recognize what you are describing. For example, Welty mentions the pines, live-oaks, and sweet-gums Phoenix sees in the forest. She also talks about the vulture the old woman encounters and the bob-whites the hunter has killed.

You can include such details as you go through the process of drafting and revising. Once you are satisfied that you have produced an interesting and well-developed paper, review your writing once more to correct errors in grammar, punctuation, and spelling which will reduce its effectiveness.

5. The selections in this chapter show that admirable people make interesting characters in fiction. Try your hand at writing a short story that includes a main character based upon someone you know and respect greatly. Tell your story in a way that shows why this person deserves admiration. In other words, use what you know about your subject's personality to predict how well he or she will react to problems, situations, and people in the world of the story.

One way to start is to recall an exciting, tragic, frightening, or otherwise dramatic event you learned about on television, read about in a newspaper, or experienced yourself. More or less, use this event as the outline of your story, but change the plot so that the person you admire becomes its main character. Have fun predicting how this new main character will react to the story's people, problems, and events. However, remember that you want to show how admirable your subject is. To do this, you might need to change the story and its outcome. So be bold and creative! Alter the original plot as much as you like to achieve your purpose.

Before you begin writing, consult your journal, especially the entries for Singer's "The Son from America" and Welty's "A Worn Path." Before you stop writing, remember that short stories require as much revision and editing as other types of assignments.

6. As a variation on the suggestion above, use the plot of one of the stories in this chapter as inspiration for a short story of your own.

Borrow the general outline of the original story and, if you like, some of its minor characters. However, replace the main characters with those based upon people you know or upon those you create in your imagination. Write your own dialogue, describe the setting in your own words, and add characters you think will make the story more interesting. As a matter of fact, change things as much as you like to give your work the theme and purpose you want.

For example, the setting for "A Worn Path" might become a large city like Philadelphia, Atlanta, Dallas, or San Francisco. And Phoenix Jackson might be replaced by an old woman from your neighborhood or even by a member of your family. In any case, make sure the words you use are your own. Don't borrow vocabulary from the story on which you are basing yours.

You can have great fun with this assignment, so be as imaginative as you like. Of course, you owe it to yourself and your readers to follow the same careful process of drafting, revising, and editing you use when writing a formal essay.

SECTION FIVE

EXPOSITION AND PERSUASION

Many new writers begin to develop their skills by practicing the kinds of writing in Sections Three and Four, description and narration. As you learned in previous chapters, description and narration usually involve writing about subjects that are concrete and, often, very specific—people, places, events, or objects that the reader can picture or understand easily. The primary purpose of description, of course, is to explain what someone or something looked like, sounded like, and so forth. The primary purpose of narration is simply to tell what happened, although many short stories and narrative essays do a great deal more.

At times, however, new writers face the challenge of discussing abstract ideas that can't be explained through narration and description alone. They may even be asked to support opinions, take convincing stands on controversial issues, or urge their readers to action. In such cases, they must rely on a variety of methods of development and techniques associated with exposition and persuasion. *Exposition* is writing that explains. *Persuasion* is writing that proves or convinces.

Each essay in Chapters 13, 14, and 15 explains an abstract idea by using illustration, comparison and contrast, or process analysis as its *primary* method of development. However, these selections also rely on other methods explained earlier in this book (see Chapter 3). The persuasive essays in Chapter 16, which support an opinion or urge readers to act, also use a variety of techniques. In fact, most writers of exposition and persuasion combine methods to develop ideas clearly and convincingly. Comparison-and-contrast papers frequently contain definitions, anecdotes, and examples; process analyses include accurate, sometimes vivid, descriptions; and illustration essays sometimes use comparisons, anecdotes, and descriptions. Persuasive writing is usually developed through examples, statistics, and other factual details, but anecdotes, comparisons, definitions, and descriptions also make useful tools for persuasion.

Whatever your purpose and however you choose to develop ideas, one thing is certain if you want to be successful at exposition and persuasion: you will have to know your subject well, you will have to include enough accurate information to make your writing convincing, and you will have to present that information in a way that is clear and easy to follow.

EXPLAINING THROUGH ILLUSTRATION

One of the most popular ways to explain an idea is illustration, a method of development you read about in Chapter 3. Illustration uses examples to turn an idea that is general, abstract, or hard to understand into something readers can recognize and, therefore, grasp more easily. As the word implies, an illustration is a concrete and specific picture of an idea that would otherwise have remained vague and undefined.

For instance, if you wanted a clearer and more definitive notion of what your friend meant when she claimed to have met several ''interesting characters'' since coming to school, you might ask her to describe a few of those ''characters'' specifically and to show you in what ways they were ''interesting.'' Each of the people she discussed would then serve as an illustration or picture of what she meant by the abstract word ''interesting.''

EXPLAINING THROUGH COMPARISON AND CONTRAST

This method of development involves pointing out similarities and/or differences between two people, objects, places, experiences, ways of doing something, and the like. Writers compare (point out similarities between) and contrast (point out differences between) two things to make one or both more recognizable or understandable to their readers. Let's say you want to explain a computer monitor to someone who had never seen one. You might compare it with a television set. After all, both have glass screens on which electronic images appear. To make your explanation more complete and accurate, however, you might also need to contrast these two devices by pointing out that only on television can one watch a baseball game, a soap opera, or reruns of *I Love Lucy.* Contrast also comes in handy when you want to explain why you believe one thing is better than another. For example, ''Watch the Cart!'', an essay in Chapter 14, points out differences to explain why the author thinks women are more adept at grocery shopping than men.

There are many reasons for comparing or contrasting the subjects you wish to write about. Whatever your purpose, you may find that comparing or contrasting will help you bring abstract ideas into sharper focus and make them more concrete than if you had discussed each of your subjects separately.

EXPLAINING THROUGH PROCESS ANALYSIS

Process analysis is used in scientific writing to help readers understand both natural and technical processes such as the formation of rain clouds, the circulation of blood through the body, or the workings of a stereo tape player. However, it also has a place in nonscientific writing. For example, you might want to use process analysis to explain how U.S. Presidents are elected, how money is transferred from one bank to another electronically, or even how your Aunt Millie manages to turn the most solemn occasion into a party!

Process analysis is also useful when you need to provide the reader with directions or instructions to complete a specific task. Subjects for such essays include "how to change the brakes on a Ford Mustang," "how to bake lasagna," or even "how to get to school from the center of town."

In each of these examples, the writer is assigning him- or herself the task of explaining, as specifically and as clearly as possible, an idea that might be very new and unfamiliar to the reader. And, in each case, the essay will focus on "how to do something" or "how something is done."

Though it may often seem deceptively simple, writing a process paper is often a painstaking task and must be approached carefully. Remember that your readers might be totally unfamiliar with what you're explaining and will need a great deal of information to follow the process easily and to understand it thoroughly.

As a matter of fact, the need to be clear and concrete often causes writers of process analysis to rely on other methods of development as well. Among them are narration, description, illustration, and comparison and contrast. Of these, writers of process analysis rely most heavily on narration. After all, a process is, in fact, a story. Like narratives, process papers are often organized in chronological order and explain a series of events. Unlike narratives, however, process essays don't simply tell *what* happens; they also explain *how* something happens or *how* something should be done.

PERSUADING

Persuasion is the attempt to convince readers that your position on an issue is valid. Sometimes it even involves urging them to take an action supported by the evidence you have presented.

To be persuasive, you will find that it is necessary to explain reasons or ideas thoroughly and clearly. Therefore, exposition is always involved in persuasion, and many of the methods of development you will use to explain an idea will also come in handy when you need to defend an opinion or take a stand.

After reading Chapter 16, you will have a better idea about how to use illustration, contrast, narration, and the like as tools for presenting evidence that will convince readers your point of view has merit. You should also have a clearer notion of the kind of analytical reasoning writers of persuasion use to think through complex issues and to draw logical conclusions. Two kinds of reasoning, *deduction* and *induction,* play important roles in building an *argument,* the heart of any persuasive paper. Chapter 16 will show you how to combine such thinking with convincing evidence to construct an effective argument.

Of course, logical arguments are not enough to convince some readers, especially those whose opinions on a subject are the very opposite of yours or whose lack of excitement about an issue makes them unwilling to act. In such cases, you may have to go beyond pure argument and appeal to their emotions, their pride, their values. Whatever you are trying to prove and whatever kind of audience you face, the selections in Chapter 16 will help you begin developing the expertise to write persuasively on almost any topic.

Essays that illustrate, that compare and contrast, that explain processes, or that persuade are only a few of the types of assignments you will read and write as you continue your education. Nevertheless, they will teach you the important skills of organization and development that are the foundation upon which to build success as a college writer.

CHAPTER 13

ILLUSTRATION

You have learned that the most interesting and effective writing uses specific and concrete details to *show* rather than to *tell* the reader something. One of the best ways to show your readers what you mean is to fill your writing with clear, relevant examples. Examples are also referred to as *illustrations*. They act as pictures—concrete representations—of the abstract idea you are trying to explain, and they make your writing easier to understand and more convincing to your readers. In fact, illustration can be used as the primary method to develop a thesis.

Effective illustrations can help you make reference to specific people, places, and things—concrete realities that your readers will recognize or understand easily. Say that you want to convince them that your 1992 ''Wizbang'' is an economical car. Instead of being content to rely on their understanding of a vague word like ''economical,'' you decide to provide examples that show exactly what you think this term means. Therefore, you explain that the Wizbang gets about 65 miles per gallon around town, that its purchase price is $4000 less than its least expensive competitor's, and that it needs only one $50 tune-up every 40,000 miles. Now that's economical!

Several types of examples are discussed below. The important thing to remember is that the examples you choose must relate to and be appropriate to the idea you're illustrating. For instance, you probably wouldn't cite statistics about the Wizbang's safety record if you wanted to impress your readers with how inexpensive the car is to own and operate.

SPECIFIC INSTANCES OR OCCURRENCES

A good way to get examples into your writing is to use specific instances of the idea you are explaining. Let's say you want to prove that the Wizbang doesn't perform well in bad weather. You can say that it stalled twice during a recent rainstorm or that it didn't start when the temperature fell below freezing last week. If you want to show that people in your town are community-minded, you might mention that they recently opened a shelter for the homeless, that they have organized a meals-on-wheels program for the elderly, or that they have increased their contributions to the United Way campaign in each of the last five years. If you want to prove that the 1960s were years of turmoil, you can recall the assassinations of John and Robert Kennedy and Martin Luther King, Jr., the antiwar marches, and the urban riots.

Many of the selections in this chapter use specific instances or occurrences to develop ideas. Edwin Way Teale's "Winter Folklore," though only a paragraph long, is chock-full of fascinating examples of country superstitions associated with the coming of winter. You can also find specific instances and occurrences in Irina Groza's "Growing Up in Rumania," in John Naisbitt and Patricia Aburdene's "The Culture of Cuisine," and in Jonathan Kozol's "Untouchables."

STATISTICS

Mathematical figures, or statistics, can also be included to strengthen your readers' understanding of an abstract idea. If you want to prove that the cost of living in your hometown has increased dramatically over the last five years, you might explain that the price of a three-bedroom home has increased by about 30 percent, from $100,000 to $130,000, that real estate taxes have doubled from an average of $1500 per family to $3000 per family, and that the cost of utilities has nearly tripled, with each household now spending about $120 per month on heat and electricity. John Naisbitt and Patricia Aburdene's "The Culture of Cuisine," which you can read later in this chapter, makes excellent use of statistics to show that, across the globe, people from very different cultures are falling in love with each other's cooking.

SPECIFIC PEOPLE, PLACES, OR THINGS

Mentioning specific people, places, and things familiar to the reader can also help you make abstract ideas easier to understand and more convincing. If you want to explain that the American South is famous for the Presidents and statespeople it has produced, you might bring up George Washington, Thomas Jefferson, Henry Clay, Lyndon Johnson, Martin Luther King, and Jimmy Carter. If you need to convince readers that your city is a great place to have fun, you will probably mention its amusement park, professional football stadium, brand-new children's zoo and aquarium, community swimming pool, camp grounds, and public golf courses. If you are discussing how fascinated people in this country have become with gadgets, you might specify labor-saving devices found in a typical American home, just as Carol Biederstadt does in "Electrical Appliances," which appears in this chapter.

ANECDOTES

As you probably know, anecdotes are brief, informative stories that develop an idea or drive home a point. They are similar to and serve the same purpose as specific instances and occurrences, and they are sometimes used with such illustrations to develop an idea more fully. However, anecdotes often appear in greater detail than other types of examples.

Jonathan Kozol includes several anecdotes in ''Untouchables'' to comment on the public's reaction to homelessness. You will also find anecdotes, among other examples, in Irina Groza's ''Growing Up in Rumania.'' Like the illustrations found throughout this chapter, they make the abstract ideas they explain more interesting, more believable, and more easily understood. Keep this in mind as you read the essays that follow and especially as you begin using illustration in your own writing.

Winter Folklore*

EDWIN WAY TEALE

A writer for Popular Science *magazine, Edwin Way Teale (1899–1980) combined his talents as an essayist and a photographer to explain the wonder of the natural world. His best-remembered works are books describing the seasons. Among them is* Wandering Through Winter, *from which ''Winter Folklore'' is taken and for which Teale was awarded a Pulitzer Prize.*

Looking Ahead

This selection uses several specific instances to explain an idea. That idea is made clear and convincing because of the careful detail Teale uses to build each of these illustrations.

Vocabulary

abundant   Plentiful.
credulous   Gullible, willing to believe or trust too easily.
folklore   Traditional knowledge or beliefs of a people handed down from generation to generation.
gird   Prepare, fortify, strengthen.
Ozarks   Mountain range in Arkansas, Missouri, and Oklahoma.
severe   Harsh, extreme, very difficult.

In the folklore of the country, numerous superstitions relate to winter weather. Back-country farmers examine their corn husks—the thicker the husk, the colder the winter. They watch the acorn crop—the more acorns, the more severe the season. They observe where white-faced hornets place their paper nests—the

* Editor's title

higher they are, the deeper will be the snow. They examine the size and shape and color of the spleens of butchered hogs for clues to the severity of the season. They keep track of the blooming of dogwood in the spring—the more abundant the blooms, the more bitter the cold in January. When chipmunks carry their tails high and squirrels have heavier fur and mice come into country houses early in the fall, the superstitious gird themselves for a long, hard winter. Without any scientific basis, a wider-than-usual black band on a woolly-bear caterpillar is accepted as a sign that winter will arrive early and stay late. Even the way a cat sits beside the stove carries its message to the credulous. According to a belief once widely held in the Ozarks, a cat sitting with its tail to the fire indicates very cold weather is on the way.

Questions for Discussion

1. From what you read here, what can you conclude about Teale's attitude toward country folklore?
2. In Looking Ahead, you learned that Teale's main idea is convincing because of the many detailed examples he uses to explain it. Which examples do you find most convincing? Why?
3. How does Teale maintain unity in this paragraph? Where does he express his central idea?

Suggestions for Journal Entries

1. Make a list of short sentences or phrases about popular beliefs you associate with a particular time of year, a holiday, or a celebration. For instance, put down what you know about the folklore of spring or summer, about popular beliefs associated with Halloween or Valentine's Day, or about rituals and traditions people follow on birthdays or wedding days.
2. Think of a superstition you once held but have now given up. Use focused freewriting to explain what you believed in and why you believed in it. Then, give at least one example to show how that belief affected the way you lived your life. If you don't want to write about yourself, write about a superstitious friend, relative, or neighbor.

   Another way to approach this assignment is to write about a phobia—an irrational but very real fear—that you or someone you know suffers from. Show how this fear affects you or the person you are writing about. Examples include fear of heights (acrophobia), fear of closed spaces (claustrophobia), fear of open places (agoraphobia), and fear of water (hydrophobia). But there are many more.
3. Teale concentrates on country people, but all sorts of people are superstitious. Brainstorm with two or three classmates about superstitions held by a group of people you know well. For example, focus on city people, college students, gamblers, athletes, children, old people, members of your family or community, or people who work at a particular trade or occupation.

Electrical Appliances

CAROL BIEDERSTADT

Carol Biederstadt majored in history at Middlesex County College and Rutgers University in central New Jersey. "Electrical Appliances," which she wrote for a freshman composition class, discusses a number of gadgets that were familiar, if unnecessary, items in the Biederstadt household. Her essay reminds us of the importance of relying on our own experiences and observations as sources of information for all types of writing, including illustration.

Looking Ahead

1. In many respects this selection is organized like a descriptive essay, for Biederstadt tells us a great deal about her home as she points out examples of gadgets her family has accumulated over the years.
2. One reason this essay is so interesting and effective is that Biederstadt makes a point of including numerous concrete and specific details. Another is that she uses irony to poke fun at herself. As you probably know, irony is an often humorous device that allows you to communicate an idea by saying or writing the very opposite of what you mean.

Vocabulary

capitalizing on   Taking advantage of.
excessive   Too many.

Lately I have been noticing how many electrical appliances there are on the   1
market. It seems to me that there are more now than there were a few years ago. I'm not really sure why this is so but I do have a few ideas. The first reason is that Americans are just too lazy to do things manually anymore. For every little odd job we once had to do, there is now a mechanical "gadget" to do the job for us. The second reason is that appliance companies like General Electric, Norelco, Whirlpool, and Toro are capitalizing on the people's laziness and are just trying to make more money.

With all of these electrical appliances around for me to use, I wonder how   2
I would have survived fifty years ago. How would I have cleaned my floor, for example? I guess I could have used one of those things called a "broom," which I rarely see any more. We have one for sweeping the driveway, but I can't remember ever seeing it used anywhere else. And how would I have gotten the dirt out of my car without my "car-vac"? A whisk brush? What's that?

The kitchen is just one of the rooms in our house that has an excessive   3 number of unnecessary electrical appliances. Take the electric can opener, for example. Personally, I think it's easier to use a hand can opener, but the rest of my family seems to like it. I often see them use it, unlike the blender that sits next to it on the counter. I can't remember the last time I saw anyone use that gadget. It's been there for years and collects dust. Luckily for me, we do not own a food processor, yogurt maker, or milkshake machine. Hopefully, we never will own any of them. They would just be more things for me to dust. We do have an electric popcorn popper, but that's a necessity, isn't it?

The garage certainly has the greatest number of unnecessary appliances.   4 There's something in there for every kind of outdoor job I can think of: rototiller, snow blower, car vacuum, hedge clipper, and probably more that I have forgotten. It seems almost ridiculous to have all of those tools, and I think that I would probably feel embarrassed to use most of them. I'd rather rake leaves than hold that leaf blower. I'd also rather get down on my hands and knees to clip weeds than use the electric weed trimmer. However, it is obvious that my father doesn't feel the same way that I do about these things. Maybe he thinks it's fun to buy a new gadget and then come home and try it out.

I'm not trying to say that I don't depend on electrical appliances; I certainly   5 do. I don't know what I would do without my hair dryer! However, I do think that a lot of modern appliances aren't needed and that people may be becoming even lazier by using them. Maybe we'll have a catastrophic electric failure some day and find out just how much we really have been depending on our appliances!

Questions for Discussion

1. What is Biederstadt's central idea?
2. Why, according to Biederstadt, are we becoming more and more dependent on electrical gadgets? Why does she mention such companies as General Electric and Norelco by name?
3. What examples of "unnecessary" appliances has the author found in her kitchen? In her garage?
4. What does Biederstadt have against electric leaf blowers and weed trimmers? Why does she prefer their manual versions?
5. What appliances does Biederstadt use regularly?
6. Where does she use irony and humor to help make her writing more interesting?

Suggestions for Journal Entries

1. Look around your bedroom, kitchen, garage, attic, basement, or storage closet. Do you find examples of the kinds of gadgets that Biederstadt is talking about in this essay? Describe a few of these.

2. The author suggests that her father "thinks it's fun to buy a new gadget and then come home and try it out." Do you feel the same way? If so, list some of the "gadgets" you've bought recently, and determine whether you've been able to make good use of them.

3. Are Americans "just too lazy to do things manually anymore," as Biederstadt explains in paragraph 1, or can you cite examples that might disprove this idea? Think of times when you or someone you know well did something the "old-fashioned way" instead of relying on a more modern tool or appliance to do the job.

The Culture of Cuisine

JOHN NAISBITT AND PATRICIA ABURDENE

John Naisbitt and Patricia Aburdene have been called "futurists." Working closely with leaders in government, business, and science, they try to describe the future effects of important trends and developments in politics, manufacturing, the environment, education, economics, popular culture, and other fields. In 1982, Naisbitt published Megatrends, *which discusses new directions for American society in the 1980s. It was so successful that he and Aburdene followed up with* Megatrends 2000 *in 1990. "The Culture of Cuisine" is taken from this book. You will find another paragraph from* Megatrends 2000 *in Chapter 1.*

Looking Ahead

1. The authors develop the main idea of this selection by using illustrations like those you learned about in the chapter's introduction. Try spotting various kinds of examples as you read "The Culture of Cuisine."

2. Much of the information in this selection is expressed in direct quotations from people Naisbitt and Aburdene interviewed or from written materials they researched. As such, you can use "The Culture of Cuisine" as a model for putting quoted material into your own work.

Vocabulary

armadillo   Animal common in the American Southwest; it has skin that resembles armor.

chic   Stylish.

confectioneries   Places that sell sweets.

cravings   Desires, yearnings.

cuisine   Style or type of cooking or of food preparation.

delicacies   Treats, rare and delicious foods.

exotic   Interesting because it is unfamiliar or foreign.

gusto   Interest, excitement, zeal.

symbol   Sign, representation.

West Los Angeles is the home of Gurume, a Japanese-run restaurant whose 1
speciality—Gurume chicken—is Oriental chopped chicken and green beans in
an Italian marinara sauce, served over spaghetti, with Japanese cabbage salad,
Texas toast, and Louisiana Tabasco sauce. It is a symbol of what is happening
to world lifestyle and cuisine.

We are tasting one another's cuisines with great gusto. Americans are 2
exporting seafood delicacies to Japan, Tex-Mex is all the rage in Paris, and the
United States is importing sushi bars as if they were Toyotas.

"Three years ago the world had never tasted soft-shells [crabs] and now we 3
export to twenty-two countries," said Terrence Conway, owner of the John T.
Handy Company, a Chesapeake Bay firm that in 1986 exported 270,000 pounds
of crabs, mainly to Japan. (In 1988 the company was bought by a Japanese
firm.)

Tex-Mex cuisine is prepared kosher in Israel, where former Houstonian 4
Barry Ritman's Chili's restaurant comes complete with a Lone Star beer sign,
armadillo art, and cactus garden.

"There just wasn't anyplace here to buy the tacos, chili, or chips I ate back 5
in Texas," says Ritman, who satisfied his Southwest cravings while introducing
Israelis to tacos, tortillas, and margaritas.

In 1985 San Antonio-based Papa Maya, one of a handful of Tex-Mex 6
restaurants in Paris, received the city's Best Foreign Food award. Since then
Tex-Mex has become Paris's hot new exotic cuisine. Chic young Parisians now
fill the house at La Perla, Café Pacifico, and the Studio.

There were 19,364 Oriental restaurants in the United States in 1988, accord- 7
ing to RE-COUNT, a service of the Restaurant Consulting Group, Inc., in
Evanston, Illinois. Oriental restaurant growth outpaces all other restaurant cate-
gories, having increased 10 percent just in 1987 and 1988 while restaurants grew
4 percent overall, says RE-COUNT.

In 1975 there were only about 300 sushi bars in the United States; by 1980 8
there were more than 1,500, reports *Palate Pleasers,* the first Japanese food
magazine for Americans printed in the United States. Today there are thousands.

"At least five to ten new sushi bars open in New York City and Los Angeles 9
every month," according to Susan Hirano of *Palate Pleasers.* And the sushi
craze has broken out of the big city.

You can order sushi in American beef country: Des Moines, Iowa; Wichita, 10
Kansas; and Omaha, Nebraska. The Japanese Steak House, in Grand Rapids,
Michigan, boasts a floating sushi bar. The Kroger supermarket in Buckhead,
Georgia, sells sushi. More adventurous Georgians order the octopus and eel.

If Americans are crazy about sushi, the Japanese have shown they have an 11 all-American sweet tooth. Tokyo is overflowing with the latest American confectioneries: Häagen-Dazs, Famous Amos, Mrs. Field's, and David's Cookies stores. Even lesser-known outlets like Steve's and Hobson's ice-cream shops are open in Tokyo.

In the United States ethnic food is one of the hottest segments in the restaurant business. Eating out in Middle America used to mean steak and potatoes. Now it is Mexican, Chinese, Korean, Afghan, and Ethiopian. Between 1982 and 1986 overall restaurant traffic in the United States increased 10 percent, but Asian restaurants saw business grow 54 percent, Mexican restaurants 43 percent, and Italian restaurants 26 percent. In a one-block area of the Adams Morgan neighborhood of Washington, D.C., you can eat Ethiopian, Jamaican, Italian, Mexican, French, Salvadorean, Japanese, Chinese, Caribbean, Indian, or American. 12

Questions for Discussion

1. Why is Gurume chicken "a symbol of what is happening to world lifestyle and cuisine" (paragraph 1)?
2. What evidence do Naisbitt and Aburdene give to illustrate that American cuisine is becoming popular across the globe?
3. What statistics do they include to show that the American appetite for foreign food is growing?
4. Does this selection make use of contrast? For what purpose?
5. Find examples of figurative language in "The Culture of Cuisine."
6. Like Carol Biederstadt, the author of "Electrical Appliances," Naisbitt and Aburdene mention brand names. They also include names of places, businesses, restaurants, and organizations. Does doing this make their writing more convincing than if they had left those names out? Explain.
7. Why do they bother to mention that we can "order sushi in American beef country" (paragraph 10)? Why do they tell us we can buy it in a supermarket in Buckhead, Georgia?
8. Is the introduction to this selection effective? Defend your answer.

Suggestions for Journal Entires

1. Are Americans becoming more international in their cooking and eating? Make a list of the foods you like that originated in another country. Then make a list of foods you like that you are *sure* originated in America. If you have trouble gathering information, brainstorm about this topic with a few classmates or friends. Before you begin, try to guess which list will be longer.
2. Do you agree that people the world over are sharing in each other's cultures? Make a list of things—consumer products, foods, sports, types of art or music, customs or traditions, trends or fads, and the like—that are popular in America but originated elsewhere. For example, mention sushi from Japan, the sauna bath from Scandinavia, or various types of music from Africa, the Caribbean, and other parts of the world.

Growing Up in Rumania

IRINA GROZA

*When Irina Groza was a girl, Rumania was a Communist country, where per-
sonal freedom and economic opportunity were in short supply. Like other countries behind the iron curtain, Rumania made it difficult for people to leave. But
Groza was one of the lucky ones, and she was able to immigrate to the United
States. Today, she is studying for her associate's degree in nursing in addition
to raising a family and working full-time.*

Looking Ahead

1. Groza shows that personal experience can be a rich source of illustrations to develop an abstract idea. She fills her essay with specific
instances and anecdotes that explain how horrible life in Rumania
had become under a tyrannical and incompetent government.
2. Several types of writing can be used together to make a successful
essay. Groza relies heavily on examples but also includes narrative
and descriptive details.
3. In 1990, Communist governments across eastern Europe fell from
power. In Rumania, dictator Nicolae Ceauşescu, his wife, and several members of his government were tried and executed for crimes
against the people they had oppressed for over thirty years.

Vocabulary

brutalize   Treat cruelly or violently.
classics   Important and lasting works of literature.
compliance   Submission, agreement.
cult   Excessive or unnatural devotion to a person or idea.
egomania   Extreme pride and self-concern.
flawed   Defective, faulty.
ideology   Ideas, beliefs, philosophy.
impoverishing   Making poor.
indoctrinate   Drill into, force to believe.
inflicted   Imposed.
jeopardy   Danger, risk.
magnitude   Size, extent.
prey on   Persecute, attack, victimize.
purge   Remove, eliminate.

regime   Government, rule.
stature   Standing, reputation.
suppress   Dominate, control.

I grew up in a beautiful Transylvanian city called Arad, just a few miles from   1
the Hungarian border. In the mid-fifties, when I was born, Rumania was still
recovering from the Second World War, and people were working hard to
rebuild their country. I was in the third grade when our beloved president,
Gheorghe Gheorghiu-Dej, died. He was succeeded by Nicolae Ceauşescu, a
young and ambitious general who promised us a bright future. At his election,
no one was able to foresee the magnitude of his egomania, ruthlessness, and
incompetence. The tyranny that followed nearly destroyed Rumania and inflicted widespread suffering on its people for many years.

At the beginning of Ceauşescu's presidency, life was still good. I remember   2
going into town with my mother. The streets were busy places, filled with people
who were smiling and laughing as they went about their business. The shops
contained plenty of food; people stood in line only to buy fresh milk and bread.
Slowly, however, certain foods began to disappear from store shelves and coun-
ters. It became much harder to get meat and fresh vegetables. Consumer goods
such as clothing and small appliances became scarce. I heard my mother complain about the new president, but as a child I did not find these problems
significant.

Then I started noticing a change in our school books. National heroes like   3
Michael Eminescu and George Cosbuc, who had once been glorified, were
deleted from our history texts. George Enescu and other great Rumanian writers,
artists, and musicians, who had been the symbols of our culture, were hardly
mentioned. Classics were removed from our school library, and its shelves were
overloaded with books about the new president and his regime. He was portrayed
as a hero of the people who had fought for Communism, but he was a hero we
had never heard of before. School children had to take courses in politics
designed to indoctrinate them with Ceauşescu's diseased ideology. We were
forced to memorize his speeches, which were full of lies about the progress and
prosperity his government had brought to Rumania. Before long this sickening
personality cult became obvious to everyone, and we knew that our country and
our culture were being polluted by this madman.

Before long, new laws restricting people's personal freedom were put into   4
effect. One of these prohibited travel outside the country, and Rumanians found
themselves prisoners in their own country. Another law required every family to
have at least four children. Ceauşescu believed that increasing the population
would make Rumania powerful and increase his stature in the world. All con-
traceptives were removed from the shelves, and doctors who performed abor-
tions were severely punished. But many people could not afford to support large
families and were forced to turn their children over to state orphanages. As
shown in recent news releases, these places were badly run and unsanitary. In
fact, many of the children housed there contracted AIDS.

In another attempt to suppress the people and to destroy their spirit, the government began a campaign to discourage church attendance. Celebrations of religious holidays were prohibited, and people who openly expressed their faith put themselves in jeopardy. One day a police officer stopped me and ridiculed me in front of my friends because I was wearing a cross around my neck. I felt embarrassed and angry, but there was nothing I could do. I had heard that many people had been beaten by the police, and we lived in constant fear of them. Those who continued to oppose the system were thrown into jail or put into mental institutions.

As soon as Ceauşescu took office, he began to purge those in the government who might oppose him, and he surrounded himself with his supporters. He also established the *Securitate,* a secret police force, which drew to its ranks many misfits who were greedy for power and who had the stomach to swallow the government's lies. No special training was required of these people, just blind compliance to the will of the regime and a desire to brutalize people. Members of the *Securitate* were privileged: they shopped in their own well-supplied stores, and their salaries were about six times those of medical doctors.

The *Securitate* was Ceauşescu's tool for holding down opposition to a regime that the people knew was a miserable failure and that had succeeded only in impoverishing the country and subjecting us to extreme economic hardship. People worked hard, but the lines at food stores became longer and longer. There were severe shortages of meat, milk, butter, flour, soap, detergent, toothpaste, gasoline, and medical supplies. No one could understand why a country that was so rich in natural resources and that possessed so many acres of fertile farmland was unable to feed its people or supply them with simple necessities.

One reason was that Ceauşescu had broken the people's spirit. Another had to do with his insane plan to crowd Rumania's growing population into large cities. On the outskirts of Arad were many private homes, each of which sat on land of between half an acre and an acre. One year, the government decided to take this land from us and to build high-rise apartments on it. Neither we nor our neighbors got paid for our property. On top of everything else, we had to clear the land ourselves by cutting down our many fruit trees. Up to that point, we had been able to supplement our food with the fruits and vegetables we grew in our garden and with the animals we raised. But then the situation became desperate, and we were barely able to feed ourselves. The president's iron hand was felt by everyone, and hatred of him grew in everybody's heart.

Like everyone else, I missed the necessities that Ceauşescu's flawed economic policy had taken from us. But I did not realize how badly the government had mismanaged its finances and how corrupt it had become until my mother became ill. Already retired by the time I left high school, she was suffering from high blood pressure and had a heart condition. In an emergency, when I had to call an ambulance, I was told to lie about my mother's age. Medical emergency squads had been instructed not to pick up retired people. If they were left to die, the government would no longer have to pay their pensions.

As the economic crisis got worse and shortages of important supplies increased, the crime rate began to soar. Alcohol abuse became a problem, as did theft, burglary, and assault. But the *Securitate* were busy searching for people who committed political crimes, and real criminals were given a free hand to prey on decent people. In fact, the police often paid common criminals to act as their informants.

I was seventeen and still in high school when I started working in a huge 11 textile factory. Once in the factory, no one was able to leave before quitting time unless he or she got a special pass from the boss. Every two weeks, we had to stay late to attend Communist Party indoctrination sessions. During these absurd meetings, the factory doors were locked, and no one was permitted to leave.

Our regular work week was six days long, but my boss often required us to 12 work on Sundays as well. In the beginning, I refused the overtime, reminding the boss that, according to our constitution, I had to work only six days a week. He in turn reminded me that if I refused overtime I could be assigned to the worst area in the factory. At this point, I had no choice but to accept the overtime, which paid the same wages as work on any other day.

Each day before we left the factory, we had to go through a room where 13 women guards body-searched us. One day, a guard thought that I was acting suspiciously and brought me to a special room where she asked me to remove all my clothes to see if I was hiding stolen material. I could not have concealed much under the thin summer dress I was wearing. She knew that because she had already body-searched me and had found nothing. I refused to obey. To clear myself, I called on another guard to search me again. At that moment, I felt embarrassment and outrage; I knew that the guard's purpose was only to exercise her power by humiliating whomever she wanted to.

My story is not unique. Ceauşescu's government tried to strip all Rumanians 14 of their dignity, pride, and freedom. Everyone suffered in some way, and everyone has a personal tragedy to tell. As for me, I could not continue to live under the constant humiliation and the severe restrictions on personal freedom that I have described. I remember looking at the birds and envying them because they were free to go anywhere in the world.

I promised myself I would never have children in Rumania because I did not 15 want them to suffer as I had. In 1977, with the help of a brother who was living in the United States, I had the opportunity to leave. The day I emigrated, the course of my life changed for the better though my heart broke for those I left behind. Now, however, new hope blossoms for Rumania. In December 1990, as part of the overthrow of corrupt Communist governments across eastern Europe, the people deposed the Ceauşescu regime and established a democracy.

Questions for Discussion

1. Find Groza's thesis statement. What are the three main points she makes about Ceauşescu's government?

2. Which examples in this essay do you think best illustrate each of those three points?

3. How does Groza explain that Rumania, a land rich in natural resources, was unable to feed its people?

4. What kind of people did the Ceauşescu government employ to carry out its policies? What examples of such people does Groza provide?

5. Why does she include details about life in Rumania before Ceauşescu came to power?

6. How does Groza show that life in Rumania was difficult for other people as well as for her?

Suggestions for Journal Entries

1. The government Groza describes is monstrous. Have you ever lived under, read about, or heard about a government that suppresses personal freedom and keeps its people in fear and poverty as Rumania did? If so, use focused freewriting to record one or two well-developed examples of how that government treats or treated its people.

   Another way to approach this assignment is to interview a person who has lived under a dictatorship. Find out what freedoms and opportunities your subject was denied, and explain his or her reaction to living in a country with such a government.

2. A major difference between a democracy and the place Groza describes is the freedom to criticize the government. Think of a law, policy, or practice of the government—federal, state, *or* local—with which you disagree. Brainstorm with others who share your opinion. Together, discuss the way(s) this law, policy, or practice affects people you know. Then, write down reasons it should be changed. If this topic doesn't interest you, focus on a school policy or regulation you want changed.

Untouchables

JONATHAN KOZOL

Jonathan Kozol writes about the effects of social problems such as illiteracy, poverty, and homelessness, especially as they affect children. He has received the National Book Award twice. "Untouchables" is from Rachel and Her Children, *which is based on Kozol's interviews with homeless people. In 1988, when this book was published, 70,000 people in New York City were homeless. Some lived in dangerous public shelters or in filthy, run-down welfare hotels, but most were forced to wander the streets. Today, families with small children make up the fastest-growing portion of the homeless population. The reasons for this, Kozol believes, are the government's inability to deal with the problem and the public's resentment of people who have come to be regarded as "untouchables."*

Looking Ahead

1. Early in this selection, we learn that many homeless people would rather live on the streets than in public shelters. As Kozol explains in other parts of *Rachel and Her Children,* some shelters are violent, filthy, disease-ridden places where there is little privacy and where difficult regulations allow only short stays.
2. This selection uses specific instances and anecdotes to illustrate a central idea. Look for such examples as you read ''Untouchables.''

Vocabulary

accommodations Place to stay or live.

akin Similar.

barricade Barrier.

charred Burned.

defecate Eliminate solid waste.

directive Order.

disrobes Undresses.

ejected Thrown out.

forage Search for food.

intimidated Discouraged, frightened.

score Group of twenty.

skid row Run-down part of town inhabited by vagrants and drunkards.

vermin Destructive or annoying insects or rodents.

Many homeless people, unable to get into shelters, frightened of disease or violence, or else intimidated by the regulations, look for refuge in such public places as train stations and church doorways. 1

Scores of people sleep in the active subway tunnels of Manhattan, inches from 600-volt live rails. Many more sleep on the ramps and station platforms. Go into the subway station under Herald Square on a December night at twelve o'clock and you will see what scarce accommodations mean at the rockbottom. Emerging from the subway, walk on Thirty-second Street to Penn Station. There you will see another form of scarce accommodations: Hot-air grates in the area are highly prized. Homeless people who arrive late often find there is no vacancy, even in a cardboard box over a grate. 2

A man who's taken shelter from the wind that sweeps Fifth Avenue by sleeping beneath the outstretched arms of Jesus on the bronze doors of St. Patrick's Cathedral tells a reporter he can't sleep there anymore because shopkeepers feel that he is hurting business. He moves to the south side of the church where he will be less visible. 3

Stories like these are heard in every state and city of the nation. A twenty- 4
year-old man in Florida tells me that he ran away when he was nine years old
from a juvenile detention home in Michigan. He found that he was small enough
to slip his body through the deposit slot of a Good Will box. Getting in was easy,
he explains, and it was warm because of the clothes and quilts and other gifts
that people dropped into the box. ''Getting out,'' he says, ''was not so easy. I
had to reach my arms above my head, grab hold of the metal edge, twist my body
into an *S,* and pull myself out slowly through the slot. When I was fourteen I was
too big to fit into the slot. I believe I am the only person in America who has
lived for five years in a Good Will box.''

Thousands of American people live in dumpsters behind restaurants, hotels, 5
and groceries. A woman describes the unimaginable experience of being awak-
ened in the middle of a winter's night by several late-arriving garbage trucks.
She nearly drowned beneath two tons of rotting vegetables and fruit.

A thirty-four-year-old man in Chicago found his sanctuary in a broken trash 6
compactor. This offered perhaps the ultimate concealment, and the rotting food
which generated heat may have protected him against the freezing weather of
Chicago. One night, not knowing that the trash compactor had in his absence
been repaired, he fell asleep. When the engine was turned on, he was compressed
into a cube of refuse.

People in many cities speak of spending nights in phone booths. I have seen 7
this only in New York. Public telephones in Grand Central Station are aligned
in recessed areas outside the main concourse. On almost any night before
one-thirty, visitors will see a score of people stuffed into these booths with their
belongings. Even phone-booth vacancies are scarce in New York City. As in
public housing, people are sometimes obliged to double up. One night I stood
for an hour and observed three people—man, woman, and child—jammed into
a single booth. All three were asleep.

Officials have tried a number of times to drive the homeless from Grand 8
Central Station. In order to make conditions less attractive, benches have been
removed throughout the terminal. One set of benches has been left there, I am
told, because they have been judged ''historic landmarks.'' The terminal's 300
lockers, used in former times by homeless people to secure their few belongings,
were removed in 1986. Authorities were forced to justify this action by declaring
them, in the words of the city council, ''a threat to public safety.'' Shaving,
cleaning of clothes, and other forms of hygiene are prohibited in the men's room
of Grand Central. A fast-food chain that wanted to distribute unsold donuts in
the terminal was denied the right to do so on the grounds that this would draw
more hungry people.

At one-thirty every morning, homeless people are ejected from Grand Cen- 9
tral. Many have attempted to take refuge on the ramp that leads to Forty-second
Street. The ramp initially provided a degree of warmth because it was protected
from the street by wooden doors. The station management responded to this
challenge in two ways. First, the ramp was mopped with a strong mixture of
ammonia to produce a noxious smell. When the people sleeping there brought
cardboard boxes and newspapers to protect them from the fumes, the entrance

doors were chained wide open. Temperatures dropped some nights to ten degrees.

In a case that won brief press attention in December 1985, an elderly woman   10
who had been living in Grand Central on one of the few remaining benches was removed night after night during the weeks preceding Christmas. On Christmas Eve she became ill. No ambulance was called. At one-thirty the police compelled her to move to the ramp outside. At dawn she came inside, climbed back on bench number 9 to sleep, and died that morning of pneumonia.

At Penn Station, fifteen blocks away, homeless women are denied use of the   11
bathroom. Amtrak police come by and herd them off each hour on the hour. In June of 1985, Amtrak officials issued this directive to police: "It is the policy of Amtrak to not allow the homeless and undesirables to remain. . . . Officers are encouraged to eject all undesirables. . . . Now is the time to train and educate them that their presence will not be tolerated as cold weather sets in." In an internal memo, according to CBS, an Amtrak official later went beyond this language and asked flatly: "Can't we get rid of this trash?"

In a surprising action, the union representing the police resisted this directive   12
and brought suit against Penn Station's management in 1986. Nonetheless, as temperatures plunged during the nights after Thanksgiving, homeless men and women were ejected from the station. At 2:00 A.M. I watched a man about my age carry his cardboard box outside the station and try to construct a barricade against the wind that tore across Eighth Avenue. The man was so cold his fingers shook and, when I spoke to him, he tried but could not answer.

Driving women from the toilets in a railroad station raises questions that go   13
far beyond the issue of "deterrence." It may surprise the reader to be told that many of these women are quite young. Few are dressed in the familiar rags that are suggested by the term "bag ladies." Some are dressed so neatly and conceal their packages and bags so skillfully that one finds it hard to differentiate them from commuters waiting for a train. Given the denial of hygienic opportunities, it is difficult to know how they are able to remain presentable. The sight of clusters of police officials, mostly male, guarding a women's toilet from its use by homeless females does not speak well for the public conscience of New York.

Where do these women defecate? How do they bathe? What will we do   14
when, in her physical distress, a woman finally disrobes in public and begins to urinate right on the floor? We may regard her as an animal. She may by then begin to view herself in the same way.

Several cities have devised unusual measures to assure that homeless people   15
will learn quickly that they are not welcome. In Laramie, Wyoming, they are given one night's shelter. On the next morning, an organization called "The Good Samaritan Fund" gives them one-way tickets to another town. The college town of Lancaster, Ohio, offers homeless families one-way tickets to Columbus.

In a number of states and cities, homeless people have been murdered,   16
knifed, or set on fire. Two high school students in California have been tried for the knife murder of a homeless man whom they found sleeping in a park. The man, an unemployed house painter, was stabbed seventeen times before his throat was slashed.

In Chicago a man was set ablaze while sleeping on a bench in early morning, 17
opposite a popular restaurant. Rush-hour commuters passed him and his charred
possessions for four hours before someone called police at noon. A man who
watched him burning from a third-floor room above the bench refused to notify
police. The purpose was "to get him out," according to a local record-store
employee. A resident told reporters that the problem of the homeless was akin
to that of "nuclear waste."

In Tucson, where police use German shepherds to hunt for the homeless in 18
the skid-row neighborhoods, a mayor was recently elected on the promise that
he'd drive the homeless out of town. "We're tired of it. Tired of feeling guilty
about these people," said an anti-homeless activist in Phoenix.

In several cities it is a crime to sleep in public; in some, armrests have been 19
inserted in the middle of park benches to make it impossible for homeless people
to lie down. In others, trash has been defined as "public property," making it
a felony to forage in the rotted food.

Grocers in Santa Barbara sprinkled bleach on food discarded in their 20
dumpsters. In Portland, Oregon, owners of some shops in redeveloped Old Town
have designed slow-dripping gutters (they are known as "drip lines") to prevent
the homeless from attempting to take shelter underneath their awnings.

Harsher tactics have been recommended in Fort Lauderdale. A city council 21
member offered a proposal to spray trash containers with rat poison to discourage foraging by homeless families. The way to "get rid of vermin," he observed,
is to cut their food supply. Some of these policies have been defeated, but the
inclination to sequester, punish and conceal the homeless has attracted wide
support.

"We are the rejected waste of the society," said [one homeless man]. "They 22
use us, if they think we have some use, maybe for sweeping leaves or scrubbing
off graffiti in the subway stations. They don't object if we donate our blood. I've
given plasma. That's one way that even worthless people can do something for
democracy. We may serve another function too. Perhaps we help to scare the
people who still have a home—even a place that's got no heat, that's rat infested,
filthy. If they see us in the streets, maybe they are scared enough so they will
learn not to complain. If they were thinking about asking for a better heater or
a better stove, they're going to think twice. It's like farmers posting scarecrows
in the fields. People see these terrifying figures in Penn Station and they know,
with one false step, that they could be here too. They think: 'I better not
complain.'

"The problem comes, however, when they try to find a place to hide us. So 23
it comes to be an engineering question: waste disposal. Store owners certainly
regard us in that way. We ruin business and lower the value of good buildings.
People fear that we are carriers of illness. Many times we are. So they wear those
plastic gloves if they are forced to touch us. It reminds me of the workers in the
nuclear reactors. They have to wear protective clothing if they come in contact
with the waste. Then you have state governors all over the United States refusing
to allow this stuff to be deposited within their borders. Now you hear them

talking about dumping toxic waste into the ocean in steel cans. Could they find an island someplace for the homeless?''

Questions for Discussion

1. What does Kozol's title tell us about his central idea? Express that idea in your own words.
2. Where in this essay are specific instances used to illustrate the central idea? Where are specific people and places used as examples?
3. Where does the author use anecdotes? Which of these do you find most effective?
4. What is Kozol's opinion of ''the public conscience'' in regard to homelessness? Is he being fair and accurate?
5. Why have so many cities ''devised unusual measures to assure that homeless people will learn quickly that they are not welcome'' (paragraph 15)? What are some of these measures?
6. What does the man quoted in paragraph 22 mean when he says the homeless are ''the rejected waste of the society''? What details in the essay support his view?
7. Why, according to this individual, does the sight of the homeless strike fear in poor people who live in substandard housing (paragraph 22)?
8. Like Naisbitt and Aburdene in ''The Culture of Cuisine,'' Kozol quotes directly from several sources. Does this practice make his writing convincing? Explain your answer.

Suggestions for Journal Entries

1. A homeless person sleeping over a sewer grate is only one sign that some of our large cities are in trouble. What other signs have you seen? Think of the city you live in or one you visit often. Are shop fronts boarded up? Are roads and bridges in disrepair? Are people afraid to go out at night? List as many examples of urban decay as you can.
2. Think of another group of people you think deserve better treatment than they receive from the rest of society. The elderly, the handicapped, the working poor, or members of a particular minority group might make good subjects. Brainstorm with classmates or do some focused freewriting to gather examples that show how badly this group has been treated.
3. Kozol offers convincing examples of the negative attitude some folks have toward the poor and the homeless. Discuss steps people in your community have taken to help the poor, the homeless, or anyone in need. Are such measures examples of a more positive ''public conscience'' than the one Kozol describes?

SUGGESTIONS FOR WRITING

1. Take any *simple* idea or statement of fact that you know a lot about. Prove this idea or statement in an essay of four or five paragraphs by using examples like the kinds you have learned about. Start by writing a preliminary thesis that expresses the idea or fact plainly. For instance:

Winters in my state can be *treacherous.*
The hurricane that smashed into town last summer *devastated our community.*
A student's life is *hectic.*
Doing your own sewing (carpentry, plumbing, car repair, typing, or the like) can *save you a lot of money.*
Casual sex can be *harmful to your health.*

The main point in each statement is in italics. As you know, the main point in a thesis is what an essay should focus on. Keep this in mind as you write your first draft. Then, review your paper to determine whether each example you have included relates directly to your main point. If not, replace it with a better example or revise your thesis. Add other examples to develop your main point even further as you complete later drafts.

When the time comes to correct spelling, punctuation, and grammar, check for coherence and clarity as well. Strengthen connections between sentences and paragraphs. Replace words and phrases that seem vague, general, or dull with more concrete, specific, and colorful choices.

2. Look back to the journal entries you made after reading Edwin Way Teale's "Winter Folklore." You may have begun writing about an irrational belief—superstition or fear—that you or someone you know has experienced. Use this information in an essay with a thesis that sums up how this belief affected the life of the person you are writing about.

Include specific instances and anecdotes to illustrate your thesis. For example, say you are claustrophobic—afraid of being closed in. You can begin with a thesis that explains how difficult, embarrassing, and costly your fear makes getting around a big city. To illustrate this idea, you might explain how scared you become in rooms without windows, how loudly friends laugh when you climb twenty flights of stairs just to avoid the elevator, and how often you spend the extra money for a taxi so you won't have to ride a crowded bus. You might even write an anecdote or two about being trapped in an elevator or a closet.

One way to end this essay is to explain how you or the person you are writing about overcame or plans to overcome this fear or superstition. Other techniques for writing conclusions are discussed in Chapter 4.

To make your paper convincing, develop your examples vividly and completely. As you rewrite and edit, make sure you have included details and vocabulary that will show how dramatically your subject was affected by the fear or superstition you are discussing.

3. In "Electrical Appliances," Carol Biederstadt says Americans may be "just too lazy to do things manually anymore." What do you think? Are modern tools and appliances causing us to become lazy, or are they making our lives easier, more efficient, and more productive?

Support your opinion by describing gadgets you use around the house or on the job to save time and effort. The journal entries you made after reading "Electrical Appliances" may provide illustrations for this paper. Other sources of ideas are popular magazines and newspapers in your college library. Leaf through three or four, paying special attention to the appliances and tools in their advertisements.

Remember that you want to support a specific opinion expressed in a thesis statement. As you draft and revise your paper, include enough examples to make that opinion convincing, and develop them in detail. At the same time, make sure that all examples relate directly to your thesis. Remove those that don't, and add appropriate information as you go along.

4. Is the world shrinking as John Naisbitt and Patricia Aburdene suggest? Review your responses to the Suggestions for Journal Entries after "The Culture of Cuisine." Use them as inspiration for an essay explaining that the products, ideas, or customs of another land or culture have found a home in America.

Limit your paper to a country or culture you know a lot about, perhaps the one your family came from. Discuss examples of food, automobiles, films, styles and works of music, games and sports, furniture, clothing, social customs, religious practices, and so on.

This is a good opportunity to use specific instances and occurrences or to mention specific objects. Include as many as you can in your first draft. As you revise your paper, try making your point even stronger with statistics.

Of course, your college librarian can help you find special information, but you can draw on your own observations, knowledge, and experience. Let's say you write about Mexico. You might explain that three of the five health-food restaurants where you eat feature Mexican food because it is nutritious and low in fat; that ten of the twenty buildings on your campus use styles and materials from Mexico; that techniques for making textiles and ceramics invented by Mexicans have been adopted by a company you work for; and that a show of contemporary paintings, silverwork, and pottery from Mexico is touring your state.

5. Have you ever lived in a land whose government was a dictatorship? Do you know someone who did? Write an essay that uses examples from personal experience—yours or someone else's—to explain what living in that country was like.

Collect information before starting your first draft. If you are writing about yourself, brainstorm with a family member who remembers as much about that time in your life as you do. If you are writing about someone else, try interviewing this person to gather examples about the kind of life he or she endured. In addition, read your response to the first journal suggestion after Irina Groza's ''Growing Up in Rumania.''

Like Groza, use anecdotes and specific instances to explain what the government did to limit people's personal and economic freedom. Your essay doesn't have to be as long as hers, but it should be filled with examples that show how difficult living under a dictatorship can be.

Groza cared enough about her readers and her subject to complete the writing process step-by-step. She made several drafts, each of which developed her thesis in greater and more startling detail. Then she revised and edited her work to make sure it was well-organized, coherent, and free of mechanical errors. Follow her example.

6. As an alternative to suggestion 5, write a letter to the editor of a local or college newspaper complaining about a law, regulation, policy, or practice in your community or on campus. Using examples from personal experience, explain why you are against it; show how negatively it affects you and others in your town or school.

Let's say your college library closes on Saturdays and Sundays. You decide to explain that this policy is hard on students who can't go to the library at other times. To develop your central idea, you might:

- Talk about the long trips to other libraries you and friends are forced to make on weekends.
- Discuss your many attempts to find a quiet place to study on Sunday afternoons.
- Explain that ten of the twenty students in your history class didn't finish their midterm essays on time because they could not get information they needed.

You are trying to convince your reader of a particular opinion. So, pack your letter with examples, but remember that each example should relate directly to that opinion. As always, state your point clearly in a thesis.

Begin this assignment by looking to your journal. Your response to the second suggestion for journal writing after Groza's ''Growing Up in Rumania'' may be useful as you complete the first draft of your letter. Once again, be thorough and careful when revising and editing your work.

7. In ''Untouchables,'' Jonathan Kozol says that one sign some cities need help is the sight of homeless people sleeping over hot-air grates, in alleys, and in dangerous public shelters. But there are many signs our cities are decaying. Perhaps you wrote about one in your journal. If not, respond to the first of the Suggestions for Journal Entries after Kozol's essay now.

Turn that journal entry into an essay filled with examples to show that the city you are writing about needs improvement. Include details about what readers can expect to see and hear on a typical day there. Describe the many boarded-up stores and factories; talk about the poor condition of bridges, tunnels, streets, and sidewalks; mention the graffiti on buildings, the litter in parks and playgrounds, and the garbage in empty lots. If your memory of the place is weak, walk its streets—journal in hand—to gather details.

If you don't like this assignment, try another approach. Write an essay arguing that, in fact, some cities are healthy. Focus on one you know well, and use examples to show it is a good place to live. Again, you might explore its busy streets and make journal notes to get yourself started.

Use as many of your observations as you can when writing your first draft. Add to and develop them as you complete later versions. After all this work, of course, don't forget to put the finishing touches on your final draft by correcting problems in grammar, punctuation, spelling, and other areas.

CHAPTER 14

COMPARISON AND CONTRAST

Comparison and contrast are methods of organizing and developing ideas by pointing out similarities and differences between subjects.

A comparison essay identifies similarities between subjects that on the *surface* appear to be quite different; for instance, Tom Wolfe's "Columbus and the Moon" in this chapter compares Columbus's voyages with the U.S. space program. A contrast essay identifies differences between subjects that on the *surface* appear to be very much alike; usually, these subjects belong to the same general class or are of the same type. Such is the case with the male and female shoppers in James Langley's "Watch the Cart!"

Contrast can also be used to point out the positive and negative aspects of a particular subject. In "If at First You Do Not See . . . ," for example, Jessie Sullivan contrasts the harsh reality of living in her community with the bright promise it holds for the future. In a similar way, you might discuss the pros and cons of living in a particular city, the advantages and disadvantages of getting married, or the strengths and weaknesses of your college basketball team. Explaining what you like and dislike about going to college, working at the supermarket, or visiting relatives will also make a good contrast paper. You might even discuss why you both loved and hated a certain film, television program, concert, or novel.

One of the greatest advantages of using comparison or contrast is the simplicity with which it allows you to organize information. In fact, putting together a successful comparison or contrast essay doesn't have to be difficult if you follow either of the two standard methods of organization: point-by-point or subject-by-subject.

THE POINT-BY-POINT METHOD

Using the point-by-point method, you compare or contrast a particular aspect (or characteristic) of *both* subjects, often in the same paragraph, before moving on to the next point to be discussed in another paragraph. For example, if you were demonstrating how economical your 1992 Wizbang is by contrasting it with another car, you would outline your essay like this:

Introduction with thesis statement
The 1992 Wizbang is far more economical to own and operate than its leading competitor.
First point of comparison or contrast (purchase price)
    Discussion of subject *A* (Wizbang)
    Discussion of subject *B* (competitor)
Second point of comparison or contrast (maintenance costs)
    Discussion of subject *A* (Wizbang)
    Discussion of subject *B* (competitor)
Third point of comparison or contrast (fuel efficiency)
    Discussion of subject *A* (Wizbang)
    Discussion of subject *B* (competitor)
Conclusion

THE SUBJECT-BY-SUBJECT METHOD

Using the subject-by-subject method, you discuss *one* subject completely before going on to compare or contrast it with another subject in the second half of the essay. For example, you would outline the essay about the Wizbang and its competitor like this:

Introduction with thesis statement
The 1992 Wizbang is far more economical to own and operate than its leading competitor.
Discussion of subject *A* (Wizbang)
    First point of comparison or contrast (purchase price)
    Second point of comparison or contrast (maintenance costs)
    Third point of comparison or contrast (fuel efficiency)
Discussion of subject *B* (competitor)
    First point of comparison or contrast (purchase price)
    Second point of comparison or contrast (maintenance costs)
    Third point of comparison or contrast (fuel efficiency)
Conclusion

Which of the two methods for organizing a comparison-or-contrast paper is best for you? That depends on your topic and your purpose.

The subject-by-subject method of organization is often used in short essays. You can see it in Hal Borland's "Hunger Moon," a selection containing just two paragraphs that reveal very different views of the eastern moon in February. However, the subject-by-subject pattern also works well with long essays. A good example is Jessie Sullivan's "If at First You Do Not See . . . ," which presents opposite views of the author's community in great detail. Therefore, regardless of your essay's length, you will find the subject-by-subject pattern useful when contrasting qualities or characteristics of the same subject.

The point-by-point method, on the other hand, generally works well with essays that compare or contrast several qualities or characteristics of two subjects. This arrangement allows readers to digest a large body of information bit by bit. As such, it helps eliminate the risk that readers will forget what you said in the first half of your essay before they finish the second half! James Langley's ''Watch the Cart!'' (contrast) and Tom Wolfe's ''Columbus and the Moon'' (comparison) use the point-by-point pattern.

As you just learned, how you organize a comparison-or-contrast essay depends on your topic and on the reason you are writing about it. In general, there is no absolutely right or wrong method for arranging the details in such a paper. Sometimes you may simply want to use the pattern you find easier. Just remember that comparing and contrasting are powerful tools for discovering ideas and expressing them effectively. In fact, the very act of pointing out similarities and differences may lead to important discoveries about your subjects that will make your writing richer in detail and more interesting.

Hunger Moon

HAL BORLAND

''Hunger Moon'' is one of the many columns on nature and the outdoors that Hal Borland (1900–1978) published in the Sunday New York Times. *''January Wind,'' another selection by Borland, appears in Chapter 6.*

Looking Ahead

Borland uses language that is both concrete and vivid. He develops this essay with carefully chosen nouns and adjectives and with exciting images and figures of speech.

Vocabulary

awe Combination of deep respect and fear.

burnished Polished, shining.

charred Burned, blackened by fire.

constellations Groups of bright stars that take the shapes of animals, objects, and mythological people.

sequins Small, shiny disks used as decorations on clothing.

stark Sharp, clear.

strewing Scattering, spreading, sprinkling.

traceries Elegant patterns of lines like those seen in a large church window.

To see the full moon as it rose in the brittle eastern sky last night was to know 1
both awe and shivering wonder. It was round as a medallion, bright as burnished
brass, and its light had no more warmth than the frost cloud of a man's breath.
It was a false and lifeless sun that made false daylight of the night. It killed the
lesser stars and reduced the constellations to fundamentals. It burned the darkness with neither heat nor smoke, strewing the snow with charred skeletons of
the naked trees. No wonder the Indians knew the February full moon as the
Hunger Moon.

Yet, as it mounted the icy sky the moon set stark patterns of beauty. 2
Footsteps in the snow became laced traceries of purple shadows. Starless
ponds of night sky lay in the meadows' hollows. Roads became black velvet
ribbons with winking frost sequins. Pines became whispering flocks of huge,
dark birds on the hilltop and pasture cedars were black candle flames. Warm-
windowed houses and frost-roofed barns were all twins, each with its counter-
part beside it on the snow. And no man walked alone as he hurried toward
warmth and shelter.

Questions for Discussion

1. Earlier you learned that this selection uses the subject-by-subject method to
   present two views of the February moon. Explain these two views.
2. What does Borland's calling the moon a "false and lifeless sun" (paragraph
   1) tell us about his subject?
3. Explain what he means when he says that the moon "killed the lesser stars
   and reduced the constellations to fundamentals" (paragraph 1).
4. Pick out two metaphors in paragraph 2. How do they help develop the
   paragraph's topic sentence?
5. Explain the image in the last two sentences.

Suggestions for Journal Entries

1. Make two lists of details that reveal your feelings about a particular time: a
   season or month of the year, a day of the week, a time of day, your birthday,
   or a specific holiday. This is a pro-and-con assignment. In the first list, tell
   what you like about the time you are writing about. In the second, tell what
   you dislike about it.
2. Spend five minutes freewriting on the things you dislike about a job, task,
   or assignment you complete regularly at home, school, or work. After a
   short break, freewrite for another five minutes and discuss what, if anything, you like about this activity or explain why you think it should be
   done.

Watch the Cart!

JAMES LANGLEY

As a student majoring in English, James Langley wrote "Watch the Cart!" after having worked as a supermarket stock clerk and observing the shopping habits of people for several years. The essay contrasts approaches to shopping by discussing a number of interesting and often humorous differences between the ways that men and women buy groceries. "Watch the Cart!" was written while Langley was a college freshman, but it demonstrates a sensitivity for detail usually seen in the work of professional writers.

Looking Ahead

1. This essay uses the point-by-point method. As you read it, write down a list of the differences Langley describes.

2. In the introduction to Section Five, you learned that writers often combine various methods of development to support important points. Notice how often Langley uses illustrations (examples) to develop contrasts between the male and female shoppers he discusses in "Watch the Cart!"

Vocabulary

confines Limits, boundaries.

dictate Demand, make it mandatory.

fluidly Smoothly.

havoc Ruin, confusion, wreckage.

invariably Without fail, without exception.

menace Threat, danger.

preponderance Larger number or quantity.

proficient Skillful.

There is nothing similar in the way men and women shop for groceries. Believe 1
me, I know, because I work in a major supermarket. After watching scores of people shop for food day in and day out, I have become somewhat of an expert on the habits of American consumers. I have noticed many things about them, but nothing stands out more clearly than the differences between men and women when they shop.

First of all, men never know where anything is. Despite the recent trends in 2
equality, which dictate that a man should share the domestic chores, there is still a preponderance of women shoppers in America's grocery stores. And these women know what they're doing. Women are exceptional food shoppers, who

always know where something is. Nine times out of ten, it will be a man who asks an employee to find a product for him. I don't know how many guys come up to me in the course of a night to ask me where something is, but 50% of those who do invariably return to me in five minutes still unaware of the product's location. Men have no sense of direction in a supermarket. It's as if they're locked up within the confines of some life-sized maze that is impossible to solve. It has always been my contention that men who shop should be provided with specially trained dogs to sniff out the products they desire. It would certainly save me valuable time that is too often wasted as I explain to some idiot for the tenth time that soup is in aisle 9.

Women, on the other hand, rarely ask for an item's location. When they do, it is usually for some obscure product that only they have ever heard of and whose name only they can pronounce. Whenever a woman asks me where some such item is, I always tell her to go to aisle 11. Aisle 11 is the dog food aisle. Send a man there and he'll forget what he was looking for and just buy the dog food out of desperation. Send a woman there and she'll be back in five minutes with the product in hand, thanking me for locating it for her. It's really weird. I think women control supermarkets in a way that men are unaware of.

Another difference between men and women is that women shop at speeds that would get them tickets on freeways, while men shop with all the speed of a dead snail. A woman who's really good can get her shopping done in the same amount of time every time she goes. A man who shops just as often will get worse and worse every time.

The biggest difference between the sexes in regard to shopping, however, involves the manipulation of carts. A woman guides a cart through the store so fluidly and effortlessly that her movements are almost poetic. Men are an entirely different story. A man with a shopping cart is a menace to anyone within two aisles of him. Men bounce their carts off display cases, sideswipe their fellow patrons, and create havoc wherever they go. They have no idea of how to control the direction of carts. To a man, a shopping cart is some sort of crazed metal monster designed to embarrass and harass him.

Overall, then, women are far more proficient shoppers than men. Women are safe and graceful, while men are dangerous and clumsy. I know these things because I work in a supermarket. I also know these things because I am a man.

Questions for Discussion

1. What is Langley's thesis? What central idea does he convey in contrasting the shopping habits of women and men?

2. According to Langley, there are three major differences between the ways that men and women shop for groceries. What are they?

3. Langley relies heavily on examples. One of the most effective is "Men bounce their carts off display cases, sideswipe their fellow patrons, and create havoc wherever they go" (paragraph 5). What other illustrations do you find in this essay?

4. One good metaphor is the description of male shoppers ''locked up within the confines of some life-sized maze'' (paragraph 2). What other examples of figurative language do you find in the essay? (To review figurative language, see Chapter 6.)

Suggestions for Journal Entries

1. Choose an activity common to women and men. Begin to compare or contrast the ways they go about this activity. You might want to point out similarities or differences between the ways they drive, act at parties, study for exams, do housework, shop for birthday gifts, keep physically fit, mend a broken heart, shop for automobiles, or get ready for a night out on the town.
2. Langley contrasts the ways that men and women shop. Pick two other groups—adults and teenagers, for instance, or rich people and poor people—and make a few notes about the ways their shopping habits differ.

Temptations of Old Age*

MALCOLM COWLEY

Malcolm Cowley (1898–1989) was a writer, editor, literary critic, and historian noted for his energy and productivity even until his death at 90. In the last decade of his life, Cowley wrote The View from 80, *a book that explains his very positive attitude toward aging and that offers excellent advice about the latter stages of life. Another selection from* The View from 80 *appears in Chapter 7.*

Looking Ahead

1. This selection is from a chapter of Cowley's book that discusses several temptations of old age and explains ways to avoid them. Among these temptations are greed, vanity, and a desire to escape life's problems through alcohol. But the greatest temptation, as shown in the following paragraphs, is ''simply giving up.''
2. Renoir, mentioned in paragraph 4, was a French painter of the nineteenth and twentieth centuries. Goya was a Spanish painter of the eighteenth and nineteenth centuries.

Vocabulary

ailments   Illnesses, disorders, diseases.
compelling   Convincing, strong, valid.
distinguished   Well-respected.

* Editor's title

distraction   Amusement, diversion.

infirmities   Illnesses, weaknesses, ailments.

lithographs   Prints.

outwitted   Outsmarted, outmanuevered.

Rolls-Royce   Expensive British automobile.

senility   Forgetfulness and decrease in mental powers affecting some elderly people.

stoical   Brave, uncomplaining.

Not whiskey or cooking sherry but simply giving up is the greatest temptation   1
of age. It is something different from a stoical acceptance of infirmities, which
is something to be admired.

   The givers-up see no reason for working. Sometimes they lie in bed all day   2
when moving about would still be possible, if difficult. I had a friend, a distinguished poet, who surrendered in that fashion. The doctors tried to stir him to
action, but he refused to leave his room. Another friend, once a successful artist,
stopped painting when his eyes began to fail. His doctor made the mistake of
telling him that he suffered from a fatal disease. He then lost interest in everything except the splendid Rolls-Royce, acquired in his prosperous days, that
stood in the garage. Daily he wiped the dust from its hood. He couldn't drive it
on the road any longer, but he used to sit in the driver's seat, start the motor, then
back the Rolls out of the garage and drive it in again, back twenty feet and
forward twenty feet; that was his only distraction.

   I haven't the right to blame those who surrender, not being able to put myself   3
inside their minds or bodies. Often they must have compelling reasons, physical
or moral. Not only do they suffer from a variety of ailments, but also they are
made to feel that they no longer have a function in the community. Their families
and neighbors don't ask them for advice, don't really listen when they speak,
don't call on them for efforts. One notes that there are not a few recoveries from
apparent senility when that situation changes. If it doesn't change, old persons
may decide that efforts are useless. I sympathize with their problems, but the
men and women I envy are those who accept old age as a series of challenges.

   For such persons, every new infirmity is an enemy to be outwitted, an   4
obstacle to be overcome by force of will. They enjoy each little victory over
themselves, and sometimes they win a major success. Renoir was one of them.
He continued painting, and magnificently, for years after he was crippled by
arthritis; the brush had to be strapped to his arm. ''You don't need your hand to
paint,'' he said. Goya was another of the unvanquished. At 72 he retired as an
official painter of the Spanish court and decided to work only for himself. His
later years were those of the famous ''black paintings'' in which he let his
imagination run (and also of the lithographs, then a new technique). At 78 he
escaped a reign of terror in Spain by fleeing to Bordeaux. He was deaf and his
eyes were failing; in order to work he had to wear several pairs of spectacles,
one over another, and then use a magnifying glass; but he was producing

splendid work in a totally new style. At 80 he drew an ancient man propped on two sticks, with a mass of white hair and beard hiding his face and with the inscription "I am still learning."

"Eighty years old!" the great Catholic poet Paul Claudel wrote in his journal. "No eyes left, no ears, no teeth, no legs, no wind! And when all is said and done, how astonishingly well one does without them!" 5

Questions for Discussion

1. Various methods can be combined to develop one idea. Where in this piece does Cowley use examples?
2. Do you think the conclusion of this selection is effective? Why or why not? If necessary, review ways to write conclusions in Chapter 4.
3. Why, according to the author, do some elderly people simply give up?
4. What does he mean when he says that others see "every new infirmity" as "an obstacle to be overcome by force of will" (paragraph 4)?
5. Is there a reason Cowley uses Renoir, Goya, and Claudel to explain his idea of people who "accept old age as a series of challenges" (paragraph 3)? Why didn't he refer to famous scientists, athletes, or entertainers instead?
6. Cowley uses the subject-by-subject pattern. Why does he begin with the "givers-up" and not end with them? Should he have discussed Renoir, Goya, and Claudel first?

Suggestions for Journal Entries

1. What Cowley says might apply to folks of all ages. Do you know someone who seems to face all the challenges life has to offer? Spend five minutes freewriting about the way this person reacts to such challenges. Then do the same for someone you might call a "giver-up." Try to include facts about their lives that will describe their personalities.
2. In what way are you like the people in your family who have come before you? Think about a parent, grandparent, great-aunt, or other older relative. Use listing or focused freewriting to explain what is similar about your personalities, interests, lifestyles, or your opinions about music, politics, other people, or anything else you can think of.

If at First You Do Not See . . .

JESSIE SULLIVAN

When Jessie Sullivan began this essay for a college composition class, she wanted simply to describe what her inner-city neighborhood looked like. As she developed her work, however, Sullivan discovered that what is important about her community is beyond what the eye can see. Slowly, her purpose for writing changed, and after many drafts she produced this fascinating picture of the sorrow and the promise of her world. Sullivan majors in liberal arts and business. She plans to attend graduate school to study business administration.

Looking Ahead

The author uses contrast skillfully. As a realist, she describes what is wrong with her community, but she doesn't forget to show us signs of hope for the people and place she loves. In the process, she reveals much about herself: her courage, her vision, and her desire to make a difference.

Vocabulary

bewilderment   Astonishment, confusion.

condone   Make excuses for.

defaced   Made ugly, disfigured.

diversified   Varied, different.

illicit   Illegal, prohibited.

infamous   Dishonorable, known for evil or wrongdoing.

obscenities   Words or drawings that are indecent and offensive.

oppressive   Harsh, severe, hard to bear.

paraphernalia   Gear, equipment used in a particular activity.

pathetic   Pitiful, wretched, miserable.

preconceived notions   Prejudices, opinions formed before having accurate information about something.

sober   Reliable, serious, steady.

superficial   Quick and careless, shallow, on the surface.

A look of genuine surprise comes over some of my classmates when I mention   1
where I live. My neighborhood has a reputation that goes before it. People who have never been there tend to hold preconceived notions about the place, most of which are negative and many of which are true. Those who actually visit my neighborhood usually notice only the filth, the deterioration of buildings and grounds, and the crime. What they fail to see isn't as apparent, but it is there also. It is hope for the future.

I live in an apartment on the outskirts of New Brunswick, New Jersey. To   2
the right of my building is Robeson Village, a large low-income housing project with about two-hundred apartments facing each other on opposite sides of a wide, asphalt driveway that runs the length of the complex. Here, drug dealers and buyers congregate daily, doing business in front of anyone who cares to watch. Sometimes, children who have witnessed these transactions look over the crack vials, hypodermic needles, syringes, and other paraphernalia the dealers and their customers have left in their wake.

To the left of my building is Henry Street, which has become synonymous   3
with illegal drugs. It is a pathetic place. The block consists of a half dozen vacant
and condemned buildings, all of which are lived in or frequented by addicts and
dealers. The latter have set up stores there in much the same way legitimate
merchants choose particular locations where they think business will be profit-
able.

It is this area, three blocks in radius, that is infamous for illicit drugs,   4
prostitution, and violence of every sort. Known as the "Vil," it is regarded as
the city's hub of criminal activity and immorality.

With the growing popularity of crack, the appearance of the community has   5
gotten worse and worse, as if it were on a collision course with destruction.
Fences that once separated one property from another lie in tangled rusted
masses on sidewalks, serving now only as eyesores. Almost all of the buildings
are defaced with spray-painted obscenities and other foul messages. Every street
is littered with candy wrappers, cardboard boxes, balled-up newspapers, and
broken beer and soda bottles.

But Henry Street is undeniably the worst. The road is so covered with broken   6
glass that the asphalt is barely visible. The way the glass catches the sunlight at
every angle makes the street look almost magical, but there is nothing magical
about it. Henry Street is a dead-end in more than the literal sense. In front of
apartment buildings, the overgrown lawns, which more closely resemble hay
than grass, are filled with old tires, cracked televisions, refrigerators and ovens
with missing doors, rusted bikes, broken toys, and worn chairs and tables without
legs. Dozens of abandoned cars, their windows shattered and their bodies
stripped of anything of value, line the curbs. The entire block is so cluttered with
refuse that strangers often mistake it for the junk yard, which is five blocks up.

To the eye of the visitor, the community appears to be in a chronic state of   7
depression. Even trees, symbols of life and vitality, seem to bow their heads in
sorrow. Rather than reaching up in praise, their branches are twisted and ill-
formed, as if poisoned by the very soil in which they are rooted. The pungent
odors of urine, feces, and dead, wet leaves are made worse by the stench of
rotting food, which spills from overturned garbage cans onto the sidewalk and
cooks in the heat of the sun.

Most people familiar with the neighborhood are aware that the majority of   8
us residents are virtual prisoners in our homes because of the alarming crime
rate. Muggings, rapes, and gang-related shootings, many of which do not get
reported in newspapers, are commonplace. Many residents live in such fear that
they hide in their apartments behind deadbolt locks and chains, daring to peer
out of their peepholes only when a frequent gunshot rings out.

Many of my neighbors have adopted an I-mind-my-own-business attitude,   9
preferring to remain silent and blind to the goings-on around them. This is the
case for so many of them that many nonresidents believe everyone feels this
way. Unfortunately, most outsiders learn about our community from people who
have been here only once or twice and who leave with unfair and dangerous
misconceptions about us. They see the filth and immorality, and that is all they

see. They take one quick look and assume none of us cares about the neighborhood or about the way we live.

I see my neighborhood from the inside, and I face all of the terrible things 10
I have mentioned on a day-to-day basis. I also see aspects of my community that
cannot be appreciated with a superficial first glance. If you look at the place
closely, you will find small strong family units, like my own, scattered amid the
degeneration and chaos. Working together, struggling to free themselves from
oppressive conditions, these families are worth noticing! We are sober, moral
people who continue to live our lives according to the laws of society and, more
important, according to the laws of God Himself.

Look closely and you will find those of us who pick up the trash when we 11
see it scattered on our small lawns, sidewalks, and doorsteps. We discourage our
children from disrespecting the area in which they live, and we see to it that they
don't litter or deface public property. We emphasize the importance of schooling, and we teach them about the evils of drugs and crime, making certain that
they are educated at home as well.

Most important, we practice what we preach. We show the children with our 12
actions that we do not condone the immoral and illegal acts around us, and we
refuse to take part in any of them. We call the police whenever we hear gunshots,
see drug transactions, or learn of any other unlawful activity. The children know
that we care and that we are trying to create a brighter future for them.

However, the most visible sign of hope is that young people from my 13
neighborhood—and from many neighborhoods like mine, for that matter—are
determined to put an end to the destruction of our communities. It angers us that
a minute yet very visible group of negative individuals has come to represent the
whole. It saddens us that skills, talents, and aspirations, which are so abundant
in our communities, should go untapped. Therefore, we have decided to take
matters into our own hands; we will get the education we need and solve the
problems of our neighborhoods ourselves.

Many of us attend the local county college, where we come together often 14
to share ideas for a better future for our community. We also give each other the
moral support we need to achieve our educational goals. Our hope binds us
together closely and is itself a sign that things will get better.

This May, I was proud to see a number of friends receive associate's degrees 15
and get admitted to four-year colleges and universities for advanced degrees. I
hope to do the same soon. We are studying for different professions, but no
matter how diversified our goals, we will use our knowledge for the benefit of
all. This means returning to the community as doctors, lawyers, teachers, entre-
preneurs. We will build programs to assist the people of our community directly:
day care centers for children with working mothers; family mental and physical
health clinics; job-training and placement facilities; legal service centers; youth
centers; and drug/alcohol rehabilitation programs. Given the leadership of educated people like those we will become, such facilities can eventually be oper-
ated by community residents themselves. Most important, we intend to serve as
visible and vocal role models for our children—for the leaders who will follow

us and keep our hope alive. Eventually, we will bring about permanent change and make it impossible for a misguided few to represent a proud and productive community.

When friends visit me in my apartment for the first time, they frequently ask 16 in awe and bewilderment, "How can you live in such a bad place?" I always give the same reply: "It isn't where you live, but how you live and what you live for."

Questions for Discussion

1. What does Sullivan mean in paragraph 1 when she says that her "neighborhood has a reputation that goes before it"? Does this statement help introduce what follows in the rest of the essay?
2. How do most outsiders learn about Sullivan's neighborhood? Why does she tell us that many shootings there never get reported in the newspapers?
3. What contrasting attitudes about the community do her neighbors hold?
4. What causes the most harm in Sullivan's community? What is its greatest source of hope?
5. As you learned earlier, this essay is organized subject by subject. Should Sullivan have used the point-by-point pattern? Why or why not?
6. When in this contrast essay does she include descriptive details to develop ideas? When does she use examples?
7. What image does she create in paragraph 7? What figure of speech does she use to develop this image?

Suggestions for Journal Entries

1. Make a list of the qualities you admire most about the neighborhood in which you live or grew up. Then make another list of ways it might be improved.
2. Spend a few minutes freewriting about the kind of community in which you grew up. Then freewrite some more about the kind of place it has become. Finally, write a short paragraph that explains major similarities and differences between what it was then and what it is now.
3. Use any of the techniques discussed in "Getting Started" to gather information about what your home, neighborhood, or town might look like to someone seeing it for the first time. Then, go beyond appearances and discuss the real character of the place as you know it. In other words, like Sullivan, describe what's on the "inside."
4. Think of a community, a family, or any group of people struggling to grow, improve, or even survive. What makes their life a struggle? What hope do you see for this place or these people?

Columbus and the Moon

TOM WOLFE

Tom Wolfe is the author of The Right Stuff, *a book about the U.S. space program that was made into a major motion picture. He is also widely known as a writer of books and articles in which he demonstrates a powerful talent for social criticism. Wolfe is one of the creators of the "new journalism," a style of news reporting in which writers express personal (subjective) reactions to the events they're covering.*

"Columbus and the Moon" compares Columbus's voyages with the exploration of space by the National Aeronautics and Space Administration (NASA).

Looking Ahead

1. At the end of paragraph 5, Wolfe writes that some of the spinoffs of the space program were "not a giant step for mankind." This is a humorous reference to what Neil Armstrong said when he set foot on the lunar surface in 1969: "That's one small step for a man, and one giant leap for mankind."

2. Neil Armstrong, Michael Collins, and Buzz Aldrin were on the Apollo 11 mission, which made the first landing on the moon.

Vocabulary

albeit   Although, though.

appropriations   Financing, money.

awed   Amazed.

evangelical   Religious fundamentalist.

ignominy   Shame, disgrace.

lurid   Racy, suggestive, strange.

psychic phenomena   Extrasensory objects or events.

quest   Search.

testy   Irritable.

traumatized   Shocked, emotionally confused.

The National Aeronautics and Space Administration's moon landing 10 years   1
ago today was a Government project, but then so was Columbus's voyage to America in 1492. The Government, in Columbus's case, was the Spanish Court of Ferdinand and Isabella. Spain was engaged in a sea race with Portugal in much the same way that the United States would be caught up in a space race with the Soviet Union four and a half centuries later.

The race in 1492 was to create the first shipping lane to Asia. The Portuguese expeditions had always sailed east, around the southern tip of Africa. Columbus decided to head due west, across open ocean, a scheme that was feasible only thanks to a recent invention—the magnetic ship's compass. Until then ships had stayed close to the great land masses even for the longest voyages. Likewise, it was only thanks to an invention of the 1940's and early 1950's, the high-speed electronic computer, that NASA would even consider propelling astronauts out of the Earth's orbit and toward the moon.

Both NASA and Columbus made not one but a series of voyages. NASA landed men on six different parts of the moon. Columbus made four voyages to different parts of what he remained convinced was the east coast of Asia. As a result both NASA and Columbus had to keep coming back to the Government with their hands out, pleading for refinancing. In each case the reply of the Government became, after a few years: "This is all very impressive, but what earthly good is it to anyone back home?"

Columbus was reduced to making the most desperate claims. When he first reached land in 1492 at San Salvador, off Cuba, he expected to find gold, or at least spices. The Arawak Indians were awed by the strangers and their ships, which they believed had descended from the sky, and they presented them with their most prized possessions, live parrots and balls of cotton. Columbus soon set them digging for gold, which didn't exist. So he brought back reports of fabulous riches in the form of manpower; which is to say, slaves. He was not speaking of the Arawaks, however. With the exception of criminals and prisoners of war, he was supposed to civilize all natives and convert them to Christianity. He was talking about the Carib Indians, who were cannibals and therefore qualified as criminals. The Caribs would fight down to the last unbroken bone rather than endure captivity, and few ever survived the voyages back to Spain. By the end of Columbus's second voyage, in 1496, the Government was becoming testy. A great deal of wealth was going into voyages to Asia, and very little was coming back. Columbus made his men swear to return to Spain saying that they had not only reached the Asian mainland, they had heard Japanese spoken.

Likewise by the early 1970's, it was clear that the moon was in economic terms pretty much what it looked like from Earth, a gray rock. NASA, in the quest for appropriations, was reduced to publicizing the "spinoffs" of the space program. These included Teflon-coated frying pans, a ballpoint pen that would write in a weightless environment, and a computerized biosensor system that would enable doctors to treat heart patients without making house calls. On the whole, not a giant step for mankind.

In 1493, after his first voyage, Columbus had ridden through Barcelona at the side of King Ferdinand in the position once occupied by Ferdinand's late son, Juan. By 1500, the bad-mouthing of Columbus had reached the point where he was put in chains at the conclusion of his third voyage and returned to Spain in disgrace. NASA suffered no such ignominy, of course, but by July 20, 1974, the fifth anniversary of the landing of Apollo 11, things were grim enough. The public had become gloriously bored by space exploration. The fifth anniversary celebration consisted mainly of about 200 souls, mostly NASA people, sitting on folding chairs underneath a camp meeting canopy on the marble prairie outside the old Smithsonian Air Museum in Washington listening to speeches by Neil Armstrong, Michael Collins, and Buzz Aldrin and watching the caloric waves ripple.

Extraordinary rumors had begun to circulate about the astronauts. The most lurid said that trips to the moon, and even into earth orbit, had so traumatized the men, they had fallen victim to religious and spiritualist manias or plain madness. (Of the total 73 astronauts chosen, one, Aldrin, is known to have suffered from depression, rooted, as his own memoir makes clear, in matters that had nothing to do with space flight. Two teamed up in an evangelical organization, and one set up a foundation for the scientific study of psychic phenomena—interests the three of them had developed long before they flew in space.) The NASA budget, meanwhile, had been reduced to the light-bill level.   7

Columbus died in 1509, nearly broke and stripped of most of his honors as Spain's Admiral of the Ocean, a title he preferred. It was only later that history began to look upon him not as an adventurer who had tried and failed to bring home gold—but as a man with a supernatural sense of destiny, whose true glory was his willingness to plunge into the unknown, including the remotest parts of the universe he could hope to reach.   8

NASA still lives, albeit in reduced circumstances, and whether or not history will treat NASA like the admiral is hard to say.   9

The idea that the exploration of the rest of the universe is its own reward is not very popular, and NASA is forced to keep talking about things such as bigger communications satellites that will enable live television transmission of European soccer games at a fraction of the current cost. Such notions as "building a bridge to the stars for mankind" do not light up the sky today—but may yet.   10

Questions for Discussion

1. What is the central idea of this essay?
2. What are some of the similarities between Columbus's voyages and NASA's space program that Wolfe identifies?
3. Wolfe uses anecdotes about Columbus and about the space program to help explain the similarities between the two. Which anecdotes show that both Columbus and NASA had trouble with finances? Which explain the loss of popularity that both suffered?
4. In what way were Columbus's "desperate claims" about the new world (paragraph 4) like NASA's publicizing the " 'spinoffs' of the space program" (paragraph 5)? What were some of these spinoffs?
5. How did Columbus's career end? What does Wolfe predict for NASA?
6. What transitional words and expressions does Wolfe use to keep his essay coherent and easy to read?

Suggestions for Journal Entries

1. One important use of comparison is to let readers discover startling new things about familiar subjects. List a few facts and ideas that this essay taught you about the space program. Then mention a few things it taught you about Columbus.

2. Wolfe's essay compares two great programs of exploration from two very different time periods. Jot down some notes about how people from different centuries have coped with the same problems or accomplished the same tasks.

   For example, list similarities between the way you celebrate a traditional holiday (Thanksgiving, Christmas, Chanukah, the Fourth of July) and the way your grandparents did. Or consider how people now and long ago have coped with the same type of misfortune (the death of a loved one, the loss of a job) or have marked important events in their lives such as marriage, the birth of a child, or the purchase of a home.

SUGGESTIONS FOR WRITING

1. The first of the Suggestions for Journal Entries after Hal Borland's "Hunger Moon" asks that you make two lists revealing what you like and dislike about a particular time: a season or month of the year, a day of the week, a time of day, your birthday, a special holiday, for example. Write this information in your journal if you haven't done so already. Then, use it to begin a short essay that explains your mixed feelings about your topic.

   A good way to organize this essay is subject by subject. Write a rough draft divided into two sections. In the first, explain what you like about this time; develop each of your reasons in a separate paragraph. In the second section, explain what you dislike about it; again, develop each reason in its own paragraph. Then, read this draft carefully to decide whether you need to add detail or to improve coherence in and between paragraphs. Make these changes when you rewrite your paper.

   Once you have a draft that is well developed and organized, summarize your overall or dominant reaction to your topic in a thesis. Do you like it this time more than you dislike it? Is the opposite true? Or is it just impossible to decide? However you answer, put your thesis in an attention-grabbing introduction. Then write an effective conclusion. You can review how to write introductions and conclusions in Chapter 4. Finally, revise the entire paper once more and edit it thoroughly.

2. Use the advice in the previous suggestion to write an essay that might be entitled "It Was the Best of Times; It Was the Worst of Times." Pick an important period in your life about which you have both positive and negative memories. A time during which you had to make changes in your lifestyle or ideas might provide interesting details. Here are a few examples: your first term in a new school; the summer you started working; the time you got braces on your teeth or a cast on your broken leg; your first weeks in the military; the semester you learned to love math; your first year of marriage; the day your child began to walk; the months you spent recovering from an illness or operation.

3. Did you respond to item 1 in the suggestions for journal writing after "Watch the Cart!" by James Langley? If so, you have probably listed several similarities and/or differences about the ways men and women go about a particular activity. Expand your notes into a well-developed essay.

   If you did not respond to this suggestion, consider the following as the kinds of topics you might want to explore in an essay that compares or contrasts the behavior of men and women:

   How men and women shop for birthday gifts for friends, relatives, and loved ones

   What men and women do to keep physically fit

   What men and women do to mend a broken heart

   How men and women shop for automobiles

   How men and women get ready for a night out on the town

Before writing the first draft, decide whether to arrange your ideas point by point or subject by subject. (Langley's essay uses the point-by-point pattern.) Then, write a preliminary thesis statement to guide you as you develop the rest of the paper. You can always revise this thesis or choose a new one as you go through the process of rewriting and editing.

4. In talking about people who are eighty, Malcolm Cowley describes two different types: those who fight on and those who give up. But we see these types in every generation, even our own. In fact, you may have begun discussing such people in your journal. Use these notes in an essay about people you know who fit Cowley's personality types: those who face life bravely and those who just give up.

   On the other hand, if you don't like this topic, you can start from scratch and choose your own basis for contrast. For example, discuss two very different types of students: those who are serious about getting an education and those who are not. Here's an example of a thesis for such an paper:

   > While serious students study hard, do extra reading, and compare notes with classmates, those who just want to get by spend much of their time playing cards or watching television!

   Cowley uses the subject-by-subject method; you might want to do the same. However you decide to organize your essay, discuss two or three people you know as examples of *each* personality type. Begin with a rough draft, adding details with each revision to make your paper clearer and more convincing. In the process, include an effective introduction and conclusion.

   Then, rewrite your paper once more. Make sure it has a clear thesis, it is easy to follow, and it is free of mistakes in grammar, punctuation, spelling, and the like.

5. If you read "If at First You Do Not See . . .," follow Jessie Sullivan's lead: write an essay that contrasts your opinion of a place you know well with the opinion of people who visit it only occasionally. In other words, contrast its surface appearance with the reality behind that appearance. A good subject might be your own community, your high school or college campus, a part of town you visit often, a run-down but beautiful building, or the home of an interesting relative or friend.

   While your paper need not be as long as Sullivan's, it should contain vivid detail to convince your readers that you know what you are talking about. An effective way to organize it is subject by subject. However, you can also use the point-by-point method, especially if you want to explain how you react to various aspects of the place—sights, sounds, smells—in contrast to how strangers might see *each* of them.

   Check the journal entries you made after reading Sullivan's essay. They should help you begin your first draft. Once you have completed several versions of your paper and have made the contrast clear, write an introduction that captures the readers' attention and expresses your main point in a thesis.

Put the finishing touches on your writing by correcting errors that might reduce its effectiveness or distract your readers.

6. In "Columbus and the Moon," Tom Wolfe drew similarities between the discovery of the New World and NASA's exploration of outer space. Consider similarities between the way people from different times have:

- Celebrated an important holiday (Christmas, Chanukah, Thanksgiving);
- Coped with the same types of misfortune (the death of a loved one, the loss of a job); or
- Marked the same major events in their lives (marriage, the birth of a child, the purchase of a home).

Now, write an essay explaining these similarities in detail. When you draft and revise your paper, make sure it has a clear thesis and is well organized. Use either the subject-by-subject or point-by-point method. Improve coherence, clarity, and development as you go along. Then, put the finishing touches on your work by correcting distracting mechanical errors.

As with other assignments, you may have already begun gathering information in your journal. So, before you begin writing, review the notes you made after reading Wolfe's essay.

7. What was your hometown, neighborhood, or street like when you were a child, and what it is like now? Has it changed for the better or for the worse?

Describe important changes in a well-developed essay that uses the subject-by-subject method. If you want, begin by describing what the place was like before, then discuss what it has become. Rely on your senses, and use language that is specific, vivid, and concrete. Examples of such language are found throughout this chapter but especially in the work of Borland and Sullivan. Other selections that describe places and things well appear in Chapter 8.

As you write your first draft, focus on a thesis that expresses your approval or disapproval of the changes you have seen. Put that thesis in your introduction or conclusion. Here are two examples:

What's happened to the downtown area in the last ten years has convinced me that even the most rundown city can be saved.

What's happened to Elm Street in recent years has made me an opponent of urban renewal.

If you responded to the second journal suggestion after Jessie Sullivan's "If at First You Do Not See . . . ," you probably already have information and inspiration to begin this project. Follow Sullivan's example. Be as careful and conscientious as she was when you draft, revise, and edit your essay.

CHAPTER 15

PROCESS ANALYSIS

Like illustration and comparison and contrast, process analysis is a way to explain complex ideas and abstract concepts. It can be used to show how something works or how something happens. It also comes in handy when you want to give readers instructions.

ORGANIZATION, PURPOSE, AND THESIS

Process explanations are organized in chronological order, much like narrative essays and short stories. In narration, however, the writer's purpose is to tell *what* happens. In process analysis, it is to explain *how* something happens (or happened) or *how* it is done.

You would be explaining a process if you wrote an essay discussing how the body uses oxygen, how electric light bulbs work, how a CD player produces sound, or how the Grand Canyon was formed. An example of such an essay in this chapter is Mildred Mastin Pace's ''The Making of a Mummy.'' You can find another, Devoe's ''The Hibernation of the Woodchuck,'' in Chapter 3.

As you can tell from the titles and topics above, process analysis is an important tool in scientific writing. But it can also be applied to topics in history, sociology, economics, the arts, and other subjects. For example, a process paper might be a good way to explain how the U.S. Constitution was ratified, how the stock market works, how people celebrate a holiday or tradition, or how a particular type of music developed. As Kenneth Kohler shows in ''How I Came Out to My Parents,'' this type of writing can even explain how people deal with important personal issues.

Process analysis is also used in the writing of instructions. Scientists, doctors, engineers, and computer experts, for example, must often write careful directions to show their readers how to use a tool or machine, how to complete a procedure safely, how to conduct a test to achieve accurate results, or how to run complicated computer software. As a beginning writer, you might want to discuss a more limited subject by showing your readers how to change a tire, hang wallpaper, stop smoking, lose weight, study for a math exam, or accomplish another important task or goal. In this chapter, selections that instruct readers are Florence Pettit's ''Sharpening Your Jackknife or Pocketknife'' and Triena Milden's ''So You Want to Flunk Out of College.''

The thesis in a process analysis essay is usually a statement of purpose; it explains why a process is important, why it occurs or occurred, or why it should be completed. For example, if you want to explain how to change the oil in a car, you might begin by saying that changing oil regularly can extend the engine's life. In addition to a statement of purpose, writers often begin with a broad summary or overview of the process so that readers can understand how each step relates to the whole procedure and to its purpose.

CLARITY AND DIRECTNESS

As with all types of writing, clarity and directness are important in process writing. You must explain the various steps in your process specifically and carefully enough that even readers who are unfamiliar with the subject will be able to follow each step easily. To be clear and to maintain your readers' interest, keep the following in mind:

1. *Use clear, simple language:* Use words that your readers will have no trouble understanding. If you *must* use terms your readers are not familiar with, provide a brief definition or description. Depending on how much your readers know about how to change a tire, for example, you might have to describe what a lug wrench looks like before you explain how to use it.

2. *Use the clearest, simplest organization:* Whenever possible, arrange the steps of your process in chronological order. In addition, use plenty of connective words and phrases between paragraphs (especially to show the passage of time); this will keep your writing coherent and easy to follow.

3. *Discuss simultaneous steps separately:* If you need to explain two or more steps that occur at the same time, write about these steps in separate paragraphs. To maintain coherence between paragraphs, use connective elements like "At the same time," "Meanwhile," and "During this stage of the process."

4. *Try not to combine steps:* Reserve at least one entire paragraph for each step in the process. Explaining more than one step at a time might confuse your readers and cause you to leave out important information. For instance, imagine how well you'd change a tire for the first time after reading this:

   • After having set the handbrake (and/or put the car in PARK) and jacked up the car, raising the tire about an inch off the ground, use the tapered end of the lug wrench to remove the hubcap, and place the hubcap nearby; it will come in handy.

   • Next, apply the wrench to the lugs and remove them by turning the wrench counterclockwise.

These instructions are much easier to follow and more complete when arranged in separate, detailed steps:

- First, apply the handbrake. If your car has an automatic transmission, also put it in PARK.
- Next, jack up the car high enough that the flat tire is about 1 inch off the ground.
- Then use the tapered end of the lug wrench to pry off the hubcap (the wheel cover).
- After you have pried the hubcap off the wheel, place the hubcap nearby on the ground. You will be using it like a bowl to hold the *lugs,* the nuts that are fastened to the bolts and hold the wheel in place.
- Next, place the socket (the open end) of the lug wrench over any one of the lugs, and loosen the lug slightly by turning the wrench counterclockwise.
- In the same manner, loosen all the other lugs.
- Continue turning each lug by hand until you have removed them all. As you remove each one, place it in the hubcap.

5. *Give all the necessary information:* Always provide enough information to develop each step in the process adequately, and don't forget the small, important details. For instance, if you're explaining how to change the oil in a car, remember to tell your readers to wait for the engine to cool off before loosening the oil-pan nut; otherwise, the oil could severely burn their hands.

6. *Use the right verb tense:* If you're explaining a recurring process (one that happens over and over again), use the present tense. In writing about how your student government works, for instance, say that "the representatives *are elected* by fellow students and *meet* together every Friday afternoon." But if you're writing about a process that is over and done with, such as how one individual ran for election, use the past tense.

7. *Use direct commands:* When giving instructions, make each step clear and brief by simply telling the reader to do it (that is, by using the imperative mood). For example, don't say, "The first thing to do is to apply the handbrake." Instead, be more direct: "First, apply the handbrake."

Enjoy the four selections that follow. They are well written and should provide you with effective examples of the techniques found in writing that makes good use of process analysis.

Sharpening Your Jackknife or Pocketknife

FLORENCE H. PETTIT

Noted for her clear and engaging style, Florence H. Pettit is the author of a number of books for young readers. "Sharpening Your Jackknife or Pocketknife" is from How to Make Whirligigs and Whimmy Diddles and Other

American Folkcraft Objects. *This fascinating book explains how to make replicas of dolls, toys, blankets, and other objects used by native Americans and Eskimos as well as by early European settlers in this hemisphere.*

"Sharpening Your Jackknife or Pocketknife" is typical of the writing found in the best technical or maintenance manuals. It is prose that has a clear and practical purpose and that remains direct and easy to follow throughout.

Looking Ahead

1. In her third sentence, Pettit mentions "gouges and chisels." These are common woodworking tools.
2. When giving instructions, it is important to mention the tools, supplies, and materials the reader will need to complete the process. As you read this essay, make a list (perhaps in your journal) of the things required for sharpening a knife.

Vocabulary

burr   Rough spot that sticks up from the sharpened surface.
oval   Egg shape.
strop   Leather strap used for sharpening.

If you have never done any whittling or wood carving before, the first skill to learn is how to sharpen your knife. You may be surprised to learn that even a brand-new knife needs sharpening. Knives are never sold honed (finely sharpened), although some gouges and chisels are. It is essential to learn the firm stroke on the stone that will keep your blades sharp. The sharpening stone must be fixed in place on the table, so that it will not move around. You can do this by placing a piece of rubber inner tube or a thin piece of foam rubber under it. Or you can tack four strips of wood, if you have a rough worktable, to frame the stone and hold it in place. Put a generous puddle of oil on the stone—this will soon disappear into the surface of a new stone, and you will need to keep adding more oil. Press the knife blade flat against the stone in the puddle of oil, using your index finger. Whichever way the cutting edge of the knife faces is the side of the blade that should get a little more pressure. Move the blade around three or four times in a narrow oval about the size of your fingernail, going *counterclockwise* when the sharp edge is facing right. Now turn the blade over in the same spot on the stone, press hard, and move it around the small oval *clockwise*, with more pressure on the cutting edge that faces left. Repeat the ovals, flipping the knife blade over six or seven times, and applying lighter pressure to the blade the last two times. Wipe the blade clean with a piece of rag or tissue and rub it flat on the piece of leather strop at least twice on each side. Stroke *away* from the cutting edge to remove the little burr of metal that may be left on the blade.

Questions for Discussion

1. Writers often begin describing a process by explaining its purpose. Why, according to Pettit, is learning how to sharpen a knife important?
2. What tools and materials does Pettit tell us we'll need to sharpen a knife properly?
3. What are the major steps in the process of sharpening your jackknife or pocketknife?
4. Does Pettit use any connective words and phrases (transitions) in this selection? Identify them.
5. Like any good set of instructions, "Sharpening Your Jackknife or Pocketknife" is written in the imperative mood, using direct commands, as discussed earlier in this chapter. Find examples of such commands in this selection.

Suggestions for Journal Entries

1. Think about a simple process that you've had to complete at home, at work, or at school. For instance, recall the steps you went through the last time you shampooed a rug, painted a wall, cooked macaroni and cheese, cut grass, set the table for dinner, waxed a floor, ironed a load of laundry, or got dressed up for an important date. Make a list of the tools, equipment, utensils, ingredients, and/or materials that you needed to complete this process.
2. Try brainstorming with a friend or two to come up with the steps most people go through to complete a common, everyday activity, such as getting dressed for school or work, preparing for bed, studying for a test, getting a child ready for school, polishing shoes, or shopping for a week's groceries. Briefly list these steps in your journal.

So You Want to Flunk Out of College

TRIENA MILDEN

This selection is Triena Milden's tongue-in-cheek response to an English assignment that required her to explain various rules or procedures that first-year students might follow to be successful in college. Milden saw this as an opportunity to create a "teaching tool" for herself and her classmates. However, she knew that no one would take her advice if she treated the subject seriously and began "preaching."

That's why she decided on an ironic approach. "I thought about all of the things I'd have to do to get good grades," explained Milden, "and then I simply reversed them."

Looking Ahead

1. Milden isolates each step in the process of flunking out of college in a paragraph of its own. Nonetheless, the essay remains coherent because she uses connective words and phrases to create effective transitions between paragraphs.

2. As you've learned, writers of process analysis use the imperative mood (direct commands) to direct or instruct their readers to do something. For instance, Milden says, "never raise your hand" (paragraph 3). Find other examples of the imperative mood in her essay.

Vocabulary

conveys   Communicates.

detrimental   Harmful, injurious.

ultimate   Final, most important.

Flunking out of college is a relatively easy task. It requires little effort and   1
might even be considered fun. Though it is hard to imagine why anyone would purposely try to flunk out of college, many people accomplish this task easily. In fact, whatever the reason one might want to flunk out of college, the process is quite simple.

First, do not show up for classes very often. It is important, however, to   2
show up occasionally to find out when tests will be scheduled; the importance of this will become apparent later in this essay.

When in class, never raise your hand to ask questions and never volunteer   3
any answers to the teacher's questions. If the teacher calls on you, either answer incorrectly or say "I don't know." Be sure your tone of voice conveys your lack of interest.

Another thing to avoid is homework. There are two reasons for this. First   4
and most important, completing homework assignments only reinforces information learned earlier, thereby contributing to higher test scores. Second, although teachers credit homework as only part of the total grade, every little bit of credit hurts. Therefore, make sure that the teacher is aware that you are not doing your homework. You can do so by making certain that the teacher sees you writing down the answers as the homework is discussed in class.

The next area, tests, can be handled in two ways. They can either not be   5
taken, or they can be failed. If you do not take them, you run the risk of receiving an "incomplete" rather than a failing grade. In order to flunk out of college, failing grades are preferable. Therefore, make sure to take and fail all exams. Incidentally, this is where attendance and homework can really affect performance. Attending class and doing homework regularly can be detrimental to obtaining poor test scores.

Since you won't know the correct answers to test questions, make sure to 6
choose those that are as absurd as possible without being obvious. Even if you
guess a few correctly, your overall grade will be an *F* as long as the majority of
your answers are wrong. By the way, one sure way to receive that cherished zero
is to be caught cheating; all teachers promise a zero for this.

The same ideas pertain to any reports or term papers that you are assigned. 7
If you fail to turn them in, you might get an "incomplete." Therefore, it is
important to hand in all papers, especially if they're poorly written. Make sure
to use poor organization, to present information in a confused manner, and to
write on the wrong topic whenever you can. The paper should be handwritten,
not typed, and barely legible. Misspellings should be plentiful and as noticeable
as possible. Smudged ink or dirty pages add a nice touch to the finished product.
Finally, try to get caught plagiarizing.

By following these few simple suggestions, you will be assured of a failing 8
grade. Try not to make it too obvious that your purpose is to fail. However, if
a teacher shows concern and offers help, be sure to exhibit a poor attitude as you
refuse. Should you decide to put extra effort into failing, you may even finish
at the bottom of the class. Someone has to finish last. Why not you?

Questions for Discussion

1. Except for Milden's introduction and conclusion, each paragraph identifies at
   least one action, or step, that a student should or should not take to flunk out
   of school. What are these steps?

2. What connective words and phrases does Milden use to maintain coherence
   between her paragraphs?

3. Each of Milden's steps in the process of flunking out relates to a central idea
   expressed in the essay's thesis. What is this thesis?

4. What examples of the imperative mood (direct commands) do you find in the
   essay?

5. What makes her essay especially effective is that Milden takes a tongue-in-
   cheek (ironic) approach to a serious subject. Which parts of the essay do you
   find most humorous?

Suggestions for Journal Entries

1. Has Milden covered her topic completely, or can you offer additional advice
   to those who wish to flunk out of college?

2. Taking a tongue-in-cheek approach, jot down a few suggestions to help a
   friend *fail* at something important. For instance, offer some advice on one of
   the following:

   How to make sure that the person you're dating never wants to go out with
   you again

   How to irritate a police officer who has stopped you for a traffic violation

How to get fired from a good job

How to be the most unpopular person in your neighborhood, class, dormitory, or apartment house

How to make sure that the set of tires you just bought will last only 5000 miles

3. Explain how *not* to do something. For instance, list a few ways not to lose weight, not to ask for a raise, not to stop smoking, not to treat a pet, or not to impress your future in-laws.

4. If you've just made it through a strict diet, gotten a good grade on a test, quit smoking, or completed some other project successfully, list some ways to help a fellow student do the same.

The Making of a Mummy

MILDRED MASTIN PACE

A graduate of Cornell University, Mildred Mastin Pace won fame as a radio and magazine writer in the 1930s and 1940s. However, her reputation rests on her books for young people. Among the most important of these are Wrapped for Eternity, *from which this selection is taken, and* The Pyramids. *Both reflect her interest in ancient Egypt.*

Looking Ahead

1. Ancient Egyptians believed in life after death. One of their greatest concerns was that, left untreated, the body would decay and be unable to rejoin the soul in the "other world." Thus, they developed mummification, a process to preserve corpses.

2. Canopic jars (paragraph 5) held the dead person's vital organs and were buried with the mummy.

3. The Egyptians pictured the god Horus (paragraph 22) as a falcon. As the story goes, Horus lost an eye in battle. After it was restored, it became a symbol for healing and was represented by "amulets," charms that protected the wearer.

4. Pace uses chronological order. She maintains coherence with transitional words and expressions common to process analysis. Look for connectives like "Now" and "The first actual step toward mummification."

Vocabulary

abhorrence   Loathing, disgust, hatred.
adze   Tool for shaping wood.

bier Platform on which a coffin is carried.

deftly Skillfully.

derision Scorn, contempt, ridicule.

dirges Funeral songs.

disheveled Untidy, in disorder or disarray.

interludes Episodes, occurrences.

intoned Sang.

jackal Wild dog.

loathsome Detestable, disgusting.

lustration Cleansing.

resin Preservative.

sarcophagus Coffin of stone.

unguents Creams, ointments.

viscera Vital organs.

It would take about ten weeks to create the mummy. During that period the   1
family would remain, as much as possible, in their home, in seclusion, chanting
dirges and mourning their loss.

The place where the body was taken for mummification was a large tent.   2
Sometimes the embalmers' workshops were in permanent buildings. But in this
country of heat and sun and almost no rain, tents were practical. They could be
moved easily when necessary, and were more comfortable for the embalmers to
work in than the walled and confined space of a building.

The tent had cooled off during the night, and when the priests and workers   3
gathered to begin their job, the air was pleasant.

The body, freshly bathed, was laid out on a long, narrow table, high enough   4
so that those administering to the body need not bend over.

Beneath the table stood four stone jars, each about a foot high. These were   5
the Canopic jars and later they would hold the embalmed larger organs of the
man's body: the intestines, liver, stomach, lungs. The lid of each jar was topped
with a figure carved of stone: one the head of a man, one a dog's head, one the
head of a jackal, and one the head of a hawk.

The priest who was in charge of the embalming represented the god Anubis,   6
who presided over mummification and was the guardian of the tombs. Since this
god had the body of a man and the head of a jackal, this one priest wore a head
mask of a jackal.

The priests were all freshly shaven; their heads, their faces—even their   7
bodies beneath the fine, crisp linen robes—had been shaved to remove all hair.
Led by the priest in the jackal mask, they intoned chants that announced the start
of the work and the ritual.

The first actual step toward mummification was about to begin. This was the   8
removal of the brain.

A specialist, highly skilled in his work, approached the head of the corpse. **9** In his hand he held a long, slender hooklike instrument. Deftly he pushed this up one nostril, and working in a circular movement, he broke through the ethmoid bone, up into the cavity of the brain.

Withdrawing the hooklike instrument, he chose another. This one was a **10** narrow, spirally twisted rod that had a small spoonlike tip. Pushing this up into the cranial cavity, he began, slowly, bit by bit, to draw out the brain through the nose, discarding each piece as he went along.

This was an operation of skill and patience. When at long last he was **11** finished, satisfied that all of the brain had been removed from the cranial cavity, leaving it clean and clear, he prepared to leave. His job was done, and he was pleased to have done it well. Once in a while a clumsy operator crushed a bone or broke the nose, disfiguring the face forever. But he had completed the delicate operation leaving the strong bone structure, the well-shaped face, as it had been when he started.

Now the mouth was cleansed and in it were placed wads of linen soaked in **12** sweet oils. The nostrils were cleansed and plugged with wax. The face was coated with a resinous paste. A small piece of linen was placed over each eye, and the eyelids drawn over them.

The body was now ready for the second important operation toward mum- **13** mification. This was the removal of the viscera from the body cavity.

The man who was to perform this operation stood outside the tent, waiting **14** to be called in. He held in his hand a fairly large, flat black stone, one edge of which was honed to razor sharpness. It was called an Ethiopian stone. His job was not a pleasant one, and gruesome to watch. Hence the other workers and the priests held him in abhorrence.

As he waited, the priest wearing the jackal mask approached the body, which **15** had been turned slightly on its right side, exposing the left flank. The tent throbbed with the sound of the soft, rhythmic chantings of the priests.

The jackal head bent toward the body, and the masked priest dipped a small **16** rush pen into a pot of ink, then drew on the left side of the body a spindle-shaped line about five inches long.

The priest stepped back and the man with the stone was called in. Following **17** the line the priest had drawn, he cut, with great strength, through skin and flesh. Then, reaching through the incision, he severed and removed each organ: the stomach, liver, kidneys, lungs, intestines.

Only the heart was left in place. It was thought to be the seat of intelligence **18** and feeling, and so must remain forever intact within the body.

The other vital organs would be wrapped in resin-soaked cloth and each **19** placed in the proper Canopic jar. Their lids sealed on with wax, the jars would be set aside to await the day of burial.

His loathsome job finished, the man fled from the tent, followed by shouts **20** of derision and contempt from all the others. He was considered unclean, and their angry outcries, the curses they called down on him, would rid the tent of his taint.

The priests, the embalmers, might pretend to despise him. But they all knew 21
his job was an important one. Left in place, the internal organs would deteriorate
rapidly, making the drying out of the body and successful mummification impossible.

The body cavity was cleansed with palm wine. The incision was pulled 22
together, and a priest performed the ritual of placing on it a wax plate bearing
the all-powerful symbol, the Eye of Horus. For a wealthier man the plate might
have been of silver, or even of gold. But in any case, always, the Eye of Horus
was depicted on it. Next, thin wires of gold were fastened around each fingernail
and toenail to keep them in place. And once again the corpse was bathed.

The body was now ready to be dried out. 23

The powder called natron came from the Libyan Desert. It was known to be 24
a great drying agent and had cleansing and purification powers as well. Laid out
on a fresh, clean mat woven of plant fibers, the body was covered with natron.
In the hot, dry atmosphere, with the heat of the sun to help, day after day the
drying-out process in the natron went on.

The day came when the body was wholly dry—the skin stretched on the firm 25
frame of bone, the face thin but still the face of the man who had died.

The body was very light when the men lifted it onto a high table. It was 26
bathed once more. It was anointed with ointments and rubbed with sweet-
smelling spices and herbs.

Priests now poured out libations—liquid that symbolically restored moisture 27
to the body. They lighted incense, which they burned—also symbolically—to
restore the body's warmth and odor.

The body was ready to be wrapped. 28

About 150 yards of linen cloth had been prepared, torn into strips of varying 29
widths. On some of the bandages the man's name was written. Thus his identity
would be preserved. On some there were figures of the gods and on others were
religious writings and words of magic. All of these would give the man help and
power when he reached the other world.

The bandaging was intricate, and those doing the work were highly skilled. 30
But only the priests knew where the magical bandages, with their words of
power, should be placed. Only the priests knew the words to be chanted when
the man's ring was placed on his finger, the gold earrings hung in his ears. Only
the priests could direct where, amongst the bandages, the amulets should be
hidden to protect the deceased on his journey into the next world.

So as the bandaging began, and as it went on, there were frequent interludes 31
when the wrapping ceased while the priests, with great ceremony, intoned their
words of wisdom and chanted religious formulas.

Thus the wrapping, with its wealth of religious significance, took some time. 32
And seventy days elapsed between the day of the man's death and the day when
the wrapping was finished. On that day the mummy was taken back to the house
of mourning where the man had died.

From the house the final procession set forth. The mummy, in its elaborately 33
painted mummiform coffin, lay upon a lion-headed bier which was placed on a

sledge drawn by men and oxen. Walking before the sledge, on each side, were two women who impersonated the goddess Isis and her sister goddess, Nephthys, guardians of the dead. Behind the bier came another sledge, drawn by men. On this was a chest that held the four Canopic jars.

The women mourners followed, wailing in grief, their hair disheveled. Then 34 came the men mourners, beating their breasts in sorrow. Behind the mourners were the servants, carrying the objects the dead man would need for living in the other world: chests filled with clothes, toilet articles, jars of salves and unguents, and some of his favorite possessions. Others bore the funerary furniture: a bed, a chair, small stools.

When the procession reached the entrance of the tomb, the mummy was 35 taken from its bier and set in a standing position on a mound of sand, facing the mourners.

While the mourners watched and waited, the priests began the long, compli- 36 cated series of rituals that would assure the man success on his long journey into the next world. Small vessels of burning incense were waved, rites of purification, lustration, were performed. The ceremonies went on and on. Finally came the most complex and important rite of all, known as the Opening of the Mouth.

One priest, holding a miniature *adze* that possessed special mystical powers, 37 approached the mummy. To the chanting of religious formulas, he touched the mummy's head: the eyes, to open them so the man could see; the ears, so he could hear; the mouth, so he could speak; the jaws, so he could eat.

He could now live in the other world as he had on earth. He would need the 38 contents of his carved chests, the furniture placed in his tomb, the food and drink that would be provided for him.

Even as the coffined body, sealed in its sarcophagus, was being placed in its 39 tomb, the man's journey into the next world had begun.

The mourners, weary from their hot and dusty procession to the tomb and 40 the long-lasting ceremonies that followed, were now ready to enjoy the great feast that had been prepared for them. Knowing that the dead man was on his way to a second happy life that would never end, they partook of a joyous banquet. The foods were the finest, the wines and beer plentiful. There were entertainers and musicians, and guests sang songs in praise of the man just buried.

The mourning was over.   41

Questions for Discussion

1. What were the major steps in the process of mummification?
2. Why did the priests only "pretend to despise" the one who removed the "internal organs" (paragraph 21)?
3. Why was the heart not removed from the corpse?
4. Why did the mourners enjoy a "joyous banquet" after the mummy was in the tomb?

5. What transitional devices, other than those mentioned in Looking Ahead, did you find?

6. Earlier you learned that many process papers contain descriptive details. Where in this essay does Pace use description? Is her writing too descriptive?

7. What would be a good thesis statement for this essay?

Suggestions for Journal Entries

1. What similarities do you see between the funeral rights of the ancient Egyptians and modern funeral rites you know about? List as many of these similarities as you can.

2. Recall a wake or funeral you attended. Use listing or freewriting to discuss things we do to mourn or bury the dead. The process differs from religion to religion and from family to family, so write only about those traditions, ceremonies, and rites about which you have personal knowledge.

How I Came Out to My Parents

KENNETH KOHLER

When his freshman English instructor encouraged the class to "write from the heart," Ken Kohler decided to explain how he accomplished one of the most difficult and meaningful tasks in his life—telling his parents he was gay. Kohler's recollection of the process by which he came to the decision and finally confronted his parents shows how deeply concerned he was about their feelings and about the kind of relationship he would have with them once they knew of his sexual preference.

This essay represents the best of what process writers can achieve, for it combines the author's emotional commitment to his subject with clear, logical analysis. Ken Kohler is now a computer programmer completing his bachelor's degree.

Looking Ahead

1. Like other process essays, "How I Came Out to My Parents" is organized as a narrative. But this is not just another story. What is really important here is not *what* happened, but *how* it happened— the agony Kohler endured to tell his family about his homosexuality.

2. This selection is divided into two sections. The first explains how Kohler made the decision and found the courage to tell his parents he was gay. The second discusses the results of that decision.

Vocabulary

acknowledged   Admitted.

acutely   Greatly, sharply.

alienation   State of loneliness, exclusion.

congregation   Church members.

disclosure   Announcement, revelation.

irreparably   Beyond repair.

pending   Upcoming, expected.

predict   Know ahead of time.

rejection   Disapproval.

Being a minority within your own family can be a source of conflict. I had always known that I was different from my brother and my sister. My parents, too, may have sensed the difference, but they never acknowledged it to me. For many years, I had struggled with the idea of letting them know how different I was from my older brother. I was gay and didn't know how they would react if they ever found out.

My struggle to "come out of the closet" grew out of several needs. First, I wanted to be closer with my parents and to be honest about who I was. Second, I needed to let them know that there was someone special in my life. Finally, I had agreed to speak at my church about being gay, and I felt it important to tell my parents about my lifestyle before informing my congregation.

Rejection was my greatest fear. At the time, I had friends who had not spoken to their families for years after revealing they were gay. Their parents could not understand how their children could be "fags" or "dykes." These were terms their families had previously applied only to strangers. Some friends even told me about the violent reactions their families had had to the news. One of them said his father chased him around the house with a butcher knife. I had also known people who had used their homosexuality as a weapon against their families. Never did I want to hurt my parents; I merely wanted to break down the barriers between us.

I had no idea how they might react when I came out to them. I knew that if they responded violently or negatively it could take years to heal the damage. I also knew that I might never see them again. It was for this reason that I had avoided coming out to them before. However, because of my pending public announcement, the time had come to let them know.

I planned what I had to say carefully. Something so important could not simply be announced and forgotten. I had actually begun to prepare for this moment years before by reading as much as I could about homosexuality and by talking to gay friends. It was necessary for me to accept myself as a gay man before expecting others to do so. I had to develop a positive self-image, and this took several years. Then, in the week prior to my announcement, I began to rehearse my lines. I made notes for various approaches I could take. I wanted to feel secure in my delivery and didn't want to appear ashamed of my lifestyle. "Why should I be?" I thought. I had never felt differently. I imagined my parents' every reaction and tried to predict my responses. I even prepared myself for the worst, afraid they would tell me to "Get out and never come back!"

I also knew it was possible that none of the negative things that had hap- 6 pened to my friends would happen to me. In fact, I thought my parents might have already suspected I was gay. After all, I had been living with a man for three years. My partner at the time said, "They probably already know about you, the way you swish around!" I knew he could be right, but I was still afraid. Would my disclosure actually draw me closer to them as I had hoped, or would it push me away? Would they accept my partner as they had in the past? How would I cope with the loss of their love? These were just a few of the many questions that swept through my mind as I called my mother to ask if I could visit and talk about something important.

My heart was racing and my palms were sweating as I stopped the car in 7 front of their house. I turned off the ignition, took a deep breath, and stepped out. "This is it," I thought. "This is what I've been thinking about doing for years." The walk to the front door had never seemed so long. I was acutely aware of my heartbeat pounding in my ears. My breath seemed suspended in the frigid February night air. Time seemed to stop as I nervously straightened my jacket, threw my shoulders back, swallowed hard, and opened the front door.

My father was sitting in the recliner watching the television. My mother was 8 folding laundry. "Hi, how are you doing?" I said, trying to hide my nervousness. They both looked up and smiled. As I walked over to give each of them a hug, I wondered if they would ever smile at me again.

I took off my coat, sat down next to my mother, and began to help her fold 9 the laundry. We talked about how fast my niece was growing up. While we spoke, I tried to form the words that I feared would hurt them irreparably, but I realized there was only one way to say it. "Mom. Dad. I've been thinking about telling you this for some time now." I swallowed hard and took a good look at them. "I'm not telling you this because I want to hurt you. I love you. Please try to understand." I paused and took a deep breath. "I'm gay."

There was silence. Finally, with much hesitation, my mother asked, "Are 10 you sure?"

There was still no response from my father. I wondered what was racing 11 through his head. His silence was deeper than I could remember. Again my mother spoke. "Are you happy?"

"Yes," I replied with hesitation. I was not sure what would happen next. 12 I could almost hear the silent screams that I imagined howling in each of them.

"Well," she paused, "you've always been good to us, and you've never 13 given us any problems."

"Here it comes," I thought, "the guilt trip." 14

"I guess if you're happy," she continued slowly as if weighing every word, 15 "then I'll try to understand."

A smile spread over my face as I leaned over and gave her a long, warm hug. 16 Never had I felt so close to her. It was only then that my father piped up, "I hope you aren't sleeping with someone new every night." I assured him that I wasn't as I gave him a hug.

"You know, it's funny," my mother said. "We always thought your friend 17 was gay, but we didn't know you were." I tried hard to keep from laughing as I thought of my partner's remarks. Deep down, I suspected that they had always known but had denied it.

When I explained that I was going to speak at my church about what it was 18 like to be gay, my mother's brow became dark and furrowed. "Do you think you should? What if you lose your job? What if someone tries to hurt you?" she responded.

I tried to assure her that everything would be all right, but I really had no 19 idea what might happen. Of course, I knew my parents would struggle with my gayness just as I had, but I was overjoyed that they were asking such questions. A great burden had been lifted from my shoulders; I felt like laughing and dancing around the room. I realized I no longer had to hide my private life, to change pronouns, or to avoid questions about whom I was dating. More important, I had discovered how deeply my parents loved me.

Questions for Discussion

1. Why did Kohler feel the need to "come out of the closet"?
2. Discuss the fears he dealt with before deciding to tell his parents he was gay.
3. What steps did he take to prepare *himself* for the moment when he would tell his parents he was gay?
4. What steps did he take to prepare his *parents* for this moment? Should he have done more to get them ready?
5. Why does the author tell us how the parents of his friends reacted when they announced they were gay? Does including this information help him explain a process?
6. Both Kohler's essay and Pace's "The Making of a Mummy" explain how something was done. What similarities and differences do you see in the ways these processes are presented?

Suggestions for Journal Entries

1. Recall a time when you told someone something he or she did not want to hear. Perhaps you had to tell your parents that you wrecked the family car, to persuade a sweatheart that your relationship was over, or to inform a friend

or relative that a loved one had died. Freewrite for about five minutes to explain how hard this was.

2. Kohler's decision to tell his parents he was gay came from a strong desire to be honest with them. Write about a time when you needed to reveal something about yourself to a loved one who might find it difficult to accept. List a few steps that explain how you did this.

SUGGESTIONS FOR WRITING

1. Florence Pettit's "Sharpening Your Jackknife or Pocketknife" explains how to do a common chore. If you read this selection, use your journal notes to begin drafting an essay that provides instructions on how to complete a simple but important task.

   Make your paper as detailed as you can so that even someone with no knowledge of the process can follow it. The best way to do this is to write about a task you are familiar with, something you do often or regularly. Try to pick a simple activity, one that has only a few steps and that can be covered thoroughly in a short paper. Stay away from topics like "how to paint a house," "how to raise prize-winning dogs," or "how to improve your health." Instead, explain "how to prepare the walls of a small bedroom for painting," "how to bathe a cocker spaniel," or "how to fight a cold."

   Like Pettit, begin by explaining why the process is important or how your readers will benefit from your instructions. Describe any tools or supplies needed to complete the job in your introduction as well.

   After completing two or three drafts, put your instructions to the test. Ask a friend or classmate to read and follow them *exactly* as written. If he or she has trouble, add information or revise your instructions to make them clearer or more logical. Then, edit your work to remove distracting errors in grammar, spelling, and the like.

2. Triena Milden takes an ironic (tongue-in-cheek) approach to academic studies in "So You Want to Flunk Out of College." You too may be able to provide advice to help someone *fail* at something important. Write an ironic but complete set of instructions for this purpose. Put them in a letter to someone you know well.

   Item 2 of the Suggestions for Journal Entries after Milden's essay contains some workable topics. If you don't like any of these, choose one of your own. In any case, check your journal for useful information to start the assignment.

   If you follow Milden's lead, begin your letter by explaining how hard or easy it is to fail at the task you are discussing. Somewhere in your letter, perhaps in the introduction or conclusion, you might also explain why anyone would want to fail at it in the first place! In any case, revise and edit your letter to make sure it's clear, easy-to-follow, and fun to read!

3. If Suggestion for Writing 2 doesn't appeal to you, write an essay that explains how *not* to do something. Here are some topics you might choose:

   How not to study for an important exam
   How not to do laundry
   How not to light a barbecue grill
   How not to start exercising
   How not to lie to your parents, children, spouse, or sweetheart
   How not to drive a car if you want it to last
   How not to become depressed when life gets difficult

How not to become addicted to tobacco, drugs, alcohol, or other substances
How not to get hooked on watching TV or any other activity

Other topics to write about can be found in item 3 of the Suggestions for Journal Entries after ''So You Want to Flunk Out of College.'' You can take a serious or a humorous approach, but you don't have to explain the correct way to do the thing you're discussing. Just include enough detail to convince your readers that not doing something correctly can produce unhappy results.

4. If you have been able to stick to a diet, get a good grade on a test, quit smoking, or achieve another important personal goal, provide a few suggestions to help others do the same. You can put your suggestions in an essay that several people might want to read. Then again, you might write a letter to an individual in particular need of your advice. If you address one person, explain ways in which your suggestions can be applied to his or her life specifically.

One way to introduce your paper or letter is with an overview that explains how difficult or easy the task is and that reveals the benefits of following your instructions. A good thesis might go like this: ''Kicking the nicotine habit requires courage, will power, and perseverance, but it will help you live longer, breathe easier, and smell better!''

Before writing your first draft, check any notes you made after reading ''So You Want to Flunk Out of College,'' especially those in response to journal suggestion 4. Once you have provided enough detail in the body of your paper or letter to develop the thesis, review your work carefully. Be sure you have used vocabulary that is interesting and convincing. When it comes time to edit the final draft, ask yourself whether you have maintained coherence in and between paragraphs. If not, add transitions, include linking pronouns, or repeat words and ideas as necessary.

5. Mildred Mastin Pace's ''The Making of a Mummy'' traces the steps in an ancient funeral rite. One of the Suggestions for Journal Entries that accompanies this piece asks you to recall a wake or funeral you attended and to list important steps you observed in the way your friends, family, or community mourns and buries the dead. Use these notes to write the first draft of an essay that explains one way people today grieve the loss of loved ones.

If you need to add detail to later drafts, try brainstorming with or interviewing family members who can provide additional information. Since the process of grieving differs from religion to religion, culture to culture, and family to family, discuss only those traditions, ceremonies, and rites about which you have personal knowledge. Use your introduction or conclusion to explain what the rites you are describing reveal about the people who practice them.

Show your respect for the topic and the people you are writing about by developing your ideas slowly and carefully. Then, as always, correct any distracting mechanical problems to produce the most effective paper you can.

6. Ken Kohler's "How I Came Out to My Parents" explains the painful process of telling people a truth they might not want to hear. Have you ever been in a similar situation? Did you ever have to confess that you smashed up the family car, misplaced an important document or tool at work, or lost your younger brother in a shopping mall? Have you ever said good-bye to a loved one or told somebody a close relative or friend died?

   Write an essay explaining how you did what had to be done. As you draft and rewrite, include details to show how painful the process was. Remember that this is not simply a narrative. Don't just say that you got the courage to face the situation or that you overcame emotional hurdles. Show *how* you did these things step by step.

   You can begin by explaining how you got yourself ready. Next, recall the things you did to prepare your listener(s) for the news. Then, tell how you made the announcement, and describe the way your listener(s) reacted. Finally, like Kohler, explain how you felt when the experience was over.

   Check your journal for notes that will help you get started. As you write your paper, remember that Kohler's essay is so powerful because he revised and edited it carefully. Do the same with yours.

7. Explain a process that human beings have learned or invented to improve the quality of their lives or to help them survive. For example, take the process by which an air conditioner works, an automobile engine burns gasoline, a food crop is grown or harvested, artificial respiration is given, an incandescent lamp turns electricity into light, a washing machine cleans clothes, a broken bone is set, a serious disease is treated, a lawn mower cuts grass, or a microwave cooks food.

   Write your first draft by listing steps in the process. As you revise, develop each step in greater detail until you are sure the process you have described is clear and complete. Then write an introduction to convince readers that learning about this process is worth their time. Check for coherence—adding connectives and linking pronouns as necessary—when you edit your final draft.

CHAPTER 16

PERSUASION

All writers of persuasion have one thing in common: they want to convince their readers. How they do this differs depending upon their purpose and their audience.

BEGINNING WITH AN ARGUMENT

At the heart of all persuasive writing is a good argument. Of course, an argument does not have to be a loud and excited discussion of a controversial issue. In fact, when it comes to writing, argumentation is just the attempt to prove a point or support an opinion through logic and concrete evidence.

Two types of thinking are used in argumentation: *induction* and *deduction*. Both support an opinion or belief the writer expresses as a *conclusion*.

Inductive thinking involves collecting separate facts and ideas, then drawing a general conclusion from that information. Say you come down with a case of food poisoning—cramps, vomiting, a headache, the works! When you call the five people with whom you shared a pot of stew the night before, each tells the same horrible story about cramps, vomiting, and so on. It's safe to say that the stew made you sick! That's your *conclusion*.

Induction is the kind of reasoning behind the conclusion-and-support method of developing paragraphs and essays, which is explained in Chapter 3. In writing developed through this method, the conclusion is often expressed in a formal thesis statement. A good example is Howard Scott's "Vegetable Gardens Are for the Birds," an essay in Chapter 2. The author begins with a thesis statement, which he uses to express a *conclusion,* the point he wants to make. He hates vegetable gardens and prefers "store-bought veggies" to those grown in the backyard. In the rest of the essay, Scott develops eleven reasons that *support* this unusual *conclusion.*

While induction involves drawing a general idea from specific pieces of evidence, deduction moves from the general to the specific. Using deduction, writers start with a general statement or idea they believe their readers will agree with. Next, they apply a specific case or example to that statement. Finally, they draw a conclusion from the two. You would be using deduction if you argued:

General statement: All full-time students can use the college exercise room free of charge.
Specific case: I am a full-time student.

Conclusion: Therefore, I can use the college exercise room free of charge.

Diane Ravitch uses deductive reasoning to organize "The Decline and Fall of Teaching History," which appears later in this chapter. Ravitch's argument goes something like this:

General statement: Making political decisions that will keep democracy strong requires a knowledge of history.
Specific case: Many Americans know little about history.
Conclusion: To make political decisions that will keep our democracy strong, Americans must learn more about history.

Induction and deduction are two different ways of reasoning, but they almost always complement each other. In fact, logical and well-supported arguments often reflect both types of thinking.

DEVELOPING IDEAS IN AN ARGUMENT

Back in Chapter 3 you learned that, whether your purpose is to explain or persuade, you can choose several ways to develop a piece of writing. One of the most popular is *conclusion and support,* a method you just read about. As the essays in this chapter show, writers of persuasion often use a combination of methods to develop evidence that proves a point or supports an opinion. In "The Decline and Fall of Teaching History," Diane Ravitch develops the ideas in her deductive argument by quoting experts in the field—college history teachers, by mentioning facts she researched, and even by including an anecdote. In "In Our Own Image," De'Lois Jacobs combines an anecdote with illustrations to persuade us that the media has too great an influence on young people. In addition to using illustration and narration, Jack G. Shaheen relies on comparison, analogy, and the cause-and-effect method to argue for a change in the media's portrayal of Arabs.

The most important thing to remember about an effective argument is that it is *both* logical and well supported. You can use inductive reasoning, deductive reasoning, or both, but your argument must be reasonable and easy to follow. You can support ideas with examples, facts, statistics, the knowledge or opinions of experts, analogies, comparisons, definitions, first-hand observations, and the like. But your writing must contain enough supportive information to be clear, convincing, and easily understood.

GOING BEYOND ARGUMENT

You just learned that persuasive writing is aimed at convincing and that at the heart of persuasion is argument: the use of logic and evidence to support an opinion. Sometimes, you will simply want to convince readers that your stand on a controversial issue has merit or that a conclusion you have drawn about a complex question is correct. In such cases, a reasoned argument supported by concrete detail will be enough.

When you need to change people's attitudes or urge them to action, however, logic and evidence alone may not get the job done. Therefore, while remaining clear-headed and fair, you might also appeal to the readers' emotions, pride, and personal values.

Let's say your college is having a problem with litter. The dean asks you to write a letter to your fellow students persuading them that they can help by cleaning up after themselves in the cafeteria and by keeping litter out of classrooms, lounges, and parking lots. You can begin by arguing that janitorial costs help raise tuition, that keeping the college clean is easy and inexpensive if everyone pitches in, and that a clean campus is a pleasant place to study. But those arguments appeal to reason, and they alone might not convince your readers to change their attitudes and behavior.

To get them to act responsibly, therefore, you may have to appeal to their sense of community and their self-image. Explain, for example, that the way students behave reveals much about their respect—or lack of it—for the college, for professors and classmates, and for themselves. If you are dealing with a group that is especially hard to convince, ask them to put themselves in the shoes of other students, faculty, and visitors—not to mention the janitors—who enter the cafeteria to find tables covered with soiled paper plates and napkins, half-eaten sandwiches, and dirty coffee cups. Express your disgust over cigarette butts and glass bottles dropped from cars in the parking lots. Complain about cans, yogurt containers, and waste paper left in lounges. In the process, use colorful figures of speech: ask your readers not to turn the place into an ''academic pigsty''; or compare the cafeteria at day's end to a ''small village that has been looted and trashed by an invading army.'' If that doesn't work, appeal to their pride by reminding them that they are college adults, not adolescents who lack table manners.

ADDRESSING OPPOSING ARGUMENTS

At the beginning of this chapter, you learned that how persuasive writers go about their work depends upon their purpose and their audience. In some cases, your readers may be sensitive about certain opinions that you believe are perfectly reasonable and that you can defend through logical argument. Say you are trying to convince bargain-hunting consumers that there should be no limit on the number of foreign cars we import. You might simply argue that competition keeps prices down. But what if your audience is a group of unemployed U.S. auto workers? Your job will be far more complicated, and you will first have to show that free, fair, and open trade can benefit workers worldwide.

At times, however, you will address readers whose opinions are the very opposite of yours, and you will be forced to discuss their point of view before defending your own. In some cases, you may be able show that the opposing argument is weak, illogical, or untrue. In others, you will have to admit that it has merit while explaining that yours makes even better sense.

Let's say you believe cars should come equipped with front-seat air bags. You know your readers can argue that air bags add a lot to the price of a new car. Therefore, you begin by admitting this fact, but you argue that saving lives is more important than saving money. As such, you are able to answer a serious objection that, otherwise, would have lingered in your readers' minds. Now, you can develop your argument by including statistics about the many lives air bags save and by showing that drivers whose cars have air bags pay lower insurance rates than other drivers. You might even appeal to your readers' emotions by describing what happens to people in the front seat of a car during a collision.

In the last few pages, you have read a lot about how to write persuasively. As with all kinds of writing, the most important ingredient in persuasion is your knowledge of the subject. Think of yourself as a lawyer. To argue a case or defend a client effectively, you will need to know the evidence well. Otherwise, you will have a hard time convincing judge or jury. Wise readers approach new opinions cautiously. Some will be open to persuasion. Others may even be eager to accept your point of view. But all will expect you to present evidence logically, clearly, and convincingly before they make your opinions their own.

The Right to Be Let Alone

BARRY GLAZER

Barry Glazer became interested in writing when he enrolled in a basic-skills composition class during his first semester in college. He went on to major in history and English, to become editor of his college newspaper, and to take a bachelor's degree. He now directs a tutoring program for developing writers and is planning to start a career in teaching after continuing his studies in graduate school.

Looking Ahead

1. This essay is logical, clear, and well developed, but it goes beyond pure argument and often appeals to the emotions.
2. Glazer organizes his work around three principles by which he would restrict the government's ability to interfere with our lives. Identify these principles as you read "The Right to Be Let Alone."
3. Louis Brandeis, mentioned in paragraph 2, was associate justice of the United States Supreme Court (1916–1939). He was a champion of individual rights.

Vocabulary

adversely   Negatively.

alleviate   Reduce, lessen, relieve.

anarchy   Chaos, disorder, lawlessness.

bureaucrats   Government officials.

constrain   Restrain, hold in check, bind.

constrict   Bind, choke, squeeze.

endure   Suffer, bear, submit to.

entrust   Give to for safekeeping.

impotence   Lack of power.

reflect   Think.

refrain from   Stop, cease, avoid.

throes   Agony, pain.

Government is the instrument of the people, says the United States Constitu-   1
tion. Those to whom the people entrust power are charged with maintaining
justice, promoting the general welfare, and securing the blessings of liberty for
us all. Recent newspaper opinion polls, however, suggest that many Americans
are dissatisfied with the men and women running our communities, our states,
and our nation. More and more of us have come to believe that our leaders are
isolated from the realities ordinary people face. We fear we are losing control.

Instead of helping to alleviate this feeling of impotence, however, politicians   2
and bureaucrats continue to make and enforce regulations that constrain our lives
and constrict our freedoms. To help people regain a rightful measure of control,
government—whether national, state, or local—should stay out of our private
lives whenever possible. As Supreme Court Justice Louis Brandeis noted, Americans treasure their "right to be let alone."

There is no reason for the government to interfere in our lives if our behavior   3
does not adversely affect others or if there is no immediate necessity for such
interference. Were I in the painful throes of terminal cancer or facing the horror
of Alzheimer's disease, I should be allowed to kill myself. Faced with the
agonizing degeneration of my memory and personality, I would probably want
to end my life in my own way. But the government says this is illegal. Indeed,
were I to call upon a doctor to assist me on this final quest, she would stand a
good chance of being charged with murder.

The government should also stay out of an individual's life if there is no   4
reason to believe he is doing wrong. The Bill of Rights protects us from unlawful
searches and seizures. Yet if I drive home from work in the early morning, I
stand a reasonable chance of being stopped without cause at a police roadblock.
While armed, uniformed officers shine flashlights in my face, I can be subjected
to questions about my destination and point of origin. I can be told to produce
my papers and to step out of my car. I can be made to endure the embarrassment

of performing tricks to prove my sobriety. Allowing the police such powers is hardly in keeping with our government's mission to promote justice, security, and liberty.

Finally, the government should refrain from creating unnecessary burdens for the American people. It should stay out of a person's private business if such involvement burdens the individual unnecessarily or unfairly. Recently, my faithful dog Linda was dying. Because of years of abuse at the hands of her previous owner, she was no longer able to walk and had to be carried in my arms. At that time, the dog warden knocked on my door and threatened me with fines for my continued refusal to license the animal. When I told him that Linda was unable to walk, let alone leave my property, he threatened to return with the police.

Similarly, when I wanted to convert my garage into a den, I was overwhelmed by official red tape. The cost of construction permits and of measures to meet complex building codes cost more than the lumber, wall board, and other supplies for the project. Another example of governmental red tape became evident when I attempted to enroll in a Japanese language course at a community college. I was told the state required that I take a mathematics placement test or pass a course in elementary algebra first!

Clearly, government is a necessity. Without it, we would face anarchy. Yet those who roam the halls of power should remember from where their power originates and should find ways to reduce the burden of unnecessary regulations heaped on the backs of the American people.

Questions for Discussion

1. What one sentence in this essay best expresses Glazer's purpose and central idea?
2. In Looking Ahead, you learned that the author defends three principles by which he would limit government interference. What are these principles?
3. What method of development does Glazer rely on most?
4. Pick out vocabulary that appeals to the readers' emotions.
5. Why does Glazer bother to tell that Justice Brandeis is the source of the quotation in paragraph 2 (and of the essay's title)?
6. Find examples of deductive and inductive reasoning in this essay.
7. Where does the author address an argument that an opponent might use to dispute his?

Suggestions for Journal Entries

1. Glazer calls up several examples from experiences similar to those you or people like you might have had. Use focused freewriting to narrate an incident that explains how a government rule or regulation interferes with the right of privacy. Interpret the word ''government'' broadly; write about the

federal, state, local, or college regulation you most disagree with. You might even address a rule followed by your family, your athletic team, or other group to which you belong.

2. Play the role of Glazer's opponent by responding to at least one of the examples he uses to support his thesis. Explain why requiring licenses for all dogs is reasonable; why strict building codes are important; why the police should have the right to stop and question drivers without cause; why doctors should not be allowed to help terminally ill patients commit suicide; or why states should set academic standards in public colleges.

3. Even if you agree with Glazer, you may know of instances in which people welcome government "interference." List as many examples of such beneficial interference as you can.

In Our Own Image

DE'LOIS JACOBS

"In Our Own Image" was fist published as an opinion column in a 1986 issue of Essence, *a magazine whose readership is primarily African-American women. Jacobs is a freelance writer who lives in New York City.*

Looking Ahead

1. Although Jacobs addresses an African-American audience, readers of all races will find her advice useful.

2. This selection contains several rhetorical questions. As you probably recall, rhetorical questions are those to which readers already know the answers.

Vocabulary

aquiline Curved.
beckon Call.
chastise Criticize, scold.
cosmetic For the sake of appearance only.
extolling Praising.
innate Inborn, native.
inundated Flooded, overwhelmed.
lineage Ancestry.
renounce Reject, deny.

revered   Honored.

siblings   Brothers and sisters.

Recently one of my greatest concerns and fears was realized when my younger   1
sister told me about a story she had read in a popular Black publication: A
teenager committed suicide because his mother would not allow him to have
cosmetic surgery on his nose in imitation of his idol, Michael Jackson. This story
is more than just sad; it is an outrage. What is it about this society that gets us
so completely involved in the material and physical world? Why is it that our
Black public figures, particularly in entertainment, tend to be turning more and
more to this way of presenting themselves? What are these false images they
worship and aspire to look like?

When I look in a mirror, I can clearly see where I come from—the influences   2
of my father's genes and my mother and grandmother in me. It gives me a feeling
of warmth, pride and reassurance to be able to see my roots every single day of
my life. There is nothing there that needs "fixing."

Yet I've had at least one lover (now "ex") tell me that my nose "spoils"   3
my looks. This was a man who was constantly talking about Black unity,
solidarity, beauty and pride. Well, I asked him whether it would please him to
see me with a straight or aquiline nose, or maybe one like a popular white
model's. This response not only surprised him, but it also shut him up on the
subject forever when he realized the absurdity of his remark.

Here in America we are increasingly buying and selling goods and services   4
based on "face value." We are inundated with images that beckon us through
advertising, shape attitudes through film and television, and influence thinking
through the printed, recorded and spoken word. Before we lay down our hard-
earned cash and our principles, let's take a close look at who is selling us this
bill of goods and why. As the ads have changed from extolling the wonders of
Afro-hairstyle products to those of "curl" activators, so has our idea of ourselves and what we look like.

Now, I have heard many defensive arguments in justification of the things   5
we do to our hair and skin color. Why are some of us so embarrassed by our
natural physical traits? I like to look into other Black faces and see the tribes
from which we have descended. Lineage is something to be aware of, and pride
in it is something to pass on to our young, from generation to generation. I will
not renounce that, ever. And here is my question: When we try to change our
looks so drastically, what messages are we conveying to our young? Think about
it—think long and strong. Think about that young teenager, and then let your
conscience be your guide.

This innate insecurity that drives us to change our images must come to an   6
end. Surely we must realize that such changes will not make our most popular
and revered singers sing any better, our musicians perform any more brilliantly,
or when you take a really close look, appear any more attractive. For instance,
although I like Michael Jackson's music, as I always have, I must admit I now

feel a remoteness when I look at him, since there is not much there that I can relate to and admire anymore. I do not wish to chastise any particular entertainers, but I am curious about the reasons behind their decisions regarding their looks. Do they even know?

It is sad that our children's heroes seem to want to look like images from 7 which we Black people are the farthest removed. Straighten your nose, then your lips are too full; fix that, then your hips are too wide; tuck those, then your hair is too kinky; relax that, then your hair is too short; wonder-weave that, then your skin is too dark; and on and on it goes.

Although the 20-inch Afro is a thing of the past, the feeling of Black pride 8 that accompanied it was fortifying. Let us not lose that feeling. The once often-heard phrases from the sixties—''I'm Black and I'm proud'' and ''Black is beautiful''—are sorely missed. I thought we didn't need to proclaim them so loudly in the eighties because, finally, we truly believed them. Do we? Look at the conflicting signals our young people get every day about their self-images. We who are parents and grandparents, aunts and uncles, godparents and older siblings have a responsibility to our young. Let us take the time to examine and explain to them those things that have real value and those that do not, so that they can make sounder judgments and better choices in conducting their own lives. Let us help them develop strong self-esteem by setting examples they can follow that are in our own images.

Questions for Discussion

1. What is the author's purpose? What does she want her readers to do?
2. The anecdote about the teenager who wanted to look like Michael Jackson establishes the essay's tone, the writer's attitude toward the subject. How would you describe Jacobs's tone? In what other ways does she make her attitude clear?
3. Which aspects of the essay are directed specifically to African-American women, its intended audience? Which appeal to all readers?
4. Does Jacobs address an opinion contrary to her own? How does she respond to it?
5. Which ideas does she develop through logic and evidence alone?
6. Which does she develop by appealing to the readers' emotions?
7. The author frequently addresses the reader directly. In paragraph 5, for example, she asks us to ''think about that young teenager.'' Does this technique make her writing more persuasive? Why or why not?
8. Rhetorical questions appear throughout the essay. Why does Jacobs include them in her introduction? What function do they serve in other parts of this selection?
9. According to Jacobs, what are some of the influences that make young people want to change their looks? Can you discuss others?

Suggestions for Journal Entries

1. Do you know people who pattern their appearance, behavior, or lifestyle after what they see on television, in the movies, or in other types of media? Use focused freewriting to discuss one such person. Include your reaction to or opinion about the media's influence on your subject.

2. Are you happy about the way members of a group to which you belong—be it racial, ethnic, religious, or other—are portrayed on television, in films, in magazines, and the like? For example, if you are female, are you pleased with the current image of women in rock videos? If you are Chinese, Indian, Mexican, or a member of another ethnic group, would you like to correct the way people of your race or nationality are portrayed in films? If you are over fifty, can you tell certain TV producers a thing or two? Explain your dissatisfaction by using focused freewriting to record details about the way a particular film, music video, television show, or magazine, for example, treats members of your group.

The Decline and Fall of Teaching History

DIANE RAVITCH

Diane Ravitch teaches at Columbia University's Teachers College and, with Chester E. Finn, wrote What Do Our 17-Year-Olds Know? *Ravitch and Finn believe the teaching of literature and history needs significant improvement. One of their suggestions is that all high school students complete at least two years of world history. As you learned in the introduction to this chapter, Ravitch argues that, without an increased emphasis on the study of history, American voters will find it harder and harder to make the independent and informed judgments required to keep our democracy strong.*

Looking Ahead

1. The essay's title recalls Edward Gibbon's *The History of the Decline and Fall of the Roman Empire,* written in the eighteenth century.

2. Ravitch establishes her expertise by presenting results of a nationwide study she conducted. She also relies on the expert testimony of other college history professors, whose opinions she quotes directly.

3. This selection uses methods to write effective introductions that you probably read about in Chapter 4. Look for them in the first two paragraphs.

Vocabulary

abysmal   Terribly low and empty (like a huge pit or cavern).

assessment   Evaluation.

causation   Relationship between causes and effects, study of why events occur.

chronology   History, series of events in time.

civics   Study of how government works.

collaboration   Cooperation, joint effort.

derives   Issues or originates from.

eminent   Famous, important, distinguished.

evolved   Developed, grew.

indifference   Lack of interest.

perspective   Point of view, way of looking at something.

premise   Principle or assumption upon which actions, ideas, or other principles are based.

sequenced   In an order, in a continuous series.

vocational   Occupational.

During the past generation, the amount of time devoted to historical studies   1
in American public schools has steadily decreased. About 25 years ago, most
public high-school youths studied one year of world history and one of American
history, but today, most study only one year of ours. In contrast, the state schools
of many other Western nations require the subject to be studied almost every
year. In France, for example, all students, not just the college-bound, follow a
carefully sequenced program of history, civics and geography every year from
the seventh grade through the twelfth grade.

Does it matter if Americans are ignorant of their past? Does it matter if the   2
general public knows little of the individuals, the events and the movements that
shaped our nation? The fundamental premise of our democratic form of government is that political power derives from the informed consent of the people.
Informed consent requires a citizenry that is rational and knowledgeable. If our
system is to remain free and democratic, citizens should know not only how to
judge candidates and their competing claims but how our institutions evolved.
An understanding of history does not lead everyone to the same conclusions, but
it does equip people with the knowledge to reach independent judgments on
current issues. Without historical perspective, voters are more likely to be
swayed by emotional appeals, by stirring commercials, or by little more than a
candidate's good looks or charisma.

Because of my interest as a historian of education in the condition of the   3
study of history, I have been involved during the last year, in collaboration with
the National Assessment of Educational Progress, in planning a countrywide

study of what 17-year-olds know about American history. In addition, my contacts with college students during the last year and discussions with other historians have led me to believe that there is cause for concern.

On the college lecture circuit this past year, I visited some 30 campuses, 4 ranging from large public universities to small private liberal-arts colleges. Repeatedly, I was astonished by questions from able students about the most elementary facts of American history. At one urban Minnesota university, none of the 30 students in a course on ethnic relations had ever heard of the Supreme Court's Brown v. Board of Education decision of 1954, which held racial segregation in public schools unconstitutional. At a university in the Pacific Northwest, a professor of education publicly insisted that high-school students should concentrate on vocational preparation and athletics, since they had the rest of their lives to learn subjects like history "on their own time."

The shock of encountering college students who did not recognize the names 5 of eminent figures like Jane Addams or W.E.B. Du Bois led me to conduct an informal, unscientific survey of professors who teach history to undergraduates. "My students are not stupid, but they have an abysmal background in American, or any other kind of, history," said Thomas Kessner, who teaches American history at Kingsborough Community College in Brooklyn. "They never heard of Daniel Webster; don't understand the Constitution; don't know the difference between the Republican and Democratic parties."

This gloomy assessment was echoed by Naomi Miller, chairman of the 6 history department at Hunter College in New York. "My students have no historical knowledge on which to draw when they enter college," she said. "They have no point of reference for understanding World War I, the Treaty of Versailles or the Holocaust." More than ignorance of the past, however, she finds an indifference to dates and chronology or causation. "They think that everything is subjective. They have plenty of attitudes and opinions, but they lack the knowledge to analyze a problem." Professor Miller believes that "we are in danger of bringing up a generation without historical memory. This is a dangerous situation."

Questions for Discussion

1. What does the author mean by "informed consent," and why is learning history important to keeping our system of government "free and democratic"?

2. In the introduction to this chapter, you learned that Ravitch uses deductive reasoning. You also learned that writers often use both deduction and induction in the same piece. Find an example of inductive reasoning in this essay.

3. In several instances, the author relies on the testimony of experts to support her thesis. However, the professor of education quoted in paragraph 4 opposes her point of view. Why does she bother to quote this person?

4. The words of her colleagues provide the author with examples that show how little some students know about history. Are these examples convincing? Why or why not?

5. Where does Ravitch use rhetorical questions? Where does she use contrast? How do such techniques help her achieve her purpose?

6. This essay contains clear thinking and convincing logic. Does it ever appeal to our emotions?

7. Is the introduction effective? Why or why not?

Suggestions for Journal Entries

1. Other than history, what do you think high school and college students should learn more about? Rely on your own experiences, brainstorm with a few classmates, or interview one or two professors to compile a list of the academic subjects or skills with which young people should become more familiar. Then, briefly list reasons students should study or practice each of them.

2. A strong democracy relies on the ''informed consent'' of its people, Ravitch believes. Given the important political and social concerns of our day, what specific problems or issues do you think American voters should be reading and learning more about? Mention the three or four you believe are most important; then, briefly explain and defend your choices. In other words, include a few details that might convince others they should be as concerned about these issues as you are.

3. What can you say to dispute the claim that students should learn history ''on their own time''? What, if anything, can you say to support this claim?

The Media's Image of Arabs

JACK G. SHAHEEN

Jack Shaheen's parents came to the United States from Lebanon, a country with a large Arabic population. Although he focuses on the stereotype through which the American media pictures Arabs, Shaheen helps us understand the danger in all stereotyping regardless of the group. This essay first appeared in Newsweek *in 1988.*

Looking Ahead

1. In paragraph 3, Shaheen creates an analogy by calling TV wrestling ''that great American morality play.'' Used in the Middle Ages to teach people morality, such plays portrayed the forces of good and of evil battling for possession of someone's soul.

2. Besides analogy, the author uses several of the methods of development you have learned about: illustration, comparison and contrast, cause and effect, and narration. All of them contribute to the persuasiveness of this essay.

3. In paragraph 5, Shaheen asks if it is "easier for a camel to go through the eye of a needle" than for the media to portray Arabs fairly. This is a variation on the New Testament's "It is easier for camel to pass through the eye of a needle than for one who is rich to enter the kingdom of God."

4. The Semites, mentioned in paragraph 8, are people of the eastern Mediterranean; both Jews and Arabs are Semites. At the end of this paragraph, Shaheen asks that we "retire the stereotypical Arab to a media Valhalla." In Nordic mythology, Valhalla was a heaven to which warriors killed in battle were sent.

Vocabulary

caricatures   Images or pictures that exaggerate and poke fun at the subject's features or qualities.

cliché   Saying so overused it becomes boring and often meaningless.

conspires   Schemes, connives.

deplore   Criticize, lament.

mosques   Muslim houses of worship.

neutralize   Act as balance to, counteract.

nurtures   Feeds, nourishes.

prevail   Predominate, command our attention.

swarthy   Dark-skinned.

America's bogyman is the Arab. Until the nightly news brought us TV pictures of Palestinian boys being punched and beaten, almost all portraits of Arabs seen in America were dangerously threatening. Arabs were either billionaires or bombers—rarely victims. They were hardly ever seen as ordinary people practicing law, driving taxis, singing lullabies or healing the sick. Though TV news may portray them more sympathetically now, the absence of positive media images nurtures suspicion and stereotype. As an Arab-American, I have found that ugly caricatures have had an enduring impact on my family. 1

I was sheltered from prejudicial portraits at first. My parents came from Lebanon in the 1920s; they met and married in America. Our home in the steel city of Clairton, Pa., was a center for ethnic sharing—black, white, Jew and gentile. There was only one major source of media images then, at the State movie theater where I was lucky enough to get a part-time job as an usher. But in the late 1940s, Westerns and war movies were popular, not Middle Eastern dramas. Memories of World War II were fresh, and the screen heavies were the 2

Japanese and the Germans. True to the cliché of the times, the only good Indian was a dead Indian. But when I mimicked or mocked the bad guys, my mother cautioned me. She explained that stereotypes blur our vision and corrupt the imagination. "Have compassion for all people, Jackie," she said. "This way, you'll learn to experience the joy of accepting people as they are, and not as they appear in films. Stereotypes hurt."

Mother was right. I can remember the Saturday afternoon when my son, 3 Michael, who was seven, and my daughter, Michele, six, suddenly called out: "Daddy, Daddy, they've got some bad Arabs on TV." They were watching that great American morality play, TV wrestling. Akbar the Great, who liked to hear the cracking of bones, and Abdullah the Butcher, a dirty fighter who liked to inflict pain, were pinning their foes with "camel locks." From that day on, I knew I had to try to neutralize the media caricatures.

It hasn't been easy. With my children, I have watched animated heroes 4 Heckle and Jeckle pull the rug from under "Ali Boo-Boo, the Desert Rat," and Laverne and Shirley stop "Sheik Ha-Mean-Ie" from conquering "the U.S. and the world." I have read comic books like the "Fantastic Four" and "G.I. Combat" whose characters have sketched Arabs as "lowlifes" and "human hyenas." Negative stereotypes were everywhere. A dictionary informed my youngsters that an Arab is a "vagabond, drifter, hobo and vagrant." Whatever happened, my wife wondered, to Aladdin's good genie?

To a child, the world is simple: good versus evil. But my children and others 5 with Arab roots grew up without ever having seen a humane Arab on the silver screen, someone to pattern their lives after. Is it easier for a camel to go through the eye of a needle than for a screen Arab to appear as a genuine human being?

Hollywood producers must have an instant Ali Baba kit that contains scimi- 6 tars, veils, sunglasses and such Arab clothing as *chadors* and *kufiyahs*. In the mythical "Ay-rabland," oil wells, tents, mosques, goats and shepherds prevail. Between the sand dunes, the camera focuses on a mock-up of a palace from "Arabian Nights"—or a military air base. Recent movies suggest that Americans are at war with Arabs, forgetting the fact that out of 21 Arab nations, America is friendly with 19 of them. And in "Wanted Dead or Alive," a movie that starred Gene Simmons, the leader of the rock group Kiss, the war comes home when an Arab terrorist comes to the United States dressed as a rabbi and, among other things, conspires with Arab-Americans to poison the people of Los Angeles. The movie was released last year.

The Arab remains American culture's favorite whipping boy. In his mem- 7 oirs, Terrel Bell, Ronald Reagan's first secretary of education, writes about an "apparent bias among mid-level, right-wing staffers at the White House" who dismissed Arabs as "sand niggers." Sadly, the racial slurs continue. At a recent teacher's conference, I met a woman from Sioux Falls, S.D., who told me about the persistence of discrimination. She was in the process of adopting a baby when an agency staffer warned her that the infant had a problem. When she asked whether the child was mentally ill, or physically handicapped, there was silence. Finally, the worker said: "The baby is Jordanian."

To me, the Arab demon of today is much like the Jewish demon of yester-   8
day. We deplore the false portrait of Jews as a swarthy menace. Yet a similar
portrait has been accepted and transferred to another group of Semites—the
Arabs. Print and broadcast journalists have started to challenge this stereotype.
They are now revealing more humane images of Palestinian Arabs, a people who
traditionally suffered from the myth that Palestinian equals terrorist. Others
could follow that lead and retire the stereotypical Arab to a media Valhalla.

It would be a step in the right direction if movie and TV producers devel-   9
oped characters modeled after real-life Arab-Americans. We could then see a
White House correspondent like Helen Thomas, whose father came from Leba-
non, in "The Golden Girls," a heart surgeon patterned after Dr. Michael De-
Bakey on "St. Elsewhere," or a Syrian-American playing tournament chess like
Yasser Seirawan, the Seattle grandmaster.

Politicians, too, should speak out against the cardboard caricatures. They   10
should refer to Arabs as friends, not just as moderates. And religious leaders
could state that Islam like Christianity and Judaism maintains that all mankind
is one family in the care of God. When all imagemakers rightfully begin to treat
Arabs and all other minorities with respect and dignity, we may begin to unlearn
our prejudices.

Questions for Discussion

1. If you read "In Our Own Image," explain in what way Jacobs's purpose and central idea are similar to Shaheen's.

2. Shaheen draws the evidence for his argument from personal experience, observation, and reading. Identify examples of information that come from each of these sources.

3. Why does the author tell us that "the Arab demon of today is much like the Jewish demon of yesterday" (paragraph 8)? What other comparison does he make, and how does it contribute to his argument?

4. Why does he recall what his mother said when he "mimicked or mocked the bad guys" (paragraph 2) of movies in the 1940s?

5. As you learned in Looking Ahead, paragraph 3 contains an analogy. In what other paragraph does the author place an analogy?

6. Shaheen could have directed his remarks to Arab-American readers, but he chose to address a far more comprehensive audience. How do we know that?

7. If this essay is aimed at persuading the media to change its image of Arabs, why does the author include examples of anti-Arab stereotyping from sources other than the media (paragraph 7)?

8. Is this selection pure argument, or does it appeal to the emotions as well? Explain.

9. Shaheen concludes by asking politicians and religious leaders to speak out against negative stereotyping. Is his ending appropriate to an essay that criticizes the media?

Suggestions for Journal Entries

1. Describe the way movies, television, music videos, radio, billboards, newspapers, and popular magazines portray a particular ethnic group. Is the portrait of this group flattering or negative? Examples of a group you might write about include blacks, Jews, Hispanics, native Americans, Asian Indians, Chinese, Poles, Hungarians, Russians, Scandinavians, Italians, or even white Anglo-Saxon Protestants. Good ways to gather details for this journal entry are focused freewriting and brainstorming.

2. Not all stereotyping is based on race, religion, or ethnic background. Members of certain occupations—police officers and politicians, for example—sometimes suffer from bad media images. As a matter of fact, some of the worst stereotyping is based on age, sex, or sexual preference. Think about a group of people—other than a racial, religious, or ethnic group—that you think suffers from an unfair and inaccurate media image. Use focused freewriting or listing to gather examples of the way these people are portrayed on television, in movies, and so forth. Groups you might want to choose from:

Housewives	Secretaries
Teachers	Factory workers
Beauticians	Bachelors
Senior citizens	College students
Homosexuals	Husbands
Grandparents	Intellectuals
Scientists	Athletes
Auto mechanics	Nurses
Musicians	Single women

SUGGESTIONS FOR WRITING

1. Like Barry Glazer, many of us have strong opinions about the right of privacy. Perhaps you discussed some of your own in your journal after reading "The Right to Be Let Alone."

   Write an essay arguing that some government regulations interfere unnecessarily with the way we live. Use examples of federal, state, or local laws you think limit our freedom. If you interpret the word "government" broadly, you can even focus on rules enforced by your college, your family, or another group to which you belong.

   One way to introduce this essay is to show readers that you are reasonable. Begin by admitting that some rules are necessary and should be fully enforced. For example, voice your support for tough laws against child abuse, rape, and drunk driving. At the end of your introduction, however, state your thesis forcefully: explain that some rules enforced by the government, by your family, or by another group are inappropriate and should be abolished. Then, like Glazer, develop your essay with examples from your experiences or from those of people you know or have read about.

   Read your first draft carefully, adding detail as you go along to make your opinions clear and convincing. In later drafts, try including language and information that appeal to the readers' emotions. Then, edit your work thoroughly.

2. Read "The Right to Be Let Alone" again. Then, write an essay in which you play Glazer's opponent. Argue that, while some government regulations are inappropriate, the ones he criticizes should be strictly enforced.

   One way to organize your paper is to defend the regulations Glazer attacks in the same order he presented them. As such, you might outline the body of your essay like this:

   Terminally ill patients should not have the right to commit suicide.
   Police have the right to stop and question motorists at random.
   Pets should be licensed.
   Strict building codes are necessary.
   Colleges should enforce placement requirements.

   Develop each of these points in concrete and convincing detail using any of the methods mentioned earlier in this chapter. After completing several drafts, write a conclusion that restates your thesis or that uses one of the methods for closing explained in Chapter 4. As always, be sure your final draft is organized and edited well.

3. De'Lois Jacobs wants black youths to reject artificial media images and take pride in their natural beauty and abilities. Do you have a friend or classmate—of whatever race—who is trying to look or act like someone he or she is not? Write a letter persuading this individual that modeling oneself after characters in rock videos, films, or magazine advertisements is downright foolish.

Write to someone you care about. Begin by explaining that everyone should follow his or her own star. For example, there is no reason a woman with beautiful curly hair should get it straightened just to look like a fashion model, that a man must develop the muscles of a weightlifter, or that people with poor singing voices should try to be rock stars, especially if their talents lie in math, business management, painting, foreign languages, or other areas.

Next, describe your reader's best qualities or abilities. Convince her to be proud of what nature has given and suggest ways she might develop these gifts further. Like Jacobs, also show that trying to be what we are not can be dangerous.

As you know, convincing letters demand the same care and hard work as effective essays, so complete each stage of the composing process for this assignment thoroughly.

4. Review the journal notes you made after reading ''In Our Own Image.'' Like Jacobs, you might have described someone who patterns his or her looks, behavior, or lifestyle on images from movies, television, or other media. If not, do some focused freewriting about such a person now. For example, discuss a friend who follows a strict diet just to be as slim as a model, or write about a classmate who buys only designer clothes seen in elegant magazines. Then, freewrite about two or three other people like this.

   Use this information to draft an essay arguing that the media has a great influence on the way some people live. Tell anecdotes about your subjects to show how strongly they have been affected. Mention particular magazine advertisements, rock stars, television shows, and so on that have had the greatest impact on them.

   Establish the tone for your essay early; make sure readers know how you feel about this influence from the very beginning. Jacobs's tone is negative, but you can adopt any attitude you want. Indeed, you might argue that the media's impact on the people you know is beneficial.

   In any case, support your argument logically and with concrete evidence. Whenever appropriate, use language that appeals to the readers' emotions. Add supportive details as you revise the paper from draft to draft. In addition, make sure your introduction and conclusion are effective. A good way to begin the essay is to quote a line from a popular song, television show, or commercial. Another is to make a statement or tell an anecdote that will startle your readers. Consider using a quotation, offering your readers advice, or rephrasing your thesis in the concluding paragraph(s).

5. The first suggestion for a journal entry after Ravitch's ''The Decline and Fall of Teaching History'' asked you to name skills or subjects other than history that students should learn more about. Now, gather more information about the subject or skill in your list that you believe is most important.

   Turn these notes into a letter or opinion paper for publication in your college or community newspaper. Your purpose is to persuade faculty, students, or anyone interested in education that high school and college curricula should put greater emphasis on the subject or skill you are discussing. Let's say you wish you knew more about music. You can argue that students be required to take courses in music history or appreciation, that more money be budgeted for school bands, and that every student have the chance to learn a musical instrument.

As you know, a good source of evidence for any persuasive paper is the testimony of experts. You can gather such testimony by interviewing professors on your campus who teach the subject you are discussing or who share your opinion. Of course, you might also draw convincing evidence from your own experiences and from those of classmates.

Though a reasoned argument may be the best way to approach this assignment, don't rule out an appeal to the emotions as well. For instance, after drafting the body of your paper, write an introduction that uses startling language and information to dramatize the need for the changes you propose. In your conclusion, include vocabulary that will move your readers to action. In any case, revise and edit your work carefully before submitting it for publication.

6. If you responded to Shaheen's ''The Media's Image of Arabs'' in your journal, you may have begun discussing the way television, radio, movies, magazines, and the like portray a particular group. Express your reaction to this treatment in a preliminary thesis statement for a persuasive essay. Depending upon the details you have already gathered, you might write a preliminary thesis like this:

> Green-haired carpenters can expect nothing but ridicule from the media.

Now, draft an essay containing three or four detailed illustrations of what you mean. For instance, discuss magazines, movies, television shows and commercials, and billboard advertisements in which ''green-haired carpenters'' are ridiculed. End your essay like Shaheen ends his: offer the media advice about how to correct its stereotype of the people you have discussed.

As you rewrite your paper, add details and revise your thesis statement as needed. Edit your best draft for problems in grammar and mechanics.

7. Write a letter to the producers or sponsors of a television show you think unfairly stereotypes people on the basis of age, race, religion, nationality, profession, gender, or sexual preference. Analyze various episodes of the show. Provide details about the characters, plots, dialogue, and issues presented to support your view that the group in question is being treated unfairly.

Then, persuade your readers to make some changes. You can start with the logical approach. For example, explain that many people no longer tolerate unfair stereotyping and that continuing this practice will reduce the show's viewing audience. However, you can also appeal to your readers' sense of fairness and responsibility. Like Shaheen, for example, you might explain that, as ''imagemakers,'' they have an important role in molding the character of our society.

As you go through the process of writing, rewriting, and polishing, make sure to provide evidence and use language that will persuade your readers to change their approach. You might find useful materials in the journal entries you made after reading Jacobs's ''In Our Own Image'' and Shaheen's ''The Media's Image of Arabs.''

GLOSSARY

abstract language Words that represent ideas rather than things we can see, hear, smell, feel, or taste. The word "love" is abstract, but the word "kiss" is concrete because we can perceive it with one or more of our five senses. (See Chapters 5 and 6.)

allusion An indirect reference to a person, place, thing, or idea with which the reader is familiar. Such references provide a quick way for a writer to add detail, clarify important points, or set the tone of an essay, a poem, or a short story. There are several effective allusions in Elsberry's "A Farewell to Arms" (Chapter 6).

analogy A method by which a writer points out similarities between two things that, on the surface, seem quite different. Analogies are most often used to make abstract or unfamiliar ideas clearer and more concrete. Read Hamer's "The Thick and Thin of It" in Chapter 3 for examples of analogy.

anecdote A brief, sometimes humorous story used to illustrate or develop a specific point. (See Chapters 9 and 13.)

argument A type of persuasive writing that relies on logic and concrete evidence to prove a point or support an opinion. (See Chapter 16.)

central idea The idea that conveys a writer's main point about a subject. It may be stated explicitly or implied. Also known as the "main idea" or "controlling idea," it determines the kinds and amount of detail needed to develop a piece of writing adequately. (See Chapter 1.)

chronological order The arrangement of material in order of time. (See Section Four.)

coherence The principle that writers observe in making certain that there are logical connections between the ideas and details in one sentence or paragraph and those in the next. (See Chapter 2.)

conclusion A paragraph or series of paragraphs that ends an essay. Conclusions often restate the writer's central idea or summarize important points used to develop that idea. (See Chapter 4.) A **conclusion** can also be defined as a principle, opinion, or belief a writer supports or defends by using convincing information. (See Chapters 3 and 16.)

concrete language Words that represent material things—things we can perceive with our five senses. (See **abstract language** above, and see Chapters 5 and 6.)

coordination A technique used to express ideas of equal importance in the same sentence. To this end, writers often use compound sentences, which are composed of two independent (main) clauses connected with a coordinating conjunction. "Four students earned scholarships, but only three accepted them" is a compound sentence. (See Chapter 7.)

deduction A kind of reasoning used to build an argument. Deductive thinking draws conclusions by applying specific cases or examples to general principles, rules, or ideas. You would be thinking deductively if you wrote:

> All students must pay tuition.
>
> I am a student.
>
> Therefore, I must pay tuition. (See Chapter 16.)

details Specific facts or pieces of information that a writer uses to develop ideas.

emphasis The placing of stress on important ideas by controlling sentence structure through coordination, subordination, and parallelism. (See Chapter 7.)

figurative language (figures of speech) Words or phrases that explain abstract ideas by comparing them to concrete realities the reader will recognize easily. Analogy, metaphor, simile, and personification are types of figurative language. (See Chapter 6.)

image A verbal picture made up of sensory details. It expresses a general idea's meaning clearly and concretely. (See Chapter 5.)

induction A kind of reasoning used to build an argument. Inductive thinking draws general conclusions from specific facts or pieces of evidence. If you heard the wind howling, saw the sky turning black, and spotted several ominous clouds on the horizon, you might rightly conclude that a storm was on its way. (See Chapter 16.)

introduction A paragraph or series of paragraphs that begins an essay. It often contains a writer's central idea in the form of a thesis statement. (See Chapter 4.)

irony A technique used by writers to communicate the very opposite of what their words mean. Irony is often used to create humor. An effective example of irony can be found in Milden's "So You Want to Flunk Out of College" in Chapter 15.

linking pronouns Pronouns that make reference to nouns that have come before (antecedents). They are one of the ways to maintain coherence in and between paragraphs. (See Chapter 2.)

main point The point that a writer focuses on in a thesis or topic sentence. (See Chapter 1.)

metaphor A figure of speech that, like a simile, creates a comparison between two things in order to make the explanation of one of them clearer. Unlike a simile, a metaphor does not use "like" or "as." "The man is a pig" is a metaphor. (See Chapter 6.)

parallelism A method to express facts and ideas of equal importance in the same sentence and thereby to give them added emphasis. Sentences that are parallel express items of equal importance in the same grammatical form. (See Chapter 7.)

personification A figure of speech that writers use to discuss animals, plants, and inanimate objects in terms normally associated with human beings: for example, "Our neighborhoods are the *soul* of the city." (See Chapter 6.)

persuasion A type of writing that supports an opinion, proves a point, or convinces the reader to act. (See Chapters 3 and 16.)

point of view The perspective from which a narrative is told. Stories that use the first-person point of view are told by a narrator who is involved in the action and who uses words like "I," "me," and "we" to explain what happened. Stories that use the third-person point of view are told by a narrator who may or may not be involved in the action and who uses words like "he," "she," and "they" to explain what happened. (See Chapters 10 and 11.)

simile A figure of speech that, like a metaphor, compares two things for the sake of clarity and emphasis. Unlike a metaphor, however, a simile uses "like" or "as." "Samantha runs like a deer" is a simile. (See Chapter 6.)

subordination A technique used to emphasize one idea over another by expressing the more important idea in the sentence's main clause and the other in its subordinate clause. (See Chapter 7.)

thesis statement A clear and explicit statement of an essay's central idea. It often appears in an introductory paragraph but is sometimes found later in the essay. (See Chapter 1.)

topic sentence   A clear and explicit statement of a paragraph's central idea. (See Chapter 1.)

transitions (connectives)   Words or phrases used to make clear and direct connections between sentences and paragraphs, thereby maintaining coherence. (See Chapter 2.)

unity   The principle that writers observe in making certain that all the information in an essay or paragraph relates directly to the central idea, which is often expressed in a thesis statement or topic sentence. (See Chapter 2.)

ACKNOWLEDGMENTS

Maya Angelou, excerpt from *I Know Why the Caged Bird Sings.* Copyright © 1969 by Maya Angelou. Reprinted by permission of Random House, Inc.

Michael Anthony, "Sandra Street" from *Cricket in the Road.* Copyright Michael Anthony 1973. Reprinted by permission of Andre Deutsch, Ltd. for the author.

Paul Aronowitz, "A Brother's Dream" from "About Men," *New York Times Magazine,* January 24, 1988. Copyright © 1988 by The New York Times Company. Reprinted by permission.

Ellen Bassuck, "The Homelessness Problem" from *Scientific American,* 251:1, July 1984. Reprinted by permission.

Wendell Berry, "Waste" from *What Are People For?* Copyright © 1990 by Wendell Berry. Published by North Point Press and reprinted by permission of Farrar, Straus & Giroux, Inc.

Carol Biederstadt, "Electrical Appliances." Reprinted by permission of the author.

Hal Borland, "Hunger Moon" and "January Wind" from *Hal Borland's Twelve Moons of the Year,* published by Alfred A. Knopf, Inc. Copyright © 1979 by Barbara Dodge Borland, as executor of the estate of Hal Borland. Reprinted by permission of Frances Collin, Literary Agent.

Judy Brady, "I Want a Wife." Copyright © 1970 by Judy Brady. Reprinted by permission of the author.

Suzanne Britt, "Fun, Oh Boy. Fun. You Could Die from It" from *New York Times.* Copyright © 1979 by The New York Times Company. Reprinted by permission.

Suzanne Britt, "I Wants to Go to the Prose" from *Newsweek.* Copyright 1977 by Suzanne Britt. Reprinted by permission.

Sandra Burton, "Condolences, It's a Girl" from *Time.* Copyright 1990 The Time Inc. Magazine Company. Reprinted by permission.

Rachel Carson, excerpt from *The Sea Around Us,* revised edition. Copyright © 1950, 1951, 1961 by Rachel L. Carson; renewed 1979, 1989 by Roger Christie. Reprinted by permission of Oxford University Press, Inc.

John Ciardi, "Dawn Watch" from *Manner of Speaking.* © 1972 Rutgers University Press, New Brunswick, New Jersey. Reprinted by permission of Judith W. Ciardi.

Norman Cousins, excerpt from *Anatomy of an Illness as Perceived by the Patient: Reflections on Healing and Regeneration.* Copyright © 1979 by W. W. Norton & Company, Inc. Reprinted by permission.

Ruth Schwartz Cowan, "Less Work for Mother?" from *American Heritage of Science and Technology,* Spring 1987. © 1987 Forbes Inc., 1992. Reprinted by permission of *American Heritage Magazine,* a division of Forbes, Inc.

Malcolm Cowley, "The View from 80" from *Life,* December 1978. Reprinted by permission of the author.

Countee Cullen, "Incident" from *Color.* Copyright © 1925 by Harper & Brothers; copyright renewed 1953 by Ida M. Cullen. Reprinted by permission of GRM Associates, Inc., Agents for the Estate of Ida M. Cullen.

Alan DeVoe, "The Hibernation of the Woodchuck" from "The Animals Sleep," *Lives Around Us.* Copyright 1942 by Alan DeVoe; renewed © 1970 by Mary DeVoe Guinn. Reprinted by permission of Farrar, Straus & Giroux, Inc.

Lynda Dickinson, excerpt from *Victims of Vanity,* 1989. Reprinted by permission of Gordon Soules Book Publishers, Inc.

Deborah Diglio, "Lessons Learned." Reprinted by permission of the author.

Annie Dillard, "In the Jungle" from *Teaching a Stone to Talk.* Copyright © 1982 by Annie Dillard. Reprinted by permission of HarperCollins Publishers.

Anita Di Pasquale, "The Transformation of Maria Fernandez." Reprinted by permission of the author.

Emanuel di Pasquale, "Joy of an Immigrant, a Thanksgiving" and "Old Man Timochenko" from *Genesis* by Emanuel di Pasquale. ("Joy of an Immigrant" originally published in M. C. Livingston [Ed.], *Thanksgiving Poems.*) Copyright © 1989 by Emanuel di Pasquale. Reprinted by permission of BOA Editions, Ltd., 92 Park Avenue, Brockport, New York 14420, and the author.

David Doubiler, "Ballet with Stingrays" from *National Geographic,* January 1989. Reprinted by permission of The National Geographic Society.

Richard Elsberry, "A Farewell to Arms" from *New York Times Magazine,* September 28, 1987. Copyright © 1987 by The New York Times Company. Reprinted by permission.

Linda Bird Francke, "The Ambivalence of Abortion" from *New York Times,* 1981. Reprinted by permission of the author.

Robert Fulghum, "I Was Just Wondering" from *All I Really Need to Know I Learned in Kindergarten.* Copyright © 1986, 1988 by Robert Fulghum. Reprinted by permission of Villard Books, a division of Random House, Inc.

Martin Gansberg, "38 Who Saw Murder Didn't Call the Police" from *New York Times,* March 17, 1964. Copyright © 1964 by The New York Times Company. Reprinted by permission.

Roger Garfitt, "Bogota, Colombia" from "Notes from Abroad," *Granta,* vol. 29, Winter 1989. Reprinted by permission.

Willard Gaylin, excerpt from *The Rage Within,* 1984. © 1984 by Dr. Willard Gaylin. Reprinted by permission of The William Morris Agency, Inc., on behalf of the author.

Barry Glazer, "The Right to Be Let Alone." Reprinted by permission of the author.

Mary Ann Gwinn, "A Deathly Call of the Wild" from *The Seattle Times.* Reprinted by permission of The Seattle Times.

Blythe Hamer, "The Thick and Thin of It" from *Science,* January/February 1986. Reprinted by permission of the author.

Sydney Harris, "How to Keep Air Clean" from *For the Time Being.* Copyright 1972 by Sydney J. Harris, copyright 1969, 1970, 1971, 1972 by Publishers-Hall Syndicate. Reprinted by permission of Houghton Mifflin Company. All rights reserved.

Robert Hastings, "The Station" from *A Penny's Worth of Minced Ham,* published by Southern Illinois University Press. Reprinted by permission of the author. All rights reserved.

Robert Hayden, "Those Winter Sundays" from *Angle of Ascent, New and Selected Poems.* Copyright © 1975, 1972, 1970, 1966 by Robert Hayden. Reprinted by permission of Liveright Publishing Corporation.

Gilbert Highet, "Subway Station" from *Talents and Geniuses.* Copyright © 1957 by Gilbert Highet. Reprinted by permission of Curtis Brown, Ltd.

L. Rust Hills, "How To Do Things Right" from *Writing in General and the Short Story in Particular.* Copyright © 1977 by L. Rust Hills. Reprinted by permission of Houghton Mifflin Company. All rights reserved.

Langston Hughes, "Back Home" from *The Big Sea.* Copyright © 1940 by Langston Hughes. Renewal copyright © 1968 by Arna Bontemps and George Houston Bass. Reprinted by permission of Hill and Wang, a division of Farrar, Straus & Giroux, Inc.

Shirley Jackson, "Charles" from *The Lottery and Other Stories.* Copyright 1948, 1949 by Shirley Jackson. Copyright renewed © 1977, 1976 by Laurence Hyman, Barry Hyman, Mrs. Sarah Webster and Mrs. Joanne Schnurer. Reprinted by permission of Farrar, Straus & Giroux, Inc.

De'Lois Jacobs, "In Our Own Image" from *Essence* magazine, 1986. Copyright by De'Lois Jacobs.

Alfred Kazin, excerpt from "The Kitchen" in *A Walker in the City.* Copyright 1951 and renewed 1979 by Alfred Kazin. Reprinted by permission of Harcourt, Brace, Jovanovich, Inc.

Maurice Kenny, "Going Home" from *Between Two Rivers: Selected Poems*. Reprinted by permission of White Pine Press.

Martin Luther King, Jr., "I Have a Dream." Copyright 1963. Reprinted by permission of Joan Daves Agency.

Kenneth E. Kohler, "How I Came Out to My Parents." Reprinted by permission of the author.

Jonathan Kozol, "Untouchables" from *Rachel and Her Children: Homeless Families in America*. Copyright © 1988 by Jonathan Kozol. Reprinted by permission of Crown Publishers, Inc.

Charles Kuralt, "Wanderlust" from *Life on the Road*. Copyright © 1990 by Charles Kuralt. Reprinted by permission of The Putnam Publishing Group.

James Langley, "Watch the Cart." Reprinted by permission of the author.

Li-Young Lee, "The Gift" from *Rose*. Copyright © 1986 by Li-Young Lee. Reprinted by permission of BOA Editions, Ltd., 92 Park Avenue, Brockport, New York 14420.

Ursula K. LeGuin, "The Ones Who Walk Away from Omelas" from *New Dimensions 3*. Copyright © 1973 by Ursula K. LeGuin. Reprinted by permission of the author and her agent, Virginia Kidd.

Anthony Lewis, "The System Worked" from *New York Times*. Copyright © 1979 by The New York Times Company. Reprinted by permission.

Norman Mailer, "The Death of Benny Paret" from *The Presidential Papers*. Copyright 1963. Reprinted by permission of the author and his agent, Scott Meredith Literary Agency, Inc., 845 Third Avenue, New York, New York 10022.

Mary Manning, "A Visit to Belfast" from *The Atlantic Monthly*, 1972. Reprinted by permission of The Atlantic Monthly.

Richard Marius, "Writing and Its Rewards" and "Writing Things Down." Copyright Richard Marius. Reprinted by permission of the author.

Robert K. Massie, excerpt from *Peter the Great: His Life and World*. Copyright © 1980 by Robert K. Massie. Reprinted by permission of Alfred A. Knopf, Inc.

Edgar Lee Masters, "Lucinda Matlock" and "Margaret Fuller Slack" from *Spoon River Anthology*. Originally published by Macmillan Publishing Company. Reprinted by permission of Ellen C. Masters.

Peter Matthiessen, excerpt from *The Snow Leopard*. Copyright © 1978 by Peter Matthiessen. Reprinted by permission of Viking Penguin, a division of Penguin Books USA Inc.

John McPhee, "Two Gentlemen of the Pines" (editor's title) from *The Deltoid Pumpkin Seed*. Copyright © 1973 by John McPhee. Reprinted by permission of Farrar, Straus & Giroux, Inc.

John McPhee, excerpt from *The Pine Barrens*. Copyright © 1967, 1968 by John McPhee. Reprinted by permission of Farrar, Straus & Giroux, Inc.

Triena Milden, "So You Want to Flunk Out of College." Reprinted by permission of the author.

Gail Y. Miyasaki, "Obachan" from Nancy Foon Young and Judy R. Parrish (Eds.), *Montage: An Ethnic History of Women in Hawaii*. General Assistance Center for the Pacific, College of Education, Educational Foundations, University of Hawaii, Honolulu, Hawaii, 1977, pp. 44–49. Reprinted by permission of the author.

Farley Mowat, excerpt from *People of the Deer*. Copyright © 1951, 1952 by Farley Mowat. Reprinted by permission of Little, Brown and Company.

Gilbert Muller and Harvey Wiener, "On Writing" from *A Short Prose Reader*, 4th edition. Reprinted by permission of McGraw-Hill, Inc.

John Naisbitt and Patricia Aburdeen, "The Culture of Cuisine" from *Megatrends 2000*. Copyright © 1990 by Megatrends Ltd. Reprinted by permission of William Morrow & Company, Inc.

Charles Osgood, " 'Real' Men and Women" from *Nothing Could Be Finer Than a Crisis That Is Minor In the Morning*. Copyright © 1979 by CBS, Inc. Reprinted by permission of Henry Holt and Company, Inc.

Mildred Mastin Pace, "The Making of a Mummy" from *Wrapped For Eternity.* Copyright 1974. Reprinted by permission of McGraw-Hill, Inc.

Jo Goodwin Parker, "What Is Poverty?" from George Henderson (Ed.), *America's Other Children: Public Schools Outside Suburbs.* Copyright © 1971 by the University of Oklahoma Press. Reprinted by permission.

Florence H. Pettit, "Sharpening Your Jackknife or Pocketknife" from *How to Make Whirligigs and Whimmy Diddles and Other American Folkcraft Objects.* Copyright 1972 by Florence H. Pettit. Reprinted by permission of the author.

Robert Pirsig, excerpt from *Zen and the Art of Motorcycle Maintenance.* Copyright © 1974 by Robert M. Pirsig. Reprinted by permission of William Morrow & Company, Inc.

Katha Pollit, "Georgie Porgie Is a Bully" from *Time.* Copyright 1990 The Time Inc. Magazine Company. Reprinted by permission.

Meg Potter, "The Shopping Bag Ladies." Reprinted by permission of Meg Potter.

Sylvia Rabiner, "How the Superwoman Myth Puts Women Down" from *The Village Voice* 1976. Reprinted by permission of the author and The Village Voice.

Robert Ramirez, "The Woolen Serape." Reprinted by permission of the author.

Robin Roberts, "Strike Out Little League" from *Newsweek,* 1975. Reprinted by permission of the author.

Lee Romero, "What the Gossips Saw" from *Agua Negra.* Copyright © 1981 by Leo Romero. Reprinted by permission of Ahsahta Press at Boise State University.

Kenneth Jon Rose, "2001 Space Shuttle" from *Travel & Leisure,* November 1979. © 1979 American Express Publishing Corporation and reverted to the author. Reprinted by permission of Travel & Leisure and the author. All rights reserved.

Phyllis Rose, "Mothers and Fathers" from *Never Say Good-Bye.* First published in *New York Times Magazine,* May 3, 1984. Copyright © 1991 by Phyllis Rose. Reprinted by permission of Doubleday, a division of Bantam Doubleday Dell Publishing Group, Inc.

A. M. Rosenthal, "The 39th Witness" from "On My Mind," *New York Times,* February 12, 1987. Copyright © 1987 by The New York Times Company. Reprinted by permission.

Carol Rowan, "Just Between Us Blacks" from Brunt & Rowan (Eds.), *Feminism, Culture and Politics,* 1982. Reprinted by permission of Lawrence and Wishart Ltd.

Bertrand Russell, excerpt from *Autobiography,* 1967–69. Reprinted by permission of Allen & Unwin, a subsidiary of Unwin Hyman Ltd.

Carl Sagan, "The Measure of Eratosthenes" from *Harvard Magazine,* September/October 1980. Copyright © 1980 by Harvard Magazine. Reprinted by permission of Harvard Magazine and the author.

Carl Sagan, "The Nuclear Winter." Reprinted by permission of the author.

Carl Sandburg, excerpt from *Abraham Lincoln: The Prairie Years,* Vol. I. Copyright 1926 by Harcourt Brace Jovanovich, Inc., and renewed 1953 by Carl Sandburg. Reprinted by permission of the publisher.

Carl Sandburg, "Child of the Romans" from *Chicago Poems.* Copyright 1916 by Holt, Rinehart & Winston, Inc., and renewed 1944 by Carl Sandburg. Reprinted by permission of Harcourt Brace Jovanovich, Inc.

Adrienne Schwartz, "The Colossus in the Kitchen." Reprinted by permission of the author.

Howard Scott, "Vegetable Gardens Are For the Birds" from *New York Times,* May 1985. Copyright © 1985 by The New York Times Company. Reprinted by permission.

Richard Selzer, "A Mask On the Face of Death: As AIDS Ravages Haiti, a U.S. Doctor Finds a Taboo Against Truth" from *Life,* August 1987. Copyright © 1987 by Richard Selzer. Reprinted by permission of Georges Borchardt, Inc., for the author.

Philip Shabecoff, "Congress Again Confronts Hazards of Killer Chemicals" from *New York Times,* October 11, 1987. Copyright © 1987 by The New York Times Company. Reprinted by permission.

Jack G. Shaheen, ''The Media's Image of Arabs'' from *Newsweek* 1988. Copyright 1988 by Jack G. Shaheen. Reprinted by permission.

Mary Taylor Simeti, excerpt from *On Persephone's Island: A Sicilian Journal.* Copyright 1986. Reprinted by permission of Alfred A. Knopf, Inc.

Isaac Bashevis Singer, ''The Son from America'' from *A Crown of Feathers.* Copyright © 1970, 1971, 1972, 1973 by Isaac Bashevis Singer. Reprinted by permission of Farrar, Straus & Giroux, Inc.

John Steinbeck, ''America and Americans'' by John Steinbeck. Copyright © 1966 by John Steinbeck, text. Copyright © 1966 by Viking Penguin. Used by permission of Viking Penguin, a division of Penguin Books USA Inc.

John Steinbeck, ''The Chrysanthemums'' from *The Long Valley.* Copyright 1937, renewed © 1965 by John Steinbeck. Reprinted by permission of Viking Penguin, a division of Penguin Books USA Inc.

Rockwell Stensrud, ''Who's On Third?'' from Teaching Guide to the film series, *The Search for Solutions.* Reprinted by permission of the author.

Henry Stickell, ''Sinnit Cave.'' Reprinted by permission of the author.

Jessie Sullivan, ''If At First You Do Not See.'' Reprinted by permission of the author.

Kathleen M. Tanskey, ''The Best of Times.'' Reprinted by permission of the author.

John Tierney, with Linda Wright and Karen Springen, ''The Search for Adam and Eve,'' *Newsweek,* January 11, 1988. © 1988, Newsweek, Inc. All rights reserved. Reprinted by permission.

Carrie Tuhy, ''So Who Needs College?'' from *Money,* September 1982. Copyright 1982 the Time Inc. Magazine Company. Reprinted by special permission.

Eudora Welty, ''Worn Path'' from *A Curtain of Green and Other Stories.* Copyright 1941 and renewed 1969 by Eudora Welty. Reprinted by permission of Harcourt Brace Jovanovich, Inc.

E. B. White, ''Twins'' from *Poems and Sketches of E. B. White.* Copyright 1948 by E. B. White. Reprinted by permission of HarperCollins Publishers.

William Carlos Williams, ''The Use of Force.'' Copyright 1938 by William Carlos Williams. Reprinted by permission of New Directions Publishing Corp.

Michael Witt, ''Gambling.'' Reprinted by permission of the author.

Alice Wnorowski, ''Longing.'' Reprinted by permission of the author.

Tom Wolfe, ''Columbus and the Moon'' from *New York Times,* July 29, 1979. Copyright 1979 by Tom Wolfe. Reprinted by permission of Janklow & Nesbit for the author.

INDEX